"The healthcare industry is undergoing a transformati
that bears daunting challenges. To incorporate groundbreaking technologies, we as leaders are building our people, skills, cultures, and leadership to capitalize on and refine those technologies to address the urgent needs of today and tomorrow. This timely work is written by a world-class multidisciplinary team in Healthcare IT, medicine, and business. This breadth and collaboration is what's required to deliver this very timely cross-functional discussion and fantastic action planning resource. This book is required reading for any organization looking to lead the next wave of healthcare technology to improve care quality, patient safety, and clinician satisfaction to help us save more lives and keep people healthy across the entire care continuum."

Aaron Miri
Chief Information Officer for Dell Medical School and UT Health Austin &
Co-Chair for the US Department of Health and Human Services'
Federal Health IT Advisory Committee

"New technologies can improve healthcare, but not without improved leadership and organization. The authors of *Mobile Medicine: Overcoming People, Culture & Governance*, a multi-disciplinary team of practitioners and users of Health IT together with researchers make a significant contribution by applying lessons from the latest technology challenges: mobility, privacy, and security that can best be addressed by developing the kind of learning organization and leadership my colleagues and I describe in our book *Transforming Health Care Leadership, A Systems Guide to Improve Patient Care, Decrease Costs, and Improve Population Health.*"

Michael Maccoby, PhD
President, The Maccoby Group, Washington, D.C.

"This outstanding book is a rich resource that will enable many leaders to initiate and structure those difficult cross functional collaborations. This is necessary to get value out of and through new technologies including mobile. In my own personal passion to improve and further the healthcare industry through ongoing education efforts, I welcome this book to greatly catalyze these efforts."

Scott Becker
Publisher, Founder of Becker's Healthcare & Partner at McGuireWoods LLP

"The will has always been there to continue to enable our clinical staff and deliver for patients through ongoing modernization of our use of technology. With the pandemic, the need to deploy mobile solutions became undeniable. As an executive who has been working to solve the gaps for this over many years, I'm thrilled that this book, *Mobile Medicine* lays out most of the challenges with solutions in a highly detailed and practical way so that any health system leadership team could have concrete discussions and develop useful plans to operationalize leading edge technology to improve the performance of our health systems."

John Orsini
SVP and CFO at Northwestern Memorial Healthcare

"Due to the international focus of my work, mobility has always seemed essential to making medical care more efficient. Because of the pandemic, we now know the value of mobile computing in medicine here in the US as well. The domain experts and researchers, coauthors of *Mobile Medicine: Overcoming People, Culture, and Governance*, provide an incredible resource to all organizations that intend to make a real impact by implementing leading edge technologies, including mobile."

Anurag Mairal, PhD
Director, Global Outreach Programs, Stanford Byers Center for Biodesign Lead Faculty, Technology Innovation and Impact, Center for Innovation in Global Health Adjunct Professor, Stanford School of Medicine Executive Vice President, Orbees Medical

"Healthcare has struggled to implement new software and digital technologies and there is great frustration that the digital revolution in healthcare has not followed the same trajectory as it has in other industries. This book helps the reader to understand what makes the healthcare environment fundamentally different with discussions on how to address many of these barriers. Understanding these differences and how to address them is the difference between a shining promise that fails and a solid solution that revolutionizes care. This should be required understanding for those that want to create new healthcare technologies, to implement new technologies, or to invest in new healthcare technologies."

Joshua Tamayo-Sarver, MD, PhD, FACEP
Vice President of Innovation at Vituity & Inflect Health

"To transform healthcare, we need to be able to strategically partner with experts from multiple domains. Mobile Medicine masterfully brings together leading researchers and industry insiders who, together, provide valuable insights on how to drive ongoing change."

Laura Huang
Professor at Harvard Business School & Author of Edge: Turning Adversity into Advantage

"Every passionate leader needs to identify and build an ecosystem of multi-disciplinary and multi-functional expertise around them to turn their vision into reality. The expert, industry insiders and research scientists, coauthors of *Mobile Medicine: Overcoming People, Culture, and Governance*, provide a compass on how to go about doing just that. Take your innovation plans from aspirational to operational by leveraging a lot of the heavy lifting done for you and provided in this book."

Dr. Shafiq Rab
Serial Healthcare CIO & Chief Digital Officer, System CIO and EVP, Wellforce

"Through my work and passion for developing business leaders through leading edge business education, this book's co-author team is an incredible example of the kind of multi-disciplinary and cross-functional teams that are needed to lead through today's challenges. With the pandemic leaving an indelible mark on our collective psyche, many professionals and graduate students will be interested in learning from those doing the real work of innovation in healthcare. For that, I highly recommend this book for those business leaders who have a passion for improving healthcare and making an impact not just in the industry, but on humanity."

Caryn Beck-Dudley
President and CEO at AACSB International

"There are so many great ideas to help digitize healthcare. What's needed beyond bright ideas is a practical understanding of what must be done to deliver results to patients, their families, and clinicians. This requires much more than cool UI or UX: this demands that we understand the risks and, as technologists and leaders, we have to take responsibility for the challenges and lead to help solve them. To help guide you, leverage the insights from the key, multiple disciplines of this world-class team of coauthors and researchers who wrote this book, *Mobile Medicine: Overcoming People, Culture, and Governance*."

Paddy Padmanabhan
Founder & CEO Damo Consulting
Co-author of Healthcare Digital Transformation and the Big Unlock

"Removing the hype and focusing on a fact based approach, this is a must read book for executives, policy makers, and entrepreneurs. Sherri and her team take the time to separate the signal from the noise in one of the most important advances for the delivery of healthcare, mobile."

R. "Ray' Wang
CEO Constellation Research and Best Selling Author "Everybody Wants To Rule The World"

"As a member of the board of directors with technology background at several public companies and member of an extended family with many loved ones who are in the medical field, I fully understand that groundbreaking technologies are often difficult to deploy, particularly for the medical industry. I'm excited for the potential of this book to provide meaningful insight and practical guidance to all partners looking to make a real impact."

Duy-Loan Le
Retired Texas Instruments Senior Fellow, Board Director at CREE-WolfSpeed,
National Instruments, Ballard Power Systems, Atomera, and Medigram

"As a veteran Silicon Valley tech executive passionate about the success of the customer and interested in medicine, this book is a great resource for me in my role as an advisor and board member to early stage tech companies. Every vertical presents a different set of challenges as a different kind of sport, if you will, and this book provides an insider's view of the landscape. The diversity of disciplines and functions, all essential in medical technology, would be hard to find anywhere else other than this book, *Mobile Medicine: Overcoming People, Culture, and Governance*."

Joe Pinto
Chief Customer Experience Officer, Pure Storage

"The pandemic has accelerated many technology trends in medicine and has both highlighted and heightened the need for mobile computing solutions. Doing this well requires a new level of collaboration across many disciplines and functions. This book provides a great roadmap for how to think about implementing leading edge solutions with mobile computing at its core."

Caretha Coleman
Founder & CEO Coleman Consulting Seasoned Health System Board Director

"As a seasoned finance, tax, and advisory board leader, I've focused on the technology sector throughout my career. Though having an extended family full of clinicians and empathy for their incredible experiences, I'm now focusing my skills and experience to help enable transformational technologies to make an impact on patients and clinicians. This book, co-authored by industry insiders and top researchers, provides incredible, practical context to move forward and make a difference in medicine through technology."

Tom Bondi
Tax Partner, Armanino LLP

"Universally, we all agree that now is the time to transform healthcare with technology; however, the healthcare industry in the United States has unique characteristics and barriers that can make it difficult to deploy innovative technologies. As a former wireless and electrical engineer and now patent attorney working with numerous connected/digital health companies, this book is an excellent resource to further understand how to solve deployment, implementation, and adoption challenges unique to medicine. While challenging, the rewards are worthwhile; the industry leaders, insiders, and researchers, all coauthors of *Mobile Medicine: Overcoming People, Culture, and Governance* show us the roadmap."

Noel Gillespie
Partner, Procopio, Cory, Hargreaves & Savitch LLP

"The COVID-19 global pandemic renewed focus on the need to bring quality healthcare outside of the traditional setting while maintaining quality and patient focus and not tripping over any regulatory wires. This book is a great resource with every chapter proving solid framing of the challenges and ideas for how to solve them. Uniquely, this book also discusses people and culture, an often overlooked part of the technology ecosystem."

Kenia Rincon
Cybersecurity Executive

"This extremely important book is right on time! Never, in the history of medicine or in the history of the world, have we had such an incredible opportunity to not only dramatically improve but also radically change the practice, availability and positive results of medicine in general with mobile medicine. Effective leadership for mobile medicine is all about engaging, inspiring and empowering people, organizations, and societies throughout the entire world. Mobile medicine is a world-class massive opportunity and challenge! The vision, knowledge and wisdom of superb thought-leaders and experts featured in this book will help us identify and apply the most effective, efficient structures, technology and processes to take full advantage of the inevitable mobile medicine movement throughout the world!"

Dan Nielsen
CEO/Founder America's Healthcare Leaders (AHL), former VP at Vizient and hospital CEO

Mobile Medicine
Overcoming People, Culture, and Governance

Dear Zom,

Kris speaks so highly of you, it's delightful to see you speak. Congratulations on all of your incredible successes!

Best wishes,
Sheri Rinéle
February 21, 2023

Mobile Medicine
Overcoming People, Culture, and Governance

Edited by Sherri Douville

Foreword by Ed Marx, Former CIO at Cleveland Clinic
Chief Digital Officer, Tech Mahindra Health & Life Sciences

Routledge
Taylor & Francis Group

A PRODUCTIVITY PRESS BOOK

First Published 2022
by Routledge
605 Third Avenue, New York, NY 10158

and by Routledge
2 Park Square, Milton Park, Abingdon, Oxon, OX14 4RN

Routledge is an imprint of the Taylor & Francis Group, an informa business

ISBN: 978-1-032-11564-1 (hbk)
ISBN: 978-0-367-65150-3 (pbk)
ISBN: 978-1-003-22047-3 (ebk)

DOI: 10.4324/9781003220473

Typeset in Adobe Garamond Pro
by codeMantra

I dedicate this book to my dear husband, Dr. Arthur W. Douville, a true partner and champion in every sense of the word. We also further dedicate this book to all of his colleagues working on the frontlines and behind the scenes to both heal and save American lives and patients all over the world.

Contents

SECTION 1 WHERE WE'VE BEEN WITH MOBILE IN MEDICINE AND WHAT TO LOOK FORWARD TO

SECTION 2 ENABLING ORGANIZATIONAL EFFECTIVENESS

SECTION 3 DRIVING REGULATORY AND COMPLIANCE SUCCESS

Foreword

I first met Sherri Douville in 2015. I had finished delivering the keynote address at a healthcare leadership conference when she approached me. Sherri asked a couple of questions and shared her perspectives on the key themes of the day. I was struck by the philosophical similarities we shared but more so by her passion around mobility. Specifically, that despite technological advances, mobility had yet to reach its full value in healthcare. Poor communication is a leading cause of preventable death, and it can easily be solved. This resonated with me. It still does today.

Since our first encounter that summer day in Denver, Colorado, we kept in touch. I learned more about Sherri the person and leader. I learned more about the company she leads as CEO, Medigram. We continued to encourage and help one another as we both share a similar vision, to help push healthcare into the digital age with modern tools including mobility. Sherri helped shape some of my thinking when it comes to mobility and the critical nature of clinician communications.

Sherri has an infectious personality. She is a caring person, and the leadership she provided during the pandemic has been a great service to many. As many of us were confused as to what to believe in the media, Sherri led a team that provided daily briefings based on science. Each day, numerous individuals and corporations benefited from her concise analysis and practical insights. This passion and care coupled with her technology savvy are key characteristics that make her one of the best healthcare technology CEOs.

As the CEO of Medigram for 6 years, Sherri has continued her relentless push to close the gap in avoidable deaths from lack of communication. The Medigram platform is the only mobile-first solution designed to work securely when no other healthcare apps can and with the security that medicine deserves built in at all levels of the solution. She positioned Medigram to help customer partners to drive better patient outcomes and financial results. Clinicians can communicate and collaborate quickly, reliably, and securely to dramatically reduce time to treatment and thereby save lives.

Sherri is a dynamic leader; a builder of teams, coalitions, and advisor to several organizations. In her work as a coauthor and editor of this book as well as technical standards work, she helped to build multifunctional teams of ethicists, enterprise architects, medical device and Biotech leaders, compliance experts, academic faculty, researchers, security leaders, and product engineers. She has also served on the faculty for ISC2 for mobile security Continuing Education. She was appointed cochair of the Trust and Identity Sub Group for the IEEE/UL P2933 standard for Trust, Identity, Privacy, Protection, Safety, and Security (TIPPSS) for clinical IoT and interoperability. This is not her first foray into publishing either. Sherri is a coauthor for a chapter on Trust for the forthcoming second edition Springer Nature textbook on Trust, Identity, Privacy, Protection, Safety, and Security (TIPPSS) for Clinical IoT titled *Women Securing the Future with TIPPSS for Connected Healthcare*. All these experiences provide the background and multicultural coalition-building required to connect the right people for this endeavor.

Sherri's passion, vision, and CEO leadership experience uniquely qualify her to edit this book, *Mobile Medicine: Overcoming Culture, People and Governance Challenges*. This book is a must read for any person in a leadership position in healthcare, regardless of industry vertical. Mobility specifically is held back for lack of cultural preparedness, people, and governance blockers, each of which is explained in detail along with solutions. The insights and practical recommendations are simply foundational table stakes for those in the provider, payer, retail, tech, or pharma spaces. Together, we will eliminate communication as the number one cause of preventable deaths.

Edward Marx
Author of best-selling books Healthcare Digital Transformation *and* Voices of Innovation

Preface: Today Is Not Your Father's Desktop World

Many people in tech, including engineers, envision mobility as an extension of legacy or current desktop workflows and products, many times by default and even subconsciously. The authors of this book, in particular the editor, do not see it that way. We believe mobile medicine needs a well-thought-out, "from the ground up" approach to managing usability and risk. There are plenty of worthwhile problems to solve in big data, high-performance computing, AI, and other web app desktop and stationary computing use cases like analytics or search; however, this book, while touching on some stationary web app use cases, such as AI, is generally not about those. As the editor, I worked to encourage thoughtful and requirements-based, highly specific thinking for enabling mobile workflows. While we did not eliminate every general web app-based, desktop, and stationary computing reference, they do not dominate this book. The rethinking and solving needed for practical useful mobility in medicine is what does. We want to acknowledge that desktop computing is still and will remain relevant to many use cases, including process trends such as the "no-code" and "low-code" platforms. These latter approaches can be adequate for many consumer-facing or lighter-weight B2B administrative or stationary computing use cases where the underlying infrastructure is already known to meet the target requirements or perhaps there are none or little in the way of requirements. However, we believe that mission-critical and novel mobile use cases require a more precise approach based on context-specific requirements, not envisioned in this kind of development, whereas "challenges to current low- and no-code development include data security and trouble with proper programming techniques, and handling of data" (McKendrick 2021).

A simple analogy used for data is often "pipes" to characterize the movement and storing of that data as the plumbing for it. Data underpins AI, and if we do not have command of our data, we cannot know if the related AI is valid or useful. Data practices have a long way to go to become accurate enough for medicine much of the time as can be inferred by the article that calls out the ubiquitous "error riddled data sets that dominate today's AI landscape" (Hao 2021).

In essence, when it's not mission critical and it doesn't matter, it's ok if your data sets are rife with errors. But what if our lives and the lives of our loved ones depend on this accuracy? This is what data, the foundation for AI and mobility, has in common in medicine specifically. The low-code and no-code trends cover the purview of user experience, but they do not address how data flows to make mobility work reliably in a mission-critical context. Solving the technical challenges for mobile medicine requires an accurate technical approach synthesizing multiple industries of wireless, hardware, software, and informatics. The value of solving this technical challenge can only be realized and executed by addressing the abundance of challenges and solutions that are outlined in this book.

One counterintuitive element of this book is the limited, albeit future-facing, focus on discussing realistic interoperability and application programmable interfaces, though not in depth. However, some elements and possibilities of interoperability are broadly touched on in the last chapter and others throughout the book. Because there are so many systems that rely on or could rely more on interoperability and many of those use cases are suited to stationary and desktop computing, that is not the primary focus of this book. However, it is touched on broadly in the last chapter when looking ahead at the future. Further, while there is much promise for newer APIs, such as Fast Health Interoperability Resources (FHIR), there are "whole of ecosystem" and likely government interventions needed to stabilize both current safety and liability concerns of physician users to enable widespread trust and adoption. There are many other interoperability tools and standards that are a necessary part of any part of the Healthcare IT ecosystem and much material on this subject exists, while this book focuses on mission-critical gaps where existing resources are scarce. There also needs to be maturity for FHIR developed in the kinds of data and addressing patients with complex conditions, which it doesn't do well today. Though applications leveraging FHIR may be marketed as mobile apps, they may have actually been designed as desktop apps initially and do not work reliably at target service levels on mobile and therefore would be primarily outside the scope of mobile medicine whereas "time is tissue."

While we are excited by the eventual further adoption of FHIR, we also felt this huge topic was outside the scope of this book. This book focuses on medicine with a capital M. Our view is that FHIR is an excellent future technology for direct-to-consumer tools, also outside the scope of this book.

One area of confusion for patients is what to expect from consumer-grade wearables compared to medical-grade devices that may also be "wearable." This is an analogy of consumer-grade vs. medical-grade technology. Take for example your everyday fitness smartwatch that is unregulated by the FDA largely because it's not expected to inform medical care. Most physicians would not perceive or treat smartwatch readings with the same weight as electrocardiography (ECG) readings that show detailed electrical signals from the heart. A cardiologist might suspect a patient has atrial fibrillation – an irregular and often rapid heart rate – and as part of the workup, decides to send the patient home with a Holter monitor for cardiac event monitoring. This patient already has a smartwatch, but the doctor needs something more rigorous and specific to help with the diagnosis that informs medical decision-making. This monitor is then attached with leads to a patient's upper body. The device is regulated in one of two ways in this scenario:

> Sometimes, the cardiac monitor acts only as a signal acquisition device and transmits via radio frequency telemetry (or hardwire) the detected ECG waveforms to a central station for processing. If the processing at the central station is only for generating heart rate alarms, the cardiac monitor remains in regulatory Class II (as 74 DRT/ II). However, if the processing at the central station involves real-time arrhythmia detection and alarms, the cardiac monitor and the central station are both placed into Class III (as 74 DSI/III).
>
> *FDA (2020)*

This level of regulatory refinement, potential legal liability, and patient risk is simply not part of the equation for consumer devices, a fact sometimes lost on some companies, investors, and developers targeting mobile medicine. Many international regions have a US regulatory equivalent, in some cases more rigorous, and other regions may have a less mature regulatory scheme.

However, what every single viable market has in common are regulatory frameworks based on risk-based classifications.

We also believe that mobile software in medicine needs this kind of attention if it is going to earn the trust of stakeholders and be useful in medicine. Both the EU and the US do have a software as medical device designation though the details differ. For example, in the EU, the classification system for software is expressed as several classes (I, Im, IIa, IIb, and III) (Fillmore 2018). We expect these classifications and their definitions for software regulated as medical devices to change in favor of increased scrutiny and rigor, particularly first in the EU and some parts of Asia.

Further, for those of us responsible for mobile medicine, we always need to ask ourselves exactly where the person is physically when they're using an application and from what kind of computer or device they're doing their work. We also need to know if a constant, ubiquitous internet connection is always possible or impossible for all devices in that setting, the latter is the norm and will remain for some years to come in many medical environments (O'Dowd 2018). Solving for this requires a new mindset and new way of thinking. Mobile medicine is not your father's desktop computing.

Intended Audience

The audience for this book is intended to be diverse, multidisciplinary, and multi-industry, addressing the teams and roles best positioned to move mobile medicine forward. In particular, leaders in those industries with the tacit knowledge, comprehension of all related systems, and who possess the networks to make the fastest impact such as health system management, health insurance management, technologists, academics, policymakers, medical device and BioPharma executives, investors, physician executives, and researchers.

- CIOs
- CTOs
- Chief Medical Officers
- Technical Fellows
- Chief Transformation Officers
- Chief Innovation Officers
- Chief Digital Officers
- Chief Strategy Officers
- Physician executives and physician champions of technology innovation
- Nursing champions of technology innovation
- Health system executives, general managers: CEO, CFO, and COO
- Health system board members
- Medical device company executives
- Biotech executives
- IT staff, managers, and executives
- CISO and strategic Infosec managers
- Privacy counsel
- General counsel
- Graduate students passionate about Health Tech innovation
- Professors and Deans of engineering, law, medicine, and business
- Provosts

- Leaders of academic accreditation organizations
- Policymakers
- Investors
- Informaticists
- Strategic clinical service line owners
- Organizational psychologists
- IT and leadership researchers

Knocking on Doors

The development of this book was driven by the search for experts. This editor has been gripped by the problem of mobile medicine for several years. Why does a delay of information remain as a stubborn leading cause of preventable death? Further, physicians frequently must wait for information that is needed and not available or did not get delivered in a timely manner, and certainly not to their mobile devices. At the beginning of this journey in 2013, we spoke to several experts in IT and computer science and could not find any who worked within or as part of a team or teams dedicated in a thoughtful way to solving this specific problem. This inspired our work to be the solution we sought. The "expert" for mobile medicine had to be a team of teams; no individual can encompass such a complex and multidisciplinary endeavor. That is what this book represents.

The Inspiration

The need and motivation for this book were driven by four pivotal situations. First, there was the moment the editor didn't feel alone in seeing the problem clearly when a prominent voice in the Healthcare IT space made it clear. As Donald Rucker, informatician, emergency physician, and National Coordinator for Healthcare IT under the US Department of Health and Human Services from 2017 to 2020, so insightfully stated, "Current software is designed for office workers at a desk, not a healthcare provider on the move. Computer science needs to adapt for this" (CCM Recap 2021).

Just as Rucker was calling out the gap in mobile medicine, a venture firm in Silicon Valley saw the gap in mobility generally including but not limited to healthcare, coining the term "deskless workforce." In a survey of over 1,500 deskless workers, Venture investor Kevin Spain, General Partner and colleagues at Emergence Capital found that "they'd been given software designed for another purpose (desktop and stationary computing), but which has been repurposed for their jobs, and that 62% of deskless workers are unsatisfied and call for improvement." Respondents also reported frustration with slow, lagging software as their primary gripe (44%), with "inefficient" as the second (20%), followed by "broken communication" as the third (18%) (Mendoza 2021). Now that they have shined a light on the 2.7 billion persons in the deskless workers market, we believe other investors will also be drawn to the field and specifically to mobile medicine.

Third, I am known for saying that "I live with the problem." My husband is a neurologist and seasoned healthcare administrator and executive, Dr. Arthur W. Douville. His effectiveness as a physician hinges on timely communication (mobility) with other team members, and he notes that effective, efficient, and timely communication is still all too often limited by reliance on telephone voice mail, faxes, and pagers. Physicians and their patients are in motion, with life-or-death decisions needed in minutes. Protocol-driven care paths smooth the way, but there are still barriers that mobile medicine technology could clearly help solve. Just as a chef determining a dining experience is only as good as the supply chain and staff around him or her or a star in a play depends on the whole production, a physician's performance and job satisfaction are constrained by the timeliness of information available to him or her. You can feel how frustrating it could be for a physician in those critical, higher-risk clinical service lines to wait for essential information. One can also imagine how this imposes a huge well-being tax on the clinician while increasing clinical risk-related anxiety.

Lastly, we're thrilled to partner with some of the top leaders in all the relevant technical and operational areas, including healthcare privacy and security such as Lucia Savage, Peter Mclaughlin, and Mitchell Parker. Their "coaching as a lifestyle" and sincere passion for governing privacy and securing our medical system helped us as innovators to understand why building and addressing privacy and security from the ground up is an enormously key component to solving for mobile medicine. There are many leaders in many fields to thank which you can find in the acknowledgment that follows.

The people, culture, and governance emphasis of this book represents the how in terms of making all of these disciplines work in concert to deliver mobile medicine.

Who Wrote This Book?

This book was conceived of and developed by a diverse team of 27 industry leaders and researchers in the areas of, but not limited to, engineering, IT, security, compliance, privacy, medicine, informatics, clinical operations, human capital, organizational psychology, and IT research.

How Is This Book Organized?

This book is organized into six Sections. Please find them listed with the related 16 chapters here and how to use them.

1. *Where We've Been with Mobile in Medicine and What to Look Forward To: Chapters 1 and 2*
   In these chapters, we explore why adoption has been so low and how modern leaders can attract and collaborate with leading mobile technologists.
2. *Enabling Organizational Effectiveness: Chapters 3–6*
   Innovators, IT, security, informatics, organizational psychologists, and physician leaders scope their cultural and social landscapes and how you might navigate them to ensure that culture enables, rather than derails, mobile medicine.
3. *Driving Regulatory and Compliance Success: Chapters 7 and 8*
   In these two chapters, legal, privacy, and compliance experts suggest ways to both leverage and transcend the classical legal training to enable innovation with tips on how to best partner with legal counsel.
4. *Managing Risks to Success: Chapters 9–12*
   Given that most software is built for maximizing profit and scale without reliability or resilience in mind, these chapters help us to define and manage risks to mitigate for the development and deployment of mobile medicine into the clinical environment.
5. *Aspirational to Operational: Rapidly Upgrade People Skills: Chapters 13 and 14*

These chapters provide tools to develop people toward unprecedented levels of self-aware-ness and elevate our capabilities to work in the diverse teams that mobile medicine requires.

6. *Envision Your Organization's Mobile Tech-Enabled Future: Chapters 15 and 16*

A team of world-class renowned researchers in Chapter 15 help us to understand how to think about what a leading human capital strategy should entail. Chapter 16 is about build-ing upon the framework standard in our shared journey toward a sustainable and useful future of mobile computing in medicine.

We recommend that you read the summary of each of the six sections in the following introduc-tion for a characterization of the problem space and solutions. It's fun and informative to then read individual chapters at the same time and discuss them with your colleagues. You can read them in any order.

What's Next

Thank you for purchasing this book. We hope that it radically accelerates your success in deploy-ing and implementing mobile medicine and improves your satisfaction with strategic planning and clarity in terms of your role in that. Please let us know when an insight from this book helps to shape your journey. Let's keep learning, growing, and solving together.

References

"Ccm-Recap-Report-Top-of-Mind-2019-Summit-Themes-Speakers.Pdf." 2021. Accessed April 4, 2021. http://s227096.gridserver.com.s227096.gridserver.com/wp-content/uploads/2019/04/ccm-recap-report-top-of-mind-2019-summit-themes-speakers.pdf.

FDA, Center for Devices and Radiological. 2020. "Cardiac Monitor Guidance (Including Cardiotachometer and Rate Alarm) - Guidance for Industry." US Food and Drug Administration. FDA. March 18, 2020. https://www.fda.gov/regulatory-information/search-fda-guidance-documents/cardiac-monitor-guidance-including-cardiotachometer-and-rate-alarm-guidance-industry.

Fillmore, R. 2018. "Is Your Software a Medical Device?" Regulatory Focus. March 8, 2018. https://www.raps.org/news-and-articles/news-articles/2019/3/is-your-software-a-medical-device.

Hao, K. 2021. "AI Datasets Are Filled with Errors. It's Warping What We Know about AI." MIT Technology Review. April 1, 2021. https://www.technologyreview.com/2021/04/01/1021619/ai-data-errors-warp-machine-learning-progress/.

McKendrick, J. 2021. "What Is Low-Code and No-Code? A Guide to Development Platforms | ZDNet." March 3, 2021. https://www.zdnet.com/article/special-report-what-is-low-code-no-code-a-guide-to-development-platforms/.

Mendoza, N.F., 2021, and 6:00 Am Pst. n.d. "Despite Working on the Front Line, Deskless Workers Lack the Tech They Need during the Pandemic." TechRepublic. Accessed April 4, 2021. https://www.techrepublic.com/article/despite-working-on-the-front-line-deskless-workers-lack-the-tech-they-need-during-the-pandemic/.

O'Dowd, E. 2018. "Planning for Coverage, Capacity in Healthcare Network Upgrades." HITInfrastructure. August 30, 2018. https://hitinfrastructure.com/news/planning-for-coverage-capacity-in-healthcare-network-upgrades.

Acknowledgments

A book is a journey in and of itself and comes to life in a larger context. I'm incredibly honored to learn with and from these extraordinary coauthors whom you will meet by way of their bios and whose wisdom you should seek out when they do interviews, write articles, through their next books, and for you to consider hiring their companies to partner with. They are incredibly intelligent, thoughtful people, many of which are, if not undoubtedly one of, the top persons in their domain. My inspiration and husband, Dr. Arthur W. Douville, also a coauthor, deserves much of the credit for this book and the work that informed the development of the book and the team that built it. Another foundation for this journey was 10 years spent at Johnson & Johnson working in field sales, marketing, and serving as a National Sales Trainer. The company invested in a formal management development program, and these are tools I still use every day with a career largely built on friendships that developed during that time. I also developed a healthy respect for compliance there and have a lifelong, constant radar tuned to regulatory environments thanks to that training. While I was an unconventional hire at the time, having a STEM degree and a retail background, it was all made possible because Nordstrom had given me my first management role in college. The tools from my retail management days include a continued obsession with workflows and "huddles" which I still use, including in the development of this book. My college, Santa Clara University (SCU), has been and still continues to be, as an institution and also a team, a source of support and development, in particular my academic advisor, the former Physics Department chair, the late Dr. John Drahmann and my crew coaches including the Farwell family. Sue Farwell encouraged me to attend SCU during a difficult time in both my and my family's life.

A few of the coauthors took on multiple chapters out of their passion to further the field, and we want to express gratitude to Mitchell Parker, also a coach on this book; Lucia Savage and Peter Mclaughlin, our legal coaches for the book; Brittany Partridge the talented applied informaticist; and William C. B. Harding, the deep medical technologist. This book itself would not exist without two people: first the kind mentoring of serial healthcare CIO Edward Marx both leading by his example as an author and through his encouragement of the creation of this work, including authoring the foreword, and the second essential person is the Publisher's editor, Kristine Mednansky, whom we can't thank enough for all of her patient coaching. There are many others to thank with gratitude, in particular Wim Roelandts and his wife Maria, a legendary leader and serial Board Director and the mentors motivated to change the world. Serial Board Director and committee chair Duy-Loan Le and finance coach Tom Bondi have been critical. There have been many more game-changing mentors and collaborators, including Medigram CTO Eric Svetcov who among many topics taught us passionately about the importance and value of building a robust security program, even if it is ahead of the curve. Jeff Bargmann, a serial entrepreneur and mobile technology expert, has been a critical guiding force in this journey in his patient willingness to adapt our mobile technology work to medicine's requirements. Karen Jaw-Madson is a very talented organizational psychologist and culture-building consultant who has lent her expertise and book-building experience to this book. Speaking of culture, vast gulfs exist that have to be bridged between the cultures of medicine, IT, and Silicon Valley. We're grateful to Allison J. Taylor and Sarasina Tuchen for brainstorming and processing with us on these subjects. In the pandemic, we've been struck by the parallels between mobile computing requirements in medicine and pandemic risk management. They both require a novel synthesis of multiple disciplines. We were so inspired by many leading aerosol scientists, such as Dr. Linsey Marr, Dr. Jose Luis-Jimenez, Dr. Shelly Miller, Dr. Kimberly Prather, and their colleagues furiously working to keep us all safe. I am deeply grateful to and inspired by their work as an example of persistence to save lives.

Others we want to thank who have been critical to this journey include former Medigram CTO Dean Shold, Kirsten Sachs, Mike Caffey, technical advisor Bill Collins, ethics experts Dr. Jodyn Platt and Ann Mongoven, my dear friend Kristi Markkula Bowers, the star communications coach Anthony Lee, the customer success advisor Irene Lefton, Dan Warmenhoven, Frank Marshall, Andrew Khorin, Julia Miller, Dennis Lanham, Thane Kreiner, Doug Sinclair, Keith Taylor, Charlie Perrell, the Douville family, Quinn Tran, Karrie Grasser, Mary Johnson, Stefanie Lingle Beasley, Stephanie Joslyn, Juliette and Jerry Davis, Michele Kirsch, Chuck DeVita, Ronnie Lott, Scott Becker, Bill Russell, Bob Zukis, Noel Gillespie, Mike Ng, Ryan Staatz, Marc Carignan, Rosie Goddard, Gloria DiIorio, Craig Hyps, David Rotenberg, Nicholas Sturgeon, Sandy Miller, Cae Swanger, Dr. Mitesh Rao, Dr. Malathi Srinivasan, Dr. Arash Padidar, Dr. Paul Beaupre, Indu Navar, Dr. James Guetzkow, Ryan and Janet Dohemann, Elizabeth O'Dowd, Camille McCormack, Andy Wen, Kara Egan, Ian McNish, Greg Lafin, Dr. Richard Ferrans, and Dr. Lisa Hsieh. There are many others who have contributed in some way and we ask for forgiveness for any oversight. Last but not least, much gratitude goes to Ms. Maunder, my chemistry teacher in Junior High, who told me that I was great at science and to stick with science, and that's one real reason why this book is here today.

Editor

Sherri Douville is CEO & Board Member at Medigram and is a sought-after speaker and author in mobile medical technology, other healthcare-related industries, leadership, risk management, mobile security, and governance. Ms. Douville is honored to strategically build, grow, and lead multidisciplinary, multi-industry teams at Medigram and in the market to solve the leading cause of preventable death – a delay in information. Ms. Douville is cochair of the technical trust and identity standard subgroup for the healthcare industry through IEEE and UL, and has been published and quoted in both mainstream and industry media such as CIO.com, *The San Jose Mercury News*, NBC, *Becker's Hospital Review*, This Week in Health IT, and HITInfrastructure.com. Other industry leadership has included serving on the board of the NorCal HIMSS and teaching continuing education credit in mobile security for CISSP, the information security certification. She is coauthor for a forthcoming Springer book chapter on Trust in Clinical IoT, has coauthored several technical articles and papers, and is the lead author and editor for *Mobile Medicine: Overcoming People, Culture, and Governance* (Taylor & Francis). Ms. Douville led the development of this industry guide to mobile computing in medicine and built the team behind it. Prior to her current work in the mobile medicine, privacy, security, health IT, and AI industries, Sherri worked in the medical device space consulting in the areas of physician acceptance and economic feasibility for medical devices. Prior to that, she worked for over a decade with products addressing over a dozen disease states at Johnson & Johnson and was recognized for industry thought leadership by McGraw-Hill and won a number of awards. Ms. Douville has a Bachelor of Combined Science degree from Santa Clara University and has completed certificates in electrical engineering, computer science, AI, and ML through MIT. She advises or serves startups, boards, and organizations, including as a member of the Board of Fellows for Santa Clara University and an advisor to the Santa Clara University Leavey School of Business Corporate Board Education initiatives, the Black Corporate Board Readiness, and Women's Corporate Board Readiness programs.

Contributors

Jeff Bargmann

Jeff Bargmann – Medigram's Director of Product Management–is a repeat startup founder, investor, and user behavior expert. He is also a seed-stage investor: working in the medical, mental health, and education venture capital space, Jeff evaluates dozens of pitch decks and founding teams per week to help shape investments and to help guide startup teams forward. Before his current role, Jeff was the founder of PhotoDrive, a personal photo management platform acquired by Flickr; cofounder at Impulse, a game distribution platform acquired by GameStop; and the author of Fences, a Windows productivity application reaching over 15 million users. Experiment-minded by nature, Jeff has created dozens upon dozens of products in a wide variety of categories, and advocates for experimentation, diversity of thought, and willingness to try. Mentorship is an important part of Jeff's life, working regularly with minority founders he meets through the course of life, on Twitter, and through his relationships with the University of Michigan Center for Entrepreneurship and the Rochester Institute of Technology Center for Innovation. In the broader workforce, Jeff has held leadership positions running teams at Flickr as Product Owner of Flickr's Camera Roll and Uploader products, and at Yahoo as owner of all Mail/Media (Sports, Finance, Weather) team collaborations, including Olympics, World Cup coverage, and others. Teams managed span web engineering, server, mobile, design and marketing, and projects lead have reached over 300M users. With an MBA from the University of Michigan Ross School of Business, an undergraduate in Computer Science from Rochester Institute of Technology, CBT training from UCSF Langley Porter Hospital, and as a Certified Mediator in the state of California by the SF Bar Association, Jeff's wide-spanning background makes him an effective communicator of product needs from every perspective, and an expert collaborator helping unlock potentials within any team.

Asha S. Collins

Dr. Asha S. Collins is a biologist, strategist, and operational leader focused on transforming and scaling biopharma businesses. She is trained as a cancer biologist and has leveraged that training with diverse management experiences that provide her a robust view of healthcare and biopharma. Specifically, her experiences span science policy, management consulting, operational leadership roles at a Fortune 5 company and ground-up operations in Ethiopia, and angel investing, as well as being an independent corporate Director at an S&P 500 public company. Her breadth of experience, exposure, and people leadership capabilities have enabled her to repeatedly drive accelerated growth and value creation across diverse healthcare settings.

Currently, she is the head of US Clinical Operations at Genentech, a member of the Roche Group. In this role, she is accountable for all in-sourced, late-stage clinical trials conducted in the United States across the entire portfolio, i.e., oncology, infectious diseases, ophthalmology, immunology, neuroscience, and rare diseases. Prior to this role, she was Vice President/General

Manager for the US Clinical Trial Sourcing business at McKesson Corporation, one of the largest healthcare organizations in North America. In the past, she has leveraged her virology background to work in bioterrorism at the national academies. She has also served as a management consultant focused on life sciences strategy and operations at Deloitte and Quintiles Consulting, driving some of the most innovative engagements for these practices.

In addition to her passion for transforming biopharmaceutical and healthcare companies, Asha is equally passionate about using her skills and experience to build communities. She is a mentor for Backstage Capital, an Aspen Institute Health Innovator Fellow, and a recognized speaker on healthcare innovation. She co-leads a community dedicated to supporting underrepresented healthcare entrepreneurs, is an angel investor, and has ongoing work focused on improving healthcare access in East Africa.

Asha is also an independent Corporate Director for IDEXX Laboratories (NASDAQ: IDXX), where she serves on the Nominating and Governance Committee. She also serves as a member of the Scientific Advisory Board for the Translational Research Institute for Space Health (TRISH), an organization that helps support human health research for NASA's space exploration efforts.

When not involved in these activities, you will find Asha out in nature, on a yoga mat, reading, or simply being outdoors adventuring.

Jennifer J. Deal, PhD

Jennifer J. Deal, PhD, is a Senior Research Scientist at the Center for Effective Organizations in the Marshall Business School at the University of Southern California; a Lecturer at the Rady School of Management at the University of California San Diego; an Affiliated Thought Leader at the Center for Creative Leadership; and a contributor to *The Wall Street Journal*'s "Experts" panel on leadership. Her work focuses on global leadership and generational differences, and has been featured in such media outlets as the *Harvard Business Review, The Economist, New York Times, Wall Street Journal, The Guardian, strategy+business, Forbes, Fortune, South China Morning Post,* and *Globe and Mail*.

Previously, Jennifer was a researcher at the Center for Creative Leadership for 23 years, helping leaders around the world more effectively address the challenges they face. In addition to her academic and popular press writing in areas such as generational differences, digital transformation, employee engagement, global management, and women in leadership, in 2002 Jennifer coauthored *Success for the New Global Manage*r (Jossey-Bass/Wiley Publishers). Her second book *Retiring the Generation Gap* (Jossey-Bass/Wiley Publishers) was published in 2007. Her third book entitled *What Millennials Want from Work* (McGraw Hill Publishers) was coauthored with Alec Levenson in 2016.

An internationally recognized expert on generational differences, she has spoken on the topic on six continents (North and South America, Europe, Asia, Africa, and Australia), and she looks forward to speaking to Antarctic penguins about their generational issues in the near future. She holds a B.A. from Haverford College and an M.A. and PhD in Industrial/Organizational Psychology with a specialty in political psychology from The Ohio State University. In 2017, she was the winner of the Raymond A. Katzell Award for "showing to the general public the importance of work done by I-O psychology for addressing social issues, that is, research that makes a difference for people" from the Society of Industrial and Organizational Psychology (SIOP).

Kristine Dery, PhD

Kristine's research in the dynamic between technology and the way that people work has been a focus of her publications and teaching for the last 15 years. Most of her research has focused on design and management of the workplace to understand how organizations use digital capabilities internally to create more effective ways of working and the impact of new ways of engaging with talent in the digital era. More recently, she has leveraged this work to gain insights into what it takes for large organizations to transition a workforce to being future-ready.

Kristine is a Research Scientist at the MIT Sloan School of Management and Center for Information Systems Research (CISR). She is based in Sydney, Australia, and, in addition to her research, is responsible for fostering CISR commercial relationships with companies in Australia, NZ, and SE Asia. Prior to her academic career, Kristine held marketing management roles in Australia, New Zealand, and the UK.

Arthur W. Douville, MD

Dr. Arthur W. Douville, CMO at Medigram and practicing Neurologist, has held numerous leadership and administrative positions in healthcare, including hospital Chief of Staff and Chief Medical Officer in two separate health systems, most recently as Regional Vice President and Chief Medical Officer at Verity Health System in Northern California. In these roles, he oversaw infection control and biohazard assessment in hospital environments, as well as physician relations, including clinical integration, patient safety and quality, regulatory compliance, and the development of innovative clinical programs. He was part of the leadership team charged with bundled payment and Hospital Consumer Assessment of Healthcare Providers and Systems (HCAHPS) initiatives. As Associate Medical Director of the Crimson Analytic program for the Advisory Board (Washington, DC), his role was helping physicians understand and leverage the data by which they are being measured. Dr. Douville has over two decades of experience in executive physician leadership and has published work in managing change in physician culture. He is in the active practice of Neurology in Los Gatos, California, and acts as a Stroke Medical Director in the Santa Clara County Health System based in San Jose, California.

Ken Fuchs

Ken is the Senior Standards Consultant at Draeger Medical Systems, Inc., a manufacturer of electronic medical devices including patient monitoring, ventilation, anesthesia, and warming therapy systems. He is responsible for the coordination of Drager Medical Systems' participation in US and international standards development activities.

He currently serves as the Chair of the Institute of Electrical and Electronic Engineers (IEEE) 11073 Standards Committee (SC) for healthcare device interoperability, is Secretary of the IEEE/UL P2933 Standards Committee, cochairs the Association for the Advancement of Medical Instrumentation (AAMI) MP working group for multi-parameter patient monitors, and is an Integrating the Healthcare Enterprise (IHE) Devices (DEV) cochair. He also participates in a number of other standards development efforts in AAMI, ISO, IHE, and HL7.

He recently was awarded the 2020 HIMSS-American College of Clinical Engineering (ACCE) Excellence in Clinical Engineering and Information Technology Synergies Award and is a past recipient of the ACCE Professional Achievement in Technology Award. He holds a number of patents related to patient monitoring systems technology.

Ken's career has focused on networking, connectivity, and system architectures at various point of care medical device companies including Draeger Medical Systems, Siemens Medical Solutions, Mindray Medical, and the non-profit Center for Medical Interoperability. He holds a M.Eng. in Bio-Medical Engineering from Rensselaer Polytechnic Institute in Troy, New York, as well as an MBA from Babson College, Wellesley, Massachusetts.

William C. B. Harding

William C. B. Harding is a Distinguished Technical Fellow with 39 years of industry experience, 22+ years at Medtronic, a Bachelor's degree in Computer Science emphasizing Electrical Engineering, a Master's degree in Information Systems, and near completion of a PhD emphasizing technology integration. William has had a very successful career in missile launch/tracking systems, drug interdiction, rechargeable cell manufacturing, and medical device manufacturing. Recognized as a leader and go-to person in extended reality (XR), 1D, 2D, RFID, OCR trace/recognition technology, and process automation, William has initiated and championed innovative manufacturing solutions and patented medical product designs that continue to have major impacts across business units in the areas of process improvement, manufacturing automation, product development/traceability, and FDA validation. With more than 60 technical conferences, symposium presentations, lectures, seminars, and workshops under his belt, William continues to establish the highest level of standards through his professionalism, ethical behavior, mentoring, and guidance both internal and external to Medtronic. Lastly, as Emeritus Chair of the Technical Fellows, Emeritus Chair of the Tempe Technical Guild, and Chair of the Tempe ABLED employee resource group, William is dedicated to improving Medtronic and the world's vision of diversity and innovation.

Florence Hudson

Florence Hudson is an inspirational leader and C-level executive in technology, business, research, and academia. She is Executive Director of the Northeast Big Data Innovation Hub at Columbia University, and Founder & CEO of FDHint, LLC, consulting in advanced technologies, diversity, and inclusion. Former IBM Vice President of Strategy & Marketing and Chief Technology Officer, Internet2 Senior Vice President and Chief Innovation Officer, and Special Advisor for TrustedCI – the NSF Cybersecurity Center of Excellence at Indiana University, she has served as an Independent Director on commercial public company and not-for-profit boards. She has developed and led multibillion-dollar business growth strategies and execution for many advanced technology innovations, including her leadership in Emerging Business Opportunities as IBM Vice President of Corporate Strategy, as noted in a Harvard Case Study.

Florence is a globally sought-after keynote speaker, academic lecturer, and author in artificial intelligence, big data and analytics, connected healthcare, cybersecurity, energy and the environment, Internet of Things (IoT), smart campus and cities, blockchain, and diversity and inclusion. She is Chair of the IEEE/UL P2933 Working Group for Clinical IoT data and device interoperability with TIPPSS (Trust, Identity, Privacy, Protection, Safety, and Security) and serves on the IEEE Engineering in Medicine and Biology Technical Standards Committee.

She is on advisory boards for Princeton University, Cal Poly San Luis Obispo, Stony Brook University, Union County College, Blockchain in Healthcare Today, the Institute of Electrical and Electronics Engineers (IEEE), and the National Cancer Institute Computational Approaches for Cancer workshops. She is a global thought leader, consultant, speaker, and author. Her TED talk is entitled "Sustainability on a smarter planet." She has published in multiple books and publications on IoT, cognitive computing, smart cities, smart buildings, wearables and medical IoT interoperability, and Trust, Identity, Privacy, Protection, Safety and Security (TIPPSS) for the Internet of Things. She is Editor in Chief for the *Women Securing the Future with TIPPSS for IoT* book series with Springer. She is an NSF reviewer and Principal Investigator on awards for End-to-End Trust and Security for the Internet of Things, Cybersecurity Transition to Practice (TTP) Acceleration, the Northeast Big Data Innovation Hub, and the COVID Information Commons.

Ms. Hudson graduated from Princeton University with a Bachelor of Science degree in Mechanical and Aerospace Engineering, beginning her career at Grumman Aerospace Corporation and the NASA Jet Propulsion Lab. She attended executive education at Harvard Business School and Columbia University.

Karen Jaw-Madson

Karen Jaw-Madson is principal of Co.-Design of Work Experience, author of *Culture Your Culture: Innovating Experiences @ Work* (Emerald Group Publishing, 2018), founder of Future of Work platform A New HR, executive coach, and instructor at Stanford University's Continuing Studies Program. She enables decision-makers to address organizational challenges that affect business performance, including leadership, company culture, talent optimization, and change management. A former corporate executive, Karen is known as a versatile leader across multiple industries with experience developing, leading, and implementing numerous organizational initiatives around the globe. She has been featured in *Inc., Fast Company, Fortune, Thrive Global*, and *Protocol*, as well as written for publications such as *Forbes, Greenbiz*, SHRM's HR People+Strategy, TLNT.com, HR.com's *HR Strategy & Planning Excellence* magazine, and *HR Professional magazine*. Karen has a BA in Ethnic and Cultural Studies from Bryn Mawr College and a MA in Social-Organizational Psychology from Columbia University.

Jeff Klaben

Jeff Klaben is a highly adaptable, multidisciplinary, cross-sector trusted advisor with networks linking all corners of the business world. He is fluent in the private sector, government, academia, and the Silicon Valley ecosystem. His primary professional focus is building, leading, and advising enterprise-scale innovation, cybersecurity, privacy, technology risk management, and research programs.

He excels in leveraging strategy while driving to execution details and also performing under pressure while being grounded in clear values. Jeff has served as Chief Information Officer and Chief Information Security Officer for leading technology-driven organizations, including SRI International, Applied Biosystems, and Cadence Design Systems. He previously held senior engineering, IT, product management, and business development roles with Neohapsis (now Cisco), SanDisk, Applied Materials, Accenture, and NCR.

Jeff is also an Adjunct Professor with Santa Clara University's Law School and Graduate Colleges of Engineering and Business, where he teaches information assurance, forensic investigation, AI ethics, and interdisciplinary collaboration. Jeff is a coauthor of *The Computer Incident Response Planning Handbook*, director of the documentary film *Orienting*, and a frequent conference speaker at leading technology conferences (e.g., RSA and Gartner) and at film and creativity festivals (e.g., Cinequest), where he ardently supports social justice projects.

He cofounded and chaired the San Francisco Bay Area InfraGard, a 501(c)(3) nonprofit and public/private partnership dedicated to information sharing for critical infrastructure protection. He also served as national ethics committee chair and was recognized by the US Department of Justice with awards for Dedicated Service and Exceptional Service in the Public Interest.

Jeff also cofounded IEEE P1735, a standard for IP security and is currently helping drive the IEEE/UL P2933 working group to enhance data management and clinical system trustworthiness. His collaborative research with SRI International's Computer Science Laboratory led to three patents:

- Multimodal help agent for network administrator (US10050868)
- Natural language dialogue-based security help agent for network administrator (US20160219048)
- Impact analyzer for a computer network (US20160218933)

Jeff enjoys putting people of all types at ease and bringing out the best in what they can do together, while leading with an open-minded, collaborative style. His future interests span ongoing support of entrepreneurship, shaping public policy, and applying advanced research in trustworthy systems development, with an emphasis on interdisciplinary communication, applied ethics in data privacy and ESG (environmental, social, and governance), modeling/visualizing risk, enhancing understandable and explainable AI, persuasive technologies, and augmenting human performance.

Mamie Lamley

Mamie Lamley is committed to moving servant leaders from "Invisible to INVINCIBLE!" She stands for culture and tradition while integrating innovative, industry disruptive technology and personality science to build trust and create lasting relationships while providing systems and structure to build communities that are people-focused and profit-driven.

Today, Mamie expertly masterminds and trains with corporations, business owners, and entrepreneurs. She provides strategic step-by-step processes to implement responsible and ethical artificial intelligence to decipher client buying behavior, elevate sales revenue, and mitigate budget risks while closing more sales in less time!

Mamie is the founder of Empowerment on Fire and a Partner at Heroic Voice Academy. Her legacy is to influence 21 million global impact leaders to lead with integrity and to authentically communicate with accuracy, precision, self-mastery, and connection to generate a return of investment in the form of money, support, and reputation.

As a top-level certified trainer for Codebreaker Technologies®, she uses the only methodology in the world scientifically validated to predict buying behavior in less than 90 seconds.

Hawaii Special Olympics honored her as a Hall of Fame Inductee. Codebreaker Technologies® recognizes her as its Nurturing Icon in its Global Community. Women Economic Forum named her an International Award-Winning Speaker and an "Iconic Woman Making a Difference in the World."

Anthony Lee

Anthony Lee is the Founder of the Heroic Voice Academy, a communications training company. He has an undergraduate degree from UC Berkeley, and an MBA from Duke University. He is also a certified trainer in Neuro-Linguistic Programming, a study of communication best practices. In his professional career, he focuses on one objective: helping leaders develop their heroic voices to solve global challenges.

The Heroic Voice Academy has prepared clients for their high-stakes presentations, including conference keynotes, TEDx presentations, conference trainings, investor presentations, and media interviews. Their clients have made a significant impact in the areas of health tech and medicine, animal welfare, employee experience, entrepreneur education, mental health, and the future of food.

Anthony's presentation and training skills were developed and fine tuned in a career that includes over 30 years with technology startups and 12 years of event production experience. His communication best practices evolved from the high-stakes presentations he gave in the fields of internet security, real estate best practices, and large-scale international partnerships. Anthony leads from the stage and also leads from the back of the room having produced major events including industry conferences and large seminar trainings.

His company offers presentation training programs, executive communications coaching, and event production consulting.

Alec Levenson, PhD

Alec Levenson is an Economist and Senior Research Scientist at the Center for Effective Organizations, Marshall School of Business, University of Southern California.

His action research and consulting work with companies optimize organization performance and HR systems through the scientific application of organization design, job design, human capital analytics, and strategic talent management.

Three areas of primary focus include:

1. Optimizing the operating model to improve strategy execution and organizational performance
2. Talent management practices for the new generation of workers and world of work
3. Integrating analytics and organization development (OD) to improve decisions around talent and work design

Dr. Levenson's work with companies combines the best elements of scientific research and practical, actionable knowledge that companies can use to improve performance. He draws from the disciplines of economics, strategy, organization behavior, and industrial-organizational psychology to tackle complex talent and organizational challenges that defy easy solutions. His recommendations focus on the practical, actionable changes organizations should take to make lasting improvements in critical areas.

He has trained HR professionals from a broad range of Fortune 500 and Global 500 companies in high-performance work design, the application of workforce (people) analytics to organizational measurement and change, and operating model optimization. He has taught and delivered keynote addresses on these topics to thousands of people around the globe.

He is the author of *Strategic Analytics: Advancing Strategy Execution and Organizational Effectiveness, What Millennials Want from Work* (with Jennifer J. Deal) and *Employee Surveys That Work.*

His research has been featured in numerous academic and business publications including *Sloan Management Review, Organizational Dynamics, Journal of Management, International Journal of Human Resource Management, WorldatWork Journal, Journal of Business and Psychology, Economic Journal, Journal of Development Economics,* and *HR Magazine.*

His research and expertise have been featured in the *New York Times, Wall Street Journal, The Economist, CNN, Associated Press, BusinessWeek, National Public Radio, USA Today, Marketplace, Fox News,* and many other news outlets.

He has received research grants from the Sloan Foundation, Russell Sage Foundation, Rockefeller Foundation, US National Science Foundation, China National Science Foundation, and National Institute for Literacy. He has served as an external evaluator for US Department of Education funded Centers for International Business, Education and Research at University of Southern California, University of Hawaii, and University of Texas – Austin.

He received his PhD and MA in Economics from Princeton University, specializing in Labor Economics and Development Economics.

Kate Liebelt

Kate Liebelt is a life sciences and healthcare leader who is passionate about strategy, technology, and innovation. She is a champion for diversity, equity, and inclusion and volunteers with a variety of civic and industry organizations that align with her personal mission to create a more equitable world for women and minorities. Kate is a Director and Chief of Staff in the Pharmacovigilance and Patient Safety Strategy Management Office at AbbVie, Inc. Prior to joining AbbVie, Kate was a management consultant and Chief of Staff at Deloitte Consulting, LLP and PricewaterhouseCoopers, serving a variety of clients across the healthcare ecosystem. Before transitioning to consulting, Kate held R&D project leadership roles at Takeda Global R&D, Inc., Baxter Healthcare Corp., TAP Pharmaceutical Products, Inc., and the Washington University in Saint Louis Office of Technology Management/ Technology Transfer. Kate earned a BA from Washington University in Saint Louis and Certificate in Health Care Innovation from the University of Pennsylvania. Kate is based in Chicago.

Edward Marx

Edward Marx is husband to Simran and father of Brandon, Talitha, Nicholas, Austin, and Shalani. He serves as the chief digital officer for TechMahindra/HCI Health & Life Sciences division. He has been blessed to serve as a CIO in many progressive organizations, including Cleveland Clinic, New York City Health & Hospitals, Texas Health Resources, and University Hospitals of Cleveland. Simultaneously, Edward began his distinguished military career starting as a combat medic and finishing as a combat engineer officer. Edward has written many books including the #1 new medical informatics release *Healthcare Digital Transformation* (2020), the best selling *Voices of Innovation* (2019), *Scenes from an Early Morning Run* (2019), and *Extraordinary Tales of a Rather Ordinary Man* (2015). He is set to release a book on sexuality in marriage cowritten with Simran (2020). In his spare time, Edward races for TeamUSA Duathlon and loves to hike and climb mountains with Simran. Edward received his Bachelor's in Psychology and Master's in Design, Merchandising, and Consumer Sciences, all from Colorado State University.

Brian D. McBeth, MD

Dr. Brian D. McBeth, an attending Emergency Physician, has worked in clinical medicine and hospital administration for more than 20 years. His degrees are from Stanford University (BA) and the University of Michigan (MD), where he also completed a residency and chief residency in emergency medicine. He has had past academic appointments as an Assistant Professor of Emergency Medicine at the University of Minnesota and the University of California, San Francisco. Recently, he served as Medical Director and Chair for the Department of Emergency Medicine at O'Connor Hospital (San Jose, CA), as well as the Chair of the hospital's Quality Improvement Committee. He completed the American Association of Physician Leadership's program as a Certified Physician Executive, and is currently Physician Executive at O'Connor Hospital in the Santa Clara County Health and Hospital System, where he oversees patient safety, hospital quality programs, and COVID strategy and response, as well as physician performance and professionalism. He has published in the areas of physician culture and administrative communication, physician impairment and wellness, infection prevention and medical ethics.

Peter McLaughlin, JD

Peter McLaughlin is a seasoned privacy and data security attorney who advises clients with respect to a broad range of technology licensing, privacy, and cybersecurity issues. He is a partner and co-chair of Prince Lobel's Data Privacy & Security practice group in Boston.

His practice focuses on innovative uses of data, especially within the life sciences and digital health sectors. He's a highly experienced technology and privacy leader with nearly 20 years in health privacy, both as the Chief Privacy Officer for Cardinal Health and in private practice. His experience includes assisting health data analytics companies to understand and develop products conforming to state privacy laws, as well as the HIPAA Security Rule; navigating the revised US Common Rule, EU GDPR, and EU Clinical Trial Regulation for health data sharing collaboratives and SaaS platforms for pharma research and analytics; and coaching health insurers on information governance strategy, data mapping exercises, and HIPAA risk analyses.

He has represented clients across industry sectors with respect to governing personal information; responding to regulators from the Federal Trade Commission, the US Department of Health and Human Services and state attorneys general; and supporting post-enforcement compliance obligations. In short, Peter holds a preeminent position in this space.

Peter regularly speaks at events sponsored by the American Bar Association, the Practicing Law Institute, the International Association of Privacy Professionals, the International Technology Law Association, HIMSS, the Boston Bar Association, and RSA, among others.

Mitchell Parker

Mitchell Parker, MBA, CISSP, is the CISO at IU Health. Mitchell has 11 years' experience in this role, having established effective organization-wide programs at multiple organizations. He is responsible for providing policy and governance oversight and research, third-party vendor guidance, proactive vulnerability research and threat modeling services, payment card and financial systems security, and security research to IU Health and IU School of Medicine. In this role, Mitch collaborates across the organization and with multiple third parties to improve the people, processes, and technologies used to facilitate security and privacy for the benefit of IU Health's patients and team members.

He also publishes in multiple publications, including *CSO Magazine, Healthcare IT News*, HealthsystemCIO.com, Security Current, Healthcare Scene, and HIMSS' blog. He also has contributed a chapter for an upcoming *Cybersecurity in Healthcare* textbook, an essay to *Voices of Innovation*, which was published in March 2019 by HIMSS, and has a chapter in an upcoming book on *Healthcare Cybersecurity* for the American Bar Association's Health Law section. Mitch has also been quoted in numerous publications, including the *Wall Street Journal, ISMG, HealthITSecurity*, and *Becker's Hospital Review*.

Mitch is also a co-vice chair of the IEEE P2933 working group, Trust, Integrity, Privacy, Protection, Safety, and Security of the Internet of Things (IoT), and a co-subgroup chair of the P2418.6, Blockchain in Healthcare and Life Sciences Cybersecurity and IoT subgroups. Mitch also participates in other IEEE working groups related to security of the Internet of Things and collaborates with researchers and professionals worldwide on establishing and understanding standards for cybersecurity.

Brittany Partridge

Brittany Partridge is a leader in technology for Clinical Communications and Telemedicine. Most recently, she has had the opportunity to join the Ancillary Applications Team at UC San Diego Health rolling out 500+ iPhones, increasing MyChart Video Visits over 1,000%, and integrating interpreters into Telemedicine offerings to assist with the COVID response. She obtained a BS in Health Care Administration from CSU-Sacramento. After graduation, she worked for the Emergency Medical Services Authority automating their Emergency Resource Reporting and fell in love with the intersection between clinical and technical. Brittany then moved to Austin, Texas, where she earned her Health IT certificate from UT and an MBA in Healthcare from UT-Tyler. Brittany worked at Seton (later grouped under the Ascension Umbrella) for 7 years. She began as a physician educator for the Electronic Health Record and brought three hospitals live from paper to electronic. From there, she was promoted to Clinical Informatics Specialist, where she ran many deployments in the EHR. Some of her favorites included ePrescribing and Merge Hemo. She has also served as the Informatics department portfolio manager, handling intake, resourcing, and governance of EHR optimization requests. She moved to Seton's Good Health Solutions Center to run CI projects for Virtual Care, Innovation, and the Patient Logistics Departments. Prior to moving to San Diego, she transitioned to Ascension Connect, expanding her Virtual Care projects from Texas to all of Ascension's health ministries. Brittany has been a long-time member of AMIA and has served on the Public Policy Committee. She also participates in the Women in AMIA working group. She has attended the National Library of Medicine Informatics Course and is involved in HIMSS education initiatives. When she is not working, Brittany enjoys programming, volunteering with Remote Area Medical, and the outdoors, where she is happiest on, in, or by the water.

Matthew Perez

Matthew Perez is a technically proficient leader with extensive information security experience, a distinguished track record, and demonstrated abilities in information assurance, risk assessment, compliance, and networking. Matthew began his career as a network engineer, spent time at the Department of Defense as an Information Security IT specialist with an emphasis on maintaining an environment that enabled compliance, confidentiality, integrity, and availability of information through Infosec Management including Continuity of Operation Plans and disaster management and backup plans. For the last 6.5 years, he has been working in the healthcare and healthcare analytics space. He has a Bachelor of Science degree in Computer and Information Systems Security and Information Assurance from Eastern Illinois University.

Neil Petroff, PhD

Dr. Neil Petroff received a doctorate in Mechanical Engineering from the University of Notre Dame in 2006, and then served a post-doctoral position in the hand rehabilitation lab at the Rehabilitation Institute of Chicago (now Shirley Ryan AbilityLab) for one year. He has 10+ years of industrial experience in steelmaking and processing and hip implant development. Neil has been in academia since 2013, first with Purdue Polytechnic South Bend and currently as an Assistant Professor in the Department of Engineering Technology at Tarleton State University where he is the Mechanical ET program director. Neil works closely with the laboratory for wellness and motor behavior in the school of Kinesiology to develop smart devices for its clients. His main teaching responsibilities include mechanics of materials and developing PLC- and microcontroller-based control systems. His research interests are in physical medicine and rehabilitation and health and human performance. He has publishing experience including with IEEE – Engineering in Medicine and Biology Society (EMBC) and Society for the Advancement of Material and Process Engineering (SAMPE). He is also an associate editor for the Neural and Rehabilitation Engineering theme for EMBC.

Willem P. Roelandts

Mr. Willem P. Roelandts, also known as Wim, has deep experience building innovative, lasting technology companies with a global business focus. He served as the President and Chief Executive Officer at Xilinx Inc. for 12 years. Prior to his tenure at Xilinx, he had a 30-year management career at Hewlett-Packard Co. Previously, he was Senior Vice President and General Manager of the Computer Systems Organization for Hewlett-Packard Company. He was responsible for all aspects of Hewlett-Packard's worldwide computer systems business, including Research and Development, Manufacturing, Marketing, Professional Services, and Sales. Previously, he was Vice President and General Manager of the Network Systems Group. Wim has also served on several boards as board Chair and/or committee Chairman. Board positions continue to include high-tech companies, research and education institutions, and professional associations, among others. He is also Chairman of the Board of Applied Materials, Medigram, Inc., and a Trustee for Santa Clara University. He has acted as a Keynote Speaker at industry conferences and trade shows hundreds of times and as a guest on financial and business television programs broadcast internationally.

He has served as a Member of the Advisory Board of the Center for Science, Technology, and Society at Santa Clara University, where he and his wife formed a philanthropic partnership with the University to support student and faculty innovations through the Willem P. Roelandts and Maria Constantino-Roelandts Grant Program in Science and Technology for Social Benefit. The grants were awarded to students and faculty researchers whose work emphasizes the use of science and technology to benefit underserved communities around the globe. Projects have included bamboo housing for Haiti, a motorized bike powered by clean compressed air, a portable solar/hydrogen fuel cell generator for off-grid electrification to meet basic needs, and a mobile application that helps pieceworkers in developing countries learn if they're getting a fair price.

Wim holds a BS in Electrical Engineering from Rijks Hogere Technische School in Anderlecht, Belgium. In addition, he holds an honorary doctorate from Santa Clara University (2004) and the University of Leuven (2009).

Some of Wim's proudest achievements outside his family and Philanthropic leadership together with his wife, Maria, include the successful mentoring of 34 CEOs in Europe, the US, and Asia. This is all while acting as a trailblazer in diversifying corporate boards and management teams.

Shreya Sarkar-Barney, PhD

Dr. Shreya Sarkar-Barney is the CEO and founder of Human Capital Growth (HCG), a firm that specializes in evidence-based talent and human-capital management. A deep conviction that the use of evidence-based methods creates fair and equitable workplaces, influences much of Shreya's work. HCG clients includes Fortunate 100, mid-size, and not-for-profit organizations including Adobe, Cisco, Ecolab, Merck, and Microsoft. In 2019, Shreya was awarded the Scientist-Practitioner presidential recognition by the Society for Industrial and Organizational Psychology (SIOP). She advises organizations on the benefits of using science and analytics to guide people decisions. Through her work, she aims to create workplaces where people and business can thrive together.

Shreya holds an affiliate research scientist appointment with the Center for Effective Organizations at the University of Southern California. She serves on the boards of the HR Strategy Forum and the City of Vacaville Economic Development Advisory Committee. She is on the editorial board of the SIOP *Professional Practice Series*, a book series that brings evidence-based practice from the field of industrial and organizational psychology to solving today's most pressing talent management issues in organizations.

Shreya is the author of the book *The Role of National Culture in Transfer of Training* based on an empirical study covering 49 countries. Her research has been published in the *International Journal of Human Computer Interaction*, *Information Technology & People*, *Organizational Research Methods*, and *Personnel Assessment and Decisions*.

She has been a visiting scholar and lecturer at the University of California, Berkeley, and tenure track professor at the Illinois Institute of Technology. Shreya earned her PhD in Industrial and Organizational Psychology from Bowling Green State University. She is an alumnus of the University of California Entrepreneurship Academy.

Lucia Savage, JD
Lucia Savage is a nationally recognized thought leader on digital health and issues of privacy, security, reimbursement, health care quality, and innovation. As Chief Privacy Officer at the US Department of Health and Humans Services Office of the National Coordinator for Health IT, she played a key strategic and expert role in HHS' drive to advance interoperable and private use of health information, tackling such issues as individual's right of access to PHI; emerging standards for API-based data exchange; privacy and genomic medicine through the Precision Medicine Initiative; and cybersecurity at the intersection of devices and hospital systems. After leaving HHS in 2017, she joined Omada Health, Inc., where she drives Omada's privacy, regulatory, and health policy agendas, including issues of reimbursement for digital products and services. She has published widely on issues such as reimbursement for digital health; interoperability, information blocking, and health care competition; and privacy. She is a frequent public speaker before audiences ranging from digital health innovators to hospital administrators. In 2019, she testified before the US Senate Committee on Health, Education, Labor, and Pensions about information blocking, interoperability, and the privacy of digital within HIPAA compared to the lack thereof for direct-to-consumer apps. She has a B.A. with Honors from Mills College and received her Juris Doctor summa cum laude from New York University School of Law.

Eric Svetcov
Eric Svetcov is CSO and CTO for Medigram. He is a recognized leader in the healthcare technology space for building highly resilient and performant solutions with security, privacy, and compliance requirements built in at all levels of the solution. His deep experience additionally includes acting as Caldicott Guardian, Chief Privacy Officer, and Data Protection Officer.

Eric has presented in seven countries, taught classes on three continents, and coauthored the CCISO Body of Knowledge. He led the first global Cloud Computing Company (Salesforce) through ISO 27001 Certification and did it again with Mede/Analytics where he also led HITRUST Certification. As a startup veteran with overseas experience, he has designed IT Operations and Security infrastructure four times from scratch. He is skilled at engendering confidence, trust, and performance with both internal and external teams to deliver within specified timeframes. He prides himself on being effective with collaborators from all walks of life including as coach and champion of rising talent.

Eric has invested in the industry through various professional associations and has been published and quoted in leading IT and Information Security magazines in the US and Asia/Pacific.

In his off-hours, Eric enjoys sports with his kids and cofounded Virussafeschools.com to assist families in understanding their risk relative to in-person learning.

Allison J. Taylor
Allison J. Taylor is a Silicon Valley technology go-to-market strategist and entrepreneur who has brought over 20 software solutions and services to market across 35 countries, representing over $3 billion in revenue. She founded her first company in Israel at age 24 and is a former Middle East journalist and New York City medical trade press editor. An award-winning cybersecurity veteran, Allison consults senior leadership and their diverse cross-generational teams on growth and transformation strategies as Founder and CEO of consulting firm Thought Marketing LLC. Clients have included Cisco Systems, EMC/Dell, Honeywell, and Juniper Networks in addition to many early and mid-stage tech start-ups worldwide. Allison's executive operating experience includes cybersecurity product leadership positions at McAfee and Nokia, strategist roles at Sun

Microsystems (now Oracle), and corporate communications leadership at Check Point Software Ltd. She is currently an author and coauthor on two security chapters for the forthcoming Taylor & Francis book, *Mobile Medicine: Overcoming Culture, People, and Governance Challenges*. Allison speaks multiple languages and holds an MS in Communications from San Jose State University in California and a BA in Spanish and Journalism from the University of Richmond. She regularly hosts her LIFT podcast for thought-provoking conversations with industry leaders.

Introduction

Like many creative and entrepreneurial endeavors, this book started with a search for something that did not yet exist. While attending the 2019 HIMSS Annual Conference in Orlando, Florida, the editor of this book, Sherri Douville, CEO and Board Member for Medigram went to the Conference Bookstore in search of an autographed copy of Ed Marx's *Voices of Innovation* (Marx 2019), hopefully autographed in person by the author, as well as a second book that might serve as a definitive survey of the field of mobile computing in medicine. Alas no Ed, who was pulled into a last-minute meeting at work as CIO of the Cleveland Clinic, but after picking out a copy of that author's groundbreaking text despite his absence, Sherri was informed by the kind lady at the booth that as far as a textbook on mobile medicine, "we don't have one on that topic, but we'd like to!" Sherri was not surprised. There was a Déjà vu flashback to finding herself giving a continuing education course for the East Bay (San Francisco) chapter of ISC2 for CISSP security certification credit in 2017. The organizer reached out to Sherri to speak and teach on mobile security. Asking who else could help, the organizer said that no names came to mind. In her work as CEO of a start-up and deeply immersed in the field of mobile computing and security, Sherri had been struck by the difficulty in finding authoritative voices in mobile medicine. Why not such a definitive text? An all-star roster rapidly flashed in her mind for who should work on it. These would be individuals with the passion and the hard-won knowledge from real-world deployments and implementations of mobile medicine technology. There are few academic courses, programs, or established experts to turn to. It is the people who are doing the work in defining the new mobile technologies and programs, such as the chapter authors of this book, who are those defining the field of mobile medicine.

It turned out that the kind woman at checkout happened to be the senior editor for this series, and a week later, Sherri was reviewing the book proposal paperwork. The rest, you could say, is history.

HIMSS has been a natural catalyst from which to create this resource. The Healthcare Information and Management Systems Society, Inc. (HIMSS) is an American not-for-profit organization dedicated to improving health care in quality, safety, cost-effectiveness, and access through the best use of information technology and management systems. Headquartered in Chicago, Illinois, HIMSS has a global presence with operations across North America, Europe, the United Kingdom, the Middle East, and Asia Pacific. Members include more than 100,000 individuals, 480 provider organizations, 470 non-profit partners, and 650 health services organizations (HIMSS 2019).

If one question is "Why Not," another is "Why Now." In looking back to the context of urgency informing this work, the current pandemic will be seen to have been a catalyst for change incubating at the heart of mobile medicine. There will not be a "return to normal." There is only a "build for the future." That future involves recovering from the COVID-19 pandemic, having capabilities to address future pandemics and other natural disasters, while addressing the catastrophic strain on the healthcare system already underway due to demographics of the growing aging population that is often coined the "silver tsunami." This book is informed by practical learned lessons from those on the frontline technologists, as well as primary academic research.

In a recent meeting of top CIO's, Dr. Andrew Rosenberg, CIO at the University of Michigan, stated, "We need to move away from brick and mortar. Mobility and automation can avoid costs and help us advance" (Scottsdale Institute 2020).

Substantiating the above statement, a recent Becker's Healthcare Report highlighted that health system leaders are de-prioritizing buildings in medicine in favor of digitization. "Uncertainty around future cash flow has pushed us to reprioritize our capital expenditures, deemphasizing any brick-and-mortar projects in favor of pushing forward with digital projects," said the CEO of the San Antonio hospital (Becker's Hospital Review 2020). To quote one of the chapter coauthors, former CEO of Xilinx Wim Roelandts, in the context of higher education, "less bricks, more clicks." To which Sherri wants to reply, "now in the mobile era, we replace a drive for clicks with taps."

In the same meeting, Doug King, SVP & CIO, Northwestern Medicine, led the CIOs in a discussion on how IT might realign itself in our post-COVID era. "The relationship between the CIO and CEO will be where we'll need to focus" (Becker's Hospital Review 2020).

As reported in a recent World Economic Forum report on health system capabilities in the COVID-19 pandemic:

> Many countries made extraordinary efforts to expand health system capacity in the first wave of the pandemic—for example, by delaying elective care, reallocating medical professionals, and building whole new temporary hospitals. However, in addition to PPE shortcomings, health systems also often overlooked the challenge of controlling infections in high-impact facilities such as care homes, where age and poor health gave rise to high numbers of deaths. In many cases, there was also insufficient forethought paid to chronic exhaustion among health system personnel, as subsequent waves of the pandemic coincided with the need to attend to other conditions that had worsened during lockdowns, e.g., for the 41% of adults in the United States who delayed or avoided medical care. In response to extreme burnout, workers have already begun leaving the profession.
>
> *Schwab and Zahidi (2021)*

A renewed purpose to help extend and protect the healthcare workforce by leveraging mobile workflows becomes urgent when the "preexisting condition" of a delay in information was already a leading cause of preventable death prior to the pandemic.

In this backdrop, there appears to be a potential crisis of critical thinking including in technology development across a variety of sectors. This is most dangerous in the medical sector. The most famous is in aerospace, in the assumption that one can extend an old technology to new use cases without understanding if the software is still fit for purpose and the related requirements. The tragedy being avoidable deaths from plane crashes due to software errors. As a leader, you must be vigilant in reviewing new technologies whether they come from established vendors or start-ups. One could ask, "does this team understand all of the requirements and have they reasonably addressed what is essential with a practical roadmap execution plan? Are the requisite talent and skills available to them with the correct culture to enable successful development and deployment of a new technology?"

In addition to focusing on the kind of teamwork and skills needed to bring new technology safely into healthcare, there is also an intentional focus on privacy and security in this book. While human rights-related arguments are common in the lay media with respect to data privacy, this issue takes on an exponentially new magnitude of meaning in medicine.

Everyone seems excited about AI and that is touched upon in a few of the chapters. While results of AI have been disappointing so far outside of imaging and some other narrow use cases in medicine, much potential remains as data quality will improve over time. Further, real value can be added in the clinical environment by AI in a security context today.

This also aligns with health systems' priorities. For example, Rod Hochman, M.D. the CEO of Providence, published his annual predictions for healthcare and coming in at his number 3 was "Cybersecurity becomes a burning priority for health systems" (Hochman 2021).

While everyone wants better, faster technological change in healthcare, it is important to remember that an IT organization of any sizable institution and its services span applications, infrastructure, analytics, informatics, call centers, and innovation. This can mean hundreds of active programs and projects for just a mid-sized health system. The organizational challenges for the CIO in these settings are enormous, and not necessarily optimally supported.

A leading cause of preventable death in healthcare is a delay in the transmission of information. One such case was 55-year-old patient L.S., who went to a heart hospital when he felt chest pains and was short of breath. Unfortunately, in this situation, care delays that are preventable can lead to further complications and even death. While he was under the care of the overnight team, medication and oxygen provided to ease breathing were ineffective. Had it been appropriately and quickly communicated, it would have resulted in admission to the intensive-care unit, intubating him, performing an echocardiogram, inserting an intra-aortic balloon, increasing his medications, and consulting with a cardiothoracic surgeon, according to the testimony of an expert witness cardiologist. However, due to the failure by the overnight care team to notify in a timely manner, the "hours of progression of the underlying heart failure" decreased his chance of survival from "over 90% percent to approximately 20%." The patient ultimately died in an emergency surgery to repair a heart muscle rupture that occurred overnight, caused by the failure to communicate quickly, according to the court opinion in Salica V. Tucson Heart Hosp.-Carondelet (Bodine 2015). In addition to the human cost of this kind of failure are the reputational and legal costs to the healthcare enterprise.

Why Is Mobility in Medicine Broken?

The point of mobility is that as neurologists and cardiologists say, "time is tissue." When a leading cause of preventable death is a delay in communication; it is undoubtedly a leading cause of disability as well. For example, a patient had a stroke and needed both TPA, the clot-busting drug as well as a neuroendovascular procedure to restore speech. Being assessed and treated within a short time window depends upon all the physicians in the care team communicating quickly. This is not just to save the patient's life, but the timeliness of care is needed to prevent disability and loss of speech in this instance. It also needs to be done in a secure and private way to maintain the trust of patients and keep the systems and devices safe from security-related harms. TPA, the clot-busting drug has to be administered within a three-hour window of the last known normal. Reducing time to treatment increases survival (Mayo Clinic 2021).

Consumer-grade text messages comprise much of the mobility taking place relative to medicine today. If used by the care team, these are not secure, and they are intentionally designed not to be reliable or provide functions such as read receipts universally. This is because consumer text messages are free. There are no service requirements for delivery or timeliness of that delivery, and it is possible to receive a text message hours, days later than intended, or not at all. This is because of the intractable nationwide connectivity infrastructure gaps and the additional challenges specific to hospital buildings, this requires a new approach. Many industries are categorizing and differentiating between consumer-grade vs. industrial-grade technologies. Health care will need to do the same.

In the work we do in mobile medicine, we must also address the fact that hospitals have many dead spots where a constant internet connection is not available. Most consumer-grade apps are designed to require a constant internet connection, in particular most web apps built with a JAVA back end or some other high-level programming language (C#, Ruby on Rails, Python), for examples. Traditional health IT apps have not been built from the ground up and from a systems perspective to solve mobile use cases. Further, in terms of the organizational psychology aspect, changing workflows requires thoughtful planning and governance to meet all the requirements. You will find helpful frameworks and examples for that in this book.

You can also think of mobile medicine as analogous to workforce diversity and inclusion. An important reason why mobile tech is so poorly adopted in enterprise settings can be unresolved cultural conflict between layers of enterprise leadership and even within the subordinate IT organization and clinical staff. The need to incorporate a diversity of perspectives to build in privacy, security, and reliability against new service level and performance requirements and within the context of new computing environments requires new and different kinds of engineers partnering together with users and medical staff – this is a challenge for the ages, which is why we wrote this book.

Mobile computing in medicine can address the problem of preventable deaths due to a delay in communication and so much more. However, many complex challenges stand in the way: technology, privacy, security, legal, regulatory, governance, cultural, and organizational. Multidisciplinary expertise is needed to not only provide integrated solutions but also ensure adoption across the healthcare industry. This is required to make a difference for patients and their families, clinicians, and other stakeholders. This book is a collaboration of leading mobile technologists, security experts, health system technology executives, industry innovators, legal experts, human capital and IT research scientists, culture and organizational thought leaders, and forward-thinking physicians. Below, we characterize the six sections of the book designed to enable your team to rapidly develop priorities and action plans for successful mobility as measured by usefulness, lives saved, and adoption of related technologies. For example, if a new product has cool features but the vendor doesn't manage or mitigate risks associated with the product, deployment, or implementation, then it is not really useful to the stakeholders in the health system, most importantly the patient. The same goes for issues of both reliability and clinical relevance.

Where We've Been with Mobile in Medicine and Where We Should Go: Chapters 1 and 2

As in all legacy enterprise settings, medicine has seen low adoption of mobile computing. However, due to the economic and public health pressures exacerbated by the COVID-19 global pandemic, we are on the cusp of an explosion of new distance-enabled mobile technologies, including mainstream computing and those tailored for clinical purposes and wearable robotics for medical care. In this section of chapters, we explore why adoption has been so low and how modern leaders can attract and collaborate with leading mobile technologists. We will articulate the shortcomings of traditional healthcare system practices that prevent optimal use of mobile computing in medicine, including technical, legal, operational, clinical, governance, and cultural elements.

Enabling Organizational Effectiveness: Chapters 3–6

Experienced healthcare executives know that success hinges on more than just finding the right technologies. Leadership, people, and change strategies are also necessary to choose, implement, and enable adoption. They must also manage the cultural dynamics, addressing potential clashes between occupations, within and outside their organizations, and across industries. Leaders must ensure that culture enables, rather than derails. In these chapters, we learn from serial board directors and executives, entrepreneurs, IT leaders, security and informatics subject matter experts, organizational psychology, and physician leaders on the social landscapes and how we might navigate them.

Driving Regulatory and Compliance Success: Chapters 7 and 8

Today's health system, insurance, BioPharma, and medical device industry CxOs need to partner with all types of innovators to bring promising technologies into production and scale. None of this can happen without a basis of trust. We will explore what trust means, and what vendors can do to earn it. Innovators, especially those in the legal fields, need to move beyond a compliance-only mentality, one that is incapable of taking appropriate risks that come with innovation. Instead, in this segment of chapters, legal, privacy, and compliance experts suggest ways to both leverage and transcend their classical training to enable innovation. Lawyers are taught to apply new facts to old and familiar rules, including the privacy and reimbursement implications of using mobile computing. Confronted with standards that may seem to a non-lawyer to be out of date but are based on well-understood principles, lawyers can help bring a vision for mobile computing to life by translating and applying the new ideas to historic principles to help executives understand how to take advantage of all that mobile computing has to offer.

Managing Risks to Success: Chapters 9–12

Whether it is the latest widespread security hack, threats, or literal virus, disruption is the norm that supply chains unfortunately were not built for. This pertains to software just as much as it did to personal protective equipment during a pandemic time. Most software is built for maximizing profit and scale without reliability, cybersecurity, or resilience in mind. Therefore, there are risks to mitigate in the development and deployment of software into medicine. This requires combining innovation capability with world-class risk management strategy, cybersecurity planning, and execution to define and manage the security and reliability of new technologies in ways that help, not hurt humanity.

Aspirational to Operational: Rapidly Upgrade People Skills: Chapters 13 and 14

Nothing gets done without the teams that need to plan, organize, and execute on the strategies that will bring the benefits of these technologies to life. With mobile computing, you are managing higher levels of privacy, security, challenges to performance, and service levels while minding the short- and long-term goals of your organization. To drive success in this context, a leader will need to attract and lead a wide coalition of internal and external talent of an enormous range of skill sets and personalities. We will need to develop people toward unprecedented levels of self-awareness and capabilities to work in diverse teams. This is required to make ideas a reality and get the best out of mobile technology's potential in medicine.

Envision Your Organization's Mobile Tech-Enabled Future: Chapters 15 and 16

We have established that there are multiple dimensions of advanced technical and performance considerations, privacy, security, people, culture, and governance issues to be solved to make mobile computing truly useful in medicine. Fully realizing the benefits of advanced technologies will require human capital transformation over the near, mid, and long terms. A team of world-class renowned researchers in this section help us to understand how to think about what our human capital strategy will entail over time. They do it by bringing us evidence. Given that physicians and other stakeholders in the ecosystem respond best to evidence-based decisions, this is a chapter that every leader needs to read. Then imagine a future where we trust that computing of all forms, is private, protected, safe, and secure.

The Institute for Electrical and Electronics Engineers Standards Association is an organization within IEEE (IEEE-SA) that develops global standards. Established for over a century, IEEE-SA is helping to design the future with a program that aims for balance, openness, fair procedures, and consensus. Technical experts from all over the world participate in the development of IEEE standards. A monthly meeting for the Clinical IoT Standard, Trust, Identity, Privacy, Protection, Safety, and Security (TIPPSS) working group, IEEE/UL P2933, will have 50 or more attendees from 10 countries, with representation from a variety of US and international government agencies, non-profits, academia, and industry. In order to share the vision and responsibility to build and execute for this future, the pioneering leadership team behind this model will describe how you can incorporate the TIPPSS Clinical IoT framework into your own work. The intent is to foster the journey toward a future of mobile computing in medicine, one that we can all be proud of because it serves our family, friends, and communities in the best possible ways. That future brings better, safer, more efficient medicine.

I am grateful to all the contributing authors and reviewers who provided their hard-won insights for this book. In the months of working with this amazing team of contributors, I have learned more than I could have possibly imagined, and I hope you, like me, will feel infinitely more confident in moving mobile medicine forward. The whole point of the book is to enable each functional leader or board member with their CEO and teams to frame and open productive discussions with their cross-functional peers. The ultimate sign of success for us as a book team and to me as editor is to enable the rapid ability for any executive team to quickly adapt to a shared vision with tighter alignment and focus on accountable, actionable objectives as well as a clear idea of how they would manage against them in fine details – all catalyzed because of reading and reflecting on this book.

This book shines a light on current key focus areas and many future topics for any enterprise leadership team serious about leading mobility for medicine. We hope you will find the book useful in helping you to accelerate your mobility strategy and achieve near-and long-term successes. When you do, please share them with us. Let's inspire one another to build a more efficient health system enabled by mobility that works for medicine.

References

Becker's Hospital Review. December, 2020. The Payer, the Provider and the Pandemic. Becker's Healthcare. https://assets.asccommunications.com/whitepapers/optum-wp-march-2021.pdf.

Bodine, L. 2015. 440,000 Deaths Annually from Preventable Hospital Mistakes. *The National Trial Lawyers Top 100* (blog). January 21, 2015. https://thenationaltriallawyers.org/2015/01/hospital-deaths/.

HIMSS. October 16, 2019. https://www.himss.org/who-we-are.

Hochman, R. 2021. Our Annual New Year's Predictions: How COVID-19 Will Reshape Health Care for the Better in 2021. *LinkedIn* (blog). January 12, 2021. https://www.linkedin.com/pulse/our-annual-new-years-predictions-how-covid-19-reshape-hochman-m-d-/?trackingId=PzNC%2FAn4pLM9aiTGdYeS7A%3D%3D.

Mayo Clinic. 2021. Stroke Diagnosis and Treatment. Accessed March 29, 2021. https://www.mayoclinic.org/diseases-conditions/stroke/diagnosis-treatment/drc-20350119.

Schwab, K., and Zahidi, S. 2021. The Global Risks Report 2021. Insight Report: World Economic Forum. https://www.oliverwyman.com/content/dam/oliver-wyman/v2/publications/2021/jan/The_Global_Risks_Report_2021-1.pdf.

Scottsdale Institute. December 8, 2020. New Alignment for IT in an Era of Rapid Change. https://scottsdaleinstitute.org/wp-content/uploads/2021/01/SI-2020-CIO-Summit-Report.pdf.

WHERE WE'VE BEEN WITH MOBILE IN MEDICINE AND WHAT TO LOOK FORWARD TO

1

Chapter 1

Why Mobile Is Missing in Medicine—and Where to Start

Jeff Bargmann

Medigram

Contents

The Evolution of Culture

We're here, at the time of this writing, in the year 2021. Mobile apps are *everywhere*. We pay for things using Apple Pay, we hear about the world on the go with Twitter, order dinner with

DOI: 10.4324/9781003220473-2

DoorDash, and take a ride with Lyft/Uber. These beautifully manicured apps only get better and better. Meanwhile, in the medical industry, we wonder: Where is this revolution?

Leaders in healthcare systems, potentially yourself, have been frustrated with the lack of progress, lack of conviction from stakeholders, and lack of clarity on how to make change happen. Why isn't that technology here, why can't we seem to make it happen? Rather than be frustrated, we do need to ask ourselves the question: Why?

Our key is in understanding the phases that brought us here, so that we can understand where we are, why we're here, and how to move forward.

Perspective: Where I'm Coming from, as a Recognized Expert in Mobile

To help set the context, some brief background on me and my motivations for writing this chapter. I'm Jeff, a serial entrepreneur, now venture investor and company operator. I have worked in healthcare and have built and sold a mobile-first company in the middle of this revolution. I spend my time acting as Product lead for companies such as Medigram to help get them to Product Market Fit and invest in healthcare startups for a living. I'm exposed to dozens of innovation pitches each week.

I know about ideation and innovating as it is my business. However, this isn't an "I" activity, and that's the point. As we'll describe in this chapter, this is exclusively a "we" endeavor. This is about what *we are all* going to build together. My business only goes forward when healthcare advances—and we only make that happen by learning to combine our expertise, contributing the unique perspectives we each have to give, to create something great. This is why I wanted to write this chapter.

Reframing the Evolution: Why Mobile Is Missing in Medicine

So, look closely: This is not a fair game I'd presented above, comparing the success of the consumer environment to the medical setting. It might also not be a fair expectation you may have set for yourself or your organization.

Those examples above of "mobile success" are of *consumer* applications, which have been iterating friction-free in the consumer marketplace for over a decade. This wave, starting in 2008, consisted of early adopters and continues to be a market characterized by (1) *low barriers to entry*, (2) *low cost of failure*, and (3) *low friction for experimentation and growth*. In this consumer space, the market gave them the time and environment to grow, succeed, and indeed lay the bedrock for everything that would come. So it seems right they've come this far. This was the initial part of the process.

As new *consumer user-interaction patterns* began to establish, emerging from this primordial soup, we saw this newfound technological comfort facilitate the next age—*B2B*. Essentially: *consumer* applications, built for *consumer-like* use patterns, which *happened to coincide with business functionality*. Rocket ship, away we go! Office employee tools like Slack, Expensify, and DocuSign. Applications built using the same casual, *consumer-centric mentality, tech expertise, and patterns* that had refined over the prior decade. Critically: In these environments, like with consumer apps, workflows are often broadly applicable to the market, and generally, failures are tolerated provided that it works eventually. Move fast, break stuff: Now in the business setting. This is the culture evolution that got us here. And this is where we are today.

If this is all feeling quite different from the environment and the solutions market you're used to seeing in healthcare, that feeling would be correct: There is a gap. This is our job now, and this is our time to adapt this technology to us.

What's Next, What's Now: Adapting Mobile and Medicine

What we need to understand are the differences between the characteristics that got us here and the characteristics of ourselves.

Let's understand: *hard-industry* businesses like ours, like many other physical trades, have much more rigorous needs, expectations, and specifications than the stages that got us here. These businesses have deeply ingrained, tedious manual processes often involving numerous specialists/experts. Experts with ad hoc processes that currently work very well for them—and nearly all proprietary. These are *highly tuned* businesses on the frontier of competitiveness.

From overseas freight (Flexport), to trucking (Convoy), to farming (FarmLogs), *each of these hard-industries face very specific mission critical needs*—where recklessly introduced technology could quickly prove catastrophic. Change is coming for these industries now only as a function of competitive pressures, successively forcing firms to look, calculate, and leap.

These hard-industry firms have demanding expectations. There is friction between the two sides: our needs as a business, and the innovation methods that got us here. "Adaption" is the process of applying and managing that friction, to wear away our differences, and to make the two sides fit. Once that friction process is complete, then on we go.

Resolving the Friction: "It's Not You, It's Me"

The most difficult part to understand is that: really, it's us. Another thing that these hard-industry firms have in common is a large gap in culture between the transforming-industry itself (us) and those most proficient at advancing these innovations (tech creatives mentioned above). It *is* the pioneers here who are the ones most unprepared. However, that's not their fault. That's just how they got there and it's what works for them. We need to understand this, appreciate their work, and help bring them in to prepare our organizations for impact. It's a question of familiarity. We're a new culture. Let's bring them in, if they're adaptable to learning and have the humility required to partner in this environment.

As consumers themselves, tech workers are intuitively familiar with consumer tech. Business tech is something they live every day as they file reports (Expensify), sign documents (DocuSign), and chat (Slack). Tech workers are smart and adaptive; *however, tech workers are not at all familiar with the insides of a hospital or health care system.* Anyone might think they know how a heart works until they're in there with a scalpel. They have no notion of the level of care, patience, security requirements, and sophistication required to deploy into that environment. An indication of our progress so far educating this workforce on our environment's challenges: There are no health systems on Forbes' list of top 100 digital employers (Forbes 2021). At any meaningful scale, *avenues for natural growth from computer culture and expertise into medicine simply do not exist.* Hospital staff meanwhile, from those on the front lines up to our top leadership, are unfamiliar—and frankly uncomfortable—with the disciplines that it took to make mobile what we have today. These best practices look a lot different than what it takes to succeed day to day in a hospital setting. Each side gaining empathy for what it looks like for the other side begins with recognizing, and respecting, that this cultural difference exists.

Better Together: A Difference of Methods

Besides the structural barriers mentioned, a keyword to focus on from the paragraph above: an innovator's "discipline". Innovation, to many, does not look like a process that resembles *discipline*.

What it *does* look like from the outside, often, is chaotic, unstructured, and ungoverned. While in ways this is true, as any technologist will share with varying degrees of credibility, there is a method to their madness. Regarding your organization's reception: When it comes to working across cultures, as we know, what you don't know actually can hurt you.

Culture wise, you'll be finding out the hard way that innovators need room to create. Your job as a leader is not "to tolerate", "to accept". It's "to embrace", "to help guide". For the sake of the innovator, setting up, revising, and maintaining guideposts on your behalf can help steer toward a productive direction.

Otherwise, as cliche as it sounds, technology is art first engineering second when it comes to building something new. The personalities of people who may come into these roles may differ necessarily from the ones we're used to in a hospital or administrative setting. On your end, as long as everyone expects this situation and is aware that it's more of a positive (diversity of thought!) than a negative, then all is well.

Just as there is a discipline in achieving the lowest possible error rate in an ER, there is an artistic discipline on making innovation where there is currently nothing. It's very reasonable to feel skepticism about this coming from the viewpoint of a rigorous health facilitator. It's not only reasonable: it's a correct and important viewpoint to express at the table. If there's one takeaway you should have from this chapter, it is this: *The key to success as a leader is in combining and coming to grasp that you are **both right**, in both your highlights and concerns. The challenge is to **respect and solve for both sets of constraints simultaneously**.*

Culture and Collaboration: Making 1 + 1 = $30B

This paragraph may sound remedial; however, it must be noted: The word "collaboration" has lost all meaning these days with its over(mis)use. Throughout this book and this chapter, I hope you'll see that by collaboration, we mean coming to an understanding that two groups do things differently, and that it's expected. It's a feature, not a bug, and with it, you can do something more. What's next to understand is that each group is coming to the table with their own unique experiences and resulting perspectives. They each bring certain superpowers to the table, as well as weaknesses and blindspots. And each piece, whether positive or negative, offers a small fragment of the whole. No one can see the whole thing themselves. *It's your job to lead the process of solving this puzzle.* This is an escape room that can only be solved together.

Medical vs. Consumer Grade

The root of why we don't see more mobile use in health system environments comes down to the difference in nature between *medical grade* and *consumer grade* production. Let's dive into what that means.

Attribute categories we'll observe:

1. Reliability
2. Physical environments
3. Security, compliance
4. Legal, risk

Project management considerations we'll touch upon:

5. Trust and perception
6. Project proposals and milestones
7. Communication skills
8. Deployment (rollout)

Something to remember here is that when we look at a *physical good we can feel in our hands*, or a process we can see with our eyes, judging it as "medical grade" is a more straightforward analysis. To most of us, however, *computer networks, user interfaces, and everything in between are a black box*. We could barely tell a knock off from the top of the line besides the marketing material or perhaps kicking the tires. Where to even start?

Consumer/B2B-natured developments are the round peg to the square hole of medical environments. Often, neither side is acutely aware of the nature of the non-fit. Hence, the problem perpetuates itself to everyone's bewilderment. The technology side thinks it's adapting to the medical side, but does not fully appreciate what this means. The medical side likewise is not sure where to look. Hospital admins, frustrated, effectively trying to jam that round peg home. This section is meant to help us assess these non-fits, communicate this information to others in the organization, and make our projects a success.

Since there are a number we'll go through, we'll be brief in this chapter and allow us to dive in further elsewhere in the book. Nonetheless, reflect on this list. Do any of them seem familiar, in terms of what might be stifling innovation in your organization? If so, what can you do regarding your vendor, your staff, or your framing to improve expectations?

Attribute: Reliability

Think about a time an app crashed for you in a personal setting. Frustrating! Maybe you even switched apps, because there was an alternative. On the mobile web, for example, it's been shown that users abandon websites that take over 3 seconds to load (Akamai Developer 2016), and at least one study has indicated 62% of users will uninstall your app if they experience crashes or freezes (DCI 2017). Keep in mind however that these observations are for getting users to start using your product ("adoption") rather than keeping them once they are users ("retention"). Once a user has become a regular user in consumer or B2B, crashes are more tolerated, with technical issues thereafter dropping to just 5% of uninstalls (Karns 2019). At that point: as long as it's roughly doing the job, most of the time, then it's doing the job.

If you're feeling your eye twitch, it's because this notion, in a hospital setting, is terrifying. "As long as it's…roughly doing its job?" In medicine, every second counts, every delay or error can cost a life. If a medical tool is not operating correctly, it is an impediment to be removed—not an aid. Reliability matters so much in the medical space that, while it's something folks in consumer-tech "think" they get, they don't begin to appreciate the full extent until they're deeply initiated in hospital understanding. If you hear someone dismiss an error scenario that happens in your environment as an "edge case", it is fair to have a concern.

Attribute: Physical Environments/Scenarios

Besides certain physically grounded specialty apps like Lyft/Uber or Augmented Reality software, consumer utilities typically do not have much influence over—nor often deeply consider—the physical environment in which their products will get used. Producers cast a wide net when designing functionality. The aim is for general usefulness regardless of the physical scenario one is in. As they will face such a multitude of scenarios, while "the best of the best" do consider the top few scenarios their users encounter, this typically cannot be a consideration.

In a hospital setting, this is flipped. Physical scenarios are critical. Tools are often targeted towards specific physical-space usage environments and scenarios. To achieve results, their producers must work directly with those environments, potentially even going hands on via service-contract components.

A resulting observation: traditional consumer app developers may not consider this option of learning more about the physical scenario, nor might they realize its importance at all. It can be a similar case with hospital admin, given that *the hospital admin is unaware **that the app producer is unaware*** of the physical environment consideration. Square peg, round hole, a mysterious wall of repetitive failure. However, with awareness and communication, one can achieve uncommon results.

Attribute: Security, Compliance

This pair of topics is at first intuitive. The key thing to highlight is that conflict will arrive here for a slightly more un-intuitive reason: timelining and expectations.

Returning to the idea of culture: the expectations of cutting-edge innovators arriving in healthcare will of course be: "This is a medical application. We've got heavy duty security and compliance work to consider." They believe they are aware. However, the second-order effects might not hit them until reality sinks in. This process is not comfortable. The process by which startups are comfortable with gaining success is to iterate quickly and build as little as possible before testing in the market. Ambitious builders may agree to these extra compliance checkboxes; however, they may not recognize how much this is going to mess with their plan of "getting it done" until they're in the thick of it. The timeline may shuffle entirely, and they may have to rethink their overall plan of attack. As they think it through, a number of these concepts they discover (security, compliance) will need to be baked in FIRST—not added on later! This is the learning, this is the adaptation, this is the industry growth.

The preferred approach, of course, is to be aware of this and to look for people already knowledgeable about this curve. Otherwise, two things to keep in mind: all we're really looking for is recognition of this situation, as to actively anticipate and manage. This is not a means to judge per se, rather to assess.

Should you be working on a project with a well-disciplined engineering team used to working with consequence-carrying compliance concerns—the situation might come easier. They might be more aware of the nature of the timelines being discussed, accompanying Gantt charts, compliance spreadsheets, blockers—or at least, the process by which they'll address these issues when they encounter them.

For an individual or a startup, just so long as they're aware and the awareness is authentic and well considered, it is often a good start. It's not necessarily prior medical experience we're looking for here. Any engineer worth their salt figures this stuff out on the go and adapts. We're looking for people with open-mindedness (vs. stubbornness), curiosity, and awareness of the unknown— so that they can enter with the right mindset and game plan. Someone with compatible culture, ready to bridge the gap between their traditional innovation methods and the new environment. If everyone enters here cognitively on the same page, without having to be "told so", you're going to be on much more solid ground.

Attribute: Legal and Risk

Short and sweet: legal and risk are intrinsically intertwined. There is (nearly) no way to be 100% free of legal liability. Every product decision call is an evaluation of risk, and agreement between the legal team's comfort and level of risk they are ready to assume. Many consumer developers will not see this and will just think by "legal" and "risk" I meant compliance. Wrong.

The correct people will be masters of risk, working with your legal team to estimate risk, advocate where important to the product, proactively generate alternatives for selection, and yield where equitable compensations can be made elsewhere to achieve a sensible product-legal-risk balance. We'll cover this further in later chapters. *More or less any website you visit that has an "Accept Cookies" GDPR banner entirely blocking their marketing landing page, has a department where legal is particularly strong, and a product team that has insufficiently managed risk vs. experience.*

Management: Trust and Perception

What people think of this process matters; management, customers, staff, patients—every stakeholder involved, and like any sales process, anyone any of those stakeholders need to be assured.

Observing trust in adoption: Just because you've signed the deal, doesn't mean much regarding successful adoption by an organization. You can even distribute it to everyone's handsets, or give them devices. Unless you've gained their trust ahead of time, your rollout is going nowhere. Success requires a campaign of trust to make sure everyone feels part of the process, making everyone an advocate and champion.

In terms of perception: Ask a tech-friendly doctor what they think about adding mobile to their routine, and they might be curious. Ask a patient what they think when they see a doctor looking at their phone. They might think the doctor is inattentive. Maybe even just looking at something else. Patient gives a mixed/negative review, citing attentiveness. Ask the doctor again what they think about using a phone on the job. Not so good anymore.

Like it or not, perception is an impediment and also the reality we face; a reality that we inherit directly from our stakeholders. In keeping with the theme of this chapter, this must be accepted and included in the solution. The device is *viewed* as a distraction by the patient, it is *treated* as a distraction by management, and around we go—without anyone brave enough to break the loop. Instead, what if we accept the situation, where it *will* be viewed as a distraction [if not properly handled], and it *can* be a distraction [if not properly used]? If we manage the situation, then perhaps we can break the loop.

Management: Project Proposals and Milestones

When planning out innovation projects, our eye is best positioned towards progress *discovering and eliminating unknowns* rather than exclusively progress toward the stated goal itself. In this process, we're looking to strike a balance that creates both pressure to reach a goal and space to create. In these situations, to "determine resourcing upfront" is to predict the future, so we'll need to consider this reality at time of the pitch. Just be sure to (1) continually re-evaluate the goal, to see if it should change based on the new information, and (2) require justifications for decisions—be it qualitative or quantitative—for the purpose of ensuring alignment, and for creating a clearer picture for connecting the dots looking backward. If you can begin to see backward, you can sometimes start to see forward.

Going too far here would be to give way to being *entirely* open-ended. Our goal is to provide structure and decision forcing functions—representing key organization goals—while also giving room to breathe for the direction changes along the way.

Management: Communication Skills

We look to build teams with a diverse set of skills, perspectives, and backgrounds when we explore a project space, including, even in regards to communication styles. In hospital settings, an individual might get placed in a role for instance based on raw skill or knowledge in their specialty, not necessarily out of communication skill. Indeed, these people can be very effective with compensation mechanisms put in place.

For exploration projects, communication and empathy are some of the key skills in play. So something to consider: if you have someone who is a poor or high-friction communicator working with your innovation team, be careful. This is too collaborative of an environment. A stubborn and poor communicator may be able to add perspective—but they may also sink the ship, as they are loaded with torpedoes in the form of comments and blocking attitudes. Communication skill is the first thing I look for when assembling a team, out and by far above talent, and I recommend you consider this as you form your team too.

Management: Deployment (Rollout)

Rolling out to your entire department? You may be underestimating just how hands on you should be when performing your rollout. Some of the most successful startups in the innovation community got off the ground by going one by one to make sure each and every customer succeeded in getting started. We view each individual as a potential point of failure, which in turn could cause the whole to fail. We also view each as a potential champion and advocate, should we deliver them something they love.

Just as "making music" doesn't sell copies without also "distributing music", your project will fall flat at the finish line without both (1) your great product and (2) a masterful, human-centric, well-attuned, and carefully proceeded rollout.

You usually only get one shot at this, and it took everything to get you to this point. Remember our comments earlier about trust. This is your shot; make it count.

Venture Capital Side Note: Sales Cycle and Funding When Working with Startups

A simple takeaway: look for startups that are ready to handle your long, long, long sales cycle.

As a repeat entrepreneur, tech investor and member of the venture capital community, I'll note that most consumer startups are built somewhat like a drag race car until they've established sufficient customer traction—and this is on purpose. The goal is to try something as hard as you can, fail fast if it doesn't work, regroup, and then run another race. Only once you have traction do you tighten the bolts for the long run.

In medicine, however, it's a known-ahead-of-time reality that traction will not come quickly. Your intuitive concerns about whether a startup will still exist in 12 months are very real. You know already that in your business, it's going to take potentially *years* of inching in, relationship building, and credibility establishment to gain full trust within your organization. So use this knowledge as a lens—not to have fear about working with younger companies, but to give you confidence you can relay to yourself and others about the ones that are doing it right.

Conclusion

In technology product management, we know that it's not about *you* (the product manager), and it's not about asserting your will, demonstrating your vision or genius. It's about organizing people, and it's about facilitating communication. In technology, this is what makes products come to life. It's a gentle and informed hand, guiding the many parts (experts) along the way, hinting and helping them to pre-align, help the smooth rough edges, so that they may naturally assemble into shape. This is a situation where every bit of learning toward this effect counts. We hope we've provided you a few hints here today, and we hope that you'll build something great.

References

Akamai Developer. 2016. "Mobile Load Time and User Abandonment." Last Modified September 14, 2016. https://developer. akamai.com/blog/ 2016/ 09/ 14/ mobile- load-time-user-abandonment.

DCI. 2017. "Why Users Uninstall Apps: 28% of People Feel Spammed." CleverTap (blog). https://clevertap. com/blog/ uninstall- apps/.

Forbes. 2021. "Top 100 Digital Companies List." Forbes (blog). https://www.forbes.com/top-digitalcompanies/ list/.

Karns, KC. 2019. "Infographic: Why Users Uninstall Your Mobile App? - Dot Com Infoway." CleverTap (blog). https://www. dotcominfoway.com/blog/ infographic-why-users-uninstall-your-app/.

Chapter 2

Wearable Technology and Robotics for a Mobile World

William C. B. Harding
Medtronic

Neil Petroff, PhD
Tarleton State University

Brittany Partridge
UC San Diego Health

Contents

DOI: 10.4324/9781003220473-3

Mobile computing has multiple dimensions, many of which are largely unknown. This is the case with wearable technology advances to extend human life and quality of life. Our book team believes that robotics in medicine needs to leverage and work with the humans' and body's capabilities. One can think of this scope in a similar and analogous way as thinking about food as medicine. We explore this extraordinary potential, comment on some of the opportunities and challenges, and imagine how wearable robotics can contribute to a more integrated future of patient care. Concurrently, healthcare teams ideally consider risk every time they encounter a patient. Risk occurs in a situational way and is a combination of the product's impact on the specific patient and that patient's personal risk profile. The former can be amplified if a product is an introduction of new technology. However, risks can be mitigated by focusing on quality. In our chapter, we aim to inspire you to collaborate with us and become empowered to help us lead in designing our future leveraging wearable robotics while also encouraging you to consider leveraging your people, employees, and your ecosystems to set the bar high for quality.

Our lead chapter author, William Harding brings decades of experience developing products and teams to build solutions in a vast array of categories including wearable robotics. As an officially designated distinguished engineer since 2011 and senior technical fellow at Medtronic since 2013, his work now focuses on human-centered biocybernetics. He brings to this experience a passion for precision, reliability, and safety which he learned through building missiles early in his career and now counts on as a patient benefiting from the use of products he helped to design and build. In this chapter, he is partnered with Dr. Neil Petroff, a mechanical engineering technology academic program director focused on health and human performance along with Brittany Partridge, an applied informaticist.

Wearables

Generally speaking, wearable tech is anything on, in, or around a living thing that performs a function such as mirroring or enhancing capabilities or improving efficiencies. Furthermore, through the lens of robotics, wearable tech does not always imply mobility. However, for the purpose of this discussion, wearable tech and robotics should represent tech that electrically stimulates, communicates, integrates, protects, or influences human behavior. Additionally, within the scope of wearable tech and robotics, it is tech that uses data and, through a wirelessly or wired connection, sends and receives data either wirelessly or wired, and works interoperably with other technology. Lastly, with consideration for energy/power, wearable tech can exist as passive, semi-passive, and active, such that power can be derived from energy harvesting, inductive, or wired (e.g., rechargeable and fixed).

In addition to considering how wearable tech uses power and data, it can also represent elements that work as parts of a larger system, such as found within mesh technology often associated with IoT and IoB (Internet of Things and Internet of Bodies). That point emphasizes the aspects

Figure 2.1   Personal mobility technologies, freepik.com image.

of technology integration associated with interoperability, data aggregation, data transformation, data security, and data analytics.

Loosely bound within the discussion of wearable tech, some elements that might be considered are those technologies that can contain a human (e.g., a spacesuit). For example, personal mobility technologies that integrate with other tech and work interoperably with the user are worth consideration. Those technologies might be viewed as something that enables the user to move from one location to another, or as tech that protects the user (i.e., military solutions and personal transport systems) (Figure 2.1).

Data is getting better, less resource intensive to procure, and there's certainly more of it! Consider manual goniometers which are used in Orthopedica to measure angles vs. what is temporarily wearable today. Any such manual device is subject to inter- and intra-rater reliability and consistency questions. However, so are the devices. We may have gotten to a point where we believe we can just slap on a device and it will record whatever is important to us. However, knowledge of where the device should be placed and the skills to properly locate the device and to collect and analyze the data are still required. It's even more critical given the Terabytes of data being moved and stored. Have we become digital pack rats, focused on collecting as much data as possible? It is important that as we continue to gather more data in volume and type, we ensure that the aggregation is actionable and understandable to the user.

To us, it may appear to be less resource intensive, but is it really a zero-sum game? More resources are required to run the cloud or the edge where automated systems are running and crunching all this data. Consider bitcoin generation – whose use of extensive power is illustrated by stories of students running vents from their computers to the outside during cold months while mining bitcoin.

As an example, consider gait analysis where nearly imperceptible changes in mechanics can hurt or heal. Such subtleties are likely unobservable to a person. However, a sensor can record this. The ability to collect massive amounts of data, and, more importantly, being able to glean useful information from it, opens up an avenue for a pay-for-performance health model supporting value-based care. Mass distribution of wearable systems allows for longitudinal studies at a scale not realizable in current clinical and academic approaches. Ultimately, this information can remove subjectivity from assessments, allow for assessments to be done remotely via Telehealth, and inform best practices, all to ultimately improve outcomes. These systems can be reconfigurable in both hardware and software such that they can be used through the continuum of care or as long-term assistive devices. Of course, the TIPPSS requirements for such devices are of great importance and are addressed in Chapter 16 (presently called "TIPPSS for Clinical IoT").

Robotics

When considering robotics that can be worn by a human or animal, it is important to consider even robotic technology that a user might enter or become partially enclosed/encased. For example, technology used in robotic surgeries can be considered temporarily worn robotics because of how a user integrates with the technology. That point emphasizes that wearable robotics are technologies that provide a user with capabilities equal to a normally enabled user or that the technology amplifies/enhances/extends a user's normal capabilities. Furthermore, some wearable robotic technologies might enable a user to fly an aircraft, control a drone, or tech that can be injected into a user, which can assist with providing healing therapies (e.g., nanorobotics). Nano is otherwise known as extra tiny robotics.

Additionally, it is probably good to think about detached robots that are controlled by humans, robots that are autonomous/semi-autonomous which assist humans, and robotics that are safe to use near humans. Specifically, many industrial robots require safety zones and interlocks to protect humans and property, where you can imagine that a robot lifting and moving an engine block like it was a feather, might not be a robot that should operate next to humans. However, there are various robots such as those made by Double Robotics and Cisco, which are designed to work in the same environments as humans. For example, imagine a robot that is able to enter a sterile environment such as a COVID-19 patient's room, for the purpose of delivering something or wirelessly communicating with the other medical devices in the room. Then think about robots or even drones that can deliver medicines or perform health assessments in geographically diverse environments.

Thinking through where and how the robots will be used can inform other important operational and design decisions. Knowing and discussing the nuances of a particular environment the robot may be entering will save frustration down the line. For example, in the case of the robot bringing the item to the COVID room, how might that robot be cleaned: Will the cleaning wipes used to disinfect most things in the hospital harm its sensors? Should we consider making its casing out of antimicrobial material? etc.

Thinking more about what wearable robotics might represent to a user, we need not only look to technology associated with mobility such as walking or climbing, we also need to consider technology that might restore sight as well as hearing. For example, within the scope of wearable robotics, we can group in technology classified as extended reality (XR) which embodies technologies such as augmented reality (AR), virtual reality (VR), and mixed reality (MR). Whereas XR technology can enable a user to interact in local and distant environments through various biometric interfaces (e.g., voice, eye tracking, gesture, and cognitive). *Note*: The term 'user' can be representative of a human (e.g., patient, healthcare professional, and caregiver) as well as a digital element (e.g., hardware and software) such as is associated with a headless client. That point also emphasizes that artificial intelligence (AI) solutions might represent the user, where device-to-device or system-to-system interactions may not involve a human user.

As for the proposal that wearable robotics might not be characterized as technology that moves (or assists with movement) there are also technologies such as electrical stimulators like those that can cause muscular contractions to assist people with cerebral palsy or tremors. In those cases, it is not the wearable solution that moves, but instead technology that stimulates or influences movement. Similarly, stimulators might actually help normalize a user's movement, such as implanted deep brain stimulators (DBS) used by individuals with Parkinson's disease. In that case, it is the user's own brain that controls the user's movement, and through the assistance of stabilizing technology, corrected neurological impulses result in user movement.

The concept of wearable robotics never held a prominent place in William's mind until he found himself in a scenario where the associated technology became a central theme toward the improvement of his quality of life. Specifically, a high-speed landing that followed one of his nearly 2,400 skydives, resulted in both his legs being turned around and his pelvis splitting open. As a result of a poor landing, 16 surgeries, nearly $2.5 million dollars in medical costs, and the below the knee amputation of his left leg, he found himself focused clearly on developing solutions that would improve his mobility and reduce the continuous pain that is a part of subsequent daily life experience. Hence, the desire to examine innovative methods for using wearable technology became the foundation for much of the elements that have emerged within this chapter.

In William's words, "Wearable robotics were no longer an abstract concept to me, they were now directly applicable to my daily life, and I had the unique opportunity to design these solutions with myself as the tester." Accordingly, the development of patented medical devices associated with improved cardiac function, external sensing of potential physiological abnormalities, technology to reduce patient pain, and AI diagnostic solutions formed the key elements of his own personal exploration of wearable solutions. Additionally, with limited ability to function normally for nearly 2 years in his home, there was an apparent need to create what his friends call "Skynet", the foundation of a home system that is nearly fully automated. That said, it has become evident that the traditional view of wearable robotics (i.e., Iron Man exo-suits) does not embrace the true scope of what might be characterized as relevant technology. For example, within the scope of wearable robotics, we might consider technology such as:

- **Sensing**, such as would be used for the detection, monitoring, and management of biological events and where those sensing devices might influence other healthcare devices
- **Electrical stimulation**, such as neurological and cardiac technology that improves cardiac function as well as enables patients to overcome issues related to seizures, cerebral palsy, and Parkinson's
- **Therapeutic**, inclusive of electrical stimulation, but might also represent other technologies associated with the application of thermal therapy often associated with pain management as well as drug pumps (e.g., for diabetes, MS, and pain)
- **Communications**, where the wearable devices might communicate with caregivers, healthcare professionals, or biocybernetics technology, which enables the interconnection between humans and machines. This also includes IoT and IoB technology that is often representative of mesh, hybrid, and heterogeneous systems
- **Mobility**, which would include wheelchairs and exoskeletons that are used in the military, for people with disabilities, and in a multitude of manufacturing industries that enable users to perform tasks that exceed normal human capacity
- **Prosthetics**, where the technology might improve a user's speed and strength, or restore functionality lost due to amputation or other disease states that hinder normal biological function

- **Safety and protection**, which might be characterized as a modern spacesuit worn by scientists on the international space station (ISS), where the user is a component of a larger system that encapsulates the user, providing them with protection from hazardous environments while measuring the user's state of health and securely transmitting relevant data across and to numerous other systems; *Note*: This element triggers a conversation associated with a system of systems (SoS), where transformative engines, data aggregation, and interoperability become a central theme
- **Autonomous, semi-autonomous, and mechanical robotics**, which can be characterized as technology that is fully or partially controlled by wearable components, either through direct human interfaces or through enhanced AI technology; Specifically, self-driving vehicles (e.g., heavy machinery, spacecraft, cars, and drones) represent wearable robotic technology, while cobots are a class of semi-autonomous and autonomous robots that are able to safely work in the same environment as humans

With that all said, we believe the information that follows will provide you the reader with an enhanced view of technology that should be considered within the scope of wearable technologies, with an emphasis on data, technology, and human protection. Respectively, in this chapter, it will become evident that there is a need to follow the TIPPSS standard (trust, identity, privacy, protection, safety, and security) during all phases of technology development lifecycle and integration (i.e., assessing, developing, deploying, testing, and sustaining wearable robotics) and that any potential technological solution must comply with TIPPSS.

Use Cases

To understand how wearable robotics are continually evolving and impacting different industries, we have outlined use cases for healthcare, military, and manufacturing.

Healthcare

Thinking about the elements that healthcare professionals and patients might consider as wearable robotics, the technology associated with sensing, diagnostics, and mobility is the perfect place to start. Specifically, the wearable technology that first comes to mind could be a powered wheelchair or a watch with the built-in EKG. However, there are many more technologies that might not first come to mind. For example, technology that restores a disabled person's quality of life would be the next more common wearable robotic technologies. Accordingly, a prosthetic device that restores hearing, mobility, and vision would be a perfect fit within the scope of wearable robotics.

That said, as discussed in the beginning of this chapter, William's own experiences with prosthetic devices have been the impetus for many of the elements presented here. Similarly, though his needs might not be associated with all forms of disabilities, the idea that tech could make him 'super enabled' has become the foundation for considering technology that might work independently from its human host. For example, you might ask yourself if a human-controlled drone used to conduct triage operations of field injuries could be considered and the answer would be 'yes'. That point can be further exemplified when we examine current solutions that mimic human motions, while extending the human controller's vision, hearing, and physical motions.

This below the knee (BK) pictured is a prosthetic leg that was designed and built with the proposal that it would become an AI-enabled device, able to provide wireless communications to

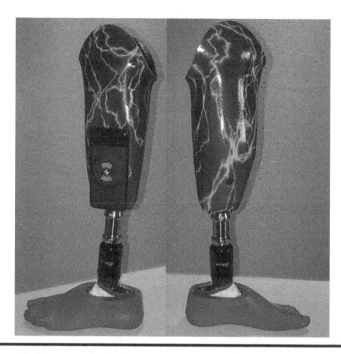

Figure 2.2   AI-enabled BK prosthetic leg (Harding, Medtronic, Inc., 2021).

an array of sensors, while controlling a fixed mounted edge computing system. The proposed AI system is an NVIDIA Jetson Nano, and the wireless power source would be a Chargetech 10 k mAh battery pack. Sensors will range from proximity, vision, thermal, pressure, accelerometer, environmental, strain gauge, SpO_2, BP, to piezo/vibration stimulation as well as multiple integrated TENS contact points. Additionally, the complete system will possess the ability to transmit notifications (i.e., via acoustic, light, BT, and Z-Wave) while also TX/RX data to/from other wearable devices and IoT-enabled mesh networks (Figure 2.2).

Next, as we think of traditional healthcare environments and patient care, an example scenario emerges. Specifically, while recovering at home following a major accident, the idea came to mind of using a semi-autonomous robot to perform the required three daily examinations. Whereas by placing a robot in the home of a recovering patient, the potential to extend a nurse's/doctor's effectiveness represents a considerable savings to the insurance provider. So, with pandemics emerging as a dominant barrier to person-to-person interactions, even in a hospital room, it would be a good idea to look at robotics as more than technology that some might personally wear.

Rural Americans, who make up 14% of the US population (Cromartie n.d.), face additional inequities due to geographical isolation. Moreover, rural areas lead urban and suburban counties in the percentage of adults who are 65 and over (Parker, 2018). This age group is at a higher risk of cardiovascular events. For various reasons, they have less access to healthcare. The broader scope of robotic healthcare can be aimed directly at alleviating inherent inequities found in rural areas. These inequities increase overall resource expenditure of receiving care, negatively impacting quality of life. So, if a person can be given a reconfigurable device to take home, this could eliminate several of the barriers to service. If the system can at least collect assessment data, then it can be relayed to a professional (therapist, doctor, etc.) for review. Next, the therapist can review and modify the rehabilitation protocol via a remote firmware update. If the system becomes more intelligent, through additional sensor technology and AI or machine learning (ML), the system can automatically adjust the rehabilitation protocol as the user progresses, or quickly note a lack of progress. Finally, if the rehabilitation is done, the system can be used as an assistive device. Internet of Medical Things (IoMT) devices support closed-loop and outcomes-based healthcare by improving communication, increasing the responsiveness of changes to care, and offering objective measures of improvement. Closed-loop healthcare is characterized by

- patient-centered collection and communication of data for improved well-being and response to trauma as well as routine physician-directed care
- in-home and wearable monitoring of personal health data, mobile collection, and reporting of data and actions
- edge analytics to assess well-being and provide responsive assistance

This ties in with communication issues. This idea is not new. As far back as 2003, the internet was being considered a tool to alleviate delivery problems with rural healthcare. Russell et al. showed knee angles measured from video captures were comparable in accuracy to those measured face-to-face with a physical goniometer (Russell, Jull, & Wootton, 2003).

Of course, speed requirements depend on the application. Lag time on the order of even days may be acceptable when doing an annual exam; however, in critical care requirements or real-time control of an assistive device where learning or actions occur off the device (in the edge/cloud) require faster and more stable communications. A 2018 report by the Federal Communication Commission reports coverage of fixed transmission rates of 25/3 Mbps has increased from 57.5% in 2014 to 68.9% in 2018 in rural United States vs. 98% in urban areas (appendix 9, 2020 Broadband Deployment Report (https://docs.fcc.gov/public/attachments/-FCC-20-50A2.pdf)). This rate is considered advanced telecommunications capability. Moreover, the rollout of next-generation networks (5G) technology should continue to lessen the connectivity gap. The USDA is also investing in E-connectivity infrastructure in rural areas (https://www.usda.gov/broadband).

Issues associated with rural healthcare can be extrapolated to compare to an astronaut on Mars where even less resources are readily available and the ability to access additional resources or communication is further delayed.

Military

When we think of military uses of wearable technologies many ideas pop into mind, such as exoskeletons that enhance personal skills or personal flying devices that enable a single human to scale obstacles, but there are many more examples that are worthy of consideration. Furthermore, the use of wearable robotics in the military is not always obvious, where much of the tech would be useless without the infrastructure that supports the technology. With that point in mind and considering that the technology enhances personal vision, strength, communications, stamina, hearing, and defense, a compromised infrastructure (e.g., hardware or software) could represent the loss of life.

For example, as we consider aligning military wearable robotic technology with health-centric systems, things like drones emerge specifically as they are used to assess dangerous environments and even triage injured individuals, but what really comes to mind is biometrics. Additionally, some wearable tech enhances the user's ability to avoid dangerous areas, navigate toward a target, triangulate weapon firing, and monitor the health of fellow users. However, the strength of those technologies is reinforced through the use of reliable and secure methods of data transfer and data analytics. That said, being able to create localized mobile networks and even communicate via high-speed bidirectional satellite represents a risk element that has to be mitigated in order for a military unit to achieve its goal and return safely.

Now, moving in a slightly different direction, wearable military tech can be characterized as protective, whereas some of those technologies can help electronically camouflage the user, defeat offensive devices, provide early warning to the user in the event of predictive danger, and even enable the user to survive in environmentally harsh conditions. Furthermore, some personal wearable military systems enable the user to integrate into more complex systems and work interoperably, which can be characterized as human mesh systems, where each user's unique equipment and capabilities are coordinated to form both an offensive and defensive system.

Lastly, though we don't often think of technology used in outer space as serving a military purpose, many early space technologies emerged from the military. The opposite can also be said, where technology prototyped and tested in space have formed the foundation for improvements associated with earth-bound military users. For example, manned maneuvering units (MMUs) have led to the development of similar personal flying systems as well as exoskeletons that enhance the user's ability to perform unique functions. Additionally, the use of lasers as a weapon is obvious, but as a communications method between individuals is something that proved practical for use with systems headed into outer space.

Manufacturing

Key concepts to consider: Wearable robotics in manufacturing can be characterized as technology that assists users with moving/lifting components (e.g., automobile industry) to tracking, controlling, and communicating with various processes and other users, as well as interconnecting with AI/ML technology that improves the quality of components built, increases yields, and assists with quality/validation actions relative to reduced scrap and human error. Such technologies can be represented as vision enhancements, gesture/voice recognition, improved sensing, and devices that amplify a user's strength and speed. Additionally, some wearable robotic technology enables users to work in environments that would normally be life threatening.

Integrating with human cognitive function, motor function, and sensing such that the technology functions intuitively (ease of use and usability) enables users to perform tasks that exceed normal human capacity. On the shop floor, this usually covers two cases: (1) strength, such as lifting heavy objects; and (2) repetition. Often, these actions may be combined, for example, lifting a heavy component in place and then being able to fix it with some type of a fastener (Think *Dave*: "I once caught a fish *this* big."). More often, the component will be supported some other way, such as a conveyor or table but the worker must still perform repeated overhead action that could lead to a repetitive stress injury. Wearables could also aid in preventing injury due to worker fatigue. Of course, this begs the question of just how reliant can we be on such devices? In the National Institute for Occupational Safety and Health, NIOSH hierarchy of controls (https://www.cdc.gov/niosh/topics/hierarchy/default.html) the most effective way to keep workers safe is to physically remove them from the hazard. Robots have already been developed to lay bricks and to hang drywall.

Devices used in the relatively fixed setting of a manufacturing environment may benefit from being tethered to provide both adequate (w/c) power and communications. Because Ethernet is a non-deterministic network (meaning variance in outputs even given potentially identical input), it is typically not used as-is for manufacturing.

Team Building

As we review these use cases and wearable technology continues to increase in prevalence throughout the world, particularly in the healthcare space, it becomes important to consider what skillsets are needed to implement and operationalize the use of this technology at scale. Leaders of healthcare organizations have realized the importance of an IT department as EHRs made computers part of every hospital room and clinic. However, as highlighted above, there were many opportunities for improvement in the rollout of desktop computing/EHRs in healthcare. How can the lessons learned from these implementations drive our staffing models as robotics technology moves forward?

One of the key points that can never be emphasized enough is the importance that the human plays when we first think of developing any wearable robotic solution. That said, there is a need to focus on two key roles that should be included in all phases associated with developing a wearable robotics concept. Those roles are the informatician and the lead systems integrator (LSI). However, it might help to first define those roles, since the individuals who possess the skills that those roles embody might not actually have those titles. Accordingly, a summary of each role is as follows.

Informatician

According to Nagle, Sermeus, and Junger (2017), an informatician is an individual working within the healthcare space, where that person possesses expertise and knowledge that enables them to mold a healthcare organization's management of healthcare information solutions, through direct contributions or indirect influences. Informaticians can be found in both the business side (e.g., Hospital Information Systems [HIS]) and patient-centered side of a healthcare organization, such that many healthcare professionals possess multidiscipline skills that enable them to focus on patient needs and the needs associated with data analytics and information management. Additionally, informaticians are characterized as individuals who possess skills in solving problems, making quality improvements associated with patient care, and are able to use change management methods in the assessment and integration of innovative healthcare solutions (Petersen, 2018).

Lead Systems Integrator

A lead systems integrator (LSI) is a role that generally came into being after 2000, when the DoD sought to have a single person in a role where the various silos that span an organization needed to be united toward a common goal. Furthermore, an individual in the role as an LSI embraces the qualities of a technologist as well as a transformative leadership style, where there is an expectation that the LSI expresses technological experience and competency in the field of healthcare solutions. That said, LSIs are professionals who are skilled in the use of innovative and often emerging technology (i.e., organic, electronic, and mechanical). Lastly, those LSI individuals who are skilled in healthcare technology are the individuals involved in the technology adoption phases associated with accessing, designing, and participative engagement, where the perspectives of those individuals are that technology and healthcare professionals coexist to care for humans (Locsin, 2017).

Considerations

Once the skill sets and teams are in place to expand on wearable robotics, we must think through the impacts to a successful implementation, what pieces if done well will create a substantial value add to the industry? As wearable technology expands throughout industries, experience shows that key factors must be considered to ensure new technology implementation is effective and seamless to the systems with which they are integrating. Through our collective work, we have identified the following areas of focus to think through in order to make a wearable robotics project impactful.

Interoperability (Interconnectivity)

Interoperability is the ability for humans, hardware, and software technology to connect and communicate using a standard protocol, where data may be transformed across dissimilar technology (Wager, Lee, & Glaser, 2017). Technology that is considered interoperable represents solutions that are able to connect with other technology and exchange data using standardized protocols through a common interface such as is characterized by a transformational engine. That proposal is supported by the Evans et al. (2017) and Slight et al. (2015) material where technology cannot be considered as successfully integrated within an environment if that technology is incompatible with existing technology.

Interoperability assumes that technology acceptance should evaluate technology and social aspects to identify methods for technology integration, while also considering five factors that influence the adoption of technology such as wearable robotics:

- Technology quality
- Integration management
- Solution ease of use and usability
- Impact on institutional development
- Sustainability

The combination of those five factors is appropriate at any phase of integration (e.g., assessment, decision making, adoption, design, development, deployment, and sustainability), where the concept of solution interoperability embodies human, hardware, and software influencers. Respectively, the integration of wearable technology with humans and other technological systems cannot be done through the use of EHR and EMR systems adequately. Whereas EHRs and EMRs originated as a billing solution, many organizations may view EHRs and EMRs as their interoperability solution. However, that point was missed during the implementation of EHRs and EMRs where technology interoperability should have been examined in the exact same way as most organizations handle the integration of any new technological solution (i.e., with an eye toward working with existing systems). For example, though most healthcare organizations seek to adopt a technology solution that would accomplish the task of interoperability across all solutions, the examination of a technology's usefulness, vs. interoperability, resulted in many technology adoption failures (Rosenbaum, 2015). According to Rosenbaum, issues associated with successfully adopting EHR/EMR solutions emerged not because of any perceived *technophobic* behavior, but instead because the solution was not fully understood nor had it been properly assessed related to its usability. From the inference that technology cannot be successfully adopted if it is not fully understood, it is proposed that theoretical models such as IASAM3 (Integrated Acceptance and Sustainability Assessment Methodology) promote an understanding of more than just the advertised usability of a technology and more toward promoting an understanding of technology interoperability (Aizstrauta & Ginters, 2017; Ginters, Mezitis, & Aizstrauta, 2018). With IASAM3 in mind, it is suggested that all future technological integration efforts be guided by the theoretical model of IASAM3.

Similarly, the negative consequences of a narrow focus on only a few phases of technology integration and the ability for a solution to function interoperably can be exposed if solution integrators looked beyond the ability for technology to solve a singular task and toward technological compatibility with existing solutions. From that point, which emphasizes increasing the scope of technology integration, it is suggested that EHR/EMR technology integrators would realize greater success if the technological experiences of all relevant stakeholders were included in the overall assessment of technology perspectives. That said, the healthcare industry lags other industries in its ability to integrate technology that functions interoperably with existing technology, which is exemplified by currently used methods, practices, electronic data, and healthcare equipment.

Quality

In many ways, at least at the consumer level, the term 'quality' can be quite subjective. We tend to work out a cost/benefit analysis to decide whether our product was quality. Something we paid more money for, we expect to perform optimally and last longer. If we paid less, we may be more willing to put up with inefficiencies in performance or design. Harbor Freight Tools is known for "quality tools at discount prices". If something were to break or malfunction for a customer "at least they didn't pay much for it". In other areas, sports for example, a baseball player may have been said to have a quality at bat even though he did not get a hit or even reach base. This connotes that there will be some reward later in the game – he saw a lot of pitches so he should be better prepared for the next at bat against the same pitcher, or the pitcher's pitch count was higher so you'll get into the opposing team's bullpen sooner. Conversely, major league baseball keeps an official statistic of quality starts for pitchers. To qualify, a pitcher must pitch at least 6 innings and give up at most 3 earned runs. This may be closer to what is considered quality from a production, or engineering standpoint, quality carries a much different meaning. Interestingly, quality certifications such as ISO 9000 say nothing about the output quality but rather tracing the process – "say what you do, and do what you say".

In manufacturing, quality is typically considered with respect to measurable parameters compared against quantifiable metrics. For example, whether a produced part is within tolerance. Depending on the complexity of the requirements and of the part, this type of check may be performed with a go/no-go gauge, an optical comparator, or a coordinate measuring machine. In a perfect world, none of this would be necessary. You would design your process in such a way that the "correct" part is produced every time. But because we live in a probabilistic world, this is not the case. Every step in a process allows for variation to enter the system, impacting whether a particular part is made to an acceptable standard/level.

It is said you can't inspect in quality. This is true. All inspection does is potentially keep defects from getting to an end user. The goal of continuous improvement is to refine a process such that parts are produced correctly and with less variability.

An example in the continuous steelmaking process, liquid steel is poured into "bathtubs" referred to as a tundish. Ports at the bottom of the tundish allow the liquid to flow out into a mold, where the intermediate shape is formed and the steel solidifies. The produced slabs are then further processed – they are rolled to reduce thickness, processed to achieve certain mechanical properties, and may be coated to provide protection against rust. However, when liquid steel is exposed to air, solid, nonmetallic inclusions are formed by the reaction of oxygen in the air with aluminum dissolved in the steel. Paint doesn't stick to inclusions well. So, if the steel containing an inclusion ends up as say a car door, that shiny new vehicle will start to spall paint where it chips off, not long after. Often inclusions are found manually or by camera systems. Improvements to the process are made by shrouding the pouring of steel. Unfortunately, if you start with a new tundish, it is full of air. One project Neil worked on was to design a cover and argon purging system to flood a new tundish with an inert gas so the steel was not exposed to air from the beginning. This allowed his team to apply the first slab to the order in which it was intended as opposed to an order with less stringent requirements (and therefore less costly). The projected savings of this project was several million (in 1990) dollars a year.

Another job Neil held was as the *quality* design engineer for a finishing plant. Among other responsibilities, he maintained the "recipes" that allowed his team to achieve certain requirements for customers. Often, they needed to meet customer requirements for chemistry and mechanical properties. The entire process was set up such that, nominally, the product would always meet requirements. They had historical data to reference and design and engineering judgment if they attempted to, for example, apply an "off-chemistry" steel to a particular order.

Further knowledge with respect to quality came through implementing design controls and risk mitigation while working as a design engineer on hip implants – design process, verification and validation, process failure modes effects and analysis (pFMEA), and design failure modes effects and analysis (dFMEA).

Approaches to continuous improvement were leveraged – green belt, yellow belt, black belt. The official quality organization site is asq.org.

Communications

When thinking of "communications", we might first be drawn to think about language and human-to-human discussions, which might not be off track, but with respect to technology, communications might best be described as an exchange of information between devices and even the transformation of that information. For example, when we consider the need for secure communications, it is a good idea to think beyond establishing standards associated with data exchange protocols and to think about the physical connections as well as the standards that enable accurate transfers of data/information. Furthermore, when the lens of communications is focused on healthcare, we need to think of the exchange of information from device to device, software to software, and even humans to systems/devices.

The point of including humans in the mix of communications is an important point that many people overlook. Whereas the human element is probably the most important element such that when we think of technology integration, we must include humans in the formula. Specifically, the human factor is critical to the successful integration of technology, where it is the element that must always be kept in mind regarding deliverables. Furthermore, when considering the concept of communications, keep in mind that it is not a singular focus on exchanging information, but also the methods for communicating. That point emphasizes that the supporting infrastructure must be kept at the forefront, where wireless and wired methods of communications represent the foundation of communications.

Furthermore, communications can exist in many states not normally thought of when considering healthcare-related applications. For example, most forms of communications might be classified as passive, semi-passive, and active, where those three classifications are generalized as push/transmit or pull/receive data. That example applies to both human and technology communications, where the method of communications might be electrical, ultrasonic, infrared and photonic, chemical, acoustic, and even symbolic. However, when we speak of healthcare communications, we are mostly focused on the transfer of data via wired and wireless data transfers. That said, as technology evolves, through the lens of the Internet of Bodies (IoB), the way in which data is transferred to and from humans will expand from audio and visual methods to embrace direct cognitive integration as well as through other human senses.

- Protocols
- IoT/IoB (e.g., mesh configurations)

While most technologists associate the term digital twin with manufacturing, there's a use for this conceptual model in medicine. From the health perspective, we are interested in a physiological model that, because it is connected, can be updated in near-real-time. Also, in either case, the goal is to improve the outcome based on intelligent reaction to and prediction from the data. This should allow for us to improve process and quality as well.

Potential issues described above (regarding power mgt) for each type of application need to be addressed. The need for portable, long-lasting power supplies is addressed as energy storage, delivery, and management improvements. 3D printing capabilities continue to transform the manufacturing process, allowing for quick and inexpensive part replacements. Ubiquitous communications guarantee that pertinent health data can be shared even from remote locations and that hardware and software can be seamlessly integrated without boundaries. Commercial electroencephalograph systems which record the electrical activity of the brain allow sufficient resolution to discern a user intent. Miniaturization makes it easier to achieve the necessary footprint for low-profile and unobtrusive devices to be placed on a human. Finally, big-data analytics can leverage the plethora of healthcare data that will become available.

Such advancements have allowed us to transition from the clinical arena for data collection, analysis, and diagnostics to what is often called "data in the wild" since we can perform the same functions with a user in her natural habitat. Consider that clothing, for example, has taken on a whole new meaning with the advent of sensors that can be woven into clothing. This information can be used to change environmental controls based on the wearers' perceived state, e.g., stressed or cold. Force and acceleration sensors embedded into running shoes or accelerometers worn on the body can measure a running event such as time and distance as well as provide real-time feedback on gait mechanics (see Figures 2.3 and 2.4). Instrumented devices abound! Lower-extremity prosthetics can provide adaptive gait or be controlled via an app; implants can measure performance and wear; and sensors can even be placed inside the body to monitor bone healing. Methods for monitoring and control inside and outside the body are numerous and interfacing all of these allow the setup of a network referred to as a body area network and the Internet of Bodies (IoB).

Such networks embody not just a wearable that is used for a specific purpose such as tracking the number of steps you take, but a litany of wearable devices or a device with various types of sensors measuring different physiological parameters that are connected to a wider network. Moreover, the IoB potentially includes multiple humans (bodies) into the ecosystem, e.g., to effect contact tracing. This brings with it all the TIPPSS issues when multiple bodies are incorporated into the ecosystem (Liu, Xiao & Merritt, 2020).

Body networks have been developed to predict traumatic events such as the onset of an epileptic seizure or an overdose. In 2017, 70,000 deaths in the United States were related to opioid overdose (Graig, Olchefske, & Alper, 2019). Such systems can be paired with a phone to notify emergency personnel. Any wearable that can share data as part of this ecosystem can be used to close the healthcare loop, providing objective and continual assessment information. Such systems may provide the concomitant benefit of providing large-scale, longitudinal data to inform better outcomes. This could have the potential to optimize resource allocation better than continued

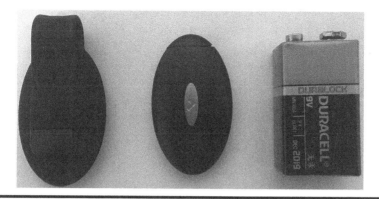

Figure 2.3 A CotS (no longer on the market) wearable (center) with attachment clip (Petroff, 2019) (based on Folland et al., 2017). A 9 V battery is shown for comparison. The wearable used accelerometers to determine running gait metrics. It could be connected with an iPhone and associated app to store summary gait data. The user had no access to his/her raw data, which begs the question of if a user purchases hardware and associated software to what extent has he/she also given consent for her data to be used?

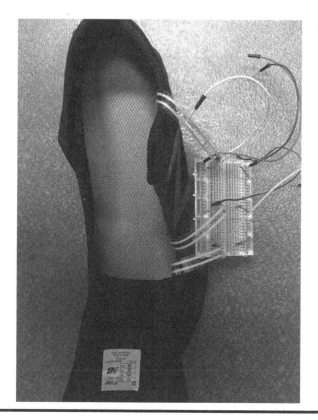

Figure 2.4 Flexiforce™ sensors embedded in a shoe to inform running gait (Petroff, 2019).

discrete device trials. It has been estimated that, worldwide, manufacturers could save $100B by data sharing of operational best practices (World Economic Forum, 2020). How much could be saved in healthcare?

Internet of Bodies

The Internet of Bodies (IoB) is a relatively new term created to describe a system where the thing connected to the internet is a human (Matwyshyn, 2019). Eventually, we may prefer to differentiate these systems from systems in which multiple humans might interact. Certain applications, like an artificial pancreas or the running wearable shown previously, we may not consider as an IoB system because only a single body is involved. The "thing" in the IoT is still the device. Ultimately, it may come down to what level of agency a user has. It's one thing to agree to let a machine inject you with a certain amount of medicine. It is true that if this machine is connected to a larger network, it may be using information about you to improve treatment, not only for you but for others like you. However, it is also true that if said device malfunctions through a hacking event, it can also kill you (Newman, 2019). It is also true that unsecure data from consumer wearables can give away an individual's location and tendencies, making it easier to perpetrate a crime against the individual.

The IoB takes on a more pernicious tone when we think of information about multiple bodies also being connected. It's a whole other level to let an entity track your whereabouts and attempt to assert some control over your behavior, e.g., tracking medical compliance (Glatter, 2015), or to track your whereabouts such as might be the case for contact tracing. In either case, we may say this is being done for our own good, but where matters of public health are at stake, to what level must anonymity be sacrificed? Unsecure data from groups have disclosed locations of installations that we may prefer to keep hidden (Morse, 2018).

Ultimately, as connected system components increase, TIPPSS (Trust, Identity, Privacy, Protection, Safety, and Security) becomes more difficult to ensure. The ideal ecosystem will operate effectively and efficiently under TIPPSS and be robust enough to deter outside attacks while allowing for the ecosystem to expand.

Integration

Integration of wearable robotics with humans should not only focus on the end solution but instead consider all elements that start from the idea of a technological solution and move to the point where the human is using the tech and it is being sustained/supported. Thus, we must approach the tactical creation of a solution with an eye toward the strategy that we use to ideate and eventually deploy the technology. Consequently, when considering the finer details associated with integrating any form of new technology/solution (even with a human), there are eleven phases that must be considered as key to the successful delivery of that new technology/solution. Specifically, those key phases are as follows and are influenced by the previously discussed theoretical model of IASAM3:

1. Project Start
   a. Requirements gathering/scope definition
   b. Technology exploration
   c. Risk assessment
2. Solution/Technology Assessment

3. Decision Making/Technology Selection
4. Adoption of New Technology
5. New Solution Design/Architecture
6. New Solution Development
7. Solution Testing/Validation
8. Deployment/Release
9. Hypercare
10. Sustainability
    a. Training
    b. Knowledge transfer
    c. Support
11. End-of-Life

Security

Thoughts to consider/talking points: When thinking of "Security" it is best to think of all elements that are touched by a wearable robotics solution, from the creation of a solution to the point where the solution is ended. Specifically, we must think of not only the physical safety and protection of humans/patients but also the security needs of data. Whereas appropriate security ensures that devices work as designed, data quality is high, data transference is timely, and that patient identity/health is paramount. Furthermore, when looking at security from the perspective of device and system manufactures, there is a need to protect sensitive organizational data such as patents and trade secrets.

- Technology/Hardware (e.g., chip level and antennas)
- Data (e.g., transmission, storage, recovery, and destruction)
- User (e.g., personal protection such as mental and physical health)
- Power
- Noninvasive blood pressure (nbp)
- Passive
- Inductive
- Active/embedded
- Energy harvesting

Power

Unlike a fixed environment where a robust supply of power is available, wearable devices will have to bring their power with them. If a battery is present, physical space required for batteries, how and how quickly batteries can be charged, battery capacity, overall power requirements, stable performance at low capacity, and whether a battery can be replaced must all be considered. Additionally, once we move self-powered technology into a patient, there is a need to protect the patient and the technology from the adverse events that might be tied to a loss of power. That point also emphasizes the need to consider what might happen if a patient's immune system attacks the technology and potentially exposes the patient to the chemicals that are contained in a battery. Lastly, some implanted technology such as pain therapy requires more power than can be contained in a single power source, whereas the technology might need to be recharged inductively from an external source.

One way to reduce power requirements is to improve the efficiency of devices that require power. Of course, this is a never-ending battle, and, as luck would have it, more autonomy requires more power. However, strides continue to be made in power management. Processors requiring less power are being produced. Communications are being made more efficient and reliable by Bluetooth Low Energy (BLE) which is better for short bursts as opposed to continuous streams of data. BLE communication is also more robust due to its use of frequency hopping. Moreover, near-field transmissions can be used for power, charging, and communications. Finally, RFID receivers can operate in "sleep" mode and are powered by an external antenna.

Inductive Charging

Inductive charging uses electromagnetic induction to perform charging wirelessly. Long after Nicola Tesla imagined a world enabled by wireless charging and communication (King, 2013), that dream is beginning to become reality. For some time now, we have had portable devices that can be recharged wirelessly, and a start-up in New Zealand is trying to take the concept full scale (Delbert, 2020). Of course, when we discuss inductive charging, there are issues that have to be overcome as it relates to the use of RF energy through biological material. That said, RF energy may be absorbed by fluids such as human blood, where there is a need to use advanced antenna designs (e.g., fractal antennas). There is also a requirement to reduce the amount of biological material that might exist between the implanted device's transceiver and the external power source in order to leverage the RF energy.

Energy Harvesting

Returning energy to the system is often mechanical which mimics the actions of tendons. For art imitating life, the RFID tags in the Jurassic Park dinosaurs were charged by the animal's motion and heat. This allowed the animals to be located long after the park had shut down. Watches charged from body movement do actually exist. Wearable textiles have been developed that can run on the wearer's sweat (Lv et al., 2018).

Think about all the times you interacted with an electrical or electromechanical system today. Did you drive to school today? If so, did you get stopped at a red light? How did the traffic light "know" cars were present at the intersection? Did you buy something from a vending machine? Did you use an automated checkout? Did you use a smartphone?

Batteries provide the power supply for circuit components. The key is understanding how long batteries can adequately power a device. Battery capacity continues to improve. Electric cars have been around much longer than most people imagine. For example, in 1890, a Scotland-born chemist living in Des Moines, Iowa, William Morrison, applied for a patent on the electric carriage he'd built perhaps as early as 1887. It appeared in a city parade in 1888, according to the *Des Moines Register*. With front-wheel drive, 4 hp, and a reported top speed of 20 mph, it had 24 battery cells that needed recharging every 50 miles (Wilson 2018). Now consumers dispose of as much as 3 billion batteries, including rechargeables, annually. Portability competes with battery capacity. The design of wearables needs to consider power in its life cycle for both performance reasons and waste reduction considerations.

Actuators are a key component of many devices and are large power drains. High-power requirements compete with battery life. Additionally, technologies that draw high amounts of power can generate considerable heat, which in itself may represent an issue for the recipient of an implanted medical device. That negative consequence of high-power medical devices can be reduced by locating the devices in areas where there is high tissue perfusion, which can help move heat away from an implanted device. Accordingly, the move to using rechargeable devices can help mitigate the issues associated with exothermic reactions leveraging the following elements.

- Communications: always on, searching for connections, low-power bluetooth
- Safety: lithium ion batteries exploding during charging, Li-Polymer
- AI/ML (includes predictive analytics, statistics, and quantum computing)
- Companies selling analytics as services

Artificial intelligence has come a long way since Alan Turing suggested a test for whether a machine could be considered intelligent, *Shakey* managed to navigate its way around a room with an unknown obstacle, or the temperature control of a cement kiln was improved based on a set of if/then qualitative rules, void of any mathematical modeling of the process (Holmblad & Ostergaard, 1982). Since then, great advances were made in the area of game playing, and when opponents said the search space of chess was not deep enough to demonstrate "intelligence" a machine went on to beat Chinese Go master Ke Jie in a tournament. In medicine, there has been promise and some success with AI, in particular with respect to image recognition and processing (Powell, 2020). Along with such rapid developments, the seedy underbelly of AI and ML has been exposed. We've seen AI and ML be farmed out as a service with untrusted use of data, in particular those that falsely promise to predict social outcomes such as job success, policing, and at risk youth to name a few (Narayanan). Healthcare has had its fair share of AI controversies, and this book's editor believes it all boils down to a fundamental lack of a true depth of understanding a clinical problem, along with the requisite data strategy inclusive of data management, data governance, data engineering, data science, and the rigor required to deliver the right data practices required for a useful AI solution. Ms. Douville believes this must be done with deeply understood, narrow use cases which are backed by superb data practices and the correctly constructed teams of skillsets: data analysts, data scientists, data engineers, data infrastructure engineers, ML engineers, medical expertise, and clinical operations. Only then can AI be applied reliably and credibly to a correct foundation. Failures of AI in medicine so far have largely stemmed from casting too wide a net (Ross and Aguilar, 2021).

After Shakey, developments in AI were, well, shaky and stagnated for quite some time. We did not see any new breakthroughs until deep neural networks entered the scene. These were enabled by major advances in computing technology, especially in storage and processing power with graphical processing units (GPUs). Now we've seen AI/ML show up everywhere; places we wouldn't expect and places we don't know about, which is also an issue. To wit, AI has been used to generate fake news text and to remove Superman's mustache. A brief history of applications includes

- Shakey (~1966–1972)
- Deep Blue beats Gary Kasparov in chess (1997)
- Watson wins on Jeopardy (2011)
- AlphaGo beats Go Master (2016)
- IBM's project debater (2018)

To show that Shakey really was foundational in developments of AI/ML, in 2017, the IEEE recognized Shakey as the world's first mobile intelligent robot. Much of what came out of that is still used today, for example, for path planning of the original Mars rover.

The combination of fusion between multiple sensors collecting information about a process and computer power has opened Pandora's box. That box is not going to close; we are going to continue to see the proliferation of data and, ideally, causations associated with the data to continue to predict what the next step in the process is going to be or to drive a particular outcome. Spurious events can confuse AI/ML systems during training, resulting in correlations being mistaken as causation events.

How we use that data is going to be key in the future of TIPPSS. We must be able to use that data ethically and transparently and also the ways in which this data is analyzed needs to be transparent as well.

Pandemic

The COVID-19 pandemic has brought to light a need for advancements in technology that helps to assess health conditions, to create solutions that interoperably consume information, and to securely transmit resulting data to other humans or AI/ML systems. However, the needs that have been amplified by the COVID epidemic have always existed. For example, as a member of the largest medical device manufacturing company, it is not always possible to jump on a plane and assist distant colleagues across the globe to resolve a critical issue. And if our Puerto Rico facility is in the eye of a hurricane or an Italian hospital is covered in snow, how do we quickly solve health-related issues? So, though the COVID crisis has made it nearly impossible to arrive on a proverbial white horse to aid our colleagues, the need to create solutions that enable a user to analyze their current state and to safely transmit their personal health data has made the need for personalized medicine and technology interconnectivity to be a critical need.

Now add in an increasing desire to remain, recover/heal, or even die in our own homes, we start to see how important it is that we develop technological solutions that are easy to deploy, use, and/or wear. Specifically, those ease of use technologies will need to help us and our caregivers (e.g., family members) to quickly determine the health of others, even if it is a simple thing like determining if someone didn't get out of bed or didn't take their medicine. To that end, it is easy to imagine some day a scenario whereas a person's clothing contains all of the technology that would sense their health, wirelessly convey their current state, and even apply therapy such as electrical stimulation as well as thermal variances that would reduce the impact of an undesired health event. Additionally, it is easy to imagine the use of autonomous or semi-autonomous robots checking on people in their home environment or delivering health-related items via a drone. Thus, events such as COVID-19 have become the impetus for creating solutions that can ultimately save time and money associated with resolving healthcare needs. Whereas we now see how important it becomes that we consider developing and deploying solutions with a focus on interconnectedness across a broad array of systems.

Future of Wearable and Robotics Technology

Future ideas to consider within the scope of wearable robotics might be: cognitive devices (i.e., thought-based communications, control, and notification); biocybernetics (e.g., human to technology integration, such as to vehicles, entertainment systems, other humans, restorative therapy devices, continuous health monitoring tech, and enhanced physiological devices that are worn or implanted within the user); immune/hormone system monitoring and control; energy harvesting technology that would provide the user with uninterrupted use of technology; technology that connects directly to visual and auditory cortex to enhance an individual's ability to better interact in their environments and even connect with other individuals through embedded VR and AR experiences.

The technology associated with what we call extended reality (XR) is the perfect example of wearable robotics, where users are able to visualize remote locations and virtually interact with the end user. For example, think about a physician performing a surgery while wearing an augmented reality (AR) headset like a HoloLens 2, a Vuzix M4000, or a RealWear device and then think about how great it would be for that physician to have a collaborator or instructor literally seeing everything they see, while annotating or emphasizing areas that the surgeon should pay particular attention to. Then think about a classroom full of future doctors being able to experience first hand what the surgeon is experiencing through sounds, haptic and cognitive feedback... Does it sound feasible? Well it should, because it already exists. Accordingly, as an innovative thought leader, it is vital that you are aware of these emerging technologies, because you are going to be asked to deploy, implement, and integrate them.

For example, even if you are not being asked to deploy some of the XR technology mentioned, there is little doubt that the people who work for you have already started using such tools to design new surgical layouts or healthcare environments, all while sitting in their home and collaborating in virtual environments. That point emphasizes the importance for CIOs to embrace a transformative leadership style, where they don't assume that all answers to technology questions must be answered by themselves, but instead those answers reside in the minds of their direct reports, such that through transparency across their group and accountability of action, all members of a CIO's team is engaged as relevant stakeholders. Furthermore, when developing potential wearable robotic solutions, many CIOs would be surprised to learn that many of their team members possess unknown interests and skills in particular technologies that are not being recognized or leveraged. However, a transformative CIO is that person who will be more successful once they establish open lines of communications and transparently share corporate strategies with their employees.

Now, thinking of what the future of wearable robotics represents, we might be tempted to think of Mr. Data from Star Trek: Next Generation, but we believe the future will focus on expanding human capabilities beyond the normal five senses. For example, as AI and ML devices evolve, so will our ability to integrate those technologies through biological interfaces. That said, we might be looking at technology that can tap directly into a human's visual and auditory cortex or that the technology can feed data directly to our conscience and subconscious centers of reasoning as part of what is described as biocybernetics. It might also be through the expansion of nanorobotics such as a hybrid design that represents bioidentical synthetic and biocompatible technology that would not be attacked by the human immune system. Furthermore, it is proposed that future wearable technology could expand human sensing by transforming digital data across neuro pathways and actually use biological elements to store information. So, don't look toward the future in search of a platform that will be the interconnector that binds the human to wearable robotics, but instead embrace the concept that the human is the platform, the data pathways, the data collector and transmitter, the storage medium, and potentially the power source for wearable robotics.

Lastly, there are some discussions that have been started around the concept of transferring a human's consciousness, but those ideas might be further in the future than we think. Whereas we might believe that we understand the human brain enough that we know what to transfer or more specifically "what is the human consciousness", but in reality, we are only a few generations from carving holes in a head to let out the evil spirits. The latter point also emphasizes that each individual is a collection of their personal experiences, where we are each unique, and that our ability to understand ourselves is equivalent to a three dimensional being trying to describe the fourth dimension. Thus, it is important for us not to think in terms of the linear transference of information (e.g., like the movement of one electron) or that information contained within the human consciousness is anything like we have accepted as data in the digital age.

Long-Term Effects?

The goal of many exoskeletons is to decrease metabolic rate during locomotion (see, e.g., Kim et al. 2019). While this may seem like a good thing, especially if gait is permanently compromised, what long-term effects might this have in the case of an exoskeleton used for augmentation, such as in manufacturing or military applications? We know that the brain and motion are inextricably linked and that complex exercise seems to promote neuroplasticity. So, if we take this away, what happens to the brain?

In this chapter, we hope that we have piqued your curiosity as you think about how your internal and external partnerships will help operationalize the deployment, implementation, adoption, and ongoing improvement of optimizing lives and function through wearable technology and robotics.

Applicable Components

Here is a non-exhaustive list of components that might be characterized as potential platforms and elements associated with wearable robotics:

- *Clothing*
  - Shoes, shirt, belt, pants, hat, coat, watch
  - Gloves (e.g., haptic, thermal, and sensing)
- *Elements internal and external to the body*
  - Implanted medical devices (e.g., cardiac, neuro, spinal, muscular, and vascular)
    - ICDs, IPGs, DBS, etc.
    - Spinal components with embedded sensing
    - Pain therapy
  - Diabetes/drug pump and diabetic monitoring devices (caregivers and patient)
    - Injectable sensing
    - Wearable sensors and pumps
  - Medical alert devices
    - EKG/ECG, BP, Pulse Ox, etc.
    - Guarded pain response
    - Body position monitoring
  - Sleep/activity monitoring
    - Rings (e.g., Motiv)
    - Earrings
    - Necklace
    - Watches
    - Shoes
    - Also might consider bedding elements (e.g., sheets, pillows, and SleepEight)

- Environmental sensors
  - UV index
  - Air quality/particulate count
  - Humidity
  - Windchill
  - Barometric pressure
- Tattoos and stick-on (e.g., sensing)
■ *Prosthetics (Legs, Arms/Hands, Fingers, Eyes, Hearing)*
  - Enhancing normal function
    - Strength, endurance, vision, hearing, and better understanding of our environment
  - Replacing normal function
    - C-Leg, ankle, arm, hand, hip, knee, eyes, ears
    - 3D printed and molded replacements (FDM, SLA, and SLS)
      Note: Some forms of prosthetics exist as integrated stimulators that electrically motivate a person's non-functioning skeletal or muscular system to restore motor function associated with motion.
■ *Exoskeletons (e.g., for hazardous environments or restorative therapy)*
  - Military
  - Protection/safety
■ *Sensing Tech*
  - Cognitive, environmental, diagnostics, proximity, pressure, range
  - SpO_2, galvanic, thermal, pain, range of motion, position, EKG/ECG, BP
  Note: Wearable tech is not just for humans, where it can also be associated with animals (e.g., mammals and marine). Additionally, robotics are not always going to be something that is easily visible or large enough to be seen by the human eye. For example, micro and nanorobots are being developed for use in medical applications, such as to attack cancers and repair damaged cells.

References

Aizstrauta, Dace, and Egils Ginters. "Using market data of technologies to build a dynamic integrated acceptance and sustainability assessment model." *Procedia Computer Science* 104, 2017: 501–508. doi: 10.1016/j.procs.2017.01.165.

Delbert, Caroline. "Does wireless power transfer work? - Wireless electricity in NZ." Popular Mechanics, August 6, 2020. https://www.popularmechanics.com/science/a33522699/wireless-electricity-new-zealand/.

Evans, Steven, Doroteya Vladimirova, Maria Holgado, Kirsten Van Fossen, Miying Yang, Elisabete A. Silva, and Claire Y. Barlow. "Business model innovation for sustainability: Towards a unified perspective for creation of sustainable business models." *Business Strategy and the Environment* 26, no. 5, 2017: 597–608. doi: 10.1002/bse.1939.

Folland, Jonathan P., Sam J. Allen, Matthew I. Black, Joseph C. Handsaker, and Stephanie E Forrester. Running technique is an important component of running economy and performance. *Medicine & Science in Sport & Exercise* 49(7), 2017: 1412–1423. doi: 10.1249/MSS.0000000000001245.

Ginters, Egils, and Dace Aizstrauta. "Technologies sustainability modeling." *World Conference on Information Systems and Technologies* 746, 2018: 659–668. Springer, Cham. doi: 10.1007/978-3-319-77712-2_61.

Glatter, Robert. "Proteus digital health and Otsuka seek FDA approval for world's first digital pill." Forbes, September 15, 2015. https://www.forbes.com/sites/robertglatter/2015/09/14/proteus-digital-health-and-otsuka-seek-fda-approval-for-worlds-first-digital-medicine/?sh=8634520603dd.

Graig, Laurene, India Olchefske, and Joe Alper, eds. *Pain Management for People with Serious Illness in the Context of the Opioid Use Disorder Epidemic: Proceedings of a Workshop.* Washington, DC: National Academies Press, 2019. doi: 10.17226/25435.

Holmblad, L. P., and J.-J. Ostergaard. "Control of a cement kiln by fuzzy logic techniques." *IFAC Proceedings Volumes* 14, no. 2, 1982: 809–814. doi: 10.1016/s1474-6670(17)63582-1.

Kim, Jinsoo, Giuk Lee, Roman Heimgartner, Dheepak Arumukhom, Nikos Karavas, Danielle Nathanson, Ignacio Galiana, et al. "Reducing the metabolic rate of walking and running with a versatile, portable exosuit." *Science* 365, no. 6454, 2019: 668–672. doi: 10.1126/science.aav7536.

King, Gilbert. "The rise and fall of Nikola Tesla and his tower." *Smithsonian Magazine*, February 4, 2013. https://www.smithsonianmag.com/history/the-rise-and-fall-of-nikola-tesla-and-his-tower-11074324/.

Liu, Xiao and Jeff Merritt. Shaping the future of the internet of bodies: New challenges of technology governance. Cologny/Geneva, Switzerland, World Economic Forum, 2020.

Locsin, Rozzano C. "The co-existence of technology and caring in the theory of technological competency as caring in nursing." *The Journal of Medical Investigation* 64, no. 1.2, 2017: 160–164. doi: 10.2152/jmi.64.160.

Lv, Jian, Itthipon Jeerapan, Farshad Tehrani, Lu Yin, Cristian Abraham Silva-Lopez, Ji-Hyun Jang, Davina Joshuia, et al. "Sweat-based wearable energy harvesting-storage hybrid textile devices." *Energy and Environmental Science* 11, no. 12, 2018: 3431–3442. doi: 10.1039/c8ee02792g.

Matwyshyn, Andrea M. "The internet of bodies." *William & Mary Law Review* 61, no. 1, 2019: 77–167. https://scholarship.law.wm.edu/wmlr/vol61/iss1/3.

Morse, Jack. "Strava Heatmap shows that fitness trackers represent a privacy threat." Mashable, January 30, 2018. https://mashable.com/2018/01/30/strava-fitness-tracking-apps-data-privacy/.

Nagle, Lynn M., Walter Sermeus and Alain Junger. "Evolving role of the nursing informatics specialist." *Forecasting Informatics Competencies for Nurses in the Future of Connected Health* 232, 2017: 212. doi: 10.3233/978-1-61499-738-2-212.

Narayanan, A. How to recognize AI snake oil. Princeton University: Center for Information Technology Policy. https://www.cs.princeton.edu/~arvindn/talks/MIT-STS-AI-snakeoil.pdf.

Newman, Lily Hay. "Hackers made an app that kills to prove a point." Wired, July 16, 2019. https://www.wired.com/story/medtronic-insulin-pump-hack-app/?mbid=email_onsiteshare.

Parker, Kim, Juliana Menasce Horowitz, Anna Brown, Richard Fry, D'vera Cohn, and Ruth Igielnik "Demographic and economic trends in urban, suburban and rural communities." Pew Research Center, Washington, DC, May 22, 2018. https://www.pewsocialtrends.org/2018/05/22/demographic-and-economic-trends-in-urban-suburban-and-rural-communities/.

Petersen, Carolyn. "Patient informaticians: Turning patient voice into patient action." *JAMIA Open* 1, no. 2, 2018: 130–135. doi: 10.1093/jamiaopen/ooy014.

Petroff, Neil. "A case study comparing running metrics determined from unshod and various shod running events." *2019 41st Annual International Conference of the IEEE Engineering in Medicine and Biology Society (EMBC)*, 2019: 3175–3178. doi: 10.1109/EMBC.2019.8857238.

Powell, A. "AI revolution in medicine." Last Modified November 11, 2020. https://news.harvard.edu/gazette/story/2020/11/risks-and-benefits-of-an-ai-revolution-in-medicine/.

Rosenbaum, Lisa. "Transitional chaos or enduring harm? The EHR and the disruption of medicine." *New England Journal of Medicine* 373, no. 17, 2015: 1585–1588. doi: 10.1056/NEJMp1509961.

Ross, C., and M. Aguilar. "Inside the fall of Watson Health: How IBM's audacious plan to 'change the face of health care' with AI fell apart." STAT (blog), 2021. https://www.statnews.com/2021/03/08/ibm-watson-health-sale/.

Russell, T. G., G. A. Jull, and R. Wootton. "Can the internet be used as a medium to evaluate knee angle?" *Manual Therapy* 8, no. 4, 2003: 242–246. doi: 10.1016/S1356-689X(03)00016-X.

Slight, Sarah Patricia, Eta S. Berner, William Galanter, Stanley Huff, Bruce L. Lambert, Carole Lannon, Christoph U. Lehmann, et al. "Meaningful use of electronic health records: Experiences from the field and future opportunities." *JMIR Medical Informatics* 3, no. 3, 2015. doi: 10.2196/medinform.4457.

Wager, Karen A., Francis Wickham Lee, and John P. Glaser, *Health Care Information Systems: A Practical Approach for Health Care Management.* San Francisco, CA: Jossey-Bass, 2017.

Wilson, Karen A., "Worth the watt: A brief history of the electric car, 1830 to present." Car and Driver. Last Modified Mar 15, 2018. https://www.caranddriver.com/features/g15378765/worth-the-watt-a-brief-history-of-the-electric-car-1830-to-present/.

World Economic Forum. "Share to gain: Unlocking data value in manufacturing." https://www.weforum.org/whitepapers/share-to-gain-unlocking-data-value-in-manufacturing, 2020.

ENABLING ORGANIZATIONAL EFFECTIVENESS

2

Chapter 3

I Can Love My Leaders (ICLML): Driving *I*nnovation through Culture, *L*eadership, Management, and *L*earning

Sherri Douville and Willem P. Roelandts
Medigram

Karen Jaw-Madson
Co.-Design of Work Experience

Contents

Introduction

It was 22 out of every 1,000 babies globally. In the least developed countries, it was 32. These were the neonatal mortality rates in 2010 when the NeoNurture was released. In his book, *Where Good Ideas Come From*, Steven Johnson (2010) explained that this infant incubator built out of car parts could be powered by an adapted cigarette lighter or a standard-issue motorcycle battery. It was

DOI: 10.4324/9781003220473-5

doubly efficient, because it tapped both the local supply of parts themselves and the local knowledge of automobile repair. These were both abundant resources in the developing world context…You didn't have to be a trained medical technician to fix the NeoNurture; you didn't even have to read the manual. You just needed to know how to replace a broken headlight.

While not state of the art, this example illustrates that innovation will fail without people at its very core: who it's for, how they live, who develops it, how they work together, how it's shared, and who adopts it. Innovation needs people. Now consider the innovators themselves. Most do not work alone. Those who are successful work together in groups. However official or unofficial, they form or participate in organizations.

In a Center for the Future of Organizations' white paper, Roland Deiser notes, "It's not technology that creates the major headaches—it's the ability of organizational structures, processes, and cultures to take advantage of the opportunities that technology provides" (2018, 7). We agree. The best technology and processes in the world fall short without the cooperation of people. This chapter will share how to leverage the people side of the business—culture, leadership, management, and learning—to drive and sustain innovation. We will codify the behaviors to demonstrate these capabilities. For many leaders and their organizations, these are mysterious and elusive.

Indeed, the very meaning behind the terminology is also unclear. There are no universally accepted definitions for "innovation," "culture," "leadership," "management," and "learning," or ICLML for short. (Remember the mnemonic, "I can love my leaders" because it will indeed require leadership to influence and motivate people.) This is not from lack of input or rigorous debate. One possible—and delightful—explanation is that so many people, from all different backgrounds and persuasions can have access, weigh in, and be involved. To at least some degree, these concepts are democratized. The same has been implied when it comes to knowledge management (Knowledge Management Tools, 2014). For each of the following sections, we will describe the intent and meaning behind each concept, explain their usefulness, and, as promised, provide examples of behaviors demonstrating the capabilities.

Innovation

Each of the authors here—a healthcare startup CEO, a former CEO/serial investor/Chairman of the Board, and an organizational psychologist/management consultant/executive coach—has their own perspectives on innovation. Sherri qualifies innovation in the business context as the use of creativity to create new products, services, or processes that allow a company to provide solutions to their customers that are better and/or lower cost than what their competitors can offer. This unique advantage allows one to build better customer loyalty and yield higher profits. Wim sees innovation as the business application of creativity where new ideas are used to create new products, services, business models, new markets, and new niches within existing markets to serve the needs of customers. For Karen,

> Innovation doesn't come from the technological discoveries and advancements themselves, but from a phenomenon that occurs when ingenuity meaningfully links to a critical mass of people. In other words, invention becomes innovation when it makes a difference in people's lives.

Jaw-Madson (2018b)

Is innovation different when it comes to healthcare? According to James Barlow, author of *Managing Innovation in Healthcare* (2016), the answer is yes.

> In healthcare, it is often less clear what the 'innovation' is than in other industries. Many innovations do not take the form of well-defined physical products and bring together elements of new technology and organizational or service model changes.
>
> *Barlow (2016, 97)*

He continues,

> The economics of technological innovations in healthcare are unlike innovations in other industries--often costs to the health system, or payers, or governments rise because new technologies allow a larger overall 'quantity' of care to be provided.
>
> *Barlow (2016, 98)*

In their literature study of digital health innovation ecosystems, Iyawa, Herselman, and Botha (2016) share Thakur, Hsu, and Fontenot's view of healthcare innovation (2012), saying it "implies that health practices that have proven to have the best approach in healthcare are used in administering health services to patients." They go on to list all the types of innovation relevant to healthcare: process innovation, product innovation, structure innovation, IT (as a component of innovation), closed innovation, open innovation and open innovation 2.0, innovation networks ecosystems, triple helix system, user innovation, and intellectual property (Iyawa et al., 248). Digital healthcare is

> ...a network of digital health communities consisting of interconnected, interrelated, and interdependent digital health species, including healthcare stakeholders, healthcare institutions, and digital healthcare devices situated in a digital health environment, who adopt the best-demonstrated practices that have been proven to be successful, and implementation of those practices through the use of information and communication technologies to monitor and improve the wellbeing and health of patients, to empower patients in the management of their health and that of their families.
>
> *Iyawa et al. (2016, 249)*

Sherri believes that the *purpose* of innovation is different in healthcare: Innovation in medicine needs to contribute to what is commonly referred to as the quadruple aim: (1) improving patient outcomes, (2) reducing healthcare costs, (3) improving the patient experience, and (4) improving the clinician experience. Our kind of healthcare innovation implements and adopts positive change that ultimately leads to better patient outcomes.

Organizations are needed to effectively combine financial and intellectual resources with infrastructure for both profit and social impact. Kim, Song, and Nerkar (2012) say that, "Innovation occurs in the context of a community, one that is evolving as a whole" (Gittelman & Kogut, 2003). The need and appetite for healthcare innovation are ravenous in all economic times, and Kim et al.'s research has shown that "R&D alliances are positively correlated with both innovation rates and impact," leading them to "suggest that exploration in the form of strengthening the external linkage to cutting-edge scientific knowledge and technology may be the only way to enhance innovation impact or improve the chances of impactful innovation" (2012, 1193). It is no surprise, then, that over the last decade a number of hospital, healthcare, and pharmaceutical organizations have established open innovation centers around the world to "find the science to solve problems in the shortest possible time…Part venture firm, part incubator, each center has a team that mixes scientists with business people" (Bluestein, 2014). The desire to establish even more still remains today (McDermott Will and Emery, 2020).

Such activities show that healthcare organizations understand the imperative to address their own Innovator's Dilemma (à la Clayton Christensen). The pressure to improve in efficiency and effectiveness is always there, but they must also look to the future: innovate or be innovated out of relevance or even existence.

> Agreement is now widespread that organizations faced with disruption need to some-how compete in mature businesses where continual improvement and cost reduction are often the keys to success (exploitation) and pursue new technologies and business models that require experimentation and innovation (exploration).
>
> *O'Reilly and Tushman (2016, 14)*

In "How Disruptive Innovation Can Finally Revolutionize Healthcare," Christensen himself, along with Waldeck and Fogg, explains just how complicated, interdependent, segmented, demanding, constrained, contradictory, and change-resistant healthcare has become. They boil it down to: "This profound disconnect between what we need and what we get from the system lies at the root of America's healthcare crisis" (Christensen et al., 2017, 5).

They suggest Innosight's "Dual Transformation" approach, where "repositioning to the core business to adapt over time to changes in the marketplace" is governed separately from business ventures

> …in pursuit of more disruptive solutions..[making] today's business more resilient while at the same time creating tomorrow's new growth engine. In the middle, they are joined by the "Capabilities Link" which owns "difficult to replicate assets and capabilities."
>
> *Christensen et al. (2017, 25)*

Unburdened by longevity, startups also have a role to play in the ecosystem, but it is just as imperfect and ever-evolving. At times, bumping up against the industry's resistance to change and their own shortcomings such as "mismatch[ing] in technical solutions and healthcare needs" (Carroll & Richardson, 2016, 2), some are making traction, but progress has been slow. Sherri believes that every technology deployment in medicine is like a startup, and therefore would have typical startup problems:

1. Most people don't understand how to build startups, especially ones that are acceptable to medical stakeholders.
2. This lack of understanding makes it a greater challenge for entrepreneurs to establish their operating systems, roadmap, leadership philosophy, vision, and playbooks as well as execute on their responsibilities to attract, align, and communicate with critical talent, customers, and other resources.

In their book *Survival to Thrival: Building the Enterprise Startup – Book 2 Change or Be Changed*, experienced entrepreneurs and venture capitalists Bob Tinker and Tae Hea Nahm outline the origins of this misunderstanding when it comes to building startups and provide perspective on how to think about it. Building in a regulated environment and working with healthcare enterprises is not typically in the wheelhouse of later stage startup CEOs. They "get hooked on value extraction, to the detriment of real value creation," to use the words of Paul Strebel and Salvatore Cantale in MIT Review (2014). They say that value extraction is about "manipulating the competitive market process to the company's advantage." Creating value, on the other hand, requires the iteration of many concurrent milestones to move forward, which is an entirely different body of work. STORM Ventures' Chemical Model depicts a startup spiral that speaks to the iterative process, where "sequencing small milestones unlocks progress" (Tinker & Nahm, 2019) (Figure 3.1).

In addition, macro-level shifts are influencing organizations from the outside, not the least of which is the years-old identity crisis for the healthcare industry that remains unresolved. In "Service Design & Healthcare Innovation: from Consumption to Co-production and Co-creation," Freire and Sangiorgi (2010, 39) described this as "a shift from the value-chain model of Michael Porter to the constellation model)" over 10 years ago. They continue,

> …in the chain model, value is added by different suppliers in a sequential process, whilst in the constellation model value is co-produced by different actors in a non-linear set of activities and interactions. Users are involved in the value creation system in the way they use 'offerings'.
>
> *Freire and Sangiorgi (2010, 39)*

Another way of illustrating this is through the three social characters. Social character is defined by Maccoby and Scudder (2011, 2)

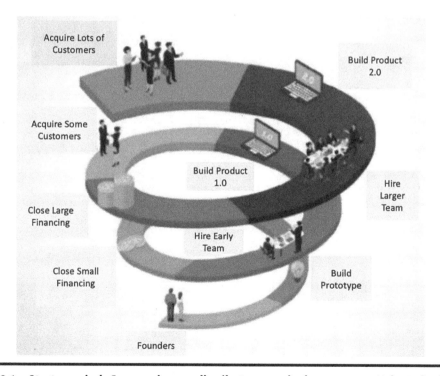

Figure 3.1   Startup spiral: Sequencing small milestones unlocks progress. (Adapted with permission from Tinker and Nahm [2019].)

as the shared part of personality of people brought up in a similar way, shaping their behavior and emotional attitudes to adapt to the dominant mode of production in that culture, so that they want to do what they need to do to prosper economically and socially.

Healthcare is struggling with what is described as a "conflict" between the Industrial-Bureaucratic and Knowledge-Interactive social characters, where the complex, hierarchical legacy organizations are clashing with employees and patients who demand "cross-functional, networked teams" (Maccoby & Scudder, 2011, 3):

> The traditional bureaucratic organization focuses on improving current products and services and meeting or exceeding internally established quality criteria, whereas the interactive-dominated organization wants to adapt the organization's products and services to a changing market or environment.
>
> *Maccoby and Scudder (2011, 4)*

See Table 6.1 for a summary of the social characters adapted for medicine.

What is happening at the end of the day is poorly managed change, where the transition between one maturity level to another is held back and stuck by resistance, tendencies to normalize disruptive innovation, risk avoidance, and slow-moving legislation and regulatory bodies. Industry organizations may attempt to move this conversation forward, but it might just take the collaboration of all such groups to intentionally strategize for the entire industry. This today remains the responsibility of individual organizations to manage within their own spheres of influence. They must define who they are and where they stand in the continuum of progress through their culture, leadership, management, and learning.

Culture

Highly innovative companies that are well managed are more competitive and profitable than other companies. Because of that, they also acquire and possess the best resources, which enable them to do even more. It's a virtuous cycle. However, there's more to it:

> …both healthy ideation and net income growth are a result of a third factor: a culture of innovation…The companies that have the greatest level of participation have the best ideas. They also have the strongest profit growth. And it all stems from a culture that recognizes that effective innovations can come from a call center worker, a clinic staffer, or just about anyone else in the organization bright enough to identify where the right ideas could make a difference.
>
> *Minor, Brook and Bernoff (2017)*

First, they are speaking of scenarios where culture is an asset. Culture can also be a liability. With the exception of newly founded startups, many organizations are burdened with the challenges of their current state, many of which have grown large and complex. When it comes to implementing innovation as many digital transformation initiatives aim to do, for example, many executives "agree on the importance of overcoming the pervasive silo culture and inward orientation that most large organizations are suffering from" (Deiser 2018, 13). This reveals the detrimental impact when culture is not just imperfect, but also an impediment.

Second, a "culture of innovation" as a concept is a bit of a misnomer. As Karen has said in the past, "There may be dominant themes or characteristics of a culture categorized by things like 'safety', 'innovation', or 'trust', but culture is never simply one thing" (Jaw-Madson, 2017). It is a complex social construct in an evolving, interconnected system. So instead of a "culture of innovation," which implies culture serves innovation, think of it as "culture that enables innovation"—innovation becomes a trait of an organization if the culture supports it. So what is culture? Culture is defined as

> All things that have the power to influence behaviors, interactions, and perception. It communicates the boundaries of what is acceptable and not acceptable and manifests itself in how people behave, interact, react, and perceive reality. Culture is created, reinforced, and experienced by people. It includes what is said and how it's lived. Simply put, culture is made up of what's acceptable, unacceptable and/or condoned.
>
> *Jaw-Madson (Co.-Design of Work Experience website)*

Culture exists in all parts of an organization, from what a company does to how it does it. Karen likes to say that it's like water—it gets everywhere as the "thing behind everything." Many organizations don't acknowledge this fact, and if they do any culture work at all, they sometimes delegate it to the HR department. This lack of discipline creates business risk.

Culture could either help or hurt the company, and it could help or hurt innovation. To make culture an asset, it must be done *intentionally* throughout the organization. The process of taking the journey is as important as the results. It begins with building the foundation of corporate identity through purpose, mission, vision, and values. Each has a role to play, but together they are the building blocks of a culture (Jaw-Madson, forthcoming). In their classic HBR article "Building Your Company's Vision" (Collins & Porras, 1996) and bestselling book *Built to Last* (Collins & Porras, 1994), Collins and Porras provided a framework for understanding how each of these is defined and relates to one another (Figure 3.2).

Figure 3.2   Corporate identity. (Adapted with permission from Collins and Porras [1996].)

Dvorak and Ott (2015) define purpose as

> more than a mission statement or a vision cast from the C-suite... At its core, a company's purpose is a bold affirmation of its reason for being in business. It conveys what the organization stands for in historical, ethical, emotional and practical terms.

Purpose answers why we exist and what we hope to achieve and serves to inspire as the core of all business activities. In turn, this also provides the organization's reason for innovating—to further this purpose.

Mission expresses how we accomplish and realize our purpose. Collins and Porras called these BHAGs (Big Hairy Audacious Goals), ones that take 10–30 years of effort:

> A true BHAG is clear and compelling, serves as a unifying focal point of effort, and acts as a catalyst for team spirit. It has a clear finish line, so the organization can know when it has achieved the goal...A BHAG engages people – it reaches out and grabs them. It is tangible, energizing, highly focused...People get it right away; it takes little or no explanation.
>
> *Collins and Porras (1994, 94)*

Values describe who we are and what guides everyday actions and behaviors. They are unique to every company. In *Built to Last*, Collins and Porras established criteria for high-quality values. They must:

- reflect the most important ideals, the worldview, and the beliefs of the company
- hold fast without reward
- remain even under penalty or competitive disadvantage
- exist if the company started from scratch today
- capture the company's core essence and are NOT aspirational

Sherri describes values as the conscience of the corporation, the things we believe are critical for the vision to be fulfilled. She agrees that these are the areas from which we don't want to deviate. "Values provide the framework for all communications and expected behaviors. Communication cannot happen without common values. If our values are different, then the words that we speak have different meanings and there can be no alignment," she says.

Built to Last-style vision comes from connecting core ideology (identity) with mission (envisioned future). When Wim was CEO of Xilinx, "Their vision is clearly forward into untapped markets and new opportunities rather than backward at competitors and naysayers" (Morris, 2004). As a result, innovation was a core focus of the organization's efforts, and it worked. Xilinx "played a major role in the advancement of programmable systems technologies...as the world's largest supplier of programmable logic products" (Morris, 2004), and the era was punctuated by a period of expansion and growth.

Vision connects who we are and where we want to go as an organization, together. Sherri says these are critical because they give direction to the innovators in which areas they need to channel their innovation. They are like the track of a train: they give the direction to the train. Without the track, the train has complete freedom but will not get anywhere. Vision not only guides but also inspires as the reason why people work at the company and are willing to work hard.

Many organizations conjure up their corporate identity in closed boardroom meetings, disconnected from important stakeholders like their employees and customers. Sometimes they copy and paste words from other institutions. Some hire external PR and branding firms to write copy for their websites *in lieu of* actual culture work. All these lack meaning and therefore will have minimal or even detrimental impact. The real company identity is co-created every day through their people. If you want alignment for something different, then you must establish it through co-creation as well.

There are numerous approaches to developing purpose, mission, vision, and values. No matter which you choose, ensure a "clean sheet" starting point with a rigorous, collaborative, thought process incorporating diverse perspectives, much like how it happens in innovation. For example, purpose can be created by incorporating stories that tap into the heart of why the company should exist and what gives meaning to people's work. Collins and Porras suggested using the "5 Whys" to peel away outer layers to get to the core. Mission emerges from many perspectives ultimately aligning around a commonly used format in the form of a statement: "Our company's mission is to provide X for Y through Z." Values also have to be boiled down to that which is most fundamental to maintaining the character and essence of the company, guiding the "how" of business no matter what. Use the criteria for high-quality values to determine what makes the grade.

Like the rest of the company, innovation teams need to connect and align around organizational purpose, mission, vision, and values. In her most innovative environment to date, Sherri and the team at Medigram deem this work to be so important that their vision and values are followed up with actual vows as coached by Anthony Lee, founder of Heroic Voice Academy. The building blocks of purpose, mission, vision, and values should be in place as a foundation before establishing or changing culture. If these elements of corporate identity don't exist meaningfully, then the initiative must be taken for teams to define this for themselves.

How to Culture

Culture is neither esoteric nor intangible, but actually real and very tangible. Talk to any job candidate about what's important to them in their next company, and culture is likely on the list. Or think about what employees share with their families and friends about their workplace. Their stories communicate their culture at work. Most people think about culture as good or bad, which translates to either an organizational asset or liability. The reality is mostly in between, with room for improvement that equates to lost potential. In addition to good or bad work conditions, many cultural issues are rooted in broken promises. Organizations don't walk their culture talk. The Mayo Clinic's "Healing the Professional Culture of Medicine" paper (Shanafelt et al., 2019) shined a spotlight on medicine's culture problem: the incongruence between behavior and espoused values. Again, every organization must rise up to the challenge of declaring and managing themselves in this respect.

This is how Highmark Health, a self-described "national health and wellness organization as well as the second largest integrated delivery and financing system in America," "embraces disruption and builds for the future": by defining behaviors as part of their operating system, integrating employee engagement into strategy, creating innovation culture that is technology-enabled but people driven, and leveraging a vast internal and external talent ecosystem (Ratanjee, 2020). On the surface, this sounds good enough to emulate. Resist the compulsion to simply copy examples set by others or implement so-called best practices. Doing so is lazy at best and dangerous at worst because it ignores your own context and the people within it. Don't expect to apply an idea

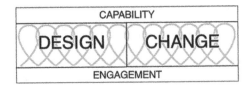

Figure 3.3 Design of Work Experience (DOWE) overview. (Adapted with permission from Karen Jaw-Madson [2018b].)

from one place to another and expect it to work the same way. Copying also fails to differentiate (a competitive no-no). When it comes to culture—or any aspect of ICLML for that matter—the approach should always be specific to your unique circumstances.

Culture serves as the enabler for innovation (or lack thereof)—but it is an enigma for many. Everyone experiences it, and yet it seems inaccessible. This is a mindset, not the reality. Karen's framework, Design of Work Experience (DOWE), was created to empower and enable people (at any job and any level) to intentionally design, implement, and sustain culture specific to their own unique context—to make something that is seemingly intangible and inaccessible very tangible and very accessible (Figure 3.3).

As explained on the Co.-Design of Work Experience website,

> The approach comprises 4 major components, the combination of DESIGN and CHANGE processes enabled by the development and use of CAPABILITY and ENGAGEMENT. DESIGN and CHANGE have specific sets of activities, organized as a series of iterative learning loops, to indicate the non-linear, but progressive nature of the process. Ultimately, the model yields an in-depth understanding of the current state [an organization's unique context], a strategy for the future state, and a plan for how to get there (Figure 3.4).

The activities are divided into five phases, as summarized on the website and presented in the book, *Culture Your Culture: Innovating Experiences @Work*

1. UNDERSTAND
   This is the first phase of design, made up of three learning loops: *People & Context, Insights*, and *Criteria*. Activities in *People & Context* include: aligning purpose and scope, identifying early assumptions and key questions, planning and implementing user research. The *Insights* learning loop begins with assuming different mindsets before developing insights from raw data collected during user research. As a result, thinking is reframed and drives the development of the provocative proposition. Learning is further catalyzed through the creation of visuals. *Criteria* takes what was learned from user research and insights to establish the most critical requirements in two sets: from the organizational point of view and the employee point of view. This becomes the decision-making tool later on in the DOWE process.

2. CREATE and LEARN
   The phase applies what's been learned "into the creative design process and combines it with generated ideas through play and experimentation" in co-creation with others. The learning loops, *Explore, Brainstorm*, and *Play*, net "brainstormed ideas to develop and refine for the new strategies and experiences." In *Explore*, the design team "builds knowledge and inspiration by learning from everything and everywhere, hunting and gathering anything that could inform their perspective...it goes beyond doing primary and secondary

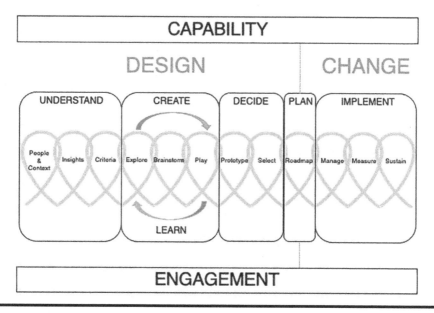

Figure 3.4 Design of Work Experience (DOWE)—detailed view. (Adapted with permission from Karen Jaw-Madson [2018b].)

research – it seeks stimulus to synthesize concepts and ideas." In *Brainstorm*, facilitation guides people to "work together to generate options, ideas, or offerings that could solve for critical needs and define or enhance a work experience." The CREATE and LEARN phase concludes with *Play*, where the team experiments with ideas to see how they relate to one another, how they work, or how they might be modified to work.

3. DECIDE

The DOWE process converges with the DECIDE phase, which is comprised of the *Prototype* and *Select* learning loops. *Prototype* is another form of exploration that further refines ideas and gathers intelligence toward bringing the team closer to decisions. *Select* brings the development of the Strategy and Design Blueprint to full fruition when the team chooses what best meets three constraints: what is viable, what is possible, and what satisfies the previously established criteria.

4. PLAN

PLAN prepares the organization for the change that inevitably accompanies the implementation of the Blueprint to (1) ensure that change reaches sufficient depth and breadth across the organization while maintaining connectivity/reinforcement across all content, actions, and activity, and (2) cover what will be done and how during IMPLEMENT. The DOWE process walks the design team through eight iterations of planning to form the Roadmap and Action Plans.

5. IMPLEMENT

In this last phase of the DOWE process, the Strategy and Design Blueprint is brought to life with the implementation of the Roadmap and Action Plans through the learning loops of *Manage, Measure*, and *Sustain. Manage* goes beyond carrying out plans, it manages meaning in the creation of a new reality at the individual, team, and organization levels. *Measure* serves to "gauge progress toward key milestones and enable timely adjustments" as well as "provides data and content for communication and contributes to the change narrative." "Both a process and an outcome," *Sustain* drives continued momentum and ensures that changes stick for as long as they're needed.

The process creates culture and the employee experience that enable innovation, answering questions such as:

- What kind of culture is needed in order for us to innovate?
- How might we transform ourselves into an innovative organization?
- How do we set the conditions for innovation in our specific context?
- How do we become known for being innovative?
- How will employees experience innovation by working here?
- How might we develop innovation as an organizational capability?
- How might we establish the behaviors that demonstrate innovation as a norm?
- How might teams collaborate for innovation?
- How do we optimize our talent for innovation?

It should not go unnoticed that practicing DOWE is also practicing innovation, for it is itself an innovation process. Also like innovation, it is best to experience DOWE rather than explain it. Allow the DOWE process to create culture and employee experience that begets more innovation. This work can happen on any scale—at the team level or across an entire organization.

On teams, culture can be co-designed as an experience using DOWE and negotiated as a social contract via a charter. Most social contracts are tacit, but Karen makes it explicit with a team charter template that enables a team to align on their way of work (Figure 3.5).

The Culture Your Culture (CYC) 30-Day Challenge on the Co.-Design of Work Experience website empowers individuals at every job or level to *initiate* the first steps in boosting company culture. The process is straightforward:

Week 1: Have a conversation with someone about your company culture. Come up with a proposition that finishes, "How might we...?"
Week 2: Find a collaboration partner to research and/or generate ideas for your "How might we...?" proposition.
Week 3: Test one idea out and refine or enhance it based on your learning.
Week 4: Share what you did with another group and answer the question, "What next?"

The "what next" can explore how to take definitive steps toward progress.

Every individual through their day-to-day interactions is contributing to the company culture, but as you can see here, there are more ways for workers and employers to collaborate on an organizational scale.

The hallmarks of a culture that enables innovation are specific to an organization, but we call out some key cultural characteristics in the following sections for leaders and managers to activate through their people.

Leadership

Plenty has been said about the differences between leadership and management. It can be summarized like this:

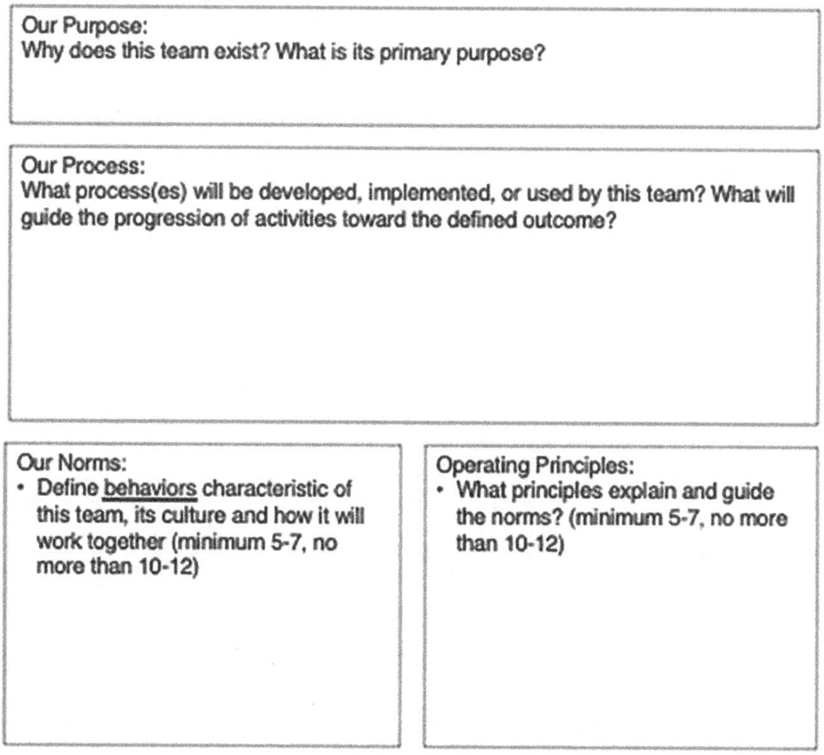

Our Purpose:
Why does this team exist? What is its primary purpose?

Our Process:
What process(es) will be developed, implemented, or used by this team? What will guide the progression of activities toward the defined outcome?

Our Norms:	Operating Principles:
• Define <u>behaviors</u> characteristic of this team, its culture and how it will work together (minimum 5-7, no more than 10-12)	• What principles explain and guide the norms? (minimum 5-7, no more than 10-12)

Figure 3.5   Team charter template. (Adapted with permission from Karen Jaw-Madson [2018b].)

> Management consists of controlling a group or a set of entities to accomplish a goal. Leadership refers to an individual's ability to influence, motivate, and enable others to contribute toward organizational success. Influence and inspiration separate leaders from managers, not power and control.
>
> *Nayar (2013)*

In *Culture Your Culture: Innovating Experiences @ Work*, Karen said, "Though there are differences between these roles, leaders should ideally be good managers, and managers should display leadership qualities" (Jaw-Madson, 2018b, 28). Wim agrees: "In some cases managers and leaders are the same, ideally they coexist in the same person. Great executives have to be BOTH good leaders AND good managers." When it comes to innovation, leadership and management are interwoven throughout. Sherri describes it this way:

> For new ideas, teams need an inspired leader to rally the troops. The leader must also have the self-awareness and the diligence to investigate and hire for gaps. For example, someone with a strength in creativity would need to work with strong project, program, and portfolio managers to deliver continuously. At a certain point the innovating stops to get the product out and to drive to milestones--this requires management. Managers have to be good executors of processes to get to results.

For both leaders and managers, a job title does not necessarily qualify—behaviors do. They also require the willingness of others to be led and managed. In other words, all leaders need followers.

Again, there are many perspectives about what it takes to lead innovation. Continually managing change is one example. Maccoby and Scudder (2011) summarize it as "strategic intelligence," consisting of four qualities "held together" by leadership philosophy and personality intelligence. They are foresight, visioning with systems thinking, partnering, and motivating and empowering (Figure 3.6).

Strategically intelligent leaders answer questions like these provided by Maccoby for illustration:

■ What is likely to happen that will mean new threats, opportunities, and demands?
■ What should I do about:
  – Designing products and services that will gain and retain customers and an organization that can create and distribute these offerings?
  – Building an effective team of people who share my philosophy and purpose, with qualities that complement mine?
  – Motivating and empowering the organization to achieve great results? (Maccoby and Scudder 2011)

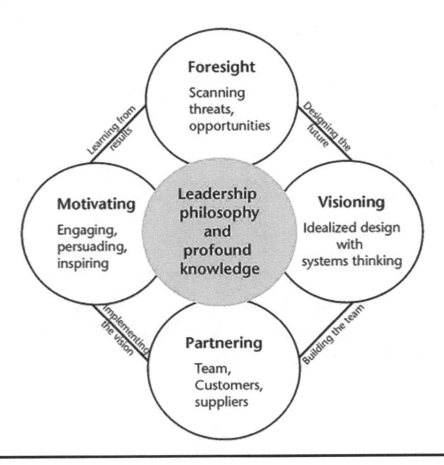

Figure 3.6   Strategic intelligence. (Adapted with permission from Maccoby [2015].)

The strategically intelligent "are able to motivate and empower them to collaborate, to achieve a shared purpose" (Maccoby & Scudder, 2011, 6). In other words, leaders with strategic intelligence can combine emotional intelligence and company identity across the entire organization. As one can infer from this discussion, managing innovation IS managing change.

As many perspectives as there are on what it takes to lead innovation, there are even more behaviors expected. So where does a leader focus? We would say it depends on the needs of the context (as defined by the UNDERSTAND phase of the DOWE process), but if we had to choose for the sake of inspiration, we would prioritize the following:

- **Showing strategic intelligence:** As defined by Maccoby and Scudder, this includes strategic visioning and systems thinking, change leadership, collaboration, and emotional intelligence.
- **Leading culture:** No strategies, plans, or technology will work without people, and they only function as well as a culture allows. Steven Johnson said, "If you look at history, innovation doesn't come just from giving people incentives; it comes from creating environments where their ideas can connect" (Johnson & Kelly, 2010). Culture is the key, and it comes from a partnership between leadership and their employees. Leadership cannot abdicate their responsibility in ensuring that culture is optimized for people and innovation.
- **Demonstrating Empathy:** In *Culture Your Culture* (Jaw-Madson, 2018b, 26), Karen shares Theresa Wiseman's attributes of empathy from the field of patient care: "the ability to see the worlds as others see it, to be nonjudgmental, to understand another's feelings, and communicate the understanding" (Wiseman, 1996, 1166). This is not just about having emotional intelligence, but genuinely connecting to people and showing it. So many failures of leadership and top-level decision-making come from a lack of empathy, which hardly inspires, nor influences followers.
- **Managing:** As said previously, good leaders should also be good managers. Do everything you are expecting your managers to do, upfront and visibly. Take heed of what we will share when it comes to innovation management in the next section.
- **Leading:** When we say "leading," we mean championing and enabling everything in this chapter and seeing innovation through to market. It's what people need you for, what you should be doing, and how you should be incentivized. Bonus points are given for influence and inspiration.

Management

Everything in a company should serve a purpose. So the oft-asked question is what is management for anyway? For Wim, managers exist for the selection of people and are responsible for the results. Sherri takes her inspiration from Wim, who introduced her to Peter Drucker's teachings. She believes that the first constant in the job of management is to make human strength effective and human weakness irrelevant (Drucker, 2018) and agrees that managers are accountable for the results—the proverbial buck stops with them. Managers might be the ones to facilitate the development of well-developed goals (i.e. OKRs, SMART), but accountability and commitment are voluntarily shared if the practice of management is done right. Karen believes managers are there *for* people, there to bring out the best in them through motivation, removing barriers, ensuring execution, driving innovation, communicating needed information, and setting the conditions for great work. Notice what's not on there—things that typically demotivate, but happen in organizations every day: micromanaging, criticizing, blame, instilling fear, pulling rank, and telling people what to do. This points to a disconnect between what employees need managers for and what managers think employees need. In *The Progress Principle: Using Small Wins to Ignite Joy, Engagement, and Creativity*, Teresa Amabile and Steven Kramer shared,

> Our research inside companies revealed that the best way to motivate people, day in and day out, is by facilitating progress—even small wins. But the managers in our survey ranked 'supporting progress' dead last as a work motivator.
>
> *Amabile and Kramer (2011, 3)*

Intentionally establishing a shared and consistently applied management philosophy can serve to repair that disconnect. At this very moment, every organization has its own management philosophy playing out in everyday employee experiences, purposefully or not. When Wim was CEO at Xilinx:

1. **People come to the company to do their best work**
   We believe people want to do a good job. They want to, and will, fulfill what's expected of them, provided, they:
   - Perform to the limit of competence with minimum supervision
   - Have a clear understanding of the expectations
   - Know how these expectations fit into the context of the company's objectives
   - Are provided with the processes, tools, and organizational support to help them
2. **Work must have meaning and value**
   - Motivated people produce better results (return on human capital)
   - Extraordinary results are produced by employees who are passionate about their job, team, work, and company
   - We want people who are proud of their achievements and the collective efforts of the company
   - People need to understand their role and its impact on the company
   - Innovation is expected from everybody
   - All employees can act, emerge, and be recognized as leaders
3. **A company must provide a sense of community**
   - Few problems can be faced by one person
   - People need to belong to a group which provides:
     • Common values, beliefs, and mental models
     • Structure
     • Support (material and emotional)
     • Psychological safety
     • Pride in achievement
     • Shared accountability
   - Without this innovation and risk taking are very difficult.
4. **A company will thrive if the people are better tomorrow than they are today.**
   - A company is responsible for creating an environment for growth and the employee is responsible for continuous learning and initiating development
   - Expectations should increase continually (the bar moves higher)
   - New learning is highest through job rotation and coaching

- Learning from others (benchmarking) and from mistakes (post mortems) is as important as innovation
5. **Everybody in the company should behave as an owner**
   - Employees who are owners understand our business (financially, technically, and structurally) and therefore make better decisions
   - Owners focus on the success of the company and not on just their part of the organization
   - Owners initiate trade-offs in the interest of the long term success of Xilinx
   - Owners will tackle a problem, if they have the competence, and not pass the bucket.

Every organization needs an effective management philosophy in place for setting expectations and ensuring consistency and accountability. Again, resist the urge to copy and paste this great example above. It should align with every organization's own context, and therefore vary from company to company, even with the same desirable outcomes. All management philosophies should also be intentionally thought through, co-created, and aligned with the end users—the employees—before being rolled out.

The role of middle management is also worth noting. As the conduit between company leadership and all workers in hierarchy-driven organizations, middle management is especially important.

> They may disseminate information vertically, from top managers to frontline employees and from frontline employees to top managers, and horizontally, across top managers and across frontline employees.
>
> *Birken, Lee, and Weiner (2012, 4)*

It's a tough position to be in with pressure from above and below. Little research has been done about the role of middle managers in healthcare but can be learned from other industries:

> This research indicates that middle managers' influence may be positive or negative. On the one hand, middle managers' commitment to innovation implementation has been linked to strategy realization, efficiency of operations and implementation speed, as well as positive organizational outcomes such as profit growth, enhanced competitiveness, and overall effectiveness in reaching established goals. On the other hand, there is evidence that middle managers may limit implementation effectiveness by speaking negatively of an innovation, choosing to withhold information about an innovation, stymying the flow of information about innovation, or preventing frontline employees from engaging in innovation implementation activities... (4).

Middle managers make a difference. Organizations need to pay attention to and ensure that they are enabled to productively contribute to innovation.

Now that we've established why management exists and our position on management philosophies, we can tell you that innovation, by its definition, cannot be managed in the traditional sense—too much is unknown, yet-to-be discovered, and can't be anticipated for planning purposes. Telling someone to "innovate" and expecting it in return, like a transaction, is nonsensical. Managing innovation has been described as "managed chaos" as far back as the 1980s (Quinn, 1985). Others have described it as the "edge of chaos-the fertile zone between too much order and too much anarchy" (Johnson, 2010, 52). For Sherri, managing innovation means delegation of

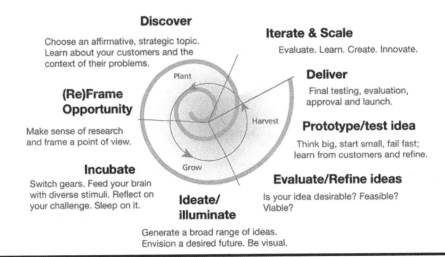

Discover
Choose an affirmative, strategic topic. Learn about your customers and the context of their problems.

Iterate & Scale
Evaluate. Learn. Create. Innovate.

Plant

(Re)Frame Opportunity
Make sense of research and frame a point of view.

Deliver
Final testing, evaluation, approval and launch.

Harvest

Prototype/test idea
Think big, start small, fail fast; learn from customers and refine.

Incubate
Switch gears. Feed your brain with diverse stimuli. Reflect on your challenge. Sleep on it.

Grow

Ideate/ illuminate

Evaluate/Refine ideas
Is your idea desirable? Feasible? Viable?

Generate a broad range of ideas. Envision a desired future. Be visual.

Figure 3.7   Creativity at work protocol. (Adapted with permission from Linda Naiman, Founder, Creativity at Work [2020].)

authority and giving the freedom for people to come up with and develop new ideas. Wim adds that learning to delegate is the most important thing to do. Define your own responsibility and delegate the authority for other things based on trust. It's a big problem when management wants innovation but doesn't give people the authority to innovate.

Driving innovation covers a lot of territory, but at a manager level it's about the environment, process, and setting direction. The innovation methodologies or processes used may be developed in house or taken from external thought leadership. A few examples include the Design Sprint, Kickbox, the Creativity at Work Protocol, design thinking, business model canvas, lean, agile, etc. Regardless of which, a manager must ensure that (1) desirable behaviors are defined for each step of the innovation process and (2) the conditions are there to successfully implement innovation (Figure 3.7).

Also, there is no single archetype or personality for innovation management despite many opinions saying otherwise. Karen reassures her executive coaching clients that they don't need to change who they are (i.e. their personal identity) or their personality to be an authentic leader. Instead, "leaders are simply obligated to take action that enables people to become inspired *as an outcome*" (Jaw-Madson, 2018b). Again, what a manager can do in their role is—just like and in alignment with culture—to *enable* innovation: creating the necessary conditions that empower employees and foster innovation in areas such as culture, creativity, idea generation, flow, learning (more on that later), mental space, autonomy, empowerment, and mindset.

An innovation manager's behaviors must elicit the best out of their people. The right mix of these (in degree and frequency) are, again, specific to the context and the team members' needs and motivations. All this being said, we have a clear point of view of where management should focus, and the behaviors that accompany them:

Understanding the landscape: This is the same advice Karen gave to executives regarding digital transformation: "Learn enough about change management, digital transformation, and your own company to speak intelligently to the landscape, anticipate the major challenges, and plan strategically. Be forthcoming with what you don't know so you can learn from others" (Jaw-Madson, 2019). Managers must have a working knowledge of innovation in order to manage it. They should understand the landscape of where they are trying to innovate, internally and externally.

A manager's own team is also a part of that landscape. What conditions need to be set in order for a team to successfully innovate? At Vanderbilt University, David Owens of The Wond'ry Innovation Center teaches about four constraints to group innovation:

1. Emotion—How I feel around others
2. Culture—How I know what to do around others
3. Environment—Where I meet and work with others
4. Process—How we do work together as a group

While they could be the reason for stunted innovation, they could also be the reason for why innovation succeeds. Therefore, these are worth at least an examination on the part of the innovation manager in reviewing the landscape. In order to do this, they need to really know their team. In "6 Things the Best Bosses Do Differently," Karen said,

> Amazing bosses demonstrate the value of true connection with their people, frequently and consistently. They know it's not about transactions. Doing one good thing or even a few good things for someone that reports to them doesn't make for an amazing boss alone… It's about a relationship where trust is continually renewed through established, positive patterns of behaviors, both ways. People look for and rely on that stability even when work becomes chaotic and unpredictable.
>
> *Abdou (2020)*

We will go so far as to say that transactional managers and leaders will more likely fail to innovate because they are missing the need for connection and meaningfulness. Karen continued, "The best bosses should never lose touch…" (Abdou, 2020). Awareness of themselves—their strengths, opportunities, and the role they play in their world is also a part of the ecosystem, as is their organizational context. To reiterate, the behavior needed to understand the landscape is this: actively seeking knowledge to remain connected to innovation as a topic, the field in which they are innovating, and the system of people and the organization around them (including themselves).

Managing to the intended culture. In the same article, Karen said,

> There's a symbiotic relationship between good bosses, culture, and career development. Good cultures develop careers and make good bosses, good bosses create a good culture and develop careers. You need good bosses for good cultures and career development. That's why they matter.
>
> *Abdou (2020)*

Managing the intended culture means continually reinforcing the co-created culture, employee experiences, and the team charter. What is written down must translate to how real life is lived. A manager must exemplify the behaviors that reflect the culture, incorporate the culture into their everyday communications, create a process or infrastructure by which they can track and connect with their people about the culture, and quickly address emerging patterns that contradict the intended culture. There are certain cultural characteristics that are particularly helpful to innovation. Here are just a few examples:

■ **Trust:** As the co-chair of TRUST and Identity for the IEEE prospective standard P2933 for Clinical IoT, Sherri has spent much time with researchers defining trust and experts that look at it from lay, technical, and system constructs. Trust is the belief that one could be vulnerable and not be taken advantage of (Jones & George, 1998). It

encourages and enables people to take risks and collaborate in pursuit of aspirational goals. Without trust, people hold back. With it, their reservations dissipate and information flows freely. People openly discuss possibilities, willingly offer their ideas, and help others.

Cross, Edmonson, and Murphy (2020, 39)

Trust should be a shared belief by all members of a team, with the manager leading the way. Everything they expect from others, they should do themselves. For Sherri, the source of management mistrust is the gap between what management says and what it does. The positive opposite is also true: the alignment between what management says and does builds trust. Another trust-building behavior highlighted by Sherri and agreed with by many: Credible leaders follow through on their promises and never make promises they can't keep. What doesn't build trust erodes it. Trust becomes a part of the culture when it is the default.

■ **Engaged, two-way communication:** On the part of the manager, they themselves must be adequately informed and in communication with leadership so that they can do the same with their teams. As Sherri says, "They have to connect the dots so they can do it for others." The aforementioned work by Birken et al. also notes that:

…middle managers have the potential to bridge informational gaps that might otherwise impede innovation implementation…By bridging informational gaps, middle managers may help to manage the demands associated with innovation implementation, align incentives, transcend professional barriers, and identify priorities to promote innovation implementation.

Birken et al. (2012, 2)

Behaviors demonstrating communication include giving people the information they need, frequently reminding them of the meaning behind what they do (purpose, mission, vision, values, philosophy/principles, strategy), and communicating what one knows and doesn't know. Communication must also bring about more clarity. As the saying goes, "the abstract kills, the concrete saves." Explain abstract concepts by examples and parables. Increase communications in difficult times.

■ **Successful collaboration:** There are lots of benefits to good collaboration. One is employee engagement, which drives up performance and extraordinary efforts: "…employee engagement is determined by the ability of leaders to foster interpersonal networks and a culture of collaboration" (Cross, Edmondson, & Murphy, 2020, 38). Collaboration also leads to better innovation, new services, greater client satisfaction, and stronger operations (Hansen, 2009, 26). According to Jim Collins as he wrote the introduction to Morten Hansen's *Collaboration: How Leaders Avoid the Traps, Create Unity and Reap Big Results*, "Good collaboration amplifies strength, but poor collaboration is worse than no collaboration at all" (Hansen, 2009, ix). Hansen himself continues, "The goal of collaboration is not collaboration, but better results" (Hansen, 2009, 15). There's a time and place for collaboration and the conditions must be ripe for it. The value must be greater or equal to the cost of the opportunity and collaboration, which uses more resources (Hansen, 2009, 41). Successful collaboration means knowing when to collaborate and ensuring that there are positive results to collaboration. A culture must set the conditions and the behaviors must reflect it.

Leveraging diversity: In "How Diversity Can Drive Innovation," Hewlett, Marshall, and Sherbin's (2013) research proved companies with diversity out-innovate and outperform others. "Employees at these companies are 45% likelier to report that their firm's market share grew over the previous year and 70% likelier to report that the firm captured a new market." Other research led by Amy Edmondson notes that leveraging diversity needs psychological safety: "… team diversity can stimulate learning if the organizational context supports open communication." Psychological safety is a critical component of a context that moderates a team's ability to overcome barriers to collaboration (Edmonson & Roloff, 2009). According to Bradley et al. (2011), psychological safety:

■ Is the shared belief that interpersonal risk take (i.e. having differences) is safe
■ Supports learning, creativity, and productive problem solving
■ Sets the conditions to leverage diversity
■ Improves team performance

There is much to discuss about diversity, especially in light of societal changes in the US. There is also much to do beyond diversity itself: ensuring inclusion and belonging, providing access, sponsorship, and allyship, etc. Start with psychological safety in your culture. Define your team charters and design employee experience with expectations of behaviors that support psychological safety, especially those that elicit genuine trust and address insecurities. Eliminate patterns that destroy psychological safety, especially those perpetrated by managers themselves. Amy Edmondson (2019) emphasizes these key behaviors in her book, *The Fearless Organization: Creating Psychological Safety in the Workplace for Learning, Innovation, and Growth*: measure and improve psychological safety, set the stage, invite participation, respond productively, walk the talk, train for fearlessness, encourage questions, listen, reward failure, build trust, and combine cultural priorities (which means to make it a part of your culture work as we suggest).

Calibrating oppositional forces: Innovation is never problem free. When there is a problem, there should be no finger pointing so much as a desire to work together as a team to resolve it. Taking reasonable risks and experiencing failures are to be expected when it comes to innovation. Make sure they are useful as learning opportunities and that mistakes are not repeated.

There are also problems that are unsolvable. To explain: managers are saddled with navigating and managing tensions simultaneously on behalf of their teams. We already called out how managers are pulled between higher ups from above and employees from below. With its own set of oppositional forces, managing innovation is arguably even more difficult in healthcare. Some are a matter of life and death. Roland Deiser of the Center for the Future of Organization at Drucker School of Management explained O'Reilly and Tushman's Ambidexterity Challenge for

> Businesses [that]… require risk minimization. Their very existence is based on a zero-tolerance for failure; procedures and products must be designed for 100% safety.…Digital innovation, on the other hand, means embracing risk-especially if it is not incremental but strives to change the rules of the game. IT requires the willingness to accept failure and to learn, as experimentation and iteration are at the core of dealing with unchartered waters.…The clash between these two paradigms is unavoidable

and lies at the heart of the ambidexterity challenge-an issue which all established organizations face.

Deiser (2018, 16)

There is no ending to the challenge, it must be constantly calibrated. Barry Johnson called the identification and management of these unsolvable problems "polarity management" (Johnson, 1992).

> Polarities to manage are sets of opposites that can't function well independently. Because the two sides of a polarity are interdependent, you cannot choose one as a "solution" and neglect the other. The objective of the Polarity Management perspective is to get the best of both opposites while avoiding the limits of each.

Johnson (1992, xii)

These "paradoxically interdependent" imperatives must be continually managed because they never get "solved," and the goal is to manage to the benefits of both without suffering their downsides. So to apply Deiser's example of The Ambidexterity Challenge to Johnson's Polarity Management framework in the context of healthcare, see the graphic below (Figure 3.8).

In the top left quadrant are the benefits of safety and in the top right quadrant are the benefits of risk. On the bottom left quadrant are the negative consequences of safety and on the bottom right quadrant are the negative consequences of risk. Every organization must define for themselves the strategies that will keep them in the top half of the 4×4 grid (on both sides), where they get the benefits of both safety and risk. Doing so indicates balanced tension, but this must be constantly managed. Vigilance is also required to watch out for "the line," where negative consequences of safety and risk begin to creep into the picture in ways that would necessitate course corrections. Behaviors that signal the successful calibration of oppositional forces are identifying the unsolvable problems, strategizing on their management, and continually assessing progress to watch out and correct for negative consequences. When a negative consequence emerges in one quadrant, take action toward eliciting the positive of the other pole. In the example above, if negative consequences of risk appear, then the team must work toward a strategy that results in the

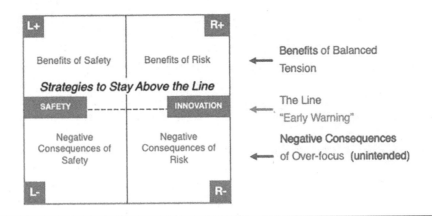

Figure 3.8   Polarity management: Safety and risk. (Adapted from Johnson [1992].)

benefits of safety—but not so much that the pendulum swings all the way to the other side. Again, it is about calibrating, which requires measured adjustments. Inherent in all these behaviors is one meta-behavior: making decisions. As Johnson describes it,

> Sometimes people see problem solving and decision making as the same thing. From that perspective, if the problem is unsolvable, there are no decisions to be made. On the contrary, managing a polarity well requires ongoing decision making based on an ever-changing reality.

> *Johnson (1992, 132)*

All of these above will enable the management of innovation.

Learning

> A culture of learning is needed more than ever when you combine vision, business objectives and the need for new capabilities when solutions are unknown and conditions are ever-changing. Under these conditions, it is clear that the only way a company can succeed is to learn.

> *Jaw-Madson (2018a)*

We are all coded to learn. With innovation, it's a requirement. Take a look at the many innovation models out there and notice how much learning is baked into the processes. You must be able to learn in order to innovate—or, more boldly—innovating is learning and learning is innovating. (This, by the way, also means that innovation can be taught as a skill.) Exploitative and explorative learning correspond to both sides of the Innovator's Dilemma as well (Kim, Song, & Nerkar, 2012, 1189). Su et al (2011, 699) summarized that exploitative learning

> ...refers to learning gained via local search, experiential refinement, and selection and reuse of existing routines; exploratory learning occurs along an entirely different trajectory through the processes of concerted variation, planned experimentation, and play.

> *Benner and Tushman (2002)* and *Gupta et al. (2006)*

Kim, Song, and Nerkar (2012, 1193) concluded from their research that

> ...if a firm wants to improve its innovative capabilities and output in terms of frequency and impact, then it should strike a balance between exploitative, localized learning and exploratory learn-by-experimentation. The idea is, in essence, the popular 'ambidexterity' premise.

> *O'Reilly and Tushman (1996)*

We mentioned ambidexterity previously, but it can also be examined as polarities.

When we talk about learning, we are referring to all types of learning at three levels: (1) Developing individuals to meet their full potentials so we can (2) connect them to others and (3) harness knowledge and collectively learn as an organization, at scale. Learning in an organization begins at the individual level, where "learning…is demonstrated by changed behavior, sustained over time, proven in observable action" (Jaw-Madson, 2018b, 219). It is the path to achieving full potential, which is relevant to everyone regardless of role. To be explicit: managers and leaders need to learn too. The transition from person to group happens where connections are made. The more connections, the more configurations, and with that, more possibilities. Steven Johnson named it high-density "liquid networks," which "make it easier for innovation to happen, but they also serve the essential function of *storing* those innovations" (Johnson, 2010, 54). Deiser agrees, adding:

> Working across boundaries-no matter if it is boundaries of the mind, function, or organization-is a key ingredient of transformational learning. Leveraging the power of difference that constitutes boundaries and embracing the unavoidable friction as an opportunity to learn and create something new is a key success factor not only for developing ideas and engage in new ways of work; it is also essential for reshaping the very essence of the structural and cultural set-up of an organization.
>
> *Deiser (2018, 13)*

A learning organization is one "that is continually expanding its capacity to create its future" (Senge, 1990, 14) by rapidly adapting to changing needs in the style of adhocracy (flexible organizational structures) or Maccoby's knowledge-interactive social character (Maccoby & Scudder, 2011, 3). They are skilled at creating, acquiring, and transferring knowledge, as well as modifying their behavior to reflect newly acquired knowledge and insights—just like learning at an individual level, but en masse.

The depth and breadth of knowledge on learning are vast. We will boil it down to prioritizing one very important prerequisite: learning how to learn. This means paying attention so that one can take learning in any way it comes. Every opportunity can be a learning opportunity. One way to learn how to learn is by developing learning agility. It has two equally important components, as described by W. Warner Burke. The first is skill. In his words, it's "what you do when you don't know what to do." The other is motivation, the "willingness to take risk in novel situations" (Jaw-Madson, 2015). There are nine dimensions to the Burke Learning Agility Inventory, each representing a cluster of behaviors:

1. **Flexibility**: Being open to new ideas and proposing new solutions
2. **Speed**: Acting on ideas quickly so that those not working are discarded and other possibilities are accelerated
3. **Experimenting**: Trying out new behaviors (i.e. approaches, ideas) to determine what is effective
4. **Performance risk taking**: Seeking new activities (i.e. tasks, assignments, roles) that provide opportunities to be challenged
5. **Interpersonal risk taking**: Confronting differences with others in ways that lead to learning and change
6. **Collaborating**: Finding ways to work with others that generate unique opportunities for learning
7. **Information gathering**: Using various methods to remain current in one's area of expertise
8. **Feedback seeking**: Asking others for feedback on one's ideas and overall performance
9. **Reflecting**: Slowing down to evaluate one's own performance in order to be more effective (Hoff & Smith, 2020).

Learning is ultimately a choice made on the part of a learner. If someone doesn't want to learn, they won't learn. People can be extrinsically motivated to learn, however. In his book, *Learn or Die: Using Science to Build a Leading-Edge Learning Organization*, Edward Hess identified five conditions for a good workplace learning environment:

1. positive environment that mitigates learning inhibitors, such as stress, fear of failure, negative emotions, and ego defenses
2. encourage mastery learning and intrinsic motivation, and be learner-centric (i.e. employee-centric) in that it would seek to engage learners (i.e. employees) emotionally by treating them with respect, dignity, and trust. It should encourage a growth mindset of discovery and exploration, self-efficacy, and experimentation
3. not punish employees for making learning mistakes or failures…so long as they learn from those mistakes or failures. Managers should role model learning behaviors, giving employees permission to speak freely and honestly
4. meet the fundamental needs…of autonomy, effectiveness, and relatedness
5. leaders and managers need to behave in a manner that earns the trust of employees and engenders employees' beliefs that they are respected as unique individuals and that their managers care about their personal growth and development (Hess, 2014, 47)

This is where the interdependence within ICLML shows up yet again—take note of where culture, leadership, and management play a role in setting these conditions for learning, especially when it comes to psychological safety. Hess went on to observe that "…an environment that promotes high employee engagement is very similar to one that promotes high-engagement learning in an educational setting" (Hess, 2014, 49) when he compared employee engagement behaviors with learning behaviors. For example, the statement "I have the opportunity to do what I do best" is associated with high employee engagement. "Learner-centricity, autonomy, effectiveness, and self-efficacy" are hallmarks of high engagement learning. The common themes are striking. So what can be done to set the conditions?

Cultivate the culture and the teams: If a company is practicing ICLML, this is already happening. Create norms and the environment around continuous improvement and learning, i.e. encouraging curiosity, asking questions, iteration and experimentation, etc. In addition to supporting psychological safety, capitalize on failures as learning opportunities. In service of driving innovation, "we try to reward failures as much as success," says Wim (Morris, 2004).

Build individual and team awareness: Using widely available assessment tools and coaching, equip individuals with an understanding of how they best learn, where they have learning preferences, and the development they need. Karen recommends Honey & Mumford's Learning Styles Questionnaire and the Burke Learning Agility Inventory (BLAI). Individual assessments mean that you can drive individualized learning—customized to a person's specific needs and motivations for maximum impact. Data can then be combined to assess the innovation capabilities of the team. The Predictive Index, a technology and data-driven talent optimization platform, takes data on individual needs and motivations and identifies the team types against four quadrants: Teamwork and Employee Experience, Innovation and Agility, Process and Precision, and Results and Discipline. The self awareness informs strategy and planning, where you can set individual and team goals for both learning and innovation.

Develop learning agility as a capability: Agile learners know how to learn. The BLAI identifies the types of behaviors to learn, practice, and demonstrate the capability every day. Create development plans and follow through with them. Measure to track success. Be consistent in developing and leveraging learning agility.

Harness knowledge from both exploitative and explorative learning to drive innovation: The key here is to actually do something with the learning happening at all levels and apply them to products, services, and the organization itself. If it makes no difference, it's not innovation. "The Ease of Inaction" is one of the traps identified by Jeremy Gutsche, CEO of Trend Hunter:

> Smart people do not intentionally resist change or adaptation, but we get so caught up with everything that needs to be done that we become less proactive about ideas that are different, are not in our department, or are not our greatest concern. A multitude of factors make it easier for us to lack urgency, and if you can address those factors, you can spark the action you need to create the future.
>
> *Gutsche (2020, 45)*

To mitigate the resistance to learning and change, he recommends:
- auditing the factors that inhibit action in the categories of structure, optimization, life, neurology, busyness, and constraints
- creating urgency
- motivating the team to achieve the impossible

All these actions support a learning organization.

Conclusion

The healthcare industry is extremely complex and fraught with challenges, and there is still so much innovation yet to achieve. We are obligated to continue until all illnesses are proactively and equitably addressed in a timely manner, thus extending the length and quality of life. In the absence of coordinated action across the ecosystem, individual organizations must uniquely define who they are, what they do, why they do it, and how according to their specific context.

Each of the authors here is fortunate enough to see innovation at its best. The common thread among our experiences are fewer barriers, supportive cultures and environments, great collaborators and teammates, possibility-driven mindsets, a lot of learning opportunities, and personal growth. If it wasn't obvious before, we will emphasize it now. Our aim for this chapter is to draw from these experiences to illuminate and advise on how the conditions—culture, leadership, management, and learning—can prove an organization's place in the world when it comes to innovation:

Culture: Purpose, mission, vision, and values are the foundational building blocks of a culture. The Design of Work Experience (DOWE) framework can guide the process of intentionally designing, implementing, and sustaining culture and corresponding experiences according to your unique context. All must be mindfully created to align an organization's people and activities for innovation.

Leadership: There are many perspectives and behaviors required of leadership for successful innovation. Our top priorities are showing strategic intelligence, leading culture, demonstrating empathy, managing, and leading.

Management: Managers, especially middle managers, play a key role in enabling innovation, so companies must be purposeful and consistent with their management philosophies. That being said, managing chaos or at the edge of chaos involves process and behaviors such as understanding the landscape, managing the intended culture, leveraging diversity, and calibrating oppositional forces.

Learning: In companies, learning happens at the individual, team, and organization levels and is critical for innovation and the survival of the business. The most important skill is learning to learn, which can be acquired through building learning agility as a competency. Cultivating the culture and the teams, building individual and team awareness, developing learning agility as a capability, and harnessing knowledge to drive innovation create the environment that encourages learning.

Our best advice is to commit to defining your leadership and carrying out your vision to build the team and ecosystem you need. Once achieved, help others to develop and implement their own visions as leaders. Scale up with other teams within the organization, and then across the industry. Understand what unique gifts you can bring to the market and how it can be orchestrated in a way that meets business objectives and benefits the greater good. Knowing is half the battle, so they say. And now the other half begins. What will you do?

References

Abdou, Anouare. 2020. "Six things the best bosses do differently." Last modified October 22, 2020. https://www.theladders.com/career-advice/6-things-the-best-bosses-do-differently.

Amabile, Teresa, and Steven Kramer. 2011. *The Progress Principle: Using Small Wins to Ignite Joy, Engagement, and Creativity at Work.* Boston, MA: Harvard Business Press.

Barlow, James. 2016. *Managing Innovation in Healthcare.* London: World Scientific Publishing Europe Ltd.

Benner, M. J., & Tushman, M. L. 2002. Process management and technological innovation: A longitudinal study of the photography and paint industries. *Administrative Science Quarterly,* 47: 676–706.

Birken, Sarah A., Shoou-Yih Daniel Lee, and Bryan J. Weiner. 2012. "Uncovering middle managers' role in healthcare Innovation Implementation." *Implementation Science* 7, no. 1: 1–12.

Bluestein, Adam. 2014. *Keeping Up with the Johnsons.* New York: Fast Company Press.

Bradley, Bret H., Bennett E. Postlethwaite, Anthony C. Klotz, Maria R. Hamdani, and Kenneth G. Brown. 2012. "Reaping the benefits of task conflict in teams: The critical role of team psychological safety climate." *Journal of Applied Psychology* 97, no. 1: 151.

Carroll, Noel, and Ita Richardson. 2016. "Aligning healthcare innovation and software requirements through design thinking." *In 2016 IEEE/ACM International Workshop on Software Engineering in Healthcare Systems (SEHS),* New York, pp. 1–7. IEEE.

Christensen, Clayton, Andrew Waldeck and Rebecca Fogg. 2017. "How disruptive innovation can finally revolutionize healthcare." Industry Horizons White Paper, Innosight. https://www.innosight.com/insight/how-disruptive-innovation-can-finally-revolutionize-h ealthcare/.

Collins, James C., and Jerry Porras. 1994. *Built to Last: Successful Habits of Visionary Companies.* New York: HarperBusiness.

Collins, James C., and Jerry I. Porras. 1996. "Building your company's vision." *Harvard Business Review* 74, no. 5: 65.

Cross, Rob, Amy Edmondson, and Wendy Murphy. 2020. "A noble purpose alone won't transform your company." *MIT Sloan Management Review* 61, no. 2: 37–43.

Deiser, Roland. 2018. "Digital transformation challenges in large and complex organizations." Center for the Future of Organization White Paper. Drucker School of Management, Claremont Graduate University. https://futureorg.org/wp-content/themes/futureorg/assets/Deiser-Digital-Transformation.pdf.

Drucker, Peter. 2018. *The Effective Executive.* London: Routledge.

Dvorak, Nate and Bryant Ott. 2015. "A company's purpose has to be a lot more than words." Last modified July 28, 2015. https://www.gallup.com/workplace/236573/company-purpose-lot-words.aspx.

Edmondson, Amy. 2019. *The Fearless Organization: Creating Psychological Safety in the Workplace for Learning, Innovation, and Growth.* Hoboken, NJ: Wiley.

Edmondson, Amy, and Kathryn Roloff. 2009. "Leveraging diversity through psychological safety." *Rotman Magazine* 1: 47–51.

Freire, Karine, and Daniela Sangiorgi. 2010. "Service design and healthcare innovation: From consumption to co-production to co-creation." *In Service Design and Service Innovation Conference*, Linköping, pp. 39–50.

Gittelman, Michelle, and Bruce Kogut. 2003. "Does good science lead to valuable knowledge? Biotechnology firms and the evolutionary logic of citation patterns." *Management Science* 49, no. 4: 366–382.

Gupta, A. K., Smith, K. G., & Shalley, C. E. 2006. The interplay between exploration and exploitation. *Academy of Management Journal*, 49(4): 693–706.

Gutsche, Jeremy. 2020. *The Innovation Handbook + Create the Future: Tactics for Disruptive Thinking.* New York: Fast Company Press.

Hansen, Morten T. 2009. *Collaboration: How Leaders Avoid the Traps, Create Unity, and Reap Big Results.* Boston, MA: Harvard University Press.

Hess, Edward D. 2014. *Learn or Die: Using Science to Build a Leading-Edge Learning Organization.* New York: Columbia University Press.

Hewlett, Sylvia Ann, Melinda Marshall, and Laura Sherbin. 2013. "How diversity can drive innovation." *Harvard Business Review* 91, no. 12: 30–30.

Hoff, David F., and David E. Smith. 2020. "Leadership and learning agility: A lifelong journey for W. Warner Burke." *The Journal of Applied Behavioral Science* 56, no. 4: 492–502.

Iyawa, Gloria Ejehiohen, Marlien Herselman, and Adele Botha. 2016. "Digital health innovation ecosystems: From systematic literature review to conceptual framework." *Procedia Computer Science* 100: 244–252.

Jaw-Madson, Karen. 2015. "The latest from W. Warner Burke on learning agility." *Co.-Design of Work Experience.* Last modified October 22, 2015. https://www.designofworkexperience.com/news/the-latest-from-w-warner-burke-on-learning-agility.

Jaw-Madson, Karen. 2017. "A culture of this or that." *LinkedIn.* Last modified March 24, 2017. https://www.linkedin.com/pulse/culture-karen-jaw-madson/.

Jaw-Madson, Karen. 2018a. "The role of leadership in creating a culture of learning." Last modified 2018. https://insights.learnlight.com/en/articles/role-of-leadership-in-creating-a-culture-of-learning/.

Jaw-Madson, Karen. 2018b. *Culture Your Culture: Innovating Experiences @ Work.* Bingley, UK: Emerald Group Publishing.

Jaw-Madson, Karen. 2019. "Change management and digital transformation: Tips for HR." Learnlight. Last modified 2019. https://insights.learnlight.com/en/articles/change-management-and-digital-transformation -tips-for-hr/.

Jaw-Madson, Karen. Definition of culture, forthcoming. https://www.designofworkexperience.com/dowe.html.

Johnson, Barry. 1992. *Polarity Management: Identifying and Managing Unsolvable Problems.* Amherst: HRD Press.

Johnson, Steven. 2010. *Where Good Ideas Come From: The Natural History of Innovation.* New York: Penguin.

Johnson, Steven, and Kevin Kelly. 2010. "Kevin Kelly and Steven Johnson on Where Ideas Come From" Last modified September 27, 2010. https://www.wired.com/2010/09/mf-kellyjohnson/.

Jones, Gareth R., and Jennifer M. George. 1998. "The experience and evolution of trust: Implications for cooperation and teamwork." *Academy of Management Review* 23, no. 3: 531–546.

Kim, Changsu, Jaeyong Song, and Atul Nerkar. 2012. "Learning and innovation: Exploitation and exploration trade-offs." *Journal of Business Research* 65, no. 8: 1189–1194.

Knowledge Management Tools, 2014. "No universal definition of knowledge management," Last modified 2014. http://www.knowledge-management-tools.net/nodefinition.html.

Maccoby, Michael. 2015. *Strategic Intelligence: Conceptual Tools for Leading Change,* First edition. Oxford, UK: Oxford United Press.

Maccoby, Michael, and Tim Scudder. 2011. "Strategic intelligence: A conceptual system of leadership for change." *Performance Improvement* 50, no. 3: 32–40.

McDermott Will & Emery. 2020. "2020 Hospital & Health system innovation summit." MWE video, November 11, 2020. https://health.mwe.com/events/2020-hospital-and-health-system-innovation-summit/.

Minor, Dylan, Paul Brook, and Josh Bernoff. 2017. "Are innovative companies more profitable?" *MIT Sloan Management Review.*

Morris, Kevin. 2004. "Wim Roelandts: Inspiring innovation at Xilinx." *Electronic Engineering Journal,* Last modified December 7, 2004. https://www.eejournal.com/article/20041207_wim/.

Nayar, Vineet. 2013. "Three differences between managers and leaders." *Harvard Business Review* 8.

O'Reilly, Charles A. and Michael L. Tushman. 2016. *Lead and Disrupt: How to Solve the Innovator's Dilemma.* Stanford: Stanford University Press.

Owens, David A. 2014. "Leading strategic innovation in organizations" A Coursera course by Vanderbilt University.

Quinn, James Brian. 1985. "Innovation and corporate strategy: Managed chaos." *Technology in Society* 7, no. 2–3: 263–279.

Ratanjee, Vibhas. 2020. "How highmark health embraces disruption and builds for the future." Last modified September 14, 2020. https://www.gallup.com/workplace/320063/highmark-health-embraces-disruption-builds- future.aspx.

Senge, Peter M. 1990. *The Fifth Discipline: The Art and Practice of the Learning Organization.* New York: Doubleday.

Shanafelt, Tait D., Edgar Schein, Lloyd B. Minor, Mickey Trockel, Peter Schein, and Darrell Kirch. 2019. "Healing the professional culture of medicine." *Mayo Clinic Proceedings*, 94, no. 8: 1556–1566.

Strebel, Paul, and Salvatore Cantale. 2014. "Is your company addicted to value extraction?" *MIT Sloan Management Review* 55, no. 4: 95.

Su, Zhongfeng, Jingyu Li, Zhiping Yang, and Yuan Li. 2011. "Exploratory learning and exploitative learning in different organizational structures." *Asia Pacific Journal of Management* 28, no. 4: 697–714.

Thakur, Ramendra, Sonya H. Y. Hsu, and Gwen Fontenot. 2012. "Innovation in healthcare: Issues and future trends." *Journal of Business Research* 65, no. 4: 562–569.

Tinker, Bob and Tae Hea Nahm. 2019. *Survival to Thrival: Building the Enterprise Startup - Book 2 Change or Be Changed.* Herndon, VA: Mascot Books.

Wiseman, Theresa. 1996. "A concept analysis of empathy." *Journal of Advanced Nursing* 23, no. 6: 1162–1167.

Chapter 4

Driving Value from Technical Innovation: Dramatic Change Management Skills and Leadership at All Levels Is Required

Brittany Partridge

UC San Diego Health

Contents

Change is a constant, and nowhere is that more true than in healthcare. The vast amounts of legislative requirements, shifting clinical guidelines, and new technology trends cause the rate of change in healthcare to be exhausting. Over the years, and countless go-lives, both successful and not, I have learned that there are ways to make change more effective and create a smoother transition for everyone. One model to consider is Dr. John Kotter's 8 Step Model of Change. I want to take you through stories from my go-lives using Dr. Kotter's lens to show how you can impact change management in healthcare. I was completely unaware of Kotter's existence going into my change management quest, however many of his steps showed up in my learnings, and it would have been amazingly helpful to have had them at the beginning (Figure 4.1).

Day One: The question racing through my mind as I climbed out of my car was "Am I going to walk into a success or total disaster?" Watching the sunrise over the capital from atop the empty parking garage, my first inclination was a disaster. For the past 16 weeks, I had poured

DOI: 10.4324/9781003220473-6

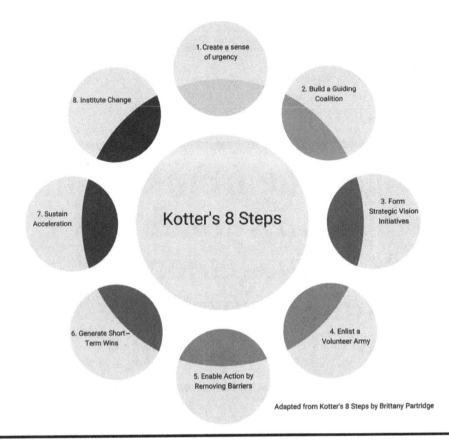

Adapted from Kotter's 8 Steps by Brittany Partridge

Figure 4.1 Kotter's 8 steps change model.

my heart and soul into the hospital that stood in front of me, working inch by inch to try and change the minds of 300 physicians. Fourteen hour days were spent in the anesthesia office, trying to educate and persuade a culture shift that had been set in stone for hundreds of years. It was the biggest test of my career thus far, the morning they flipped the Electronic Health Record (EHR) Switch, and I had no idea what the morning would hold. Looking up at the blinding red lights of the emergency room, I took a deep breath, crossed my fingers, and stepped through the sliding glass doors.

The First Step Kotter outlines is: Cultivate Urgency, Kotter suggests that for change to be successful 75% of a company's management must "buy-in" to the change (Kotter, 2012). This urgency was cultivated for us because the entire nation was going through a shift inside of physician's offices and hospitals. In 2009 the American Reinvestment and Recovery Act was signed. One of the components was the HITECH act which called for *Meaningful Use* of the certified Electronic Health Record Technology. This change was to be led by the Office of the National Coordinator. Due to the penalties attached to noncompliance with the *Meaningful Use* rules, rapid change efforts were being put into place to bring all of healthcare onto the EHR. These penalties created the buy-in we needed for the change very quickly in the senior executives, however, we still had an uphill battle to go with the physician and clinical leaders. My network, Central Healthcare[1] knew that it would have to bring technology to all ten of its hospitals and that the change would affect nearly every single employee and patient to walk through our doors.

Fresh out of college, I wandered into my new role as Clinical Informatics Specialist, just as this massive change was taking place. I was eager to show the world how technology was always the right option, and how it could truly change and optimize the workflow in the hospitals. I had used computers my entire life, typing my papers since the first grade and enjoying the intuitive comfort that can only come with that level of exposure. I was a technology evangelist and believed that it was the path, the ONLY path to the future. It had never crossed my mind that everyone didn't share the same exuberance for electronics and cutting-edge functionality that I had. I would soon find that the whole world was not as elated about the shift as I was.

I first began to realize that not everyone was as excited about the looming changes to physician workflow and medical practice when I taught my first class to a group of physicians in a large lecture hall at one of our university hospitals. About half the room was residents, around my age who had used EHRs in some of their medical school rotations. The other half was a mix of longer practicing physicians and a few that only came to our hospitals to do surgery once or twice a month. The latter group was grumbling throughout the lecture and made some snarky comments when I pointed out features that I thought were amazing or would make the work easier. "Easier" one of them exclaimed, "I am quitting medicine when this atrocity comes out." I remember thinking some less than savory thoughts about these "dinosaurs of medicine," not my proudest moment, but at least it stayed in my head.

Another hint that some of the medical staff wasn't as excited about the shift to electronic was when the schedule of the EHR rollout was posted. We shared with the hospital network, what the plan was, where we would begin and the order of the hospitals to come live. We had to bring each of our hospitals up one at a time, over 5 years, due to resource and monetary constraints. Soon the physicians that were extremely anti-EHR began to put in transfer requests to the last hospital on the list. It wasn't just a few names either, but instead more than 200 doctors wanted to avoid the transition for as long as possible. Like lemmings running from a burning ship, they systematically moved away from technology and all its changes. Their belief was so great that technology would be the downfall of medicine, that they left the hospitals that had been their homes for decades, to put off using it for a few more years. This wasn't just a phenomenon in my network, and it has been shown across the nation that physician job satisfaction had declined with the implementation of the electronic record.

It wasn't just the physicians that were against the change, there were many other staff members that were opposed. Nurses complained that they would not get to interact with the patients anymore due to the time it would take to chart electronically. They stated adamantly that with the addition of the EHR, the profession of nursing would go through an existential change, from that of a caring nurturing position to that of a secretary performing never-ending data entry. The admissions staff fussed that they wouldn't be able to track the patients, and even the kitchen was convinced that meals would get lost. Their fear wasn't completely unfounded, with all of the new processes, sometimes meals wouldn't get ordered on time, or would be delivered to the floor the patient had been on that morning.

All the way up to the top there was a wall of resistance being built against the EHR. The biggest hurdle we had to face was when the administration bowed to the physicians and refused to mandate training. I couldn't believe my ears, how were physicians going to practice medicine electronically if they never learned the system?!

As we slowly rolled out to all the hospitals in the network, we got better at the transition, we learned more about the system, and we became more comfortable with the functionality. However, as we continued to bring hospitals live, more clinicians asked to transfer to the final hospital, putting the change off a few more months. When we got to the final hospital, the one with the biggest surgeon population, the one with the most resistant clinicians, I was told that for this go-live I would support overseeing the physician adoption and training. It was time for trial by fire.

Kotter suggests change leaders initiate open dialogues and discussions to allow people to think through issues and verbalize the challenges. Overwhelmed by the animosity and cold demeanors of the staff at our final hospital, I pulled one of my favorite physicians aside. A delightful Emergency Physician who wore Hawaiian shirts over his scrubs and extremely loud Air Jordans on his feet, Dr. Brown[2] had made it known that he would be retiring once the EHR went into effect. I asked him why the hostility, why isn't this something you want to do? He replied,

> Britt, I don't do technology, I don't know how and I don't want to look stupid in front of those that I lead. None of my peers are saying this is a good shift, and it will take my focus off my patients.

I was a bit taken aback, even though I had been completely for technology, through the rollouts at the other hospitals, I came to believe that the resistance was based solely on being uncomfortable with the new skills and nothing more. Talking to Dr. Brown was my first foray into Kotter's second step of Building a Guiding Coalition. From our conversation, I learned that it is so important to listen to your "customers" and the true drivers behind their fears. I was so excited about the new technology, ready to push it on anyone and everyone, that I hadn't really stopped to listen to what clinicians were saying.

Dr. Brown had shared concerns that very closely resembled the four commons reasons people resist change, outlined in the book *What Leaders Really Do*:

> First, they do not want to lose something which they perceive of as valuable; second, a misunderstanding of change and its implications; third, their belief that change does not make any sense for the organization; fourth, a low tolerance for change.

I thought about what Dr. Brown said and I listed all the reasons he gave for not wanting to embrace the EHR. One, fear of technology and being uncomfortable with the computer in general, fear of the unknown. Two, fear of looking stupid in front of those that he taught, residents, med students and those that he led, nurses and patients. Three, this was not a peer-led initiative, there was no one from his community speaking about the EHR in a positive manner. Finally, four, there wouldn't be time left over for his patients. Once I knew what the underlying challenges were for the physicians, I could begin to implement a game plan. I also noticed a shift in my thinking, maybe my way and my technology obsession wasn't the only way, maybe what my trusted physicians were saying had merit. So, 4 months before go-live that is exactly what I did. I took each of the resistance points and made an action plan, initially to try and make them see how awesome the technology was, and eventually to help them through this drastic change to their profession and comfort zone of the past few decades. Little did I know but I was working through Kotter's fifth point of Identifying and Removing Obstacles.

By addressing the "whys" and finding what drove the physicians I was working toward the first step of change, unfreezing what they were currently doing. Sure, we had to do this implementation due to what the federal government was mandating; however, the creation of why needed to be more personal, more impactful for the clinician's workflow. To make this change possible, we needed to Form Strategic Vision and Initiatives. Maybe it was important for physicians to be able to read the notes left by their fellow clinicians without having to slog through the handwriting. There had been an error a few months prior that had almost killed a patient when the wrong drug was given due to handwriting issues. Or perhaps it was helpful to be able to graph labs and their correlation to the medications the patient was on. Some of the consulting providers may have been excited to find out that they could write orders for their patients from home so that patients didn't have to wait for care. The residents might be excited to see charts of their patients before they arrived at the hospital. It was my job to use the "why" to motivate the change, to show why what we were doing on paper wasn't the best option.

To address the challenge of fear of the unknown, I started hanging out at the hospital all the time. I went on rounds with each of our service lines, listening to their vocabulary and understanding the flow of work through the units. One morning on rounds a pediatric intensivist chose to explain to me why the EHR was an "atrocity that would be the downfall of medicine," I still have a yellow legal pad completely full of his comments that day. I attended more surgeries and procedures than I could count, to get the staff familiar with my face, and to learn my way around the OR pods. I did my homework in the physician lounge and let them know that I was available for questions or suggestions if they needed it. I watched deliveries in the middle of the night and I stood in the emergency room during resuscitation events. Roberts et al. (2016) define design thinking as a systematic innovation process that prioritizes deep empathy for end-user desires, needs, and challenges to fully understand a problem in hopes of developing more comprehensive and effective solutions. This embedding in the hospital was my first exposure to design thinking and something I would use in my implementations for the rest of my career.

Slowly, over time, the clinicians came to accept that I was learning their lives and languages. Rather than avoid me like the plague, they began to wonder where I was when I wasn't on rounds. I knew we had made major progress when on a few separate days, three physicians brought me their home computers for help and their cell phone questions. They trusted me to help them, and they believed in my ability to find the right answer. Dr. S., famous for being one of the first doctors to run away from the electronic record, dropped by one day with his Mac, telling me that he had broken it and it wouldn't turn on. While I wiped the hard drive and performed a factory reset (not at all in my job description), we began talking. He told me about some of his longtime patients, and how now he was now delivering their babies, how medicine had changed so much, and how much he loved being a doctor. I in turn listened and tried not to force my technology agenda into his musings. That trust from the providers would serve me well through the following months.

I focused on continuing to remove barriers, to address the frustration with computers, in general, I made sure there were as many class options as possible, different times of day, different days of the week. Then to combat the fear of looking stupid in front of their teams I broke the classes into self-proclaimed abilities. There was the expert class for those who had used the EHR before and just needed slight help specific to their workflow. There was the consistent user class, for those that used computers often but hadn't used an EHR where we covered all of the functionality of the system and how to find the bits of information most important to their service line. Finally, there was the "new to computers" class, which was surprisingly well attended. In this class, to avoid forcing the physicians to ask questions they deemed dumb, I taught with the assumption that they had never used the computer before. We started out with how to use the right and left click buttons on a mouse, how to copy/paste using your keyboard and many other shortcuts many of us take for granted before we progressed through the other material. I would have never thought to teach the classes like that without Dr. Brown's help, but the "New to Computers" class had the best attendance, with the most repeat attendees. One physician told me after class that while he still hated the computer, he was glad there had been a class like this for him. He said, "I have been God of the OR for 30 plus years, I know everything. I can't let that reputation crumble in one computer class." While it took everything, I had to not roll my eyes at his choice of words, I realized how important self-confidence was in the business of saving lives. The unexpected attendance demonstrates the importance of Dr. Kotter's Step 6: Create Quick Wins, with training unmandated any participation by the staff was a win, and their continued attendance created more wins.

As we move forward to mobile devices becoming more prominent in the hospitals and clinics, this introductory class will be an important consideration to repeat. Currently we are not seeing as much resistance to mobile devices as we saw to the addition of computers in the health space. My hypothesis around this is that this is twofold, one that many Physicians have gotten used to using mobile devices in their everyday lives. Two, that many of the workflows are not mandated on mobile devices and there are computer-based workarounds, so if a user has resistance to the mobile device they just aren't using it. I imagine this may change as more and more functionality is available mobile only, and we will be doing ourselves a huge disservice if we don't remember all of the lessons from transitioning to EHRs on computers.

Dr. S. came to that class, commenting that since I had listened to all of his "soapbox rantings," he would listen to me. He attended not once, not twice, but three times. He began coming to my lab and asking questions about electronic workflow. Once I showed him how to get the EHR on his Mac he began calling me at all hours of the day and night to get scenarios to practice. I was shocked at his full 180°, and it further made me realize that technology adoption was not a linear trajectory.

The next concern, lack of peer lead promotion, brought on a lot of learning moments for me. Just as I had been under the assumption that everyone was excited about technology, I also assumed that the leaders in official leadership positions were those with the most control in the hospital. I found I was so wrong when I tried to get the official leaders to coax the physicians into attending classes, which went over like a lead balloon. Then I learned about the unofficial leaders, the cornerstones of each unit. The physicians that all the other doctors trusted and looked to for advice, the ones that set best practice and were team players, the unofficial leaders. Turns out pretty much every service line (ED, women's health, acute care, etc.) had one. Once I started looking, they weren't that difficult to identify.

By finding the unofficial leaders that the physicians looked up to and trusted, I was able to build a coalition. I coached them into being the spokespeople at their respective clinical councils. We had meetings of these leaders, dubbed physician champions, to make sure we were doing what was right for their service lines. Each member of this coalition helped with the design of their groups' electronic order sets, note templates, and look and feel of the computer. The idea was that in designing it, they could be excited about it and motivate the other physicians that they led. Kotter focuses on this process with steps 2 and 4 of Creating a Guiding Coalition, and Building a Volunteer army/communicating the vision. Guiding coalitions aren't always traditional leaders and their word of mouth can be your biggest ally through any change.

Not only was a coalition created at the physician level, but in nursing as well. We pulled out volunteer self-proclaimed computer specialists from every unit in the hospital, from every floor and every specialty. We dubbed them experts and created an exclusive feeling club-like atmosphere to get them excited. They too helped with the design of the EHR. They also helped teach the classes of the other nurses and providers, all while keeping up with their clinical shifts on the units. When go-live came this gang of self-confident, positive users would be our biggest attribute. They would be on their home units with staff that was used to interacting with them speaking to the workflows that they used every day.

Through the use of both the Physician Champions and the Nurse Experts, we were able to create a Vision for Change, Kotter's step 3. We created transparent expectations of the change for the other providers and we communicated clearly with leadership about when and where each of the changes would occur. They helped me distribute cutover plans, the documents that show how a technological change will take place and what you can expect to see throughout the night of the change. When things got heated through the long hours and the change hit solid walls, they brought me humor in the form of songs and poems about the dreaded electronic go-lives.

Dr. Brown's last reason about not supporting EHRs because it took time away from the patient was the hardest to address. We would struggle with it throughout the process. I knew that at the beginning this would be a completely legitimate concern and there was really no way to say it wouldn't happen. To mitigate this concern the best, we made sure that computers were available in every form and fashion. There were computers in the rooms the physicians could use while talking to the patients. We had rolling computers, the physicians could take to the different Emergency and PACU bays, which eventually were used so creatively, with a pediatrician turning one into a scooter complete with streamers. There were also handheld tablets, the physician could use at home or in the break room. We also made sure to communicate with the patients, every day for the first 6 weeks, what the change was and how care might be affected or different. Once go-live happened some of the patients took it upon themselves to be commentators on the changes. I can still see Mr. Smith,[3] ambling down the Ortho floor with his walker, the hospital gown opened wide in the back, asking the physicians how the computers were "running their lives today?" and telling them "his granny could type faster." We worked with administration and staffing to make sure the caseloads were lighter for the first 6 weeks and we brought in traveling nurses and physicians to help staff the units, so the native clinicians would have time to learn. We also continued highlighting Quick Wins, Kotter step 6, by having a leaderboard of the physicians with the highest percentage or order entry, and a board with the best staff submitted technical tips of the week.

Once all the whys were addressed and all the training was complete it was time for day one, the actual changing, the most adventurous and trying, stretching 6 weeks of my life. As I walked through the sliding doors of the emergency room that morning, I expected chaos, but it was oddly quiet. As soon as I said the Q word in my head I admonished myself, you don't say that in a hospital, the belief is as soon as you say it is quiet, chaos and bedlam will erupt. It wasn't quite instantaneous but 2 hours later "quiet" wasn't crossing my mind. All staff was on hand and shift change had just occurred when we flipped the switch at seven in the morning.

Surprisingly, while there was a lot of angst and the energy was palpable. The first day went smoothly for the most part. There were no major meltdowns and everyone worked together as a collaborative team. While I did have a surgeon throw his laptop out a two-story window and another physician have a screaming fit in the PACU, I learned not to take it personally and to always circle back to the why. There were some tears on the nursing units, and some pretty catty remarks, however, we got through it. For the loudest of physicians, it was almost always a lack of understanding of how the EHR worked, acting out driven by fear of failure. For those that stomped and screamed we made sure they were set up with an expert for one-on-one class, or a "buddy" to follow them around at the elbow for a few days. We also submitted a list of all the staff that was acting out to the leadership team every day. For the nurses, the leadership worked with their managers to make sure they were getting the help they needed. For the physicians, sometimes a call from the Vice President of Medical Affairs or Chief of Surgery improved their perception, that someone was hearing their concerns, that we saw them and were listening. By framing the frustrations and outbursts as opportunities for change and not as punishable moments we were able to follow Kotter's step 7 and Sustain the Acceleration of the Go-Live, continuing to win over clinicians little by little.

Over the next 6 weeks, my patience would be tried over and over as I was pushed to the edge by working a 12 plus hour shift every single day. However, during that time, I learned so much about myself, my leadership style, and the rest of the human race in general. I learned how people react when faced with fear and uncertainty. I learned how to speak calmly and rationally when that was the opposite of what I felt. As we worked our way through Kotter's step 8 of Institutionalizing the Change, refreezing the behavior patterns, and cementing the use of the EHR as the new normal for the physicians and nurses, I realized we were also refreezing my behavior patterns. I now defaulted to starting with the why of doing things, I always made sure I had an informal leader as an ally, and I learned to communicate clearly where we were going and how to get there.

If I had known about Kotter's process when I was working through this initiative, I would have known that what we were doing at the end of go-live was Step 8, Instituting Change and solidifying it in the organization's culture. We continued to make the change part of everyday clinical practice, by using a model that had expert users working out of the numbers at each of our hospitals to sustain momentum and help with re-education as needed. We highlighted how electronic orders led to decreased medication errors and more standardized treatments. We had clinical councils present wins (along with the optimization requests) at the service line councils. Eventually, we were able to get EHR training to be mandatory for all incoming staff, and to support it with CMEs. Instituting EHR change will be an ongoing piece of Health IT as long as EHRs exist in the clinical setting, it will always be a work in process. However, as long as we continue to innovate, to always return to our guiding coalition, and to address the "Whys," we can only improve.

My life has been forever impacted by the 6 months I spent preparing for, leading, and solidifying the change to the EHR. I went from being dead set on forcing technology into every crevice of the hospital, to understanding that there was more to consider. The human influence on medicine and the art that had been perfected through hundreds of years couldn't be smashed into an electronic box. While some days I wanted to quit, and some days I felt hopeless, by the end we had created such an amazing team and a resounding feeling of unity that can truly only be forged in the fire. I also learned how to be patient and how to hear others' concerns, and I gained the confidence in myself and my leadership abilities that will last my whole life. Shortly after this adventure, I accepted a leadership position in my network. I have used the lessons learned in this go-live, the steps of change, and how to drive behavior over and over again. It was one of the most trying times of my life, but I wouldn't trade the experience and growth for anything.

Notes

1 Note the names of people and hospitals have been changed to protect team-members. The events in this chapter took place over multiple go-lives but have been condensed into one timeline to provide a cohesive narrative.
2 Ibid.
3 Ibid.

References

Kotter, J. P. (2012), *Leading Change*. Brighton, MA: Harvard Business Review Press.
Roberts, J. P., Fisher, T. R., Trowbridge, M. J., and Bent, C. (2016), "A design thinking framework for healthcare management and innovation", *Healthcare*, Vol. 4, No. 1, pp. 11–14. doi: 10.1016/j.hjdsi.2015.12.002.

Chapter 5

Management and Leadership Distinctions Required at Stages of Maturity in an EHR/ EMR Adoption Model Context

Mitchell Parker
IU Health

Brittany Partridge
UC San Diego Health

Contents

DOI: 10.4324/9781003220473-7

Introduction

As Information Technology continues to mature and expand in its role within healthcare organizations, there are many areas of opportunity the teams must navigate. Progressing through the Health Information and Management Systems Society Electronic Medical Record Adoption Model (HIMSS EMRAM)stages brings about both discovery and challenges. While the specific decisions and discussions are unique to each system, themes and structures that underlie them have continuity across all of healthcare. We have been in the trenches as these models have unfolded in our systems. We have made many mistakes throughout our careers and brought out our lessons learned. What we have learned from all of this is that management of mobile initiatives requires a significant change in how we manage. We look at this as exacerbating existing management challenges that healthcare already faces. When we develop solutions, we need to rethink our mindset as to how we build them to be more inclusive of the culture of the organization. Engagement is critical, along with building relationships, managing the processes used to build solutions, and managing communication and education. We have to focus more on the basics and understanding the customer's needs. This chapter focuses on those steps we need to take, and how to rethink our processes to deliver successful mobile initiatives.

Building Relationships and Focusing on Education

While all healthcare information technology organizations have big goals and exciting plans for innovation and lofty plans to be the first to implement the newest newsworthy solution, it is vital to remember the basics. At its core, Health IT is just another hopeful better way of taking care of patients and supporting those that do. We must remind ourselves that as we build newer, more technical products, not to lose sight of the basics, and to return often to engage with and educate our most valuable assets, our clinical staff.

Engaging Clinicians: Project Based

One of the biggest determinants of success in a health technology project is ensuring that the clinician users have buy-in from the very beginning. As Melissa Langhan states in *Implementations of Newly Adopted Technology in Acute Care Settings*, "The methods and reasons for adoption of new technologies described by our subjects were often varied and poorly understood by clinical staff, but new technology was more often supported when providers were involved on the ground level" (Langhan et al., 2014). Leading Information Services in Health Systems is a world of checks and balances, on the one hand, you have technology teams, excited about new technology. On the other hand, you have clinicians that actually have to use the new technology. While a prototype or solution might seem cutting edge (shiny object syndrome), if it doesn't solve the problem or fit the workflow of the clinician, if it makes their job more difficult or has a steep learning curve, chances are it will fail. To mitigate this failure, clinicians need to be engaged from the very beginning. Identifying these clinical champions early is vitally important, making sure they are viewed as partners throughout the project will garner trust between the teams and advocacy for the finished product. What follows are some examples of when and how to engage clinicians:

Before Build

1. **Current state workflow**: Have the technical team go to the clinical site and follow the clinicians around; ask questions about decision points. If there are multiple sites and multiple units be sure to validate continuity. Don't allow the technical team to make assumptions about clinical workflow, ask, and observe. Don't forget to:
   - Document the current workflow process
   - Review security and permission requirements
   - Consider device availability
   - Think through charging needs and processes
   - Identify patient touchpoints
   - Document all verbal, written, and technical communication points and handoffs. "To design technologies for teams, we need a better understanding of the critical information that team members need to share and communicate for shared team awareness"
   - Identification of challenges and opportunities
   - Ask for end-user input for optimization of current state processes before discussing new technology
   - Create a list of requirements end-users feel are needed to meet process goals
2. **Create use cases**: A written description of how users will perform tasks with the new technology. A use case is a broken down sequence of steps, beginning with the end-user's goal and ending when that goal has been met. Bringing these use-cases to clinical department meetings for brainstorming and validation allows input from the clinical users and begins to socialize the technology on a larger scale. Make sure to include:
   - Which roles (be specific, such as cardiologist or ICU nurse) are going to use the technology
   - The goal that the technology hopes to achieve
   - The steps the user must take using the technology to achieve the task
   - How the technology should perform when the user completes each task
        Tip: If you write good use cases, creating testing scripts later will be much easier.
3. **High-level future state workflows**: Use the current state workflows and the use-cases to make an overview of future state workflows. This allows clinicians to understand the scope of the project as well as what steps in the process their design decisions will be impacting.

During Build

4. Clinical representation should be included at the project level. It is important that this representation is current in the numbers of users, not just leadership or analysts with former clinical experience. Leadership and analysts are important, but they are often removed from what specifically is happening in a process, and this is where failed assumptions can occur. Use the list of requirements obtained during the current state workflow to create design options for the end-users. If possible these should include mock ups.

5. Engage clinical end-users in all design decision-making; ideally, this would be an in-person meeting for discussion. Other alternatives include surveys, leaving prototypes on the units and asking for feedback, one-on-one sessions during rounding.

Right at the End of Build

6. **End-user validation**: this is where sign off on final design decisions happens. Due to the busy nature of healthcare workers, getting everyone in a room can often be difficult. Options include:
   - Call in meetings
   - Engaging site leads to obtain sign off from their groups at service line meetings
   - PowerPoints with signature lines
   - In-Depth Future State Workflows: Flesh out your high-level document, and this will aid in the creation of testing scripts, education, and communication.
7. Make sure sign off is obtained by all clinical stakeholders (remember this may not just be physicians and nurses, think pharmacists, schedulers, MAs, OT, PT, etc.)

Once Build Is Complete

8. **Creation of test scripts**: Turn the use cases into spreadsheets with places for end-users to sign off on design and workflow validation. Leave a section for comments should the build fail.
   - Testing is a big topic, the takeaway now is that clinical users must be engaged in User Acceptance Testing (UAT).
   - If at all possible the end users doing the testing should not have participated in the design. This allows socialization to more of the clinical team and ensures that any education highlights or processes that aren't clear are further identified.
9. **Education**: Clinicians know their colleagues best and can help the technical team determine what level of education is needed for each project.
10. Go-Live Support, both formal in that super users are on site during rollouts to help their colleagues with questions as well as informal, clinicians talking favorably about the new technology with their teams is a positive outcome of clinical buy in. According to Langhan's article,

> Implementation of new technology was facilitated when a strong educational foundation and support system was available. This included initial training on a device, the availability of super-users and technology support staff to assist providers and later on the availability of a jumpstart guide or annual validation to refresh a user's memory on operating the technology.

This knowledge and ownership that is brought about by getting clinical buy-in early will help the project succeed (Figure 5.1).

Sustaining Relationships between Clinical and Technical Teams

Up until this point, the focus has been on clinician engagement for a specific project one that has a start/stop date and is looking to solve a problem, address legislative changes, or supplement new clinical guidelines. However, clinical engagement should be an ongoing focus of Information Services in a healthcare system, beyond project needs. Trust between clinicians and technical

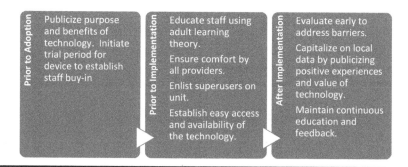

Figure 5.1   Steps to successful implementation of new technology (Parker, 2021). (Adaptation from Langhan et al. [2014].)

teams will support technical products and the healthcare system as a whole. When a relationship exists between the technical team and the clinical team, clinicians will feel comfortable reporting issues, will have faith that the issues will be solved, and will be kept in the loop with status updates. When the technical team has clinical relationships, they will feel comfortable rounding and reaching out for consistent feedback, optimization opportunity solicitation, and issue discovery. As Gellert and team suggest, we must "Respect and exploit the intelligence that our clinician customers bring from their care delivery and end user experience, and recognize their importance as partners of Health Informatics in a process of continuous EHR improvement."

How does an organization build robust relationships between clinical and technical teams? Familiarity and consistent interaction. When I was working on some of the really big go-lives, I made sure to work my regular job out of the physicians' lounge, to breed familiarity and comfort. Information Services departments within healthcare organizations can build familiarity through a targeted socialization approach.

First, determine where important information is handed out in the hospitals/clinics/healthcare systems. Often this is a morning house-wide huddle where things like staffing, bed availability, maintenance requests, and quality metrics are discussed. Add IS to this morning huddle, have an appointed team member attend with the goal of passing out vital information related to Tech (downtimes, updates, etc.) and to take feedback. This frontline approach allows for trickle-down information as well as allows the IS team to hear about problems faster than they would if relying on tickets. Other meetings beyond daily huddles that can be extremely helpful in building relationships are clinical service-line councils. IS should be a fixture in meetings like Surgical Services Council, Critical Care Council, OB/GYN Council, etc., often it can be extremely helpful to have the IS team that builds the EHR portion relevant to that council as that liaison. Not only does it allow the teams to get consistent feedback about the technology used in that service line it allows the continuous dissemination of pertinent information. Gellert says that

> Well integrated into the hospital team, CIs actively round multiple times each day, attend various facility meetings of clinicians, and are on call to providers, nurses and other end users throughout the hospital (through email, mobile telephone, or a wireless, voice-activated intra-facility communication device).

This active engagement can expand beyond clinical informatics to application analysts and other IS team members for robust clinical engagement.

Becoming a constant presence at meetings is imperative as is establishing an expected information flow. When the clinical team knows where to find the latest technical updates and what cadence the updates are disseminated, there is less frustration and confusion. An example of this information cascade is weekly or monthly newsletters from the CIO/IS Director containing high-level highlights, with links to further information and how-to guides/videos as needed for specific workflows.

Finally, the technical teams need to meet the clinical teams where they are, where they use the technology. I cannot overstate the importance of rounding, not just by the leadership teams, but by every single member of the IS staff. Rounding allows the technical teams to see the clinicians using the technology and address barriers they may not have even known were there, and they can get real-time feedback from the clinicians and cultivate empathy for the teams they are building for. Rounding should be done across shifts (the night shift is often left out, but often has the most time to engage) and throughout all areas of the hospitals, from central sterilization to the ICUs, from the emergency departments to the cardiac rehab facilities.

Effective Evaluation of Technology and Clinical engagement will allow continuous improvement of your engagement strategy and methods. As part of being a learning health system, organizations need to constantly review how the clinicians are using the technology that has been implemented and if it is effective. A study completed by Ratwani et al. (2018) looked at emergency department physicians performing multiple tasks, what they saw was an error rate between 0% and 50% across the different tasks. This variation in the use of technology reiterates that continuous education to processes and review of clinical technology skills should be identified and addressed.

Leading Your Team in Relationship Building

As a technical team, it can sometimes appear daunting to create relationships with clinical stakeholders, especially if it is a team-member's first foray into healthcare. This is an area where leadership has the opportunity to coach team members to allow them to be comfortable and confident walking into a clinical space. The following ideas offer a starting point on how to help your teams engage with clinicians.

1. **Embedding**: This is the number one reason I have been able to obtain a solid clinical baseline and succeed as a CI. When I first joined the CI team, my boss and I brainstormed the best way for me to quickly gain clinical knowledge as well as understand how clinicians interact with technology. We landed on the idea of embedding me with a residency team. Find opportunities for your teams to embed and pave the way for it to happen.
2. **Teaching**: One of the biggest hurdles for me not having a clinical background was encountered during my weekly physician onboarding classes. Each week, I would get questions such as "How do I order Sliding Scale Insulin?" or "How do I order controlled medications for prescriptions?" Teaching these workflows and how technology interacts with them has required me to know them more in-depth than any other project could. Find opportunities for your team to teach new workflows and how the technology they are designing impacts them.
3. **Cultivate curiosity:** Processes and difficulties often do not align across hospital systems or even clinical service lines, so beginning with an open mind and a questioning attitude will really allow the team to highlight pieces that may have derailed a project later on. Teach them to ask in-depth and open-ended questions and to always clarify if they are not sure, or

if a clinical term is confusing, create the culture that not-knowing/asking further questions is a good thing.

Education

Technical Education in the clinical setting could be an entire book in itself; however, there are a few consistent steps that can be focused on each time new technology is launched or a refresher course on existing technology is needed. Begin an educational initiative with a gap analysis and/or a strategic plan. If the technology is already in place but the system isn't meeting expected outcomes, a gap analysis can help determine where to focus educational initiatives and what content the education should have. A gap analysis can uncover opportunities such as the one listed above where the emergency department physicians had wide variations in processes and technical knowledge when performing tasks in the EHR.

Once a gap analysis has been completed you will know your target audience, based on which roles or individuals need further education or optimizations on their processes. However, if it is net new technology or changes to current workflow, it is important to assess job roles impacted and the level of education needed for each role. Think through what the change is and what each user will need to know to successfully perform the new workflow. This is where Start-Stop-Continue documents can be helpful in filling out educational plans. It is also helpful to engage the end-users you have built relationships with to help match the education to their learning needs, some options include:

- YouTube videos
- Web-based learning modules
- PowerPoints
- Pocket guides
- Presentations at service line meetings
- Tips and tricks
- Classroom training
- Post change FAQs for questions that consistently arise after the change is in place
- VR/AR scenarios
- Simulation labs

Some things to consider when building an educational plan:

- Budget to pay clinical staff for off-shift classroom training
- Real-time vs. ahead of time
- Cascading opportunities such as train-the-trainer, to have experts on each shift.
- Different learning styles and redundant education opportunities
- Ways to break up the information so it can be consumed is small snippets

Infrastructure

A major challenge that organizations face when it comes to bringing onboard new functionality or applications is having the infrastructure to do so. When it comes to failed IT projects, the paper *Cataloguing Most Severe Causes That Lead Software Projects to Fail* by Vikas Sitaram Chomal and

Dr. Jatinderkumar R. Saini indicates that technology is a major cause of IT project failures as part of their review (Chomal, 2014). Even if that infrastructure is in the cloud, it's not an infinite resource. Both compute and bandwidth are always at a premium, with wireless bandwidth adding even more stress to that.

When additional functions are considered for an organizational initiative, there needs to be a network and capabilities assessment completed as part of the project intake process. This assessment needs to cover the following areas:

- Local infrastructure present and available for the initiative
- Cloud infrastructure present and available
- Local infrastructure required
- Cloud infrastructure required
- Network/wireless infrastructure present and available
- Network/wireless infrastructure required for success
- Security/privacy requirements for monitoring
  - Will there be additional SIEM/Security resources required
  - Which elements have to be monitored for security?
  - Can this be integrated into the existing security monitoring system?
  - How many resources will be needed to monitor the system?
  - How will it be monitored?
- Team resources required for this project that can be made available across infrastructure, networking, and security
- Team resources required for project completion
- Team resources required for sustainment/maintenance
- Will the organization be able to accept the true budget for the initiative?
- Remember, there is no such thing as "No IT Involvement." Vendors make it up to make the overall cost appear lower.

The reason for the assessment is to get a true picture of the overall organizational impact from a technical and resource management perspective. A major reason for the failure of technical projects is the lack of proper resourcing. A major reason for security issues with these initiatives is the inability to properly maintain or monitor them (source: Verizon DBIR). Making the assumption that resources are infinite or immediately available has the side effects of starving other ones that can affect the delivery of core services. Academic medical centers are typically separate from the university structure by design and will have representation from the care delivery and educational sides. This assessment has to take into account resources and planning for both. Both sides need to be part of planning for these initiatives, especially if they include clinical research.

Even if an organization has assessed that they have the resources to finish the initiative and sustainably maintain it, how do they do so effectively? How do organizations need to manage the use of mobile devices in the environment to mitigate risk, as opposed to adding it and causing an adverse event in the process? How do they need to think about the process by which they bring these devices in?

They need to reinvent themselves as learning organizations to be able to mitigate those risks. Learning organizations are organizations where people within them continually expand their capacity at all levels to create desired results (Senge, 1990). This is an evolution of previous business models, where a small core group innovated, and the rest of the organization executed, much like Henry Ford and the assembly line. Peter Senge, in the 1990 book

Figure 5.2 Learning organization model (Adapted from Parker [2021].)

The Fifth Discipline, discussed the five key components of a learning organization. These components are (Figure 5.2):

- **System thinking**: Businesses and human endeavors are bound by invisible fabrics of interrelated actions. To understand the organization, understand the interactions and patterns to get a sense of the whole. Systems are feedback loops that feed off of these. Focusing on one discrete part ignores this and will be potentially disruptive.
- **Personal mastery**: According to Senge, this is a commitment to lifelong learning, continually clarifying and deepening personal vision, focusing energies, developing patience, and seeing reality objectively. In the healthcare world, this is part of the commitment that physicians, nurses, and specialized care providers make.
- **Mental models**: These are deeply ingrained assumptions, generalizations, images, and guidance that guide how people think. These lead to people using theories, which is what they intend to do, and their guiding credos and theories-in-use, which is what they do. Organizations and their associated artifacts and documents create organizational memories that affirm these norms, values, and customs as part of the culture. Human nature dictates that we act in self-preservation when our mental models are challenged. The article *Defensive Routines*, by William Noonan, describes how people exhibit this in the work environment to protect themselves from embarrassment or threat (Noonan, 2018).
- The unilateral control model is the term used to describe defensive routines people use to keep themselves in control. It uses existing mental models to keep a semblance of it in uncertain situations where people feel they are being threatened. However, this does not accommodate for the interactions described in system thinking and is more linear.
  - To be able to address these models, organizations need to make people feel safe and trusted enough to stop the actions causing these defensive routines to manifest, enable curiosity to view this from a different mindset, engage the differences and call them out, and pursue a line of inquiry by understanding the processes by which the other parties

came to their current decision state, get additional information, get examples of it, and change personal and corporate mental models with an eye on improvement.
  – Organizations need to accommodate and welcome change, not succumb to their own inertia.
■ **Building shared vision**: This builds the common vision that organizations need to have that common identity for focus and learning. This has to align with system thinking and focus on building ones that are achievable. This is a commitment for the long term. The shared vision has to be able to encompass system thinking, personal mastery, the organizational enablement to continually challenge and change personal and shared/manifested mental models, and team learning.
■ **Team learning**: The organization needs to facilitate structures to support organizational knowledge, personal mastery, open communication, collaboration, and the smashing of silos through shared meaning and shared understanding. Rapid collection, creation, dissemination, and sharing of knowledge are musts. The organization must grow as a whole and commit to facilitating this, even if assumptions are challenged and changed.

Being a learning organization means that organizations are focused upon continual growth and development. It means that the people within the organization see it not as a set of linear processes and silos. They see it as a set of feedback loops and interrelated processes and components that can be continually improved. There are two methods that learning healthcare organizations can build upon this to manage risks, which are the uses of Failure Mode and Effects Analysis (FMEA), and the implementation of Just Culture. FMEA provides a quantitative analysis of system thinking to facilitate process improvement when events do not go as planned. Just culture builds upon the foundations of a learning organization by extending it to the healthcare environment.

Failure Mode and Effects Analysis

FMEA is an incredibly critical component of integrating with clinical risk management. This is because it is focused on where events can go wrong. Standard project management, especially in Information Systems, is focused on where it goes right. Project plans often make the assumption that all events in a sequence will go correctly. This leads to delays in plans when errors occur. The Institute for Healthcare Improvement (IHI) championed FMEA to proactively examine processes where harm could occur. The expected output is to use this to bring in experts to identify process improvements to prevent them (IHI, 2020).

FMEA is a quantitative analysis. It uses the dimensions of Likelihood of Occurrence (1–10), Likelihood of Detection (1–10), and Severity (1–10), multiplied together to arrive at a Risk Profile Number. This is very similar to a risk assessment; however, this includes the extra dimension of Likelihood of Detection, in addition to Likelihood of Occurrence and Severity. Like a risk assessment, this identifies the highest risks (IHI, 2020).

FMEA works by breaking down processes. The first step is to identify the process mode that is likely to have a failure. Then, the failure mode, how it could go wrong, is identified. The potential causes are then described. Next, the effects are described. The Likelihood of Occurrence, Likelihood of Detection, and Severity are then calculated on a scale from 1 to 10. These are then multiplied together to come up with the Risk Profile Number (RPN). Actions to reduce the likelihood of failure are then described. These actions represent plans to address the highest-scored items. They need to be assigned to someone accountable and addressed within a certain time period (IHI, 2020).

Just Culture

Just Culture is another critical component for integrating with clinical risk management. According to the article *Just Culture: A Foundation for Balanced Accountability and Patient Safety*, by Philip G. Boysen II, MD, in *The Ochsner Journal*, it is a learning culture focused on patient improvement and safety (Boysen, 2013). It accomplishes this through several key principles. First, it holds everyone in the organization in the patient care process accountable for their behaviors and the quality of their choices. Secondly, it focuses on addressing root causes by systematically redesigning processes to reduce the likelihood of their recurrence. Third, it focuses on system redesign first before punitive personnel actions because the system may be at fault, not the people executing the processes. It also focuses on having an open and honest reporting environment for reporting actions and allowing the ability to speak up and address when something has the potential to cause an adverse event. It emphasizes a learning culture based upon having everyone continually learning, adjusting, and redesigning systems to improve safety and allow for better choices. Just Culture also promotes mindfulness among team members. It also promotes conflict resolution by focusing on collaboration to achieve systemic improvement.

Addressing Alarm and Alert Fatigue Using FMEA and Just Culture

When you have too many alarms and alerts, something critical is going to get missed. According to Leah M. Addis, Vladimir N. Cadet, and Kelly C. Graham, in the article *Sound the Alarm*, in the July 2014 edition of Patient Safety and Quality Healthcare, there can be up to 700 alarms per bed per day (Addis, 2014). When there are that many alarms, they can't be appropriately managed. This article discussed three common themes around alarm fatigue, which were:

- Alarms that did not sound
- Alarms that were not properly addressed
- Alarm-related miscommunication

This issue has been specifically noted by the Joint Commission as a significant patient safety issue (Addis, 2014). The Joint Commission has noted four key factors organizations need to take into consideration as part of an alarm management plan to address this issue:

- Necessity of the alarm
- Risk if the alarm goes unanswered or fails
- Review of related facility adverse events, current best practices, and guidelines
- Engagement of clinicians

Alarm fatigue is real, is a major patient safety issue, and can overwhelm the clinicians who are responding to them. The addition of new devices needs to be done with care given the patient safety risks.

In the 2018 edition of Cerner's publication, *Perspectives: Value in Health Care*, Dr. Seung Park, former Chief Health Information Officer for Indiana University Health, discussed another side effect. The number of alerts in their instance of Cerner Millennium, their Electronic Medical Record, was ten times the national average (Cerner, 2018). The use of a highly customized electronic medical record system caused the average transaction response time to be 0.72 seconds, and the number of transactions >5 seconds was at 1.7%, when the national average was 0.5% (Cerner, 2018). The inpatient nursing solution average transaction response time was 2.39 seconds. Customizing the build slowed it down for everyone else (Cerner, 2018).

Dr. Park received funding to update Cerner by removing the customizations and using the model solution. He was able to cut the nursing ATRT down to 0.4 seconds. Removing 90% of the alerts caused the performance of Discern Expert to go down from 0.3 to 0.19 seconds. This caused significant performance improvements (Cerner, 2018).

He also adopted a governance model to strictly monitor and regulate changes to the EMR. This addressed the issue he identified where customizations for one person slowed them down for everyone else. Changes are now evaluated to ensure that they do not go against the model build and do not cause performance issues. They are evaluated by clinicians and technical team members to ensure effectiveness (Cerner, 2018).

Further reading from Dr. Bakheet Aldosari, in the article. *Patients' Safety in the Era of EMR/ EHR Automation, from the Journal Informatics in Medicine Unlocked* provides further elucidation. In this article, he discusses how turning on a large number of alerts with little specificity leads to high rates of clinician override, which leads to "alert fatigue," making physicians accidentally ignore important information (Aldosari, 2017). This shows that alert fatigue isn't just for alarms, it also extends to electronic medical records.

The *Sound the Alarm* article, the experiences of Dr. Park at Indiana University Health, and Dr. Aldosari's article all illustrate one critical item. Alarm fatigue is real, and the number of devices that clinicians have to respond to, combined with the alerts in the electronic medical record, exasperates clinicians and presents a clear and present safety risk.

How Can We Address This Using Network and Capabilities Assessments, Learning Organizations, FMEA, and Just Culture?

One of the shared mental models that organizations perpetuate is that information systems is capable of handling any technology problems thrown at it by non-technical staff using a flat budget without any need from the rest of the organization. This model ignores the pervasive interdependencies that information systems have throughout the organization. It also ignores their strategic importance. They need to address their true capacity and capabilities through a network and capabilities assessment first. After completing this and making the determination that the organization has the resources to build and sustain the initiative, the organization needs to ask other questions. These are honest questions that need to be asked through the lens of a learning organization:

- Have we applied the principles of system thinking in building the business case?
- Have we challenged our way of thinking with a focus on improvement?
- Does this help the organization materially reach the goals inscribed by the vision?
- Does this initiative facilitate team learning and personal mastery?

If the initiative meets these four criteria, then the organization needs to model the use cases and describe the processes and steps that users will go through when implementing the initiative. The paper, *Stakeholder Identification and Use Case Representation for Internet of Things Applications in Healthcare*, by Nancy L. Laplante, Philip A. Laplante, and Jeffrey Voas, describes the use of use case diagrams to map out Internet of Things use in healthcare (LaPlante et al., 2018). The use of simple and enhanced rich pictures, and simplified and abstract use case diagrams to model processes and steps provide concrete means to decompose processes into their base sequential components and steps (LaPlante et al., 2018).

Now that these components and steps have been discovered through the modeling process, the corresponding ways they can fail need to be modeled. By conducting an FMEA on each step in the process, organizations can understand exactly where the processes have a high potential for failure and quantitatively rank them. This allows them to mitigate potential failure steps before the deployment of the initiative as part of the implementation plan.

Examine the proposed plan and its fit to just culture. Does the deployment of the system support fair and accurate reporting of issues? Is the organization structured to address them? Do people understand enough to be able to take actions to remediate issues when discovered? Has the plan accounted for policy and process evolution as part of the deployment?

Part of being a learning organization is to evolve from following what a leader says to developing a culture where organic change with the aim of fulfilling the vision exists. With this in mind, ask the question of whether or not the initiative follows existing processes, or does it evolve them forward. If the deployment of the solution does not cause team members to question other processes or policies or plans to augment existing ones, it's not an initiative meant to grow the organization. It will keep it from moving forward, and to be stagnant is to move backward when other organizations have adopted this model. If it's not disruptive or transformative, it's not worth implementing.

In the HIMSS Electronic Medical Record Adoption Model (EMRAM), there are seven stages (HIMSS, 2020). The first six stages, 0–5, focus on the basic requirements for implementing electronic medical records. Stage 6 implements the basics of Just Culture through its requirements for risk reporting and full clinical decision support (HIMSS, 2020). It does so by providing team members the means by which they can report risks and events, and provide basic feedback and assistance in performing clinical tasks. Clinical decision support pathways can be changed based on feedback from risks and events.

Stage 7, which is the top that organizations aspire to, focuses on cross-organizational boundary spanning processes and structures that facilitate learning organizations, evolution, organization-wide use of the EMR, disaster recovery, privacy, security, structured data interchange with a Health Information Exchange (HIE), and most importantly, governance (HIMSS, 2020). Data Analytics, for example, requires the implementation of data warehousing, and cross-organizational communication to be truly effective. At the core of data analytics sits data governance, which according to Gartner is the specification of decision rights and an accountability framework to ensure the appropriate behavior in the valuation, creation, consumption, and control of data and analytics (Gartner, 2020). If an organization does not use the same EMR platform for the same business processes throughout, then it becomes very difficult to have effective data analytics or governance due to the complexity of multiple systems and data harmonization. The goals are continual feedback through the ingestion and analysis of data according to effective governance patterns, and the protection of the data throughout.

Gartner defines governance as:
- Setting decision rights and accountability, as well as establishing policies that are aligned to business objectives (preservation and growth of shareholder value)
- Balancing investments in accordance with policies and in support of business objectives (coherent strategy realization)

- Establishing measures to monitor adherence to decisions and policies (compliance and assurance)
- Ensuring that processes, behaviors, and procedures are in accordance with policies and within tolerances to support decisions (risk management) (Short, 2015)

Effective governance that supports a learning organization would need to continually evolve policies, procedures, measures, and behaviors to facilitate organizational change. Data Analytics builds upon this to support system thinking and team learning through the effective use of data. Disaster recovery, privacy, and security also layer on top of governance to support risk management, compliance, and assurance.

Healthcare makes this very complicated with the multitude of complex structures that facilitate themselves through service lines, physician practices, regulatory, and joint commission requirements. Focusing on intake or prioritization as one component without looking at the effects of them on the rest of the organization through the frame of a learning organization is only one piece. Continual feedback is necessary for continued evolution.

HIMSS EMRAM Stage 7 is more than just a goal for the IS or informatics organizations, and it is an organization-wide goal that requires significant effort to build the governance basics. One of the outputs of this is the ability to send and receive structured data from a HIE. Others are robust governance and data protection and privacy standards. The data is then used to inform the organization and develop that necessary feedback loop for change.

With the advent of the 21st-century Cures Act Final Rule, the potential exists for a Stage 8 on top of the existing Stage 7 that supports data provenance monitoring, inter-organization data interchange through Application Programming Interfaces (APIs) not facilitated by HIEs and cross-organizational governance (ONC, 2020).

To build this, standards need to be followed. The current hub-and-spoke approach is marked by deviation from known standards. The Cures Act Final Rule focuses on FHIR 4.0.1 as the approved baseline standard (ONC, 2020). Data interchange formats need to be defined in agreements and consortia and have to be focused specifically on the data being transferred. If diagnostic imaging data is being interchanged, DICOM has to be specifically followed. FHIR has to be the baseline for API interchange. Standards are important for preventing lock-in.

They are also important because cross-organizational monitoring for service level agreements has to be based on agreed-upon metrics. You can't effectively monitor non-standard protocols when all the consortia partners have heterogeneous networks. Major network vendors will know how to address standard protocols well. You also can't effectively monitor these protocols for security events if it's not a common standard. Conflict resolution becomes very difficult if everyone has a different way to resolve the conflicts.

Security is built on good standards. Many health systems already have intrusion prevention and intrusion detection systems. Managed mobile devices can be wiped if lost or stolen thanks to mobile device management available from many vendors. Where the issues start with it is making sure that there is enough security staff to address root causes of alerts and threats. If team members are just clearing out alerts to lower the response time, that doesn't fix the issues. If they aren't giving explanations as to what is happening, then there is a much larger one.

This is complicated by the move from corporate-owned devices to Bring Your Own Device. This puts the devices used by team members to access organizational resources outside the scope of risk assessments because of ownership. This shifts the required risk assessments and risk management plans to focus more on how to separate and segment data so it does not fall outside the management of the organization. This means that some degree of management has to be on the device to enforce this. The scope of what organizations can legally do to the device is extremely narrow. Therefore, an approach of only keeping data on the device that is absolutely needed is considered a judicious one. Keeping data generated by an organization's applications on the device somewhere else keeps the device itself out of scope.

Policy development for a BYOD scenario needs to focus on limiting management to only what is needed to ensure that approved corporate applications function. There has to be focus on not intermingling data, securely erasing segmented data and not someone's family pictures, and ensuring that the device itself is transient application storage. These policies also have to enforce that only supported devices that get operating system updates and apply them are allowed to connect to run approved corporate applications. One of the major concerns with mobile devices is that many in use, especially the ones that run Android, do not get updates.

Governance

One of the perpetual challenges within any organization is governance; however, inside of healthcare with the multitude of competing priorities from service lines, clinical subgroups, and regulatory surprises, the challenge is heightened. The importance of a robust governance structure is vital to the continued evolution of the health system. "A process is needed to make prioritization transparent and inclusive and to help clinicians and managers understand the competing demands for resources" (Kropf, 2013).

> **Note**: The following are example processes for governance, as the appropriate structure for your organization depends on its leadership style, clinical engagement, and the Information Services Structure in the Organization's overall strategy.

Intake: A Request Is Born

Requests for technical changes come from everywhere: Clinicians that have great ideas to streamline their workflow, administrators that have regulatory requirements, capital overhaul requests, and system mandates. They are born out of Network Clinical Care Councils, 2 a.m. ready-room conversations, and everything in between. Generally, they are good, really good suggestions to solve an identified, vetted problem. Technical Teams wish that we had unlimited resources to complete all the requests; however, they don't and it is the role of the CIO and their leadership team to set and adhere to a prioritization process to both protect their teams and to ensure the most vital requests are completed.

Once a request is initiated out of innovation or necessity, an intake process (that is documented and supported by training) must be followed to ensure all requests are assessed equally and technical teams aren't juggling random, constant inputs from multiple directions pulling their focus.

There are many ways to tackle an intake process; however, throughout many systems, it consists of a centrally located form with initial discovery questions. Some systems feel that everyone should be able to fill out a request. When I served as a portfolio manager we asked directors and above to be required to be informed before a request was filled out (and named in the request), this allowed for department/service-line prioritization and transparency before the request was entered. The forms include questions like:

- What is the problem you are trying to solve?
- Is this the result of a safety event?
- What is the current process?
- What is the ideal process?

Depending on the size of the organization and the current staffing model, a Portfolio Manager may review the requests for completion prior to bringing them to an intake meeting. The first intake meeting I ever sat on was called SWAT (Sequencing Work: Assessment and Tactics), which I have brought with me to other systems and is an apt description of what occurs in the meeting, so for the remainder of the book, this meeting will be referred to as such for simplicity. SWAT should be attended by each of the clinical informatics managers (Design, Training/Ops, Orders, Portfolio, InPatient, Ambulatory), each of the information services managers (Documentation, Rules, Orders, Regulatory, RevCycle, HIM, Privacy, Security), the respective directors, and a clinical architect. This list may change based on your system's staffing model. With all eyes on the request, the following decisions are made:

1. Do we understand enough about this request to move forward?
    a. If the answer is yes proceed. If not, assign pre-discovery to the appropriate team. Pre-discovery dives into what problem the requester is trying to solve and what systems are impacted.
2. Is this request technically possible?
3. The clinical architect weighs in around if the system has the code level and functionality to complete this request. Sometimes a ticket is logged to the EHR vendor if the team believes that they may have the capability to solve it.
4. Is the request best solved through education, behavior, process, or tool changes?
5. Will fulfilling this request cause significant negative workflow changes?
6. Is this request related to a safety event?

The information above can be used to follow the prioritization matrix (Adopted from the HIMSS Prioritization Matrix) (Figure 5.3).

Once an initial score is determined, three contextual scores can be added for a robust ranking:

1. Likelihood of success (1–5)
2. Technical ease of implementation (1–5)
3. Change management ease to implement (1–5)

Another example of a ranking system was published by Roger Kropf and Guy Scalzi in *Using IT Governance to Prioritize Investments*. This one from Allina Health in Minnesota had project sponsors complete a "Prioritization Grid" that ranks the project on the criteria of:

- Patient care, outcomes/quality, safety
- Compliance/contractual/regulatory requirement
- Financial benefit and/or productivity improvement
- Strategic measure

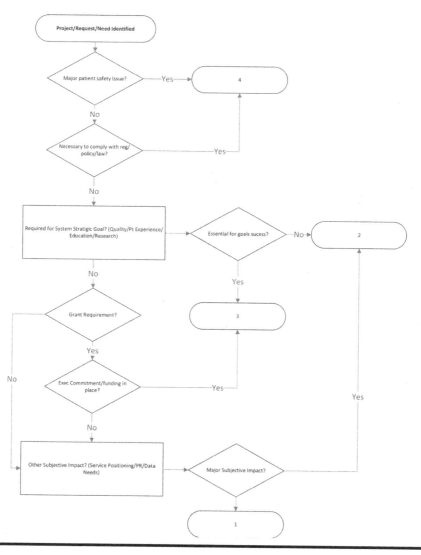

Figure 5.3   HIMSS prioritization matrix (Partridge, 2021).

■ Service enhancement/operational excellence
■ Product lifecycle and performance improvement

The sponsor provides a score for each criteria (None=0, Minimal=1, Moderate=5, High=10), and a total score is calculated.

There are many different ways to prioritize projects and requests, and the methodology is as important as leadership agreeing on the methodology and sharing it with the entire system so everyone knows how prioritization decisions were reached.

Size will also help determine the path a request will take. An example of size buckets (IS/CI time combined):

1. Small (<80 hours)
2. Medium (80–350 hours)
3. Large (350+ hours)

Once each request has been evaluated through these steps, SWAT makes a recommendation to move forward, or not. The team discusses if it is a duplicate, if the request will solve the root problem, and if the request goes against standardization/best practice. Once SWAT has made a recommendation, a SWAT report is sent to Senior leadership.

Senior leadership reviews the SWAT report weekly and either approves or denies SWAT's recommendations. This communication allows senior leadership to stay out of the weeds, to trust their SMEs but to also have the whole picture of what is coming in, and to address political situations as needed. It also allows senior leadership to ensure that projects being undertaken by their teams align with the system's goals.

If SWAT recommends to deny a request due to an identified alternative being a more appropriate solution or lack of technical feasibility and senior leadership agrees, that denial is relayed back to the requester. If SWAT recommends to move forward and senior leadership approves, the request continues through governance based on its size.

Governance of Requests

Small: You must have an expedited process for smaller projects (Kropf & Scalzi, 2012.). If a project is deemed to be a small work effort, it takes <80 hours of work between the Clinical Informatics Team and the IS team. Some CIOs make it clear they are setting aside 20% of resources for these expedited changes, which has helped with IS/Clinical relations and to highlight quick wins. Some examples of these types of projects are: changing the EHR table of contents for optimizing the pharmacist position, changing a single order, or adding a care role to a clinical communication device. These are projects that don't need many design decisions or leadership oversight but have been asked for by a Clinician and determined by SWAT to be a valid request. After sign-off, the portfolio manager puts the request into a tracking software and assigns it to the appropriate technical teams. The portfolio manager also attaches the sign-offs (so the teams know it is a valid request and has gone through the appropriate processes) and assigns a Clinical Informatics POC for any education or workflow questions. These small requests typically turn around in <2 weeks and the teams work on them as time allows. While it may seem like unnecessary work upfront to have small requests go through SWAT, there are so many of these small requests that due diligence and sign-off upfront allow the technical teams to dive right into the work.

Medium: Medium projects tend to be the most politically polarizing and have the most clinician investment, so it is important to come up with a very robust process for deciding which ones to work on. A medium project is 81–350 hours of combined work between Clinical Informatics and IS. Some examples include POC results to the ED tracking board, overhaul of restraint documentation, or turning on autoverify in the ED. These projects need some robust design sessions but the problem is pretty well defined and the solution is relatively straightforward. The challenge with these requests is the sheer magnitude. When I served as the CI portfolio manager, I had 100+ of these types of requests in my queue at any given time and it would take a few years with 100% dedicated resources to clear it out. These medium projects compete for what we call the Clinical Priorities top ten list. This list is published and reanalyzed every quarter, so even if a project makes the list, it is possible it can be bumped to the next quarter. These projects go onto the enterprise roadmap as medium placeholders and whatever request is at the top at the medium kickoff begins. These requests go through the prioritization matrix, then are then looked at for change management ease, technical ease, and educational effort, negotiations are made if the request solves for a serious safety event or legislation/regulation. Once all these scores have been tallied they are ranked on sheer numbers and brought to senior leadership, where service line impact is analyzed (try not to have all of the top ten from one area, like surgery), and time in the queue is considered. From there, the top ten list is published and work begins.

Publishing the list and the scores in a central location allow stakeholders to transparently see what information services is working on and why their project hasn't been addressed. It allows for a decrease in the amount of emails the technical team receives for status reports and it creates trust in the organization. With that being said, difficult conversations still have to take place due to resource constraints. CIOs and their leadership team can dramatically impact the experience of their technical teams by being transparent and consistent in their messaging about requests. If requesters realize they can game the system by constantly pinging senior leadership, the technical teams will suffer as the priorities are unclear and burnout ensues. The biggest asset to a technical team is having a leader who will be transparent but firm with all of the stakeholders, giving the analysts space and confidence to do their jobs.

Large: Large projects often have a different funding model. While medium and small projects are handled through operational funds out of the IS and CI department budgets, large projects must have a clinical cost center associated with them. Once a project is determined to be large, 350+ hours of combined work, it is sent to the business and strategy team for a cost work-up. Large projects include woman's health scheduling and OR control interfaces, the complete redesign of wound care documentation, and billing or implementation of bedside iPads in the ICU. The business and strategy team writes a business case of a large project and attaches all the costs, including what it would take to hire a contractor and return on Investment. In some systems, this may be the PMO doing this work and writing a case writeup called an A3 document. This business case/A3 is presented to a Business and Strategy Committee, an example of who staffs this committee is the five most senior leaders in an organization, who are ultimately accountable for all the cost centers in our network. In order for a large project to move forward, one of these five leaders has to volunteer to be the executive sponsor of the project and has to provide a cost center to charge the project cost to. If none of the five volunteers the project is killed for the year, it may be presented again the next fiscal year.

Capital projects: One size of the project that doesn't originate from our clinical end users or our SWAT meeting is capital projects. Capital projects, according to Steven Bragg at AccountingTools.com, are investments in the procurement or construction of a significant fixed asset (Bragg, 2020). These often require more investment than other projects. They are also carried on the balance sheet as an asset. More often than not, as they are large investments, return on investment or criticality is a major consideration to offset the large costs. This requires a process by which organizations need to combine both enterprise risk management results with business requirements. For example, the lack of a decent roof on a building used to take care of patients will outrank a new instrument that a doctor wants. A cybersecurity need identified as part of a risk assessment or enterprise risk management exercise will outscore a machine upgrade. These projects are scored and ranked based on cost. Organizations, as part of an annual budgeting process, will rank proposed capital projects based on cost, need, risk, and return on investment.

Organizations submit proposals for funding these strategic major projects. These can include implementing a NICU, new modules for the Electronic Health Record system, new chillers for buildings, or new roofs. These can also include major upgrades such as PACS systems. The size and scope of these projects are such that the Capital Budgeting Committees often include executive leadership. The results of this are given to the Board of Directors for final approval. The financial status of these initiatives is tracked and reported on as part of the financial statements. Capital projects are significant enough to require their own pro forma financials and projections as part of the submission process. They are also tracked separately from operational projects. Governance for these projects is different due to this.

Once again, this section is only an example of potential governance and sizing models, and there are many other options out there. However, the key takeaway is that information technology in a healthcare system must have some sort of documented process to take a request from intake through prioritization to implementation. This process must be transparent to the requesters as well as the analysts/engineers and must allow for streamlined communication around the status of a request/project. The more straightforward and socialized an intake/governance process is, the more trust all teams will have that their interests are being addressed and that they are all working toward the same goal.

Security

There are also some very important components of security that need to be tackled as part of a high-functioning organization, no matter the size of the projects that they have. These capabilities reflect their evolution to be able to address issues. They also reflect the capabilities of a learning organization, and one capable of evolving to address digital transformation, mobile, and security needs.

While organizations often have set policies, and they leverage HIPAA requirements for assessing the security of their vendors, they don't do the same for their business partners. While a relationship that involves the exchange of data still requires a Business Associate Agreement (BAA), the relationship is transactional and based on that contract (HHS, 2018). Managing a business partner relationship, however, requires constant communication between security officers to ensure protection. This is not like buying a medical device that needs to be patched and maintained. There will be constant inflows and outflows of data between organizations, and this means that security officers will have to treat each new interchange like a cross-organizational project. This isn't something that can be scripted like a plan for a new device. It involves looking at each new project and examining the security of each in collaboration with business partners to provide that degree of assurance. The best example of this is the relationship between a health system and its HIE partners, or their main supply chain partners.

Building on 1:1 relationships, organizations need to extend that to N:N relationships within a consortium. While a healthcare organization is used to working with one partner, the current focus on the 21st-century Cures Act Final Rule and APIs means that this can easily be expanded to N:N ones. This requires the ability to contract with and set standards for interfacing with multiple organizations. Data standards, basic security standards, service level agreements, fraud and inappropriate use detection, conflict resolution methods, and security agreements that temporarily remove members until they are corrected need to be standardized here. What could be done as part of relationship management as part of a 1:1 relationship is much more formal and structured as part of a consortium.

Insider threats are a major concern. According to the 2020 Verizon Data Breach Investigations Report (Langlois, 2020), 30% of threats are insider sources across all surveyed industries. In healthcare, that goes up to 48% (Langlois, 2020). With the security model of Electronic Medical

Records systems allowing for much more access by default than systems from other industries, the use of software to detect potential insider threats becomes very important (Walsh, 2014). This software operates much like the fraud detection software that banks and financial institutions use by analyzing the audit logs of electronic medical records systems (Protenus, 2016). This extends to mobile device usage and the access logs from that usage reflect the same access, and therefore log entries, as from a desktop device.

To understand who is accessing systems containing patient data, especially given the situations that healthcare providers have to deal with, there's a lot more to understand than just the login name. The HIPAA Security Rule has a requirement for managing access based on appropriateness in 45CFR 164.308 (HHS, 2020a). The rule requires covered entities to determine the appropriateness of access, periodically review it, and remove unneeded access rights (HHS, 2020a,b). They also have the requirement to implement policies and procedures for granting access. This is commonly referred to as Identity Proofing. NIST Special Publication 800-63-3, Digital Identity Guidelines, and Special Publication 800-63A, Enrollment and Identity Proofing, are the US government standards that federal agencies are required to follow (Grassi, 2017a,b). These evolving documents provide a detailed process that organizations need to follow for identifying and enrolling people in identity management systems for the purpose of gaining access. According to the US Drug Enforcement Administration, these processes are required and federal law for systems that can be used to electronically prescribe controlled substances (DEA, 2020).

Organizations normally accomplish this for their EMR systems by mapping job descriptions and roles to access roles (Zhang, 2011). Those need to map to roles in the EMR so that security can be properly assigned. Kruse, Smith, Vanderlinden, and Nealand, in their paper, Security Techniques for the Electronic Health Records, discuss the mapping of EMR roles to jobs to assign privileges based on their role in the healthcare facility (Kruse, 2017). With third parties accessing the EMR, this becomes even more important as the access granted is not just based on their role, and it also extends to what is contractually allowed as part of data interchange.

The way to understand what data roles have access to is to have effective data governance and processes for data elements in the Electronic Medical Record. Ultimately the goal is threefold with EMR data governance:

- Understand what data all users will get access to by default
- Understand what data users get access to by specific role
- Understand what data users get access to by specific workflows

The superset of these is the universe of data that each person has access to. Data governance, as discussed before, addresses the need to have accountability and the appropriate behavior in its usage to ultimately support the business. The required behavior in healthcare is to use the minimum necessary data to perform certain tasks (HHS, 2020a). Understanding the data that roles have access to provides that understanding of how it will be used in workflows by specific roles. If a user does not have access to read, change, add, or delete data elements required to measure performance or complete tasks related to their job, then that is something that needs to be addressed. It ultimately aligns with system security access, contracting, and business associate agreements to demonstrate the due diligence that an organization needs to go through to ensure that only the minimum necessary data is being utilized and that privacy and security are being appropriately protected.

Data governance also assists in making sure that the data also has appropriate provenance. The flow of data from its generation to its ultimate destination has to be protected. The HIPAA

Security Rule requires that protected health information has its confidentiality, integrity, and availability protected (HHS, 2020b). Ensuring security throughout the process and demonstrating it as part of data governance helps address that need. It also provides the assurance that reasonable and appropriate steps have been taken to ensure its accuracy.

Without accurate data, there is no way to leverage enterprise data analytics to improve service delivery, and no way to make it to Stage 7. Full analytics that captures all of the data points from the pervasive use of electronic medical records is the best way that organizations can embark upon the quality improvement journey. Data is the lifeblood that allows them to improve quality and truly become a learning organization through improved system thinking and team learning. The feedback loops from initiatives will give data that can show improvement.

A modern healthcare delivery site needs to have a failsafe EMR with sufficient redundancy to operate in a less than optimal state. If leased lines, connectivity, or other components fail, there need to be redundant components there to take their place and run until they can be repaired. These include:

■ Redundant network connections
■ Clustered virtual machine environments to support machine failover
■ Redundant distributed file server environments
■ Storage Area Networks (SANs) with Redundant Arrays of Inexpensive Disks (RAID)
■ Redundant power supplies on servers
■ Error-correcting RAM on servers

In addition, organizations need a redundant location to operate systems from in case the primary location is unreachable. Organizations need at least a warm site, which according to Baseline Data has all the systems needed (Baseline Data, 2017). However, they need to restore the latest backups to make them fully operational. Hot sites are fully redundant copies of the primary data center; however, they are much more expensive, and organizations may not have those resources available. Warm sites allow them to come back online without the expense of maintaining fully redundant systems. However, this requires good validated and tested backups to work. According to the 2020 Verizon Data Breach Investigations Report, 81% of breaches can be contained within days (Langlois, 2020). Ransomware attackers have been known to corrupt backups to incentivize their targets to pay. This also has the side effect of potentially infecting unwitting warm sites. Making sure that well-tested backups exist is critical to containing breaches and resuming normal activity.

Ransomware illustrates the importance of having good downtime procedures, paper charting, and procedures for reconciling systems to come back online. There is often significant pressure to bring systems up as quickly as possible, especially when patient care is involved. Premature restoration without validation or checking backup media for malware or ransomware can lead to reinfection. Not having good downtime procedures and processes can lead to either ransomware payment or reinfection through corrupted restorations due to pressure to bring systems back online. Even a system that pays the ransom to unlock their data has to verify and validate everything that has been restored. That data may have been corrupted by it, with this in mind, health systems need to focus on having good downtime procedures and to drill on them regularly. Many team members have never charted on paper or operated without computers. This can and will lead to degradation in care. This also can and will lead to the inability to record accurate data about what happens during incidents, leading to a loss of visibility. This can result in incomplete data, and the inability to utilize data from the incident for quality improvement and team learning.

Conclusion

Healthcare has evolved significantly with the implementation of technology to augment existing processes. Mobile technologies and telemedicine have pushed us further along. However, management techniques to address them have not progressed at the same pace. By examining engagement, governance, workflows, organizational requirements, security requirements, intake, education, relationship building, and needs analysis, we have put together a framework your organization can use to effectively manage its mobile device initiatives.

References

Addis, Leah M., Vladimir N. Cadet, and Kelly C. Graham, "Sound the alarm", May 27, 2014. https://www.psqh.com/analysis/sound-the-alarm/.

Aldosari, Bakheet, "Patients' safety in the era of EMR/EHR automation." *Informatics in Medicine Unlocked* 9, 2017: 230–233. doi: 10.1016/j.imu.2017.10.001.

Baseline Data Inc., "Your recovery site: Hot, warm, or cold?" Baseline Data, June 8, 2017. https://baseline-data.com/blog/disaster-recovery/recovery-site-hot-warm-or-cold/.

Boysen II, Philip G., "Just culture: A foundation for balanced accountability and patient safety." *The Ochsner Journal* 13(3), 2013: 400–406.

Bragg, Steven, "Capital project definition", December 18, 2020. https://www.accountingtools.com/articles/2020/6/17/capital-project-definition.

Cerner Corporation (Cerner). "The buck stops here." Essay. In *Perspectives: Value in Health Care*, vol. 2, pp. 8–15, Kansas City, MO: Cerner Corporation, 2018.

Chomal, Vikas Sataram and Jatinderkumar R. Saini, "Cataloguing most severe causes that lead software projects to fail." *International Journal on Recent and Innovation Trends in Computing and Communication* 2(5), 2014: 1143–1147.

Drug Enforcement Agency (DEA), "Rules - 2020." 2020- Electronic Prescriptions for Controlled Substances. Accessed December 28, 2020. https://www.deadiversion.usdoj.gov/fed_regs/rules/2020/fr0421_3.htm.

Gartner, Inc., "Data governance", Retrieved on December 27, 2020. https://www.gartner.com/en/information-technology/glossary/data-governance.

Grassi, Paul A., James L. Fenton, Naomi B. Lefkovitz, Jamie M. Danker, Yee-Yin Choong, Kristen K. Greene, and Mary F. Theofanos. "Digital identity guidelines: Enrollment and identity proofing," 2017a. doi: 10.6028/nist.sp.800-63a.

Grassi, Paul A., Michael E. Garcia, and James L. Fenton, "Digital identity guidelines: Revision 3," 2017b. doi: 10.6028/nist.sp.800-63-3.

HIMSS, "Electronic medical record adoption model". Retrieved on December 27, 2020. https://www.himssanalytics.org/emram.

Institute for Healthcare Improvement (IHI). "Failure Modes and Effects Analysis (FMEA) tool", Retrieved on December 27, 2020. http://www.ihi.org/resources/Pages/Tools/FailureModesandEffectsAnalysisTool.aspx.

Kropf, Roger, and Guy Scalzi, *IT Governance in Hospitals and Health Systems*. Chicago, IL: HIMSS, 2012.

Kropf, Roger, and Guy Scalzi, "We have to prioritize: But how? Defining how priorities will be Setand who is involved is essential for IT" *Journal of Health Information Management* 27(1), Winter 2013: 20–22.

Kruse, Clemens Scott, Brenna Smith, Hannah Vanderlinden, and Alexandra Nealand, "Security techniques for the electronic health records." *Journal of Medical Systems*, 2017, Springer US. https://www.ncbi.nlm.nih.gov/pmc/articles/PMC5522514/.

Langhan, Melissa L., Antonio Riera, Jordan C. Kurtz, Paula Schaeffer, and Andrea G. Asnes, "Implementation of newly adopted technology in acute care settings: A qualitative analysis of clinical staff." *Journal of Medical Engineering & Technology* 39(1), 2014: 44–53. doi: 10.3109/03091902.2014.973618.

Langlois, Philippe, "2020 Data Breach Investigations Report.", May 19, 2020, https://enterprise.verizon. com/resources/reports/dbir/

Laplante, Nancy L., Phillip A. Laplante, and Jeffrey M. Voas. "Stakeholder identification and use case representation for internet of things applications in healthcare." *IEEE Systems Journal*, 2018, US National Library of Medicine. https://www.ncbi.nlm.nih.gov/pmc/articles/PMC6512844/.

Noonan, William R., "Overcoming defensive routines in the workplace", 2018, Retrieved on December 27, 2020. https://thesystemsthinker.com/overcoming-defensive-routines-in-the-workplace/.

Office of the National Coordinator for Health Information Technology (ONC). "Cures Act Final Rule standards-based Application Programming Interface (API) certification criterion". Retrieved on December 27, 2020. https://www.healthit.gov/cures/sites/default/files/cures/2020-03/APICertification Criterion.pdf.

Parker, Mitchell, Indiana University Health (2021).

Protenus Inc. "Illuminating a black box in healthcare." September 14, 2016. https://www.protenus.com/ resources/illuminating-a-black-box-in-healthcare/.

Ratwani, Raj M., Erica Savage, Amy Will, Ryan Arnold, Saif Khairat, Kristen Miller, Rollin J. Fairbanks, Michael Hodgkins, and A Zachary Hettinger, "A usability and safety analysis of electronic health records: A multi-center study." *Journal of the American Medical Informatics Association* 25(9), 2018: 1197–1201. doi: 10.1093/jamia/ocy088.

Senge, Peter M., *The Fifth Discipline: The Art and Practice of the Learning Organization*. New York: Doubleday/Currency, 1990.

Short, Julie, Nunno, Tina, and Caldwell, French. "Gartner defines 'governance'". September 2, 2015. https://www.gartner.com/document/2145816?ref=solrAll&refval=272655848.

US Department of Health and Human Services (HHS), "HIPAA administrative simplification". Accessed October 31, 2018. https://www.hhs.gov/sites/default/files/ocr/privacy/hipaa/administrative/ combined/hipaa-simplification-201303.pdf.

US Department of Health and Human Services (HHS), "Minimum necessary requirements". Accessed December 28, 2020a. https://www.hhs.gov/hipaa/for-professionals/privacy/guidance/minimum-necessary-requirement/index.html.

US Department of Health and Human Services (HHS), "Summary of the HIPAA security rule". Accessed December 28, 2020b. https://www.hhs.gov/hipaa/for-professionals/security/laws-regulations/index. html.

Walsh, Tom and William M. Miaoulis, "Privacy and security audits of electronic health information (2014 update)" *Journal of AHIMA* 85(3), 2014: 54–59.

Zhang, Wen, Carl A. Gunter, David Liebovitz, Jian Tian, and Bradley Malin, "Role prediction using electronic medical record system audits." *AMIA 2011 Annual Symposium - American Medical Informatics Association*, 2011. https://www.ncbi.nlm.nih.gov/pmc/articles/PMC3243238/.

Chapter 6

Physician Culture and the Adoption of Mobile Medicine

Arthur W. Douville, MD
Medigram

Brian D. McBeth, MD
Santa Clara County Health System

Contents

DOI: 10.4324/9781003220473-8

Introduction

Accounting for one-sixth of the American economy, healthcare is at once an object of intense economic interest and in the last decade particularly an object of political and social conflict. The founder of modern enterprise management, Peter Drucker famously observed that the contemporary hospital is "altogether the most complex human organization ever devised," but also noted that hospital organizations had been in the previous 30 or 40 years the fastest growing enterprises in the developed world (Drucker 2002). This complexity is derived from the panoply of specialized stakeholders—doctors, patients, nurses, healthcare administrators, insurance companies, pharmaceutical companies and intermediaries, myriad kinds of hospital workers, benefits managers, and medical device vendors to name only a few of an estimated 350 types of occupations and enterprises employing 21 million healthcare workers in what remains still a highly fragmented industry. The potential for digital technology, including mobile medicine, to contribute to a way out of the chaos is compelling.

Whether the healthcare industry and the digital technologies that enable it are up to this challenge has been debated. One study examining the digital maturity of six industries found that the healthcare industry ranked third in terms of overall digital maturity, lagging especially in technologies that would help with "customer engagement" (Landi 2018). Others decry the slow development of technology adoption in healthcare, citing the difficulty in measuring the impact of technology innovation on healthcare outcomes, the complexity of funding mechanisms, a risk averse and cost-sensitive culture, and the lack of central guidance outside of the electronic health record (EHR) revolution that has occurred in the last decade. Symbols of backwardness include the reliance on fax machines that remain the backbone of communication throughout much of the healthcare system and the still ubiquitous belt pager.

On the other hand, many of the major technologies that have transformed medicine in the last 20 years are fundamentally driven by digital computing technologies. These include CT ("Computer Assisted Tomography"), MRI, robotic surgery, digital radiography with distributed imaging, the electronic health record itself, telemedicine, wireless communication technologies, and 3-D printing of prosthetic devices as just a few examples. While biological advancements will be key to improving patient outcomes (think Nextgen sequencing, immunotherapy of cancer, stem cell therapies for diabetes, single-cell genomics, and gene editing), assessments of the biggest advances in recent years have focused on big data applications, wearable devices with data analytics powered by AI, digital security and ownership, VR/AR applications in surgery and rehabilitation, expansion of point of care diagnostic technologies such as portable ultrasound and lab testing, and mobile communication applications focusing on healthcare team coordination (Becker's 2015). Meanwhile, digital technologies have consistently dominated predictions of future trends (Copeland 2016; Dyrda 2020; Marr 2019).

In the face of this stands medical culture and its inherent resistance to change, including the dominant players in the healthcare workplace itself, the doctors. There is also the adherence of increasingly consolidated healthcare systems to hierarchical systems of management that are poorly designed for the knowledge workers who account for much of the complexity of the healthcare system. The most heartbreaking evidence of failure continues to be medical error leading to injury, prolonged hospital stays, persisting disability, or even preventable death. We need not only new technologies but new behaviors. The healthcare innovation movement should include changes in the way consumers perceive and acquire healthcare, new technologies involving treatment and communication, and new business models that involve more adaptive and agile management. The perverse incentives and deadlocked self-interests so aptly outlined in Porter and Teisberg's essential work *Redefining Health Care* (Porter & Teisberg 2006) must somehow be overcome to ameliorate the tragic waste that is a defining feature of a uniquely American health care industry. What is required is a more strategic concept of structure in the healthcare system, and how physicians and other "providers" can contribute more creatively. This will help to make the role of a technological transformation such as mobile medicine even clearer.

We cannot offer a comprehensive view of all the areas touched upon in the pages below, but the authors hope to convey a point of view and the sensibility that physicians bring to the table in our common effort to find a way out of the labyrinth of cultural and technological challenges before us.

Unique Aspects of Physician Culture

One major contributing factor in resistance to change in healthcare is that of physician culture itself. Culture has been described as the "climate of an organization," incorporating fundamental beliefs, normative values, and shared social practices (Shanafelt et al. 2019a). These values are often so ingrained that they are implicit and go beyond organizational rules to influence behavior. Deeply rooted, culture includes the symbols and visible manifestations of behavior, as well as espoused values and "unwritten rules" that are pervasive in complex organizations.

Physician culture is an important component of a broader culture of healthcare organizations, and at times the two can be in conflict. For example, organizational culture may support team-based care and a collaborative care delivery model, but physician culture is built on a foundation of personal responsibility to the patient, supported by a hierarchical structure of supervision and oversight. The alignment between "subcultures" within the hospital has potential to affect efficiency, quality, and wellness of employed staff and independent physicians. System safety experts have argued that healthcare and other organizations that embrace a culture of collaboration and open communication over strict hierarchical responsibility and the paternalism of the traditional culture of medicine have greater reliability and potential to reduce errors and harm events with early identification and prevention (Dekker 2017; Nance 2008; Weick 1990). Physician culture is certainly influenced by the changing economics of medicine, but this is only one of many factors. Traditionally, medical schools have emphasized knowledge and skill acquisition, with the responsibility of quality of care attributed to the individual physician. Emphasis is placed on personal accountability in maintenance of skills, often driving expectations of perfectionism and low tolerance of human error (Shanafelt et al. 2019a). This perspective does not align well with organizational team-based care delivery and shared responsibility models. Physician culture, when driven by unrealistic and unrealizable expectations, also neglects personal wellness and self-compassion, and can contribute to the "burn out" that is pervasive in today's healthcare system (Shanafelt et al. 2019b).

Physician Culture and the Social Transformation of Healthcare

In his groundbreaking work, *Strategic Intelligence* Maccoby presents a social character concept of organizational design that in our view reflects many of the challenges of healthcare systems in uniting the professional integrity and independence of an artisan, individualistic, expert class (we would say, physicians) into a larger social transformation from industrial/bureaucratic to

Table 6.1   Summary of Three Different Social Characters

	Artisan-Craft	Industrial-Bureaucratic	Knowledge-Interactive
Values	Responsibility	Stability	Continual Improvement
	Independence	Hierarchy/autonomy	Independence/collaboration
Social Character	Family loyalty	Organizational loyalty	Free agency/networking
	Sustainable production	Production excellence	Creating value
	Inner directed	Inner-directed	Other-directed
	Identification with parental authority	Identification with parental authority	Identification with peers
	Hard-working, hoarding, conservative	Precise, methodical, obsessive	Experimental, innovative, self-marketing
Socio-economic base	Independent Practice	Market-controlling bureaucracies	Entrepreneurial companies New technologies
	Slow-changing technology	Controlled technology change	Global markets
	Stable local markets	National markets	Employment uncertainty
	Predictable hierarchical workforce	Employment security	Diverse workforce

Source: Adapted with permission from Maccoby (2015)

knowledge/interactive organizational cultures (Maccoby 2013, 2015). In our view, a major aspect of resistance to change in healthcare relates to the cultural "friction" of this transformation (Table 6.1).

Physician culture since the early part of the 20th century has been dominated by the consolidation of medical education in state-sanctioned, largely university-owned, and operated medical colleges promoting a scientific approach to medical care currently embodied in the evidence-based medicine movement. However, it has maintained much of the guild animus of personal responsibility, professional autonomy, and professional loyalty maintained by an artisan class resistant to hierarchical corporate control.

Most healthcare systems fit the industrial/bureaucratic model, which themselves are resistant to technological change because of hierarchies in decision making and their aversion to the potential cost and risk of new technologies. At the same time, healthcare organizations struggle to move toward rational technology adoption models (Cresswell, Bates, and Sheikh 2013; Rahimi et al. 2018). Whether a system is organized around an explicitly for-profit model or not, technology adoption to a great extent reflects a complicated mix of perceived marketplace opportunity and competition (e.g., joint replacement, cardiac surgery, stroke or cancer care, emergency, and urgent care services), regulatory requirements, and vendor management. Larger healthcare systems have relatively strict hierarchical supply chains and marketplace consolidation programs that funnel most new technologies into relatively narrow review channels that are sensitive to social and political influences at the very top of the organization. These may not always be disinterested or rational. Meanwhile, outside of government-subsidized EHR adoption, the three top categories of healthcare technology investment in 2018 were in consumer health education, digital gym equipment, and healthcare consumer engagement (Ghafur & Schneider 2019) where the applications are less technologically rigorous, the ROI clearer, and the requirements of technologies such as FHIR less risk prone.

A Sense of Powerlessness

In all of this, physicians have recognized their relative inability to affect the outcome of large-scale technology adoption, especially in IT systems. Most physicians have been caught in the digital transformation of healthcare as reflected in the adoption of the electronic medical record, finding themselves sitting in lengthy training sessions to learn to use desktop, PC-based systems that have profoundly affected their workflow and reduced their sense of professional autonomy and efficiency. They watched with a mix of frustration, anger, and disdain as they and the nursing professionals upon whom they relied to care for patients were moved from the bedside to the desk. In particular, the advent of "standards-based documentation" in which the medical record became fragmented into database-friendly entries based on government and financial requirements meant that the nursing record of care became far less useful and redundant with pasted reentries and pro forma statements designed to meet regulatory requirements. Gone was the ready access to a text-based summary from the bedside nurse, who was busy as a data entry clerk at the unit station and not to be found at the bedside. Moreover, the patient chart record, ideally a diary of succinct entries with pertinent observations and data, has itself become a Frankenstein's monster of redundant and often irrelevant elements aimed at effective coding of illness severity and complexity for billing purposes as well as potential legal and regulatory scrutiny.

Although trends throughout the 1990s seemed to predict corporate organizational ownership as the future of medical practice, the inefficiencies of large practice organizations and the cost of acquisition and maintenance of medical practices seemed to slow somewhat in the first decade of the millennia in favor of health system contracts with relatively smaller specialty groups that provide much of the non-integrated workforce (Starr 2017). These groups may be fragmented themselves into the competing spheres of influence of larger healthcare organizations in any given market. For example, in Santa Clara County, California ("Silicon Valley"), even large private hospital organizations find their physician workforce divided between the Sutter organization, Stanford Healthcare, and smaller private physician groups, while the larger community is further divided between Kaiser Permanente and a large Santa Clara County Health System. This has led to a very complicated regional healthcare provider community wherein the only large-scale IT integration has been provided by the market dominance of the EPIC electronic health record as a quasi-regional healthcare information exchange.

Still, the hospital acquisition of medical practices has continued wherever the corporate practice of medicine is allowed, with the percentage of hospital-employed physicians increasing by more than 78% from July 2012 through January 2018, from 94,700 to 168,800 or 44% (Physicians Advocacy Institute 2019). While government and consolidating third-party payers promulgate policies favoring hospital-owned practice models, this kind of consolidation also breeds increasing costs as the acquired practices direct more care toward hospital-owned ancillary services. Payers have adjusted through cost shifting to medicare beneficiaries and commercially insured patients alike. Since much of healthcare transformation is motivated by efforts to contain cost, this kind of consolidation is virtually certain to reach an equilibrium as government and payors push back against regional monopolies. The $575M antitrust settlement between the State of California and Sutter Health (Thomas 2019) may well be a harbinger of renewed efforts to create a federal scheme of "managed competition" to slow the growth of these kinds of corporate structures whenever their regional dominance can appear to have too great an effect on healthcare prices.

Thus, the staff model systems reflected by Kaiser, Mayo, and Cleveland Clinic as well as larger university systems such as UCLA will likely remain less dominant than the kinds of mixed regional organization structures noted above. Even where a single system may seem ascendant, a mixed staff and private practice model seems likely to be the predominant model in most large urban areas, e.g., Banner in Arizona, Intermountain in Utah.

Some observers feel that there will be an increasing opportunity for physicians to exert leadership in this variegated landscape going forward. Physicians may well find that technology in the form of social media may allow development of a commonality of shared interests and influence (Mishori et al. 2014), while observations of their interactions in patient care networking will be a useful way of improving care while empowering physicians as leaders of the patient-centered healthcare team (Uddin, Hamra, and Hossain 2013).

The Role of Government

Undoubtedly, the American Reinvestment and Recovery Act (ARRA) enacted on February 17, 2009, along with its HITECH provisions and the consequent infusion of an estimated $35B into the healthcare information system economy (Miliard 2019) has had a definitive impact on the growth of healthcare-related IT, especially in hospital system and physician practices at all levels. Policy goals included the improvement of quality, safety, and efficiency of healthcare, reducing healthcare disparities, engaging patients and families in their health, improvements in healthcare coordination, and improvement in population and public health while at the same time ensuring adequate privacy and security protection for personal health information. These were general public health policy goals, which did not specify the exact technologies by which they would be accomplished, just that they demonstrate a series of requirements for "meaningful use" (CDC 2020). The impact on healthcare has been, with emerging virtual monopolies on large-scale EHR adoption, concerns for fraud and abuse, and often a negative impact on the doctor-patient relationship as physicians type at their laptops to meet clinic requirements for visit times instead of listening and learning about their patients as individual human beings (Topol 2019). Many physicians and healthcare executives feel challenged and at times limited by expensive EHR systems that have met government specifications without advancing all of the HITECH goals of 2009 (D'Amore 2019). Having spent inordinate sums on their government mandated and approved EHR systems, prior to the COVID-19 pandemic, it wasn't clear the number of healthcare systems would have risked additional resources on IT technology development outside a "full shop," a phrase referring to complete services by a single major EHR vendor such as EPIC, Cerner, Allscripts, and Meditech. Interoperability will become table stakes for software vendors of all sizes as the fundamental restructuring of healthcare information moves away from the traditional claims-based data acquisition model. The latter changes the game and creates the need for services provided outside the EHR vendor.

Individual vs. Organization View

In the face of this kind of complexity, hospital organizational culture and physician culture can still agree on the importance of quality and patient outcomes. However, the roadmap to achieve the goals and definitions of quality can differ, and physician engagement in hospital quality leadership and process can be variable. Conceptual frameworks such as "Just Culture" may find more difficult acceptance in traditional physician cultures that are intolerant of error and emphasize individual accountability over system optimization to improve reliability (Dekker 2017). Attempts to modify the traditional role of the physician in the healthcare team with requirements to use checklists and timeouts in surgery to innovate in team design (e.g., "TeamSTEPPS®") have at times met bitter resistance from some physicians.

At the same time, professionalism is also a key component of physician culture, and physician groups that maintain a high standard of collaborative interactions with other staff, patients, and family see fewer complaints, grievances, and litigation (Boothman, Imhoff, and Campbell 2012). There has been an argument to move to greater transparency regarding disclosure of medical errors early, though this is still far from an industry standard (Gallagher et al. 2020). Many institutions struggle with ongoing challenges in physician professionalism though physician citizenship programs are an example of efforts to drive behavioral change and high standards for staff interactions (McBeth & Douville 2019).

Defining a "Commons" in Healthcare

Just as technology seeks a common language for disparate IT systems through efforts such as FHIR, different physician, nursing, and management cultures must evolve to speak a common language of quality and professionalism. This common perspective—all people being deserving of quality healthcare and mutual respect—is essentially a distillation of the Institute of Medicine's six domains of healthcare quality (Institute of Medicine – Committee on Quality of Health Care in America 2012). With the recognition that healthcare is a limited resource, it has been described as a shared "commons," managed collectively for both individual and group benefit (Jecker & Jonsen 1995; Mattke et al. 2017). The same could be said for IT investment and development for healthcare systems. Thoughtful strategy—leveraging IT Service Management (ITSM) best practices, agile methods for operating, and transparency and accountability associated with Technology Best Management (TBM)—can help limit waste and avoid a "tragedy of the commons" in healthcare tech investment, driven by unfocused consumption by the end user and lack of long-term organizational vision (Marx & Padmanabhan 2020). As well, mobile tech development should align with the vision of the healthcare system with awareness of physician and hospital culture, and thus will avoid a "shiny object syndrome," continually chasing after development ideas that distract from organizational vision.

The complexity of health technology can be overwhelming for physicians and other providers. Many experienced physicians trained and practiced in an era of paper orders and charting and have a limited foundation in computer literacy. Others, especially community physicians working at multiple hospitals with different EHR systems, face time-consuming redundancies in learning and maintaining fluency in disparate systems. Mobile technology has the potential to personalize and increase accessibility, but some physicians who are less comfortable with devices and will not necessarily embrace these options quickly, or alternate mechanisms need to be developed for them, similar to the scribe model of an assistant that interacts with the computing interface.

Physician discomfort with technology manifests in a spectrum of behavior that can range from frequent complaints to deep anxiety manifesting as insistence on IT presence for basic technology engagement such as order entry and documentation to refusal to comply with mandatory EHR use. Some physicians will even quit practice or retire early when forced to adopt technology like a new EHR rollout. According to Dr. Robert Wachter in his book, *The Digital Doctor*,

> 61% of physicians felt their EHR improved the quality of care they delivered to patients, but only 1 in 3 said it had improved their job satisfaction, and 1 in 5 said they would go back to paper if they could.

He also asserts that the complexity of the EHR is inversely proportional to physicians' satisfaction with it, "the more advanced the EHR; for example, systems that offered reminders, alerts, and messaging capability, the greater the unhappiness" (Wachter 2015).

The Quality and Safety Argument for Change

One area where there is general agreement that technology has huge potential to benefit healthcare delivery is quality. There are innumerable examples of standard technology implementation such as computerized physician order entry (CPOE) eliminating the oft-joked-about issues with poor penmanship and misinterpretation of orders. The Institute of Medicine has argued the CPOE implementation alone can reduce the frequency of medication errors by 81% (Institute of Medicine – Committee on Quality of Health Care in America 2012). Access to patient records and information, as well as new chart documentation, is expeditious and relatively seamless with a functional EHR, compared to the old days of phone calls to the file room and operating with minimal data. Medicine reconciliation, bar coding, and allergy reminders through EHR are standard in most US hospitals and have been recognized for decades now as critical for patient safety (Bates 2000). There is an underside to this story, however, with reports of "e-iatrogenesis" coined to describe patient harm from incidents related to health information technology (Weiner et al. 2007).

Acknowledging that patient safety must be a primary focus of health technology systems, both physicians and administrators recognize that these tools have enormous potential to leverage improvement in care delivery. There is an oft-quoted adage attributed to W. Edwards Deming that says, "if you can't measure it, you can't manage it" (Deming 2018). He argued that while not every outcome of value can be quantified, managers must make decisions with incomplete information, and data has potential to improve decision making by leadership and channel improvement efforts. To the large extent that physicians are data driven, this is an important approach to finding common ground between the administrative-enterprise culture and working physicians, including those early in medical training, to look to research and data to drive clinical decision making. Thus, leveraging technology within the hospital system to benchmark and highlight opportunity for improvement has natural resonance. This is true when driving institutional improvement in metrics like mortality or readmissions, or departmental metrics with individual physician performance. There is often competitiveness among physicians where data can be leveraged to encourage improved performance by lower performers (Limb 2016).

However, it is critical that physicians have trust and confidence in the data. Measures of physician quality need to include an adequate sample size to assure validity. The Healthcare Effectiveness Data and Information Set (HEDIS) is one widely used data set that measures physician quality with effectiveness of care, access to care, and resource utilization. Others include CMS Core

Measures and its Consumer Assessment of Healthcare Providers and Systems (HCAHPS) and Physician Consortium for Performance Improvement® (PCPI). Technical challenges with smaller data sets leveraged on a hospital or health-system level include the difficulty of constructing valid measures with data generated from small patient populations, as well as information systems that are not standardized and sources that are not comprehensive. Not uncommonly physician stakeholders will be wary of adoption of such tools, and there may be a lack of consensus of which measures to share with consumers (Quality 2019). The Agency for Healthcare Research and Quality (AHRQ) suggests that evaluation of physician quality on the group practice or department level assures a more robust sample size and allow calculation of benchmarks with reasonable comparison to peer groups (Quality 2019). It is important to assure transparent and accurate attribution as well as validation of data to foster physician trust and engagement in the process.

Big Data and Physician Performance Evaluation

One of the authors saw this process in action at multiple facilities during rollouts of working applications of a widely utilized "big data" program to promote "clinical excellence" at the personal, group, and facility level. Most large facilities have programs available through third-party vendors such as Health Catalyst, MedeAnalytics, Optum, or their large EHR vendor to aggregate ongoing physician performance evaluation data. Physicians can be compared individually or as a group with other hospitals in the system at various levels of hospital size and type. For most physicians on a hospital staff, the data is statistically inadequate to draw any conclusions. Our experience is that they have some marginal value in flagging individual physician-related events such as surgical lacerations or finding instances of unusual overuse of modalities such as CT scans. The latter are hard to pick out of the general background of overuse of imaging technologies for example in Emergency Departments where CT scanning for minor head injuries is heavily driven by malpractice and follow-up concerns. On one introduction of such a program in a large Central Valley hospital in California, a prime concern for hospital quality managers was a specialist with unusually high treatment complication rates and costs per hospital case. As part of an overall presentation to influential members of the medical staff, the physician was approached with his data. A discussion of his devotion to the hospital and acceptance of any patient who came to the emergency department in his specialty regardless of payment source or severity of illness led to the discovery of systematic coding issues that had led to underestimation of his calculated Case Mix Index (CMI). Subsequent coaching by a clinical documentation specialist altered the picture considerably as the physician better understood the descriptive details required for effective coding, thus properly adjusting his complication rates in light of the severity of illness of his patients. In another instance, a contracted hospitalist group took on the challenge of improvements in chart documentation aimed at improving coding, with measurable improvements in CMI by 5% in 6 months (Douville 2013). Stories like these have an impact on convincing physicians of the value of data in demonstrating care improvement, whereas the "physician scorecard" approach typically leads to resistance and resentment, often justified by poor understanding of the limitations of data management by those to whom it is reported.

Physician Satisfaction and Technology Adoption

Physicians will not infrequently describe their relationship with technology in the healthcare space as "love-hate." There is a clear appreciation by most physicians of the benefits of access to accurate documentation, expeditious record retrieval, accuracy of order entry, and mobile access to vast amounts of medical data. There is also a perception by many that technology has driven a wedge between a direct connection of care providers and patients, as well as increased the burden of documentation and compliance for physicians. It has been described as an "epidemic of burnout," which some pin largely on technology. Dr. Ashish Jha of the Harvard School of Public Health asserts that "the growth in poorly designed digital health records ... that [have] required that physicians spend more and more time on tasks that don't directly benefit patients" (Schulte & Fry 2019). Physicians at times feel alienated from their patients, and there is some research that suggests that time spent with EHR documentation exceeds that spent directly with patients (Arndt et al. 2017). Many physicians spend significant time after hours at home completing documentation, a practice that has been enabled by remote access to the EHR. Stanford Medicine's 2018 National Physician Poll suggested that while most physicians believe that EHRs have improved care, most also felt the systems had detracted from their professional satisfaction (54%) and from their clinical effectiveness (49%) (The Harris Poll 2018). At times, even younger physicians who may be more facile with computers feel that simple tasks are made significantly more cumbersome with technology.

Physicians often feel frustrated and intimidated by technology, with many having received little formal education in digital technology. In recent years, medical schools have made significant progress with incorporation of computer-based learning, simulation, mobile technology, and even gaming to further the goals of medical education (Guze 2015). However, many physicians were trained prior to the adoption of these tools, and their fluency with technology is often limited. They frequently feel alienated or disenfranchised by administrative IT initiatives such as an EHR rollout. It can be challenging to drive alignment with the medical staff of a hospital on any technology-based project. Transparency, multidimensional communication with repeated messaging, integration of physician leaders into tech planning and rollouts, and overstaffing "at the elbow support" teams during rollouts can significantly mitigate this barrier.

The Physician and the IT Department

How do physicians view their IT departments and technology experts and interact with these colleagues? There is not a lot of data on this question, and certainly it will vary depending on a health system's history with technology, resource investment, institutional priorities, staff expertise, and leadership. Over the last few decades, with the advent of search engines and easy access to information by patients as well as patient advocacy and empowerment, technology has been seen by some as a mechanism of disruption of the physician's traditional role as a source of medical expertise. Clichéd references to "Doctor Google" at times are heard scornfully dropped about a perceived devaluation of the training and sacrifice of physicians by patients who seek medical information from nontraditional, tech-facilitated sources. Many physicians realize that they are dependent on technology and technology experts for their ability to provide care in a modern healthcare environment, and for some, this can also contribute to bitterness and alienation. Hopefully, this is rarely directed at IT staff directly but may shape interactions and drive complaints generally.

Conversely, the IT department has its own point of view that physicians are hard-pressed to comprehend in their day-to-day struggles. The electronic medical record may loom large to physicians as the pre-eminent IT manifestation, but a busy CIO, CMIO, or IT director overseeing a midsized health system with several hospitals may be juggling hundreds of active projects within a portfolio of over a thousand applications. There are few programs or systems in the hospital in which an IT department does not play a role. Every clinical and organizational system seems to have its own often individual technologies, information control processes, storage demands, and risk management requirements. Examples include diagnostic imaging in all its forms, cath labs, radiation therapy machines, surgical robots, point of care diagnostic devices, infusion pumps, electrocardiogram databases, bed control programs and displays, medical staff data, HR programs, supply chain control, intra-facility web pages, pharmacy control and medication administration, clinical monitoring interfaces, and the list goes on. Most physicians tend to focus on workflow issues that affect them directly in the moment and do not see this higher level of IT responsibility, often beset with its own resource limitations.

Interoperability, Big Data, and AI

Physicians and other care providers struggle daily with the lack of interoperability in the complex systems they confront every day when they walk into the clinic or hospital.

At the facility level, the electronic health record, for all its faults, at least attempts to make available to clinicians in some form the hundreds, even thousands of data points acquired during a typical hospital stay of even a few days. These include laboratory tests, diagnostic imaging reports and image access, care orders, clinical observations of multiple caregivers, vital sign observations and flow charts, case management observations, and discharge planning efforts. In various chart summaries, clinicians find ways to integrate much of this deluge of data into care plans and treatment decisions. However, current efforts to integrate ongoing hospital-based care based on point of care data assessments have been limited. At least partially successful examples include using a list of symptoms and signs to trigger nursing orders for lactate or procalcitonin levels to assess possible sepsis or using computerized indices of vital signs to provide a "medical early warning system (MEWS)." The EPIC-based "Clinical Deterioration Index" (an unfortunate eponymous overlap with "Clinical Documentation Improvement") purports to utilize what amounts to clinically unproven AI technology (Ross 2020). A recently updated systematic review of these kinds of clinical applications of programmed algorithms found that most studies had "poor methods and inadequate reporting…and all studies were at risk of bias" (Gerry et al. 2020).

Advancing these kinds of programs inevitably will lead to new communication requirements and adjustments in traditional roles but can lead to major improvements in care beyond currently simple clinical decision support tools embedded in the EHR. A concern is whether the application of such tools before they have been vetted adequately for clinical effectiveness or even safety may create later problems with adoption. Physicians have a very long memory for new processes that fail and tend to generalize to similar processes going forward. The famous Zuckerberg aphorism "move fast and break things" does not go far in the clinic or the hospital board room. Prominent failure of an inadequately vetted and monitored AI system could set the entire field back for an extended period.

Most clinicians care for patients who are seen in multiple settings, sometimes under the auspices of two or three different EHRs. Clinics, caregivers, and hospitals, even if not technically part of the same integrated system, may share data when one large EHR is utilized by multiple healthcare systems in the same regional "market." In Santa Clara Valley in California, EPIC is used by Stanford, the Santa Clara County Health System, El Camino Health, Sutter Healthcare, and Kaiser Permanente, as well as at least one geographically dispersed medical group whose EPIC EHR is sponsored by John Muir Health. That leaves out a very significant for-profit organization, HCA Healthcare, with two major facilities subserving a large segment of the South Bay San Jose greater metro regional market. Their Meditech EHR is not part of this larger network, which leaves a major informational "black hole" in the care of patients moving between these facilities. Continuing to patch through these gaps is a fundamental challenge for interoperability. It is as much or perhaps more a leadership, governance, and political challenge than a technology hurdle. Recent estimates suggest that fewer than one in three hospitals can provide truly accessible interoperable record sharing (Holmgren, Patel, and Adler-Milstein 2017).

The Healthcare Information and Management Systems Society (HIMSS) has offered a comprehensive description of the ecosystem of interoperability and with four levels: foundational, structural, semantic, and organizational as a basis of true health information exchange and data sharing (HIMSS 2020). Standards development is a key factor, complicated by the presence of some 40 different Standards Development Organizations in the field. In the HIMSS schema, processes surrounding standards development include vocabulary/terminology, content, message formatting for transport, privacy and security, and identifier standards, all with their own implementation guides and profiles. These require testing and conformance efforts, including with such newer processes and HL7 FHIR, as well as the development of network architectures that vary in degrees of centralization and development of appropriate application programming interfaces (APIs), already ubiquitous in the web economy. The web economy itself fuels a range of false promises and starts, with technology "stacks" that offer varying degrees of reliability and security risks based on phenomena beyond the scope of training or interests of most physicians such as intra-stack latency, packet failure rates, or widespread cloud outages, which could lead to massive hacks or other malign actions ranging from simple vandalism, deliberate sabotage, or ransomware assaults, all of which have affected healthcare systems throughout the world. In contrast with these threatened harms are a host of potential benefits including care coordination, improvements in business and administrative processes, realization of value-based care and other population health initiatives, and increased patient safety and satisfaction.

The National Academy of Medicine has offered an alternative interoperability model, working with a steering committee of recognized experts in healthcare quality and management, digital health services, and technology standards development, including recommendations for an integrative architecture under development at the Johns Hopkins Applied Physics Laboratory (Pronovost and National Academy of Medicine (US) 2018). Their schema recognizes three levels of required integration, including the point of care, intra-facility, and interfacility levels. The point of care "micro-tier" involves integration of communication between caregivers, as well as integration of information from sensors, devices, and related systems. Proponents of mobile medicine would argue that much of this can be mediated through mobile medicine devices and associated applications, integrated at the larger facility level through personal connective devices such as smartphones, wearables, and activity monitors. The next level of integration would involve artificial intelligence to parse automated clinical data and provide potential warnings of clinical deterioration, deviations from accepted management programs such as stroke, pneumonia, or sepsis, and opportunities for changes in clinical management through AI-driven clinical decision support software. Point-of-care queries regarding coding issues related to care management could likely offer major advantages for healthcare enterprises in efforts to assess the severity of illness and adjust resources accordingly. The opportunity to mine extensive data derived at the point of care also seems likely to offer insights obtainable in no other way. The ONC Health Certification Program Final Rule was set for publication as of January 4, 2021, and should offer an anchor for new efforts in the interoperability arena (National Archives 2020b). This subject is covered at length in a later Chapter 8 written by attorneys, "Getting the Most out of your Counsel When Implementing a

Mobile Computing Strategy, including thorny issues like Privacy, Reimbursement, and Standard of Care."

Managing the Development of AI in Healthcare

Given the complex processes and events that guide a patient's stay at a hospital or pathway through a clinic experience, efforts have been made to reduce error and waste through the introduction of a "patient navigator." Patient care generates enormous amounts of data, and many believe that embedded within that data, including the bulk of chart materials that are represented in some form of plain text outside the standardized entries, are clues to possible errors in diagnosis and management, simplifications of care that could lead to cost savings in drug therapy, early warnings of clinical risk, awareness of cultural factors that might influence care decisions, and discharge plans that might include data and process variables. These might include hidden variables in discharge disposition and follow-up contact that if recognized could reduce admissions or prevent later adverse outcomes. This view would hold that in all this data are hidden not only keys to better care but possible new insights into how each patient's healthcare experience can be optimized and even sorted in the aggregate into new ideas about disease and care entirely. Is there a role for a kind of intelligence, a "super patient navigator" that could be integrated into the current care process? Is this just science fiction or a real possibility in a not-distant horizon? How would it be manifested—a cranky holographic doctor or a quiet but insistent voice calling the physician's cell phone or alerting a nurse or case manager? Digital hard stops in the ordered care process will not contribute. Moving beyond the relatively simple algorithms of current clinical decision support will require new paradigms of data organization and the application of artificial intelligence. (The authors have heard a voice from the back of the room, "I'll settle for intelligence.")

It seems fair to say that the intrusion of AI-driven programs into the day-to-day care process will likely require major investments in not only the digital processes underpinning them, but also the political, ethical, governance, and cultural factors that underlie the human factors in medicine. The well-known problems with autonomous driving vehicles, aircraft control systems (e.g., Max 8), and failures of mass-scale facial recognition programs are certain to collide with all the cultural factors discussed in this chapter so far. The way forward likely will be to introduce physicians and other providers at all levels of experience and training to successes in retinal screening for diabetes, pattern recognition in oncology linking tissue origin and classical pathology with genomics and drug and biological therapies, and radiology screening algorithms for chest radiographs. The combination of these increasingly sophisticated and successful programs with human supervision seems to drive the greatest success and are likely to find the greatest acceptance of these new programs as tools that can enhance rather than direct the care given by ever burdened providers. It is more likely that success will come with gradual introduction of well-vetted applications, all well communicated to physicians both inside and outside of the relevant specialties. It is our view that the process of development and application of AI must be guided by a code of ethics. Such efforts should include the requirement that proponents and users of AI programs understand and respect the limits of the data sets, algorithms, and applications underlying the AI process. Geis and others have outlined a process recommended in their "Summary of the Joint European and North American Multisociety Statement on the Ethics of Artificial Intelligence in Radiology." They write that

Regulations, standards, and codes of conduct must be agreed upon and continually updated. Key to these codes of conduct will be a continual emphasis for transparency, protection of patients, and vigorous control of data versions and uses. Continuous post-implementation monitoring for unintended consequences and loss of quality must be enforced, with protocols in place for determining causes and implementing corrective action.

Geis et al. (2019)

It is easy to find enthusiastic predictions of AI applications for virtually any field of medicine. The reader has only to run an internet search to find them. Some authors believe that AI, somewhat paradoxically, has the potential to "rehumanize" healthcare (Topol 2019). It is harder to find clear approaches to avoiding biases based on application of inappropriate databases to select populations, use of clinical decision software to maximize profits or regulatory compliance without improvements in patient care, or development of a collective clinical authority that would supersede the judgment of the clinician. At worst, diagnosis and treatment could be based on an algorithm that hides within its "black box" clinical decisions that move the locus of control from the patient and the physician to the patient and the healthcare system and whatever biases might be programmed into the support software (Char, Shah, and Magnus 2018) or worse yet lead to serious error in clinical decision-making (Liyanage et al. 2019). Physicians should be engaged with design and safe and effective deployment of AI technologies, as envisioned in the SPIRIT-AI and CONSORT-AI guidelines (Ibrahim et al. 2021).

Back to Reality

In the meantime, from the physician's standpoint, the most common official wearable in the hospital is the belt pager (O'Leary et al. 2017), and the most commonly available device for interoperability at the "micro-tier" point of care level is a smartphone with SMS. Over 90% of healthcare workers have access to smartphones, with the majority frequently using this method to communicate, often outside HIPAA-compliant applications (Hagedorn et al. 2020). Physicians use smartphones and SMS texting to communicate in some fashion regarding patient care, often about care transitions or to trigger attention of a specialist consultant and settle simple but crucial care issues. Facility warnings and HIPAA issues aside barring the use of consumer-grade text and SMS messaging, there are real concerns for proper patient identification, contributions to alarm fatigue, and substitution for more effective means of communication (Hagedorn et al. 2020). Recognition of potential drawbacks to unrestricted SMS messaging drew a stern admonition from CMS in late 2017 that all text messaging in the healthcare environment was prohibited, expressing doubt that vendors could overcome issues regarding privacy and security. In a memo dated December 28, 2017, CMS clarified its stance, stating that texting patient information among members of the healthcare team "is permissible if accomplished through a secure platform," but reiterated that texting of patient orders is "prohibited regardless of the platform utilized" (Alder 2018). Secure text messaging platforms are available, and indications are that when utilized effectively they can improve physician satisfaction (Przybylo et al. 2014), reduce the length of stay (Patel et al. 2016), and potentially reduce the overall waste and error implicit in current practices based on telephone, fax, and pager communications. This is one area of potential interaction between physicians, IT departments, and hospital administration that could readily bear fruits of increased cooperation and understanding, given the ubiquity of smartphones and their potential for application at point of care and facility levels, though encouraging realistic expectations among the medical staff and understanding the limitations of this technology will be important. As recently as 2018, however, only 8% of hospitals had achieved adoption of secure text mobile messaging for healthcare teams (Friedman & Newton 2018).

Physician Culture and IT at the Crossroads

Real-world examples of IT programs affecting physicians are ubiquitous, but as in our example of physicians coping with big data applications in quality and cost control, there are few models of true collaboration. Both authors have had experiences that are illustrative of the challenges. In a recent example from a Silicon Valley health system which integrated EPIC into two community hospitals previously utilizing a different EHR, discharge summary communication broke down when the prior EHR's automated fax function was suspended and community physicians outside the system were not integrated into a communications strategy. In many systems, primary care providers who are not members of the hospital medical staff may not have direct access to inpatient discharge and care summaries, and secure arrangements need to be made to transfer this vital information for ongoing care needs and scheduled follow up. After a handful of irate phone calls from such providers with painful descriptions of poor care transitions affecting their long-term patients, physician executive and IT leadership were able to integrate an approach to support these community physicians, and at the same time maintain integrity of PCP attribution within the EHR database, which proved to be a challenging but surmountable hurdle. Prospective and thoughtful consideration by leadership of the unique needs and perspectives of all providers and patients affected with the integration of new technology will help avoid conflict with implementation and the resulting culture clashes and alienation.

In another example, top executive leadership of a small California healthcare system of seven hospitals wished to centralize physician peer review utilizing online forms and questionnaires. Finding significant medical staff resistance as physicians in the system perceived medical staff autonomy to be at risk, the regional CMO found himself working in some isolation with system IT, a well-known vendor in the regulatory IT field, and local staff to develop a working prototype, only to see the project fail due to lack of funding and inconsistent leadership as the system faced a financial crisis.

These examples to some extent reflect challenges common in IT applications at all levels. The widely quoted Standish "CHAOS Report" from the UK, published every 2 years since 1995 and based on analysis of some 50,000 software projects found that in 2018 only 36% of IT projects met traditional metrics of success such as being on time, on budget, and meeting users' needs and specifications. This left 45% lacking in some key dimensions and 19% failing outright (Portman 2020). At the top of the list for success is user involvement. At the top of the list for failure is *lack* of user involvement. Systematic reviews for IT development in healthcare are few. One of the most comprehensive efforts to define elements of success and failure was undertaken by the American Medical Informatics Association. Very similar challenges in timeliness, value, and cost were found extensively in medical IT projects (Kaplan & Harris-Salamone 2009). Over and above their frustrations with the EHR, physicians are very aware of this slippage in IT processes as they play out in several areas in their hospitals and in large programs such as ACOs, MIPS, and Value-Based Purchasing. There is often a sense of oppression in confronting processes over which they have had little or no control, and a mix of schadenfreude if not outright relief when they fail.

Rational Adoption of HIT and Physician Culture

Given the complex cultural, technological, and institutional organizational barriers to digital technology adoption, especially mobile, what is the way forward? If the experience of frontline physicians and other providers is one of frustration and burnout in confronting digital transformation, it is certain that the organization will feel the cost at various levels in various ways. To some extent, this is a challenge for alignment of organizational goals and needs in a competitive environment with technology solutions may come to bear, but in a context of participation with clinical leadership at all levels of the hospital organization. The involvement of the organized medical staff should in our view be a key factor in development. The organization will see a requirement, say for a clinical program to integrate services for value-based purchasing or communication with post hospital care providers. The case can be made with the medical staff in terms of requirements for marketplace competition or enhancement of the health system role in the community, quality of care, and/or meeting regulatory requirements. Our experience is that medical staff will accept the need for such programs and be ready to consider them and help guide them to success. What is required for success is an explanation that is clear and direct. Physician champions can be found and developed. The role of the medical staff organization is to work with the hospital and health system leadership to *communicate* on a regular basis in terms of project development, challenges, and successes. We have found that regular reports to the medical staff through online bulletins, medical staff department, and executive committee meetings, and especially the development of physician champions to lead the way have been very successful in the development of new programs in robotic and cardiac surgery, stroke management, online electronic peer review systems, and clinical documentation of clinical excellence, to name a few examples.

Thus, the role of providers in energizing digital transformation should not be overlooked but enhanced. This starts by taking stock of the present technology landscape of the organization as a start, informed by discussions at departmental levels and with Medical Staff Executive Committees with the clinically informed participation of the facility/system technology leadership. It is crucial to recognize physician champions and avoid excluding informal leadership and talent. We recommend creation of a technology/IT committee of the Medical Staff Executive Committee with a focus on digital transformation, actively seeking ideas from medical staff, and meeting regularly with CIO and CMIO leadership. The focus would be on developing a structure of ad hoc focus groups around concerns, possibilities, and needs that can streamline ideas and proposals, interacting back and forth up and down the organization with new concepts, proposals, plans, and projects. There are any number of structural ways in which this could be done. For smaller standalone hospitals or smaller health systems, direct interaction between upper-level executive leadership and frontline staff should not be difficult. The key is communication and developing excitement around projects that might improve the lives of patients and providers. Something must be done about the disproportionate share of EHR reporting requirements that take twice the time of actual patient care. This is where artificial intelligence, for example, can utilize analysis of free text generated by patient–physician interactions to produce structured medical records meeting legal and regulatory requirements while representing useful rather than redundant and repetitive cut and paste information. Finding and celebrating successes of digital technology including use of big data, improvements in interoperability, and artificial intelligence could help heal the rift between patient care work and its digital informational representation in the EHR and other databases.

Descriptions of organizational structures that have worked should appear in the medical literature regularly in place of the consultation business advertising that occupies page after page of internet searches looking for actual projects and organizational structures supporting them at the medical staff level. Structural requirements will vary according to facility/health system size and complexity. The type of project will dictate the level of standardization required at different levels of the organization. Common requirements include involvement of staff affected at all levels of the organization, a participatory, non-arrogant leadership style, and consistent and comprehensible communication.

By the same token, physicians have in our view the obligation to make the effort to understand the technology that underlies the tools that they use every day and which they would like to see improved or developed. This might mean continuing medical education aimed at the technologies underlying digital transformation, including the basics of computing, artificial intelligence, the structure of data used in electronic health records, and basic programming ideas that inform the structural development of medical data and its analysis, for example.

Returning to the theme of professionalism, mutual respect, and emphasis on team-based structures of care delivery over hierarchical systems will facilitate an interdisciplinary professional discourse that respects contributions from technological experts, direct healthcare providers, and supportive service staff. Hospital and health system leadership must develop and support this dialogue, which ultimately will benefit patients and manifest a healthy work environment for all. As mobile medicine develops, we predict that physicians will be eager to use tools that help them perform optimally in the service of their patients and the teams that these physicians help lead.

Addendum 6.A: Mobile Medicine during and after the COVID-19 Pandemic

Since the arrival of the SARS-CoV-2 virus and the outbreak of the COVID-19 pandemic, there have been sweeping changes in the healthcare technology and integration landscape with regards to patient care and communication. The most obvious and wide-ranging initiative has been the drive to embrace telehealth and remote options for patient access to provider visits, with the immediate goal of reducing the risk of patient–provider contact for the spread of infection, as well as other face-to-face contact involved for physical office visits (registration staff, patient-patient contact in waiting areas, family exposure, etc.). As always, healthcare system interest and physician engagement follow reimbursement, and CMS significantly expanded the services payable when performed by telehealth, effective March 2020 (Centers for Medicare and Medicaid Services, 2020). Beyond remote visits, there has been an acceleration in efforts to employ mobile technology for patient–provider communication (text, email, and mobile phone applications) and home monitoring devices (Keesera 2020). Data protection and privacy regulations, such as the Health Insurance Portability and Accountability Act (HIPAA), have been cited as major impediments to implementation of digital strategies (PwC Health Research Institute 2019). The Department of Health and Human Services recently announced that they are using "enforcement discretion" and will not impose penalties for use of technologies that don't comply with HIPAA used to provide support for patients during the COVID-19 crisis (Department of and Human Services 2020). However, these exemptions are limited to specific instances such as telehealth use cases, scheduling, and uses and disclosures for public health and health oversight activities overseeing and providing assistance for the healthcare system as it relates to the COVID-19 response, consistent with 45 CFR 164.512 (National Archives 2020a). While the Office of Civil Rights, OCR under the US Department of Health and Human Services has not specified an end date to these exceptions as of this writing, it is likely to change in the near term.

Within the brick and mortar of hospital walls, mobile technology has also facilitated patient–family communication during the COVID-19 pandemic, where healthcare systems have significantly restricted visitation as part of their infection prevention strategy. Many hospitals have received donations of tablets, phones, chargers, and other equipment to distribute to hospitalized and emergency department patients, allowing them to stay connected to those outside of the hospitals (Ducharme 2020). Even with critically ill patients in intensive care unit settings and at the end of life, mobile technology has been recognized as a way of bringing families together, improving trust in quality of care, and allowing families to say goodbye to dying loved ones when there is no safe alternative to being physically together (Bergeron 2020).

The extent and lasting effects of the COVID-19 pandemic on mobile technology and healthcare operations may not be known for decades, though is certain to be far-reaching. In a broad sense, some like economist Nicholas Bloom have argued that changes necessitated by the pandemic will drive toward "working from home" economy with an overdue restructuring and relocation of the labor force (Wong 2020). In the healthcare sector, it seems reasonable to surmise that mobile technologies will be increasingly embraced for remote physician and provider access, as both patients and providers are increasingly more comfortable with the technologies. There is enormous opportunity in chronic disease management and population health, especially for patients with mobility and transportation challenges. Support of alternative healthcare settings by hospital experts—such as hospitalists working remotely to care for patients in skilled nursing facilities—is another area of opportunity. Even "home hospitalization"—supported by mobile technology and connectivity, and advanced by the driver of need around COVID-19 infection concerns—bears promise to reduce cost and add to the care and comfort of appropriately selected patients in their homes. It seems quite possible that the stress and disruption brought by the pandemic will drive innovation in mobile technology for healthcare and telehealth options, affecting large numbers of patients worldwide. In some international settings, there has been disruptive innovation and collaboration around healthcare technology between countries where previously there have not been even simple diplomatic relations. For example, the ARC Gulf Initiative is such an initiative between Israel and the United Arab Emirates, and some hope this hub of healthcare technology could help drive not only better chronic disease management and improved quality of care for many countries in the region, but could contribute to improved prospects for international relations and peace (Jaffe-Hoffman 2020).

If there is anything the pandemic has taught us thus far, it is the experience of dramatic irony as we look back on our predictions. It seems safe to envisage that the healthcare landscape will in many ways be permanently altered, quite possibly in the end for the benefit of our patients, our physicians, and other healthcare providers.

References

Agency for Healthcare and Research Quality. 2019. "Measuring the Quality of Physician Care." https://www.ahrq.gov/talkingquality/measures/setting/physician/index.html.

Alder, S. 2018. "CMS clarifies position on use of text messages in healthcare." *HIPAA Journal (blog)*. https://www.hipaajournal.com/cms-text-messages-in-healthcare/.

Arndt, B. G., J. W. Beasley, M. D. Watkinson, J. L. Temte, W. J. Tuan, C. A. Sinsky, and V. J. Gilchrist. 2017. "Tethered to the EHR: Primary care physician workload assessment using EHR event log data and time-motion observations." *Annals of Family Medicine* 15 (5). doi: 10.1370/afm.2121.

Bates, D. W. 2000. "Using information technology to reduce rates of medication errors in hospitals." 320 (7237): 788–791. doi: 10.1136/bmj.320.7237.788.

Becker's. 2015. "10 biggest technological advancements for healthcare in the last decade." Becker's Last Modified September 17, 2015. https://www.beckershospitalreview.com/healthcare-information-technology/10-biggest-technological-advancements-for-healthcare-in-the-last-decade.html.

Bergeron, R. 2020. "A non-profit is gathering laptops and other devices so hospital patients can say goodbye to their loved ones." April 15, 2020.

Boothman, R. C., S. J. Imhoff, and D. A. Campbell, Jr. 2012. "Nurturing a culture of patient safety and achieving lower malpractice risk through disclosure: Lessons learned and future directions." *Frontiers of Health Services Management* 28(3): 13–28.

CDC. 2020. "Introduction | meaningful use | CDC.". Accessed September 17, 2020. https://www.cdc.gov/ehrmeaningfuluse/introduction.html.

Centers for Medicare and Medicaid Services. 2020. Covered Telehealth services for PHE for the COVID-19 pandemic, effective, March 1, 2020.

Char, D. S., N. H. Shah, and D. Magnus. 2018. "Implementing machine learning in health care: Addressing ethical challenges." *The New England Journal of Medicine* 378 (11): 981–983. doi: 10.1056/NEJMp1714229. https://www.ncbi.nlm.nih.gov/pubmed/29539284.

Copeland, B., M. Raynor, and S. Thomas. 2016. "Top 10 health care innovations." Deloitte United States, Deloitte Center for Health Solutions. https://www2.deloitte.com/us/en/pages/life-sciences-and-health-care/articles/top-10-health-care-innovations.html files/215/top-10-health-care-innovations.html.

Cresswell, K. M., D. W. Bates, and A. Sheikh. 2013. "Ten key considerations for the successful implementation and adoption of large-scale health information technology." *Journal of the American Medical Informatics Association* 20 (e1): e9–e13. doi: 10.1136/amiajnl-2013-001684. https://www.ncbi.nlm.nih.gov/pubmed/23599226.

D'Amore, J. 2019. "10 years since Hitech: The good, the bad and the ugly." *Healhcare IT Today (blog)*, 12–19. https://www.healthcareittoday.com/2019/12/19/10-years-since-hitech-the-good-the-bad-and-the-ugly/.

Dekker, S. 2017. *Just Culture: Restoring Trust and Accountability in Your Organization.* Boca Raton, FL: CRC Press, Taylor & Francis Group.

Deming, W. E. 2018. *The New Economics for Industry, Government, Education.* Cambridge, MA: MIT Press.

Department of Health, and Office for Civil Rights Human Services. 2020. Notification of enforcement discretion for telehealth remote communications during the COVID-19 nationwide public health emergency.

Douville, A. 2013. *Improving Clinical Documentation.* Washington DC: Advisory Board Company.

Drucker, P. F. 2002. *Managing in the Next Society*, 1st ed. New York: St. Martin's Press.

Ducharme, J. 2020. "Volunteers are collecting tablets for COVID-19 patients so they don't have to suffer alone." Time, April 24, 2020.

Dyrda, L. 2020. "Mass general brigham: 12 disruptive innovations in healthcare." Becker's Health IT. Last Modified May 12, 2020. https://www.beckershospitalreview.com/digital-transformation/mass-general-brigham-12-most-impactful-technologies-innovations-in-the-next-18-months.html.

Friedman, B., and Newton, B. 2018. "A closer look at text messaging in health care?" *Health IT Investor Quarterly Winter*, 2018. http://www.burdelaw.com/wp-content/uploads/2018/12/HITIQ_Winter-2018.pdf.

Gallagher, T. H., R. C. Boothman, L. Schweitzer, and E. M. Benjamin. 2020. "Making communication and resolution programmes mission critical in healthcare organisations." *BMJ Quality & Safety.* doi: 10.1136/bmjqs-2020-010855.

Geis, J. R., A. P. Brady, C. C. Wu, J. Spencer, E. Ranschaert, J. L. Jaremko, S. G. Langer, A. B. Kitts, J. Birch, W. F. Shields, R. van den Hoven van Genderen, E. Kotter, J. W. Gichoya, T. S. Cook, M. B. Morgan, A. Tang, N. M. Safdar, and M. Kohli. 2019. "Ethics of artificial intelligence in radiology: Summary of the joint European and North American multisociety statement." *Radiology* 293: 436–440. doi: 10.1148/radiol.2019191586.

Gerry, S., T. Bonnici, J. Birks, S. Kirtley, P. S. Virdee, P. J. Watkinson, and G. S. Collins. 2020. "Early warning scores for detecting deterioration in adult hospital patients: Systematic review and critical appraisal of methodology." *BMJ* 369: m1501. doi: 10.1136/bmj.m1501. https://www.ncbi.nlm.nih.gov/pubmed/32434791, https://www.bmj.com/content/bmj/369/bmj.m1501.full.pdf.

Ghafur, S., and Schneider, E. 2019. "Why Are Health Care Organizations Slow To Adopt Patient-Facing Digital technologies? | health affairs blog." *Health Affairs (blog).* https://www.healthaffairs.org/action/doSearch?ContribAuthorRaw=Ghafur%2C+Saira.

Guze, P. A. 2015. "Using technology to meet the challenges of medical education." *Transactions of the American Clinical and Climatological Association* 126: 260–270.

Hagedorn, P. A., A. Singh, B. Luo, C. P. Bonafide, and J. M. Simmons. 2020. "Secure text messaging in healthcare: Latent threats and opportunities to improve patient safety." *Journal of Hospital Medicine* 15 (6): 378–380. doi: 10.12788/jhm.3305. https://www.ncbi.nlm.nih.gov/pubmed/31532741.

HIMSS. 2020. "Interoperability in healthcare." [Blog]. https://www.himss.org/resources/interoperability-healthcare.

Holmgren, A. J., V. Patel, and J. Adler-Milstein. 2017. "Progress in interoperability: Measuring US hospitals' engagement in sharing patient data." *Health Affairs* 36 (10): 1820–1827. doi: 10.1377/hlthaff.2017.0546. https://www.healthaffairs.org/doi/full/10.1377/hlthaff.2017.0546.

Ibrahim, H., X. Liu, S. C. Rivera, D. Moher, A. W. Chan, M. R. Sydes, M. J. Calvert, and A. K. Denniston. 2021. Reporting guidelines for clinical trials of artificial intelligence interventions: the SPIRIT-AI and CONSORT-AI guidelines. *Trials* 22(1): 11. doi: 10.1186/s13063-020-04951-6.

Institute of Medicine - Committee on Quality of Health Care in America. 2012. *Health Information Technology and Patient Safety: Building Safer Systems for Better Care.* Washington, DC: National Academy Press.

Jaffe-Hoffman, M. 2020. "Sheba hospital, UAE's apex set for joint innovation hub in Gulf." *Jerusalem Post,* September 10, 2020.

Jecker, N. S., and A. R. Jonsen. 1995. "Healthcare as a commons." *Cambridge Quarterly of Healthcare Ethics* 4(2): 207–216.

Kaplan, B., and K. D. Harris-Salamone. 2009. "Health IT success and failure: Recommendations from literature and an AMIA workshop." *Journal of the American Medical Informatics Association* 16 (3): 291–299. doi: 10.1197/jamia.M2997. https://www.ncbi.nlm.nih.gov/pubmed/19261935. https://www.ncbi.nlm.nih.gov/pmc/articles/PMC2732244/pdf/291.S1067502709000322.main.pdf.

Keesera, S., J. A. Schulman. 2020. "Covid-19 and health care's digital revolution." *New England Journal of Medicine* 382: e82. doi: 10.1056/NEJMp2005835.

Landi, H. 2018. "Study: Healthcare lags other industries in digital transformation, customer engagement tech." *Healthcare Innovation (blog).* March 30. https://www.hcinnovationgroup.com/population-health-management/news/13030021/study-healthcare-lags-other-industries-in-digital-transformation-customer-engagement-techfiles/268/study-healthcare-lags-other-industries-in-digital-transformation-customer-engagement-tech.html.

Limb, M. 2016. "Use doctors' competitive nature to drive improvement, researchers say." 352: 1021. doi: doi: 10.1136/bmj.i1021.

Liyanage, H., S. T. Liaw, J. Jonnagaddala, R. Schreiber, C. Kuziemsky, A. L. Terry, and S. de Lusignan. 2019. "Artificial intelligence in primary health care: Perceptions, issues, and challenges." *Yearbook of Medical Informatics* 28 (1): 41–46. doi: 10.1055/s-0039-1677901. https://www.ncbi.nlm.nih.gov/pubmed/31022751.

Maccoby, M. 2013. *Transforming Health Care Leadership: A Systems Guide to Improve Patient Care, Decrease Costs, and Improve Population Health,* 1st ed. San Francisco, CA: Jossey-Bass.

Maccoby, M. 2015. *Strategic Intelligence: Conceptual Tools for Leading Change,* 1st ed. Oxford: Oxford United Press.

Marr, B. 2019. "The 9 biggest technology trends that will transform medicine and healthcare in 2020." *Forbes.* Last Modified November 1, 2019. https://www.forbes.com/sites/bernardmarr/2019/11/01/the-9-biggest-technology-trends-that-will-transform-medicine-and-healthcare-in-2020/.

Marx, E. W., and P. Padmanabhan. 2020. *Healthcare Digital Transformation: An Agile Approach to Creating the Future.* New York: Routledge.

Mattke, S., H. Liu, E. Hoch, and A. W. Mulcahy. 2017. "Avoiding the tragedy of the commons in health care: Policy options for covering high-cost cures." *Rand Health Quarterly* 6 (2): 1.

McBeth, B. D., and A. Douville, Jr. 2019. "A brief report of implementation of a physician citizenship committee in a community hospital to address disruptive physician behavior." *Journal of Hospital Management and Health Policy* 3: 31.

Miliard, M. 2019. "10 years on from meaningful use, major progress despite the challenges." *Healthcare IT News*, December 30, 2019. https://www.healthcareitnews.com/news/10-years-meaningful-use-major-progress-despite-challenges.

Mishori, R., L. O. Singh, B. Levy, and C. Newport. 2014. "Mapping physician Twitter networks: Describing how they work as a first step in understanding connectivity, information flow, and message diffusion." *Journal of Medical Internet Research* 16 (4): e107. doi: 10.2196/jmir.3006. https://www.ncbi.nlm.nih.gov/pubmed/24733146.

Nance, J. 2008. *Why Hospitals Should Fly: The Ultimate Flight Plan to Patient Safety and Quality Care.* Bozeman, MT: Second River Healthcare Press.

National Archives. 2020a. "Enforcement discretion under HIPAA." Federal Register. Last Modified April, 7, 2020. https://www.federalregister.gov/documents/2020/04/07/2020-07268/enforcement-discretion-under-hipaa-to-allow-uses-and-disclosures-of-protected-health-information-by.

National Archives. 2020b. "Information blocking and the ONC health IT certification program: Extension of compliance dates and timeframes in response to the COVID-19 public health emergency. 2020. *Federal Register.*

O'Leary, K. J., D. M. Liebovitz, R. C. Wu, K. Ravi, C. A. Knoten, M. Sun, A. M. Walker, and M. C. Reddy. 2017. "Hospital-based clinicians' use of technology for patient care-related communication: A national survey." *Journal of Hospital Medicine* 12 (7): 530–535. doi: 10.12788/jhm.2767. https://www.ncbi.nlm.nih.gov/pubmed/28699941.

Patel, M. S., N. Patel, D. S. Small, R. Rosin, J. I. Rohrbach, N. Stromberg, C. W. Hanson, and D. A. Asch. 2016. "Change in length of stay and readmissions among hospitalized medical patients after inpatient medicine service adoption of mobile secure text messaging." *Journal of General Internal Medicine* 31 (8): 863–870. doi: 10.1007/s11606-016-3673-7. https://www.ncbi.nlm.nih.gov/pubmed/27016064.

Physicians Advocacy Institute. 2019. Updated physician practice acquisition study. Avalere (Online). http://www.physiciansadvocacyinstitute.org/Portals/0/assets/docs/021919-Avalere-PAI-Physician-Employment-Trends-Study-2018-Update.pdf?ver=qR5bTErhmEF5MASqe2lsyQ%3d%3d.

Porter, M. E., and E. O. Teisberg. 2006. *Redefining Health Care: Creating Value-Based Competition on Results.* Boston, MA: Harvard Business School Press.

Portman, H. 2020. "Review CHAOS report 2018." Henny Portman's Blog, January 3, 2020.

Pronovost, P. J., and National Academy of Medicine (US). 2018. Procuring interoperability: Achieving high-quality, connected, and person-centered care. Learning Health System Series. Washington, DC, nam.edu.

Przybylo, J. A., A. Wang, P. Loftus, K. H. Evans, I. Chu, and L. Shieh. 2014. "Smarter hospital communication: Secure smartphone text messaging improves provider satisfaction and perception of efficacy, workflow." *Journal of Hospital Medicine* 9 (9): 573–578. doi: 10.1002/jhm.2228. https://www.ncbi.nlm.nih.gov/pubmed/25110991.

PwC Health Research Institute. 2019. Top health industry issues of 2020: Will digital start to show an ROI? https://www.pwc.com/us/en/industries/health-industries/assets/pwc-us-health-top-health-issues.pdf.

Rahimi, B., H. Nadri, H. Lotfnezhad Afshar, and T. Timpka. 2018. "A systematic review of the technology acceptance model in health informatics." *Applied Clinical Informatics* 9 (3): 604–634. doi: 10.1055/s-0038-1668091. https://www.ncbi.nlm.nih.gov/pubmed/30112741.

Ross, C. 2020. "Hospitals are using AI to predict the decline of COVID-19 patients: Before knowing it works." *STAT Health Tech (blog)*, April 24, 2020. https://www.statnews.com/2020/04/24/coronavirus-hospitals-use-ai-to-predict-patient-decline-before-knowing-it-works/.

Schulte, F., and E. Fry. 2019. "Death by 1,000 clicks: Where electronic health records went wrong." *Fortune.* https://khn.org/news/death-by-a-thousand-clicks/.

Shanafelt, T. D., C. P. West, C. Sinsky, M. Trockel, M. Tutty, D. V. Satele, L. E. Carlasare, and L. N. Dyrbye. 2019b. "Changes in burnout and satisfaction with work-life integration in physicians and the general US working population between 2011 and 2017." *Mayo Clinic Proceedings* 94 (9): 1681–1694. doi: 10.1016/j.mayocp.2018.10.023. http://www.sciencedirect.com/science/article/pii/S0025619618309388.

Shanafelt, T. D., E. Schein, L. B. Minor, M. Trockel, P. Schein, and D. Kirch. 2019a. "Healing the professional culture of medicine." *Mayo Clinic Proceedings* 94 (8): 1556–1566. doi: 10.1016/j.mayocp.2019.03.026. https://www.ncbi.nlm.nih.gov/pubmed/31303431 https://www.mayoclinicproceedings.org/article/S0025-6196(19)30345-3/pdf.

Starr, P. 2017. *The Social Transformation of American Medicine*, Updated edition. New York: Basic Books.

The Harris Poll, National Physician. 2018. "How doctors feel about electronic heath records." https://med.stanford.edu/content/dam/sm/ehr/documents/EHR-Poll-Presentation.pdf.

Thomas, K. 2019. "Sutter health to pay $575 million to settle antitrust lawsuit (published 2019)." *New York Times*, December 20, 2019. https://www.nytimes.com/2019/12/20/health/sutter-health-settlement-california.html#:~:text=Sutter%20Health%2C%20the%20large%20hospital,well%20as%20unions%20and%20employers.

Topol, E. J. 2019. *Deep Medicine: How Artificial Intelligence Can Make Healthcare Human Again*. New York: Basic Books.

Uddin, S., J. Hamra, and L. Hossain. 2013. "Mapping and modeling of physician collaboration network." *Statistics in Medicine* 32 (20): 3539–3551. doi: 10.1002/sim.5770. https://www.ncbi.nlm.nih.gov/pubmed/23468249.

Wachter, R. M. 2015. *The Digital Doctor: Hope, Hype, and Harm at the Dawn of Medicine's Computer Age*. New York: McGraw-Hill Education.

Weick, K. E. 1990. "The vulnerable system: An analysis of the tenerife air disaster." *Journal of Management* 16 (3): 571–593. doi: 10.1177/014920639001600304.

Weiner, J. P., T. Kfuri, K. Chan, and J. B. Fowles. 2007. ""e-Iatrogenesis": The most critical unintended consequence of CPOE and other HIT." *Journal of the American Medical Informatics Association* 14 (3): 387–388; discussion 389. doi: 10.1197/jamia.M2338. https://www.ncbi.nlm.nih.gov/pubmed/17329719.

Wong, M. 2020. "Stanford research provides a snapshot of a new working-from-home economy." *Stanford News*, June 29, 2020.

DRIVING REGULATORY AND COMPLIANCE SUCCESS

Chapter 7

The Importance of Trust

Peter McLaughlin, JD
Prince Lobel Tye LLP

Contents

> The digital revolution needs a trust revolution. There has been an incredible shift in the technology industry.... We've gone from systems of record to systems of engagement and now we are about to move into a world of systems of intelligence. But none of these will retain form or have referential integrity unless the customers trust them. Trust is a serious problem. The reality is that we all have to step up and get to another level of openness and transparency.
>
> *Kennedy (2015)*

Introduction

These are the words of Marc Benioff, the founder and CEO of Salesforce, spoken at the 2015 World Economic Forum in Davos, Switzerland, and they apply as much to digital health solutions – perhaps even more so – as they do to the tools that Salesforce develops. Bright ideas too far ahead of the curve do not succeed; bright ideas and timely healthcare technologies from a company with an inconsistent medically specific product development track record are similarly challenged; and so too are timely, effective digital health systems offered by an organization whose motives are questioned. In each of these cases, the successful development and sale of a product depend upon something more than simply the features of the product itself. This is especially so when information technology has rapidly created a different kind of infrastructure

DOI: 10.4324/9781003220473-10

through which information and knowledge can be stored and healthcare organizations increasingly rely upon third parties to run algorithms, perform data analysis, and/or host huge databases of patient information (Budd 2020).

The complexity of the trust calculus in healthcare today is partly due to the intrusion of startups seeking to disrupt some component of healthcare or established technology companies entering a new space: to wit, Big Tech attempts to tackle healthcare (Taneja 2020). Microsoft has been a platform for health data analytics and administrative tools for a while; Apple is looking to expand its Health Kit and incorporating new consumer wellness-oriented apps; Amazon has purchased PillPack; and Google aims to reinvigorate Google Health as its central team for the company's efforts in artificial intelligence and related technologies. These few examples present companies with potentially tremendous computing power to search across databases and to assess radiology and other diagnostic scans. They also wish to leverage their consumer tools to engage with patients. But while these four firms may be superb at what they do in the consumer and commercial space, are their solutions effective in healthcare, do they handle patient data – identifiable or otherwise – as expected, and do they use the data they access and process for any other purposes? In other words, do we trust them?

The potential impact on those using these systems if not those selecting them is that "these technologies have the potential to transform many aspects of patient care, as well as administrative processes within provider, payer and pharmaceutical organisations" (Davenport 2019, 94). In the context of machine learning opportunities for healthcare, Davenport and Kalakota write that "The greatest challenge to AI in these healthcare domains is not whether the technologies will be capable enough to be useful, but rather ensuring their adoption in daily clinical practice" (Davenport, 97). For this, there must be a trust of the healthcare technology, of the backend systems, and of the company making the solution available.

What Is Trust?

At its most basic, trust is "assured reliance on the character, ability, strength, or truth of someone or something" or alternatively "one in which confidence is placed" (Merriam Webster). There are, of course, myriad definitions of trust, depending on whether the context is personal relationships, in a work environment, leadership (Zenger & Folkman 2019), or of a brand. For example, in a sales context, one can view the challenge as a Venn diagram where trust in the salesperson, trust in the company, and trust in the product converge. We know it or sense when that trust exists, but how to articulate it?

According to Tallant and Donati, "Though there is no firmly agreed and explicit definition within the business literature, a fairly widely adopted approach is that advocated by Mayer et al. (1995: 712)":

> Trust is the willingness to be vulnerable to the actions of another party based on the expectation that the other will perform a particular action important to the trustor, irrespective of the ability to monitor or control that other party.
>
> *Tallant and Donati (2020)*

McLeod concurs with Mayer generally and adds that whether to trust is a rational conclusion of whether trust is warranted (McLeod 2020, 1). In his 2015 book *Achieving Digital Trust*, Jeffrey Ritter presents this definition specific to a digital world:

Trust is the affirmative output of a disciplined, analytical decision process that measures and scores the suitability of the next actions taken by you, your team, your business, or your community. Trust is the calculation of the probability of outcomes. In every interaction with the world, you are identifying, measuring, and figuring out the likelihoods. When the results are positive, you move ahead, from here to there. When the results are negative, you rarely move ahead; you stay put or you find an alternate path.

Ritter (2015, 37)

Ritter underscores that notwithstanding the genuine feeling of vulnerability, the decision to trust is neither an instinct (Ritter, 36) nor an emotion (Ritter, 37). Ritter's idea of trust – viewed through the lens of a lawyer conceptualizing a new framework to make digital transactions more trustworthy – is that it is a rules-based exercise fueled by information, the resulting decisions of which are mathematical (Ritter, 39).

Regardless of which framework you, the reader, use to conceptualize trust, and regardless of how your own decisions are made, in the end "sustaining … trust means designing your products and solutions to be adaptive and responsive to changes in the rules" (Ritter, 31) and demonstrating that the trust is "warranted" certainly at the product and the company levels.

When Is Trust Warranted?

In a healthcare ecosystem with new solutions from both established health sector participants and newcomers, with big data becoming big healthcare data, with the digitization of health and patient data, we are witnessing a dramatic and fundamental shift in the clinical, operating, and business models. How then to identify a trusted product and trusted partner when so much is new? In the product sales context, one can easily imagine at least five vectors that may contribute to the development of a potential customer's trust. From the customer's view, these might be (1) expertise of the prospective vendor, (2) the vendor's customer orientation, (3) the historic dependability of their solutions, (4) the real or perceived candor of the vendor and its representatives, and (5) the technical compatibility (interoperability) and personal compatibility between the relationship leads.

All five of these trust components will come into play consciously or unconsciously and regardless of whether you conclude that trust is instinctual or the result of a Ritter-like calculation. For the purposes of this chapter, we will focus on candor because when trying to assess the trustworthiness of a technology vendor – and especially one that will be hosting and processing patient data on your behalf – there will be little opportunity for success if you and your team are not convinced that the company will do what it describes with the data and no more.

How, then, to assess candor in this context? Perhaps the best proxy is whether the solution provider has a demonstrable, robust, transparent, and auditable privacy by design program for any of its healthcare offerings. This includes how the product collects and processes data, how the data moves within a network – whether your own or increasingly likely that of a cloud provider, and how proactively transparent the technology provider is with respect to the functioning of data analytics or machine learning. Black boxes need not apply. In the *Journal of Big Data*, Abouelmehdi et al. provide extensive data to support what seems intuitive: that is, "big data analytics in healthcare carries many benefits, promises and presents great potential for transforming healthcare, yet it raises manifold barriers and challenges. Indeed, the concerns over the big healthcare data security and privacy are increased year-by-year" (Abouelmehdi 2018, 1). Privacy by design, properly implemented, addresses many of these concerns and can function as a proxy for candor or trust-worthiness in a trust but verify world.

Privacy by Design

Privacy by Design (PbD) (Wikipedia 2020) has its origins in the mid-1990s when Ann Cavoukian, the former Information and Privacy Commissioner of Ontario, Canada, developed a conceptual model for the integration of commonly held privacy principles (Dixon 2008) with systems engineering, which she later published with John Borking in *Privacy-Enhancing Technologies: The Path to Anonymity* (Hes & Borking 1995). The underlying privacy principles, which the US Department of Health, Education, Welfare initially proposed in 1973, were adopted in 1980 by the Organization for Economic Cooperation and Development (OECD) and expanded them to create a framework of eight 'Fair Information Practices' formalized in the *OECD Guidelines on the Protection of Privacy and Transborder Flows of Personal Data* (OECD 1980, 2013). The briefest way to describe the OECD privacy principles is as follows:

1. **Collection limitation principle:** There should be limits to the collection of personal data and any such data should be obtained by lawful and fair means and, where appropriate, with the knowledge or consent of the data subject.
2. **Data quality principle:** Personal data should be relevant to the purposes for which they are to be used, and, to the extent necessary for those purposes, should be accurate, complete, and kept up-to-date.
3. **Purpose specification principle:** The purposes for which personal data are collected should be specified not later than at the time of data collection and the subsequent use limited to the fulfillment of those purposes or such others as are not incompatible with those purposes and as are specified on each occasion of change of purpose.
4. **Use limitation principle:** Personal data should not be disclosed, made available, or otherwise used for purposes other than those specified in accordance with [the Purpose Specification Principle] except:
   a. with the consent of the data subject; or
   b. by the authority of law.
5. **Security safeguards principle:** Personal data should be protected by reasonable security safeguards against such risks as loss or unauthorized access, destruction, use, modification, or disclosure of data.
6. **Openness principle:** There should be a general policy of openness about developments, practices, and policies with respect to personal data. Means should be readily available to establish the existence and nature of personal data, and the main purposes of their use, as well as the identity and usual residence of the data controller.
7. **Individual participation principle:** An individual should have the right:
   a. to obtain from a data controller, or otherwise, confirmation of whether or not the data controller has data relating to him;
   b. to have communicated to him, data relating to him within a reasonable time; at a charge, if any, that is not excessive; in a reasonable manner; and in a form that is readily intelligible to him;
   c. to be given reasons if a request made under subparagraphs (a) and (b) is denied, and to be able to challenge such denial; and

    d. to challenge data relating to him and, if the challenge is successful to have the data erased, rectified, completed, or amended.
8. **Accountability principle:** A data controller should be accountable for complying with measures which give effect to the principles stated above (OECD).

Any set of principles will necessarily be abstract and high-level, but when one reads through the principles above and specifically considers them in the context of developing healthcare technology, these sound somewhat like HIPAA. If we are considering a new technology that will often involve a third-party host for data storage, analytics, diagnosis, or treatment recommendations, then would we not want that combined platform to abide by data minimization; deliver data quality and integrity; ensure proper notices and applicable consents; prohibit unapproved secondary uses of the data; safeguard the data and the system; ensure transparency in data handling, especially regarding analytics and artificial intelligence; enable patient access; and be accountable? Taken together, these begin to sound like the basis for a trusted product and company, particularly those principles of not using data beyond the intended purpose and transparency or openness.

What Cavoukian did was to lead the integration of these lofty principles with more tangible, process-oriented stages of product engineering within the product development lifecycle. Privacy by Design is the concept of embedding privacy and appropriate security into any new product, system, or process at the point it is being conceptualized and developed. At its best, one 'designs in' essential privacy measures while designing 'out' or reducing the likelihood of regulatory fines and customer rejection (at least on the basis of how the product handles information). When combined with genuine transparency (candor) as to how patient information is handled and processed, the idea of building in privacy and security from the earliest stages helps build a best-in-class reputation and concomitant trust.

The seven foundational principles of Privacy by Design, as expressed by Cavoukian, are:

1. Proactive not reactive; preventative not remedial
2. Privacy as the default setting
3. Privacy embedded into design
4. Full functionality as positive-sum and not zero-sum
5. End to end security and full protection over the product life cycle
6. Visibility and transparency – keep it open
7. Respect for user privacy; keep it user-centric (Cavoukian 2011)

The Privacy by Design principles were developed for their general applicability and not for the particular requirements of any one sector, let alone any one country. But when we consider mobile apps for patient engagement, privacy as the default setting (as opposed to sharing of data) is a win for patients and their healthcare providers. When we assess the implications of different modules or different product versions, broader functionality should not involve any compromise of patient data or any other information, such as metadata. End-to-end security over the product life cycle is critical for networked products (which is basically every tool), and being able to review and confirm that privacy and security have been baked into the product plan proactively, from the initial design concepts goes a long way to generating trust.

And again, in the context of trust, a belief in the other person's candor is critical; here, Cavoukian's principles elevate the properties of visibility and transparency as essential for a third party to review and understand how a product works, how it processes data, and how the company managing the solution abides by its promise not to use the data for any other purposes.

Other chapters of this book focus on the data security requirements and recommendations that are conducive to trust, but if a product and a company servicing the product can demonstrate that the handling of patient data is consistent with these PbD principles, then it should be a system you can trust. But remember, it is not simply a matter of a vendor demonstrating how a specific device manages sensitive data; the privacy protections, the limitations of data (re)use, the safeguards, and the transparency of analytics must be evident at all stages of the product life cycle.

References

Abouelmehdi, Karim, Abderrahim Beni-Hessane, and Hayat Khaloufi, "Big healthcare data: Preserving security and privacy," *Journal of Big Data* 5, no. 1 (2018). doi: 10.1186/s40537-017-0110-7.

Budd, Jobie, "Digital technologies in the public-health response to COVID-19," *Nature Medicine* 26, no. 8 (2020): 1183–92. doi:10.1038/s41591-020-1011-4.

Cavoukian, Ann, "Privacy by design: The 7 foundational principles: Implementing and mapping of fair information practices," *Information and Privacy Commissioner of Ontario* (2011). https://iapp.org/resources/article/privacy-by-design-the-7-foundational-principles/.

Davenport, Thomas, and Ravi Kalakota, "The potential for artificial intelligence in healthcare," *Future Healthcare Journal* 6, no. 2 (2019): 94–8. doi: 10.7861/futurehosp.6-2-94.

Dixon, Pam, "A brief introduction to fair information practices," World Privacy Forum (January 2008), https://www.worldprivacyforum.org/2008/01/report-a-brief-introduction-to-fair-information-practices/.

Hes, Ronald and John Borking, "Privacy-enhancing technologies: The path to anonymity," (January 1, 1995).

Kennedy, John, "The digital revolution needs a trust revolution, tech leaders tell Davos," *Silicon Republic* (January 22, 2015). https://www.siliconrepublic.com/companies/the-digital-revolution-needs-a-trust-revolution-tech-leaders-tell-davos.

Mayer, Roger C., James H. Davis, and F. David Schoorman. "An integrative model of organizational trust," *The Academy of Management Review* 20 (1995): 709–734.

McLeod, Carolyn, "Trust," In *The Stanford Encyclopedia of Philosophy*, ed. Edward N. Zalta. Stanford, CA: Metaphysics Research Lab, Stanford University (2020). https://plato.stanford.edu/entries/trust/.

Merriam Webster (Accessed December 16, 2020). https://www.merriam-webster.com/dictionary/trust.

OECD Guidelines Governing the Protection of Privacy and Transborder Flows of Personal Data. C(80)/58/FINAL as amended on 11 July 2013 by C(2013)79. https://www.oecd.org/sti/ieconomy/2013-oecd-privacy-guidelines.pdf; https://www.oecd.org/sti/ieconomy/privacy-guidelines.htm

Organization for Economic Cooperation and Development, "OECD guidelines on the protection of privacy and transborder flows of personal data," Paris, France (September 23, 1980). https://www.oecd.org/digital/ieconomy/oecdguidelinesontheprotectionofprivacyandtransborderflowsofpersonaldata.htm.

Ritter, Jeffrey, *Achieving Digital Trust: The New Rules for Business at the Speed of Light*, 1st ed. Montgomery, IL: Original Thought Press (2015). https://www.amazon.com/Achieving-Digital-Trust-Rules-Business/dp/0996599002.

Tallant, Jonathan and Donatella Donati, "Trust: From the philosophical to the commercial," *Philosophy of Management* 19, no. 1 (2020): 3–19. doi: 10.1007/s40926-019-00107-y.

Taneja, Hemant, "How tech companies can help fix US healthcare," *Harvard Business Review, Innovation* (2020). https://hbr.org/2020/04/how-big-tech-can-help-fix-u-s-health-care.

US Department of Health, Education and Welfare (now Health and Human Services), "Records, computers and the rights of citizens", (July 1, 1973). https://aspe.hhs.gov/report/records-computers-and-rights-citizens.

Wikipedia, "Privacy by design," (December 13, 2020). https://en.wikipedia.org/w/index.php?title=Privacy_by_design&oldid=993906321.

Zenger, Jack and Joseph Folkman, "The 3 elements of trust," *Harvard Business Review* (2019). https://hbr.org/2019/02/the-3-elements-of-trust.

Chapter 8

Getting the Most Out of Your Counsel When Implementing a Mobile Computing Strategy, Including Thorny Issues Like Privacy, Reimbursement, and Standard of Care

Lucia Savage, JD

Omada Health

Peter McLaughlin, JD

Prince Lobel

Contents

DOI: 10.4324/9781003220473-11

Part 1: Why a Chapter on Legal Issues and Dealing with Counsel

Having made it this far through the book you have no doubt noticed that most of the chapters and discussion have focused on the significance of organizational change as a necessary component of introducing new technologies. Apart from considerations of user experience, security, and risk management, your people must buy into the idea of adopting technology because one way or another any technology will impact the process and how your team functions. Leadership and change management facilitate any such adoption and are critical to the success of the project.

Before diving into the technical, operational, and risk management chapters, our goal is to lay a foundation for success by giving you a new way to think about and approach fundamental legal and regulatory issues in healthcare that are critical to success. Thus, we included a chapter on how to work with your legal counsel—whether that person is within your organization or outside. We also included an overview of key federal health rules. Like death and taxes, developing and implementing technology in the health space involve federal and potentially state rules on the use of the technology; equally important are the ways in which patient data is created, used, shared, and protected by your technology provider. This is not simply a matter of minding the HIPAA Privacy and Security Rules, though those are important. Rather, the development and selection of healthcare technology involve potentially life-saving (and thus life-threatening) decisions. Mistakes in a technology or how it is used can result in death or serious permanent injury.

To successfully implement a mobile computing strategy, you and your c-suite colleagues (CFO, COO, CIO, and CISO) will need a strong collaboration with your legal team. This is because although technology and implementation models are changing faster than the express legal rules (as we describe in Part 2, below), the right legal advisor can guide you through legal ambiguity, and point you toward a sensible risk approach to implement a mobile computing strategy. The first step is to understand how to get the best from your lawyer(s), and we provide that guidance in Part 3 of this chapter. We also explain the basic legal model or thought process (still taught to every first-year law student). While sometimes quite complex, the core methodology is figuring out how existing, absent, or potentially outdated rules apply to new situations, as might occur when you implement your mobile computing strategy. And remember that while you are the client and in a very real sense "the boss," your partnering with legal, like any successful working relationship, involves leadership, collaboration, and communication.

Next, in Part 4, we look at new and emerging issues with mobile computing for health information. These include privacy rules, reimbursement from payers; and fraud, waste and abuse standards. Finally, we close in Part 5 with an overview of how a standard of care will apply when the mobile computing product or service under consideration is not clearly subject to existing healthcare rules. The concept of the standard of care explains how and why you might incorporate those (apparently inapplicable) rules anyway. And frankly, regardless of whether or how the product is regulated, a proactive approach will serve you and your team far better than a reactive, defensive approach in the event legal issues arise.

Part 2: Managing the Fast with the Slow

Technology advances seem to occur at an impressive pace, especially in the last few decades during which the Internet, artificial intelligence and machine learning, robotics, and mobile tools have each changed how we work, how we socialize, and how we live. Have you ever wondered how or even if the development of laws keeps pace?

The answer, as you may suspect, is that technology far outpaces its legal rule sets and that law as a construct evolves slowly. There are at least two reasons for why one would expect law to evolve cautiously. First, changes in law (apart from any unintended consequences) impact societal rules and thus by design should not change rapidly and frequently. It would do no good for the basic understanding of a contractual relationship, its inherent rights and obligations, penalties, and enforcement, to change meaningfully from one year to another. To do so risks undermining the fundamental idea of a contract representing the agreement of the parties. Similarly, in the field of criminal law, the rights of victims and the accused should evolve with the foresight and caution appropriate when the liberty and perhaps even life of the accused is at stake. The second reason is more mundane; the creation and modification of laws require compromise by legislators. And over the past few decades, our political system at the federal level has been such that compromise remains less frequent than some might like.

While law changes slowly, whether we like it or not, technology has undergone changes in the last couple of decades that arguably have not been experienced since the Industrial Revolution. Moore's law describes this development pace in the context of computer processing power as doubling every 18–24 months, though Intel engineer Gordon Moore's original observation was that the number of transistors per silicon chip doubled annually (Intel, 2020). Some argue that such rapid developments risk undermining liberal democracy and even capitalism (Wheeler, 2019).

Some estimates put law at least 5 years behind technology advances (Griffith, 2019), and there is no shortage of thought contributed as to how this gap—even assuming it is only a 5-year gap—is best addressed (Malan, 2018; Fenwick et al., 2017; Schwab, 2016). In a world of horse-drawn buggies, the introduction of self-propelled vehicles created types of risks that existing laws had not addressed. The technology that produced the video cassette recorder ("VCR") was developed in the late 1950s and triggered fear throughout the movie and television industry that their revenue and intellectual property would be undermined. Even though litigation by the studios reached the US Supreme Court in a relatively quick 7 years, by that time roughly 10 million American homes had a VCR (Standler, 1998).

More recently, with the advent of the Internet, entrepreneurs developed technology and business models to sell goods online. Until then, purchases might have been in person or via postal mail in the context of catalogs. While the idea of clicking "I Accept" and having that represent your agreement to purchase and pay for a product is now commonplace, there were few legal grounds to validate the purchase transaction in the event a product was not delivered, payment was not made, or there was a problem with the delivered item. In contemporary news, the "gig" economy is overturning decades of norms on what it means to be an independent contractor or an employee, and whether the facilitation via mobile app of a car ride or an overnight stay in a stranger's property is properly governed by taxi and lodging rules or something else entirely.

According to Klaus Schwab, founder and executive chairman of the World Economic Forum, we are experiencing the Fourth Industrial Revolution.

> There are three reasons why today's transformations represent not merely a prolongation of the Third Industrial Revolution but rather the arrival of a Fourth and distinct

one: velocity, scope, and systems impact. The speed of current breakthroughs has no historical precedent. When compared with previous industrial revolutions, the Fourth is evolving at an exponential rather than a linear pace. Moreover, it is disrupting almost every industry in every country. And the breadth and depth of these changes herald the transformation of entire systems of production, management, and governance.

Against this backdrop, the application of machine learning and deep learning to health databases triggers concerns about how the algorithms work and what the technology provider might also do with the data, identifiable or not. What one might call the "Uber" model of bidding out services via a mobile app is being applied to specialist consults and potentially to the scheduling of staff in a hospital. The evolution of cloud platforms and software as a service are extensions of the prior generation's outsourcing, but sometimes this involves much more interaction by the vendor with patient data. And depending on how the data is handled, the vendor may or may not be a HIPAA business associate.

That leaves us with rapid developments in technology and new business models in healthcare and comparably glacial progress in the law, and so it can be intimidating trying to assess the opportunity and risk of a new product. The challenge, then, for those especially in the healthcare space is how to work with your counsel to ensure that the product meets appropriate requirements or conforms to the anticipated standard of care.

Part 3: Working with Counsel

The Basic Legal Method

To effectively understand, manage, and respond to the complex state and federal statutes and regulations that run through, and wrap around, our healthcare system, one [or you] must understand the legal method which most strategic lawyers will use when advising you. It has a simple mnemonic: IRAC, for *Issue, Rule, Analysis, Conclusion*. Furthermore, it has an underlying method for getting from Rule to Conclusion which is to identify if there is an explicit rule on point, and if not, find the most relevant analogous rule, apply that even if the facts are novel, and from there, reach a conclusion built on prior precedent. As an executive, you will want counsel who are adept at analogizing new facts to a law or rule that may have been around some time, in order to plan for your institution's use of mobile computing. You do not want a lawyer who cannot do this and ends up unable to effectively counsel you merely because the technology facts may require an analogy, rather than be subject to a specific or clear law. Two familiar examples will illustrate.

First, from healthcare, let's take the example of Amazon's Alexa being used in a clinical setting to provide voice-activated assistance to medical staff. *The issue* is whether the HIPAA Privacy Rule applies to Amazon's services, thereby requiring the clinic and Amazon to undertake some familiar steps to protect the privacy of the patient's data to which Amazon might be exposed via Alexa. This may seem completely novel.

Actually, however, there is a specific *rule* exactly on point: HIPAA covers "protected health information" which, in turn, is any "health information" including genetic information, whether oral or recorded in any form or medium. Thus, HIPAA applies to the recorded oral information Alexa is collecting. In fact, HIPAA is medium-agnostic and, as a result, has many rules that apply equally well in 2021 as they did in 2000 when they were first written. From there, the analysis is easy and familiar, leading to the conclusion that for a hospital wanting to use Alexa in clinic, exposed to patient information, Amazon must sign a Business Associate Agreement and adhere to HIPAA, and the hospital's use of Alexa must meet its obligations under the HIPAA Privacy, Security and Breach Notification Rules.

A harder example might be the complex facts that can emerge when a hospital evaluates how it will implement the requirements of HHS rules against information blocking, which require that a healthcare provider (like a hospital) allow a patient to get a copy of their PHI electronically using an app of the patient's own choosing (ONC Info Blocking Rule). For illustration, let's assume the issue is the hospital's desire to comply with the ONC Info Blocking Rule, but to avoid absorbing liability for poor privacy hygiene of the patient, who may choose an app that does not keep their information private or adequately secure, as has been imagined in a press release from the American Medical Association issued on March 9, 2020 (AMA, 2020).

What is the applicable rule to comply with regulations and protect the organization from someone else's bad practices? It could be HIPAA, which does not regulate how individuals handle their own health information. In fact, HIPAA's Patient Right of Access Rule requires that a healthcare provider give a patient a copy of the patient's own health information when the patient asks for it. It is clear that the discloser of health information who does that properly is not liable for others downstream use (or misuse) of that health information (Savage & Savage, 2020).

Or, the applicable rule could be the Hippocratic Oath itself, which does not stop an individual from telling people other than their physician about their health condition (it only stops the physician from telling others about the patient's health condition).

Figuring out what rule best applies is the tricky part, and in working with counsel who is going to do this analysis for you, the key will be to look for the rule that fits the issue best. Here that is whatever rule best illustrates whether a hospital legally is responsible for how a patient handles their private life outside the hospital. Here, both HIPAA and the Oath tell us the same thing: that hospitals and their leadership are not responsible for how patients do or do not blurt out information about their health outside the health care setting. Given that **Analysis**, the **Conclusion** would be that how a patient behaves in their private life is not a reason to refuse to give them their own health information.

As mobile computing comes into its own, you will want to ensure that your legal team takes full advantage of this method in two key ways. First, make sure the issue is identified correctly. The mere presence of a new invention that has never before been used in a hospital, like Amazon Alexa, does not mean there is no rule. On the contrary, there may be a very specific rule in place that applies neatly, even though the technology or how it is being used is innovative. Second, make sure the rule fits, either directly as in the Alexa example, or with a good analogy, as in the example of how the Hippocratic Oath applies to a physician but does not limit the patient's own conduct. There does not have to be an exact precedent on point; *there has to be a precedent from which your organization's response can be developed.* A strategic advisor who can think ahead with imagination, while building precedents that come out of facts that look unique but can be effectively applied to existing rules will be your best ally.

What Qualities Will You Likely Need in Your Counsel?

So where do you find the Thurgood Marshall or Louis Brandeis to help you with your plans to take advantage of mobile computing? As we described in the prior section, you will be best served by an attorney who embraces, and maybe even relishes, the complexity that new technology can bring. As attorneys who have both worked in a variety of settings (fortune ten companies, government agencies, law firms, and start-ups), this section provides our views on the qualities that will help you find counsel to advise on risks and rewards of mobile computing without becoming the naysayer your Chief Innovation Officer avoids in the cafeteria.

Outside the box thinking: We used that Alexa example on purpose because it includes both a novel technology (wireless digital recording with AI-like search behind it) and a well-established rule: PHI includes health information "recorded in any form." An attorney who can think out of the box is an attorney who recognizes this right away, rather than thinking that because a wireless digital assistant is not specifically mentioned in the HIPAA regulations, there must not be a rule on point.

An eye on the future: In 2017, one of us had the privilege of giving a talk to about 100 lawyers from the law departments of academic medical research institutions (all marquee names), and we talked about Apple Research Kit. A quick survey of the room indicated that <5% of the lawyers present knew what Apple Research Kit was, even while the academic medical literature was publishing the first results of researcher's assessment of the quality of data from Apple Research Kit and speculating about the possibility of using connectivity to Apple Research Kit to acquire data from research volunteers. In that same group of attorneys, about 80% said their institutions kept track of individuals' research consent forms in manila folders, while unpublished data from HHS showed that about 80% of Principal Investigators scanned research forms and stored the PDFs with databases like Excel®. Clearly, the lawyers in this room did NOT have an eye to the future, and their institutions perhaps suffered for that. A lawyer with an eye toward the future does not have to use the latest gadget, but at the very least, they should know what is coming down the pike in healthcare, from app-enabled continuous glucose monitors, to digitally signaling medication (Otsuka, 2017), to robotic assistants. An attorney with an eye toward the future will ask questions about how something works so that they can understand and when the time comes find the right analogous rule to apply.

Trained to assess risk: At the end of the day, the attorney's job when counseling a business (not defending or prosecuting a lawsuit—that is for another book) is to identify the issues and apply the rules to help you assess risk about decisions you have to make. Whether to take a particular risk should always be a business decision, but, if your attorney thinks you are not addressing the risk seriously enough, more conversation may be needed, because your attorney is also trained (and their license requires them) to be a fierce advocate for your organization's interests. For example, healthcare statutes and regulations are byzantine and complicated, but they do have certain themes and also under those themes are certain principles. The theme of privacy in the Hippocratic Oath, and manifest in HIPAA, is one example. An experienced, strategic lawyer will counsel you with an awareness of these themes and principles, and their job is to know them better than you so that YOU can be fully informed about the risks you choose to take for your organization.

If we apply this concept to the problem of the patient-chosen app, above, we can illustrate how it works. In that example, the two applicable rules, HIPAA and the Oath, clarify that a healthcare institution is not responsible ethically, or under HIPAA, for how a patient handles their health information. Rather, the institution is responsible for how IT handles the patient's health information. In this example, an attorney who is trained to assess risk, to think out of the box, and who has an eye on the future (and knowing the government, which closely regulates your business and may even be paying you substantial sums for the healthcare you supply, has been on a 6-year effort to let patients use their own apps to get their own data) might say:

Yes, it is true, we could give a patient's app this data, the app could be cheesy or unreliable, the patient could complain, but we actually don't have a legal duty to protect the patient from themselves outside our four walls, so I think the risk of serious liability is low. And yes, we cannot prevent a patient from bringing a lawsuit, but this one we can defend and win.

In-house vs. law firm attorneys: What are the benefits of in-house vs. law firm attorneys? We're biased. We've both worked in-house more than in a law firm, although we both have relied on law firm expertise. Here is why we are biased: If you can bring in a strategic, future-thinking, lawyer on board to your organization, she will master two things it is almost impossible to master at an affordable price point from a law firm. First, an in-house member of your leadership team will develop trusted relations with internal colleagues, like your CMO, or your Chief Innovation Officer, or your CISO. This will ensure that your leadership team is supporting you 100% as you implement your mobile strategy. In contrast, law firm attorneys, even the most experienced, rarely get to work with your whole team enough to establish those relationships. Second, with your attorney in your organization, she will have an acute and well-tuned sense of your organization's risk appetite and where your organization wants to go; in contrast, a law firm attorney may not know your organization well enough to have that sensibility.

Even the most experienced in-house health care attorney or legal team, however, may have moments where the issue is simply too technical for the level of their expertise. Or, they may be actually expert, but in an abundance of caution, additional input is appropriate from a law firm expert. These are both common and fruitful uses of the in-house/law firm lawyer relationships. Here are some as-applied examples.

■ Your Chief Informatics Officer, an MD, has written a new software app which she swears will make the search function on your EHR operate with 3× efficiency and accuracy. There are no barriers with your EHR developer exist to implementing this app. You are concerned, however, that this app is a medical device subject to FDA oversight, while your Informatics office swears it is clinical decision support software and not overseen by FDA. Your in-house team has lots of experience negotiating with device manufacturers, and they've read the FDA guidance and agree with the Informatics office. In an abundance of caution, however, you ask your legal team to check with outside counsel, who for a living helps clients evaluate if they need to submit to FDA or not. That lawyer agrees with your legal team, you implement the app, and your medical and nursing staff loves how more efficient it makes their workflow.

■ Your institution wants to develop a value-based arrangement with several other organizations under new VBA Safe Harbor rules issued by HHS OIG in November 2020. The rules are so new, no one on your legal team has ever worked on them before, but your law firm recently hired an attorney who came from the HHS OIG division that developed that rule. You and your general counsel agree to bring in that attorney on this project to partner with your in-house team, so that next time you have the expertise to do this yourselves.

Legal advice vs. compliance: for people in the legal advice vs. compliance business, this is obvious but for business people not so much. The best way to describe these two functions is as follows: Legal advice is to advise on what a law or regulation means a business should do, while compliance asks the question, "did the business do that thing?" Because compliance is inherently backward looking, a compliance function is not designed to steer you through new questions of law that are best answered by analogy (see IRAC above). Let's look at some applied examples.

■ You contract for some new devices that collect and transmit digital PHI, but do not encrypt it end-to-end. Your security officer brings this to your attention. Encryption clearly is a best practice, but the price tag for retrofitting encryption is so high that it would consume an entire year's worth of IT budget. There are some interim fixes. In an ideal world, your next stop is your attorney, to actually validate for you what the HIPAA encryption rule states, and to advise on how to apply that rule to these facts. It turns out, you can address the absence of end-to-end encryption through some of these interim fixes, save this year's IT budget, and capitalize the bigger fix in 18 months, when the capital is available. Once the interim fix is implemented, it will be your Compliance department's job to make sure it's working right, and to hold you to your commitment of a bigger fix in 18 months.

Making your in-house lawyer successful, so you can move into the future with lower risk. This last tip is easy; you have hired a great legal team, now you need to get your other executives and their teams to use them, and earlier in the process rather than later. You will always get a better result when your executive team members have strong, trusted, and frank relationships with your legal team. Here are some examples:

■ Your org wants to offer a new service to patients that includes providing them with free digital blood pressure cuffs and digital glucometers that connect directly to your EHR, so your nurses can help manage, remotely, the chronic conditions of high blood pressure or type 2 diabetes. To implement this, your organization will have to solve a variety of legal issues such as (1) are you licensed to distribute these devices; (2) will you be billing insurance for them; (3) do you have the necessary ability to have their results transmitted to your EHR by the manufacturer; (4) what about the EHR vendor's contract with you; and (5) do you need to worry about whether this is an inappropriate gift under the fraud, waste and abuse rules? Clearly, this is not a DiY project, and while not illegal, may have some specific requirements to meet. Better ask your lawyers first than have to redesign the whole effort once implemented.

Part 4A: A New Way to Think about Privacy and Security as You Implement a Mobile Computing Strategy (L. Savage, JD)

Privacy and security are likely at top of mind if you are contemplating a mobile computing strategy, and much of this book has been focused on security and risk management, two important parts of your strategy. This section covers privacy, but not as a "how to," a list of all the rules (your counsel knows them or can learn them) or even a "compliance checklist." Those are all likely readings you've done before if you are a CEO COO or CFO of a large hospital or health system. Below, we cover some high-level principles that give you a new way to think about privacy, so that you can better evaluate that great analysis you are getting from your counsel (Part 3). Furthermore, as we go to press, our nationwide health privacy law minimum, HIPAA, is undergoing some modernization, so no list we would supply could be complete.

So, we will cover:

1. Why we need health information privacy, and that principle relationship to the Hippocratic Oath.
2. Some high-level, well-established aspects of our nationwide health privacy law, HIPAA, and where there are gaps in law that make consumers nervous.

3. How to think about the principles of health information privacy and the Hippocratic Oath as you implement a mobile computing policy and navigate changing laws.
4. Ensuring your privacy analysis and security practices remain in sync.

Why We Have and Need Health Information Privacy

Health Information Privacy has long been a part of the Hippocratic Oath, which even today asks physicians to swear to "respect the privacy of my patients, for their problems are not disclosed to me that the world may know" (Savage & IAPP, 2018, quoting Tufts Medical School Hippocratic Oath). HIPAA is no different. Passed in 1996, HIPAA's source is legislation that required hospitals, physicians, and other healthcare providers to bill the Center for Medicare and Medicaid Services (CMS) electronically (Solove, 2013). As a result of creating hundreds of millions of lines of digit health information inherent in electronic claims, it was necessary to regulate who could access and use that data and for what purposes, and to set minimum standards for secure custody. Thus, the HIPAA Privacy rule was born in December 2000, and the Security rule was born in 2003.

HIPAA also was enacted as the HIV/AIDs epidemic had raged across certain communities in the US HIPAA's structure of not pre-empting more privacy-protective state law is a direct consequence of that. In the late 1990s, many states had passed special laws to protect the privacy of the health information of their residents with HIV/AIDS, or with loved ones with HIV/AIDS, to prevent discrimination against those residents due to their health status. This reflected traditional state powers to protect their population's health and privacy, and HIPAA did not disturb that. And, given the roots in the Hippocratic Oath, health information privacy was NEVER intended to keep health information from the patient themselves (Belmont Report, 1977).

But, given its roots in a law requiring that CMS be billed electronically, HIPAA reached, and to this day reaches, only to traditional and expected healthcare transactions: collecting health history examinations; writing orders, prescriptions and referrals; sending information to insurance companies for payment and related utilization and approval functions; and quality improvement, particular by examining retrospectively what happened. Since 2000, the HIPAA Privacy Rule has allowed almost all the movement of health information necessary for the ordinary functioning of the US healthcare system. But, HIPAA did not, and does not, cover peripheral health activities like pharmacological research, medical device functions (when data is not sent to the medical record), and health information collected for life insurance.

Fast forward 20 years, and what was only digital claims information has exploded into an entire world of clinical digital information collected and stored in electronic health records. Furthermore, as a result of the fourth Industrial Revolution (Schwab, 2016), we now have thousands of terabytes of "health adjacent" (McGraw & Mandl, 2021) digital information from exercise trackers, grocery purchase, geolocation on smartphones, video visits, etc., all of which are collected and used outside HIPAA (NCE Report, 2016). Consumers may or may not understand the difference. Your mobile computing strategy, then, should be built on a few key principles, found both in HIPAA and in the Hippocratic Oath.

What Is the Actual Law of HIPAA?

As mentioned above, the regulatory agency charged with writing, interpreting, and enforcing HIPAA, the Health and Human Services Office for Civil Rights (OCR) is in the midst of proposed changes to HIPAA. Given the rulemaking calendar, we won't know the final outcome until late 2021 at the earliest. To the extent relevant, proposals are included here but may be out of date by the time of publication. We list some principles below, and all references to "health information" are to the health information HIPAA protects, aka "Protected Health Information" or "PHI" unless otherwise noted.

Principle 1: If you need to disclose information to another health care organization to ensure safe, coordinated, value-based care for a common patient, you can, and vice versa. In its 2021 proposed rule, OCR asks should this type of disclosure **be required** in the interests of care coordination and more efficient care for patients (HIPAA, 2021 NPRM). That gives you a pretty good clue about how OCR is thinking about privacy.

Principle 2: Most patients trust their physicians to maintain privacy, but ALSO want their physicians to make sure that they are sharing information about the patient to improve care coordination (Privacy Tiger Team Letter to ONC, 2010; NPWF Survey, 2015). So acute is the need for more widespread exchange or disclosure of health information for care coordination that in its proposed changes to HIPAA, OCR is proposing liberalizing the amount of data that can be disclosed to another provider for care coordination (HIPAA, 2021 NPRM).

Principle 3: For almost every aspect of the Privacy rule, electronic PHI and PHI on paper are treated the same. The only real differences are that requirements to disclose electronic PHI can be faster and require more liberal disclosure rules, because of advances in nationwide standards for computing such as open-source, common data sets that enable patients to automatically get copies of the PHI from their providers (ONC API Rule; HIPAA, 2021 NPRM).

Principle 4: Patients have an absolute right to get a copy of their own PHI, including requiring an institution with an EHR to transmit PHI directly to a location/endpoint of the patient's choosing, even a competing institution (HITECH sec. 13405(e), HIPAA, 2021 NPRM). Refusing to send a copy of a patient's record to a competing institution or provider could be a violation of the HIPAA Privacy Rule right of access. In the week of February 8–12, 2021, OCR settled two violations of this right, their 15th and 16th such settlements in 18 months, for a total just that week of $175,000 in fines.

Principle 5: If you are lawfully disclosing PHI and transmit it securely, you should not be liable for what the recipient does with it. You should not have to worry about the security practices of a different organization if they are not impacting the security of your system (Fact Sheets, 2015; Savage & Savage, 2020).

Principle 6: If the COVID-19 pandemic of 2020/2021 has taught us one thing, it is that consumers will use, and may even prefer, certain digital modalities of care (synchronous video telehealth or asynchronous SMS based telehealth) because of the convenience of that smartphone in their pocket. It may not be right for every need, but it is right for many needs, and consumers are savvy enough to pick online healthcare services that work for them. Just look at the online men's telehealth company Ro is currently valued at 1.5 billion (Franklin & Spaulting, 2021).

Principle 7: HIPAA applies due to a data collector's function in the healthcare economy, but other privacy laws and principles apply even if HIPAA does not, and ALL of them are set out in the 1977 Belmont Report, which has now, 44 years later, become the international standard for privacy principles. (The Belmont Report was commissioned to advise the predecessor to the US Department of Health and Human Services about how to treat "computerized" data collected during human subjects research.)

Applying the Principles for a Mobile Computing Strategy

The above principles can be used as through-lines from a paper-based healthcare delivery system to one that has implemented a full mobile computing strategy. We illustrate by analyzing what might happen over the course of your institution's decision to use a newly approved device that collects important clinical data and sends it to your EHR.

Test case: New devices that connect to the Internet of Things and send actionable data to your EHR, including a physician's ability to view results remotely through their tablet computers and smartphones. This use case assumes you have installed these devices with appropriate security so that their connectivity to other endpoints does not (1) deliver pollutants to your security system or (2) allow unauthorized access to the health data this device is generating. The device itself is not covered by HIPAA (see above) but the data it is sending to your EHR is covered by HIPAA, once it arrives, because your institution, a hospital, is a traditional actor for delivering care. The data in your EHR, if it is being used for patient care (as seems the case here), is fully subject to HIPAA. This is no different if the device is IN your hospital, or if the device is used by the patient out in the world. Nor does it matter if the equipment is an FDA class 3 device like a continuous glucose meter, or if it is a class 1 consumer-oriented device like a fitness tracker with a heart rate monitor built in. The key fact here is that the device is sending information to your EHR.

When your physicians want to view the data via remote connection, security standards will apply, but the right (or permission) of the physician to view the data is not different because of remote access than it would be for log-in access on your premises. So, if the physician is legitimately treating the patient or being consulted about the patient, role-based access supports the login. But if the physician has no connection to the patient, and is merely curious about the latest celebrity to be admitted to your hospital, physician's remote access is just as unauthorized as would be on-premises snooping.

After discharge, the patient asks her husband, who holds the patient's Durable Power of Attorney for Health care, to get a copy of the data in your EHR that the device collected about her. HIPAA does not care that this was collected by a medical device not regulated by HIPAA— that data is now in your EHR and the patient has a right to it if it was used in her care. Although OCR is updating how to supply a copy of this electronically, the right to that copy has been in place since 2000. The husband is the patient's legitimate legal agent; his request should be fulfilled.

In addition, the data from the device is very informative about the clinical outcome, and it turns out that for this patient's condition, your institution participates in a full-risk value-based arrangement under the new HHS OIG rules (42 CFR 1001.952(gg)). Yes, HIPAA does allow you to use this data to prove the outcome for which you are at risk. You will want to make sure when you contract to buy this device that your contract or license from the device manufacturer recognizes this, but that is a matter of contract law, not what HIPAA allows. Where you and your value-based arrangement co-collaborators need this data to measure an outcome for quality improvement, HIPAA rules on disclosures for healthcare operations like quality improvement (HCO type 1) have enabled this since 2002 (HCO Fact sheets, 2015).

Even though you are in this full risk value-based arrangement, you still need to submit a claim to the patient's payer. The claim standards may not have a way electronically to include it IN the claim itself, as they have specific content. Nevertheless, if the payer asks for substantiation of what you have claimed, HIPAA has long permitted disclosure to the payer for substantiation of a right to be paid.

Finally, you are an academic medical center and your Chief of this particular specialty has received a large NIH grant to study the condition for which the device collected health information. Health information in your EHR should be treated from a privacy perspective the same for human subjects research or even retrospective studies as would any other information about humans under relevant rules. That would not necessarily be the same were your Chief studying the device itself. The device is not a human subject and the device has no privacy rights, but it does contain intellectual property of the manufacturer. To untangle that all for you, lean on our counsellor (part 3).

Part 4B: Reimbursement

Hospitals and health systems are complex businesses. In the US system, being reimbursed for the healthcare supplied is equally complex, starting with whether an item or service is "covered?"

If so, what is the rate of reimbursement, and moving on to patient responsibility, balance billing, coordination of benefits, and subrogation, to name some of the thornier issues. In this section, we will NOT be discussing those. Rather, we will highlight emerging trends in reimbursement that are implicated by the advent of digital technology and for which you will want to plan when you implement your mobile computing strategy. These issues are:

1. Movement of care outside of the hospital setting, and indeed outside the ambulatory clinic setting
2. New and evolving rules that create pathways to build new health care collaborations that use mobile computing technology to document health outcomes achieved and where the collaborators share upside and downside risk for those outcomes in sharing reimbursements for those services.
3. As mobile computing equipment expands the conditions for which is useful, moving from chronic conditions like diabetes (e.g., a digital or continuous glucose monitor) to rehabilitation services like cardiac rehab and app-supported physical therapy, to health monitoring regimens at home for the seriously ill, health systems will concomitantly want to take advantage of new coding opportunities presented by new codes for Remote Patient Monitoring, Transition of Care management, and Chronic Care management.

Since 2014, investments in Mobile Computing (aka "digital health") companies have topped $4 billion annually and hit $9 billion in the third quarter of 2020 per Rock Health. Even without the COVID-19 pandemic, healthcare was moving slowly but surely out of the hospital (Duffy et al., 2018; Asch et al., 2019; Singhal and Repasky, 2020). During 2020, with most elective care being delayed and most office visits being converted to telemedicine where appropriate, that pace has accelerated and, although it may slow, is here to stay (Keesara et al., 2020). Thus, a forward-looking mobile computing strategy will plan for a hospital or health system increasingly providing care and services, especially for those with chronic conditions (vs. those who need surgery) in people's homes. From a reimbursement perspective, coding continues to lag behind this change in modality in three ways. First, many category 1 codes (for professional services) continue to be defined by a location modifier, such as an office-based clinic, even though many services can be supplied in a patient's home, from home dialysis (Kaiser Health News, 2020) to cardiac rehabilitation (American College of Cardiology, 2019), to rehabilitative physical therapy (Mani et al., 2016), to diabetes self-management education and training (Pal, 2018).

Despite this, for commercially insured individuals (under age 65) health insurance companies and those who seek reimbursement from them for services supplied via mobile computing have already developed appropriate reimbursement mechanisms to cover efficacious services supplied this way (Horne & Savage, 2021). Where federally funded health care is not at issue (that is, for patients covered by their employers, not federal insurance coverage), a mobile computing strategy could be implemented despite the fact that CPT codes have not evolved to specifically accommodate mobile computing. For example, for its patients who are not in Medicare or Medicaid, Intermountain Health System recently finalized a contract to supply asynchronous diabetes prevention service to its patients via a mobile computing platform that includes human health coaches (MedCity News, 2020). It may take some creativity, but where there is a will, there is a way.

This brings us to the second point. It is true that catching the coding system up to mobile computing will take a while, with coding cycles taking ~36 months. Nevertheless, the reimbursement system does evolve, and on December 2, 2020, the HHS Office of the Inspector and CMS together published new rules (VBA Rules) that will foster organizations' ability to implement mobile computing strategies that do two things. First, they will allow joint efforts among healthcare organizations to share Mobile Computing resources for certain types of value-based patient care. Second, as they become better understood, they will allow hospitals and health systems to be reimbursed for certain types of mobile computing strategies for those systems' federally covered populations when they meet new safe harbors, without running afoul of the criminal Anti-KickBack Statute, without acquiring civil liability for an inappropriate referral under the Stark law, and without triggering rules against supplying things of value to Medicare Beneficiaries.

Space constraints as well as the recency of these rules prevent a complete explanation here, but we supply one example of how the new OIG VBA Safe Harbor for Care Coordination might work (Figure 8.1).

Because this area is evolving, how your organization looks at these NEW rules compared to other more traditional paths to reimbursement will depend substantially on how you work with your counsel, as discussed in the first section of this chapter.

Finally, there also is an emerging area of reimbursement in new codes that allow professionals to seek reimbursement when they use mobile computing tools that are FDA devices which automatically "upload patient physiologic data (that is, data are not patient self-recorded and/or self-reported)" ("remote patient monitoring" or "RPM" codes) and use that data to formulate or update an existing, treatment plan. In its 2021, Physician Fee Schedule (PFS) CMS updated and clarified these rules, as well as rules for new coding for managing Transitions of Care to care settings outside hospitals, including homes; and for Chronic Care Management, for monthly oversight of Beneficiaries with multiple, complex, co-occurring conditions. Again, while space precludes a detailed analysis of these changes, which take effect in 2021, how your organization can presently, or in its future depending on its business plans, take advantage of these codes is exactly the type of strategic analysis you should be looking for from your counsel.

There is no question that advances in mobile computing are occurring at a rate faster than reimbursement rules have been able to keep up with. There is also, however, some movement. First, for commercial healthcare (people under age 65, primarily with employer-sponsored insurance), providers, health systems, and technology developers have for many years been able to contract for relevant mobile computing services in ways that made business sense for those involved (Arkwright et al., 2019). And in this respect, it is important to remember that the seeming rigidity of CMS (aka Federal) reimbursement rules do not always apply to commercial populations whose care is funded by large employers and union trust funds.

Second, even CMS itself is trying to make progress, albeit slowly. In the Fall of 2020, it announced the addition (on top of existing teams) of a new team to analyze coverage and reimbursement called the "Technology, Coding and Pricing" group (Quinn, 2020). Furthermore, in announcing its final payment rules for 2021, not only did CMS finalize new rules for Remote Patient Monitoring, etc., as discussed above, it also finalized rules that financially favor reimbursing for certain types of lab and outpatient surgery in lower cost settings (2021 PFS). Therefore, because in the commercial setting creative solutions are being implemented, and because CMS regulations are slowly trying to catch up to ensure that efficacious use of mobile computing is fairly compensated, this is an area of law (statutes, regulations, and contracts) where collaboration with counsel who can enable your vision is a must.

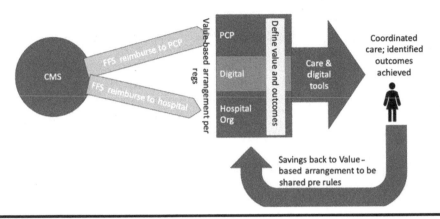

Figure 8.1   Value-based arrangements under OIG anti-kickback care coordination safe harbor 2021 rules. (Copyright© 2020 L. Savage.)

Part 5: The Importance of the Standard of Care

With a better understanding now of how best to work with your counsel and how key rules for healthcare apply, we come to the legal topic of the standard of care. Healthcare professionals and facilities often encounter the standard of care in the context of malpractice litigation, with a plaintiff arguing that a procedure was not performed at a reasonable standard of competence. And in a sense, the idea of a standard of care is just that—the baseline expectation of how something is done.

We raise the topic here, though, not necessarily in the context of litigation but rather for those times when your counsel suggests that HIPAA, for example, does not clearly apply to a novel mobile computing technique. Competent legal counsel should explain this to you in more detail and in the context of the healthcare product in question. At its most basic, the idea of the standard of care is much as one might imagine; do the right thing, regardless of whether there are rules that establish minimum requirements, such as the HIPAA Privacy Rule discussed above.

When there are rules that clearly apply, those typically set a baseline of behavior, of product functionality, of data use and protection. But because technology and business models outpace evolving legal standards, it is critical to evaluate product decisions and data use through the eyes of a skeptic with 20/20 hindsight. A legal rule might assert that a product must meet requirements A, B, and C. Then at some future point when the product is generally available and in use, it might become clear (or worse, it will not be clear) that product functionality and data use do not align with the expectations and standards of interested parties, who may be regulators, news reporters, healthcare professionals, or patient advocates. The skeptic with 20/20 hindsight will say, "Yes, you complied with the minimum requirements, but because of X, Y, or Z, you should have held yourself and your product to a higher standard." They may be right, or they may be wrong, but even if wrong, the diversion of your time and resources and perhaps even potential customers' attention may have been avoidable.

Perhaps more challenging is when there is no rule set that applies. For example, if the product in question handles individually identifiable health information but not in a way that HIPAA deems it protected health information, then what does one do to protect the information? Suppose it is a consumer-facing health app outside HIPAA's scope. The HIPAA Security Rule applies only to electronic PHI. The applicable US Federal Trade Commission rules focus on breach notification but not safeguards.

There is a good argument that one should build in compliance with the HIPAA Security Rule, even though HIPAA itself (and hence its implementing rules) does not apply. This point is equally applicable if the "industry standard"—or, what everyone else is doing—could arguably fall short of safeguarding the health information.

Court decisions have addressed these situations as far back as the 1930s. One case known as The T.J. Hooper concerned whether tugs moving barges should have radios aboard, particularly to hear weather updates, even though radios were not required for tugs and most of the industry reportedly did not have weather radios on board. The appeals court held that even though "a whole calling [industry] may have unduly lagged in the adoption of new and available devices.... there are precautions so imperative that even their universal disregard will not excuse their omission" (The T.J. Hooper at 740).

The takeaway here is that there will always be a legal standard of care to consider, whether expressly applicable through a law or when no specific law or set of rules seems to clearly apply. You and counsel should always consider the ramifications of the skeptic with 20/20 hindsight leveling accusations and the impact on a product or the company more generally.

Public resources on HIPAA (Privacy and Security)-full hyperlinks. All of these should be able to be freely used w/o permission from the agency.
Section 4A: privacy

1. ONC/OCR Fact Sheets on information exchange (Principle 1)
   a. For Treatment: https://www.healthit.gov/sites/default/files/factsheets/exchange_treatment.pdf
   b. For Health Care Operations: https://www.healthit.gov/sites/default/files/factsheets/exchange_health_care_ops.pdf
   c. For Public Health Oversight: https://www.healthit.gov/sites/default/files/1207 2016_hipaa_and_public_health_fact_sheet.pdf
2. ONC Resources on Information Blocking/Interoperability/21c Cures final regulation: https://www.healthit.gov/curesrule/resources/fact-sheets?options=f422c1d2-f743-4774-acc5-d90a5ec657eb
3. OCR videos on patient right of access to their own PHI--Principle 4
   ■ Individual's Right under HIPAA to Access their Health Information
   ■ HIPAA Access Associated Fees and Timing
   ■ HIPAA Access and Third Parties
   ■ https://www.hhs.gov/hipaa/for-individuals/guidance-materials-for-consumers/index.html
4. HHS OIG Value Based Arrangements changes to Anti Kickback Statute, Final rule Nov. 2020, fact sheet (Section 4B): https://oig.hhs.gov/reports-and-publications/federal-register-notices/factsheet-rule-beneficiary-inducements.pdf

References

American College of Cardiology, 2019. https://www.acc.org/latest-in-cardiology/articles/2019/05/07/12/42/innovation-at-acc-acc19-innovation-challenge-supporting-emerging-technology-to-transform-care-outcomes

American Medical Association, AMA reviewing interoperability rules for patient focus, privacy issues, March 9, 2020. https://www.ama-assn.org/press-center/press-releases/ama-reviewing-interoperability-rules-patient-focus-privacy-issues.

Apple Research Kit, *Apple Worldwide Developer Conference*, 2017. https://developer.apple.com/videos/play/wwdc2017/232/.

Bruce Quinn, CMS introduces new office for technology policy, coding, pricing, 2020. http://www.discoveriesinhealthpolicy.com/2020/11/cms-introduces-new-office-for.html.

Bryan T. Arkwright, Monica Leslie, Morgan Light, Telehealth finance variables and successful business models, 2019. https://telehealthandmedicinetoday.com/index.php/journal/article/view/140/164. doi: 10.30953/tmt.v4.140.

Daniel Malan, Technology is changing faster than regulators can keep up: Here's how to close the gap, World Economic Forum (blog), June 21, 2018. https://www.weforum.org/agenda/2018/06/law-too-slow-for-new-tech-how-keep-up/.

Daniel Solove, HIPAA turns 10, 2013. https://pubmed.ncbi.nlm.nih.gov/23781600/

David Asch, et al., Toward facilitated self-service in health care, *The New England Journal of Medicine* 380, 2019: 1891–1893. doi: 10.1056/NEJMp1817104.

Deven McGraw, and Ken Mandl, Privacy protections to encourage use of health-relevant digital data in a learning health system, *Nature*, 2021. https://www.nature.com/articles/s41746-020-00362-8.

Elise Reuter, Intermountain expands diabetes prevention partnership with Omada, 2021. https://medcitynews.com/2020/11/intermountain-expands-diabetes-prevention-partnership-with-omada/.

Health Information Technology for Clinical Health Act (HITECH) section 13405(e). HITECH was part of the American Recovery and Reinvestment Act, Public Law No: 111–5, February 17, 2009, 100 Stat 2548, codified throughout US Code but in particular at 42 US C. 300jj, https://www.congress.gov/111/plaws/publ5/PLAW-111publ5.pdf.

Intel, Over 50 Years of Moore's Law, accessed December 20, 2020. https://www.intel.com/content/www/us/en/silicon-innovations/moores-law-technology.html.

Joshua Franklin, and Rebecca Spaulting, Telehealth company Ro explores deal to go public: sources, Reuters, 2021. https://www.reuters.com/article/us-roman-health-m-a/telehealth-company-ro-explores-deal-to-go-public-sources-idUSKBN29W30R.

Julia Griffith, "A losing game: The law is struggling to keep up with technology," The Journal of High Technology Law (blog), April 12, 2019. https://sites.suffolk.edu/jhtl/2019/04/12/a-losing-game-the-law-is-struggling-to-keep-up-with-technology/.

Kaiser Health News, Feds pave the way to expand home dialysis: But patients hit roadblocks, 2020. https://khn.org/news/feds-pave-the-way-to-expand-home-dialysis-but-patients-hit-roadblocks/.

Kingshuk Pal, et al. Digital health interventions for adults with type 2 diabetes: Qualitative study of patient perspectives on diabetes self-management education and support, 2018. https://www.ncbi.nlm.nih.gov/pmc/articles/PMC5931778/.

Klaus Schwab, "The fourth industrial revolution: What it means and how to respond," World Economic Forum Global Agenda (blog), January 14, 2016. https://www.weforum.org/agenda/2016/01/the-fourth-industrial-revolution-what-it-means-and-how-to-respond/.

Kris Hauser and Ryan Shaw, How medical robots will help treat patients in future outbreaks, Institute of Electrical and Electronics Engineers Spectrum, https://spectrum.ieee.org/automaton/robotics/medical-robots/medical-robots-future-outbreak-respons.

Lucia Savage, Why we must remember where informed consent comes from, International Association of Privacy Professionals, September 2018. https://iapp.org/news/a/why-we-must-remember-where-informed-consent-comes-from/.

Mark Fenwick, Wulf A. Kaal, and Erik P.M. Vermeulen, "Regulation tomorrow: What happens when technology is faster than the law?" *American University Business Law Review* 6, no. 3, 2017: 561–94. doi: 10.2139/ssrn.2834531.

Mark Savage, and Lucia Savage, Doctors routinely share health data electronically under HIPAA, and sharing with patients and patients' third-party health apps is consistent: Interoperability and privacy analysis, *Journal of Medical Internet Research*, 22, no. 9, 2020. https://www.jmir.org/2020/9/e19818/.

Medicare and State Health Plan Program: Fraud and Abuse; Revisions to the Safe Harbors Under the Anti-Kickback Statute, and Civil Monetary Penalty Rules Regarding Beneficiary Inducements, published at 85 Federal Register page 77684, December 2, 2020 and amending Title 42 Code of

Federal Regulations, Parts 1001 and 1003. https://www.federalregister.gov/documents/2020/12/02/2020-26072/medicare-and-state-health-care-programs-fraud-and-abuse-revisions-to-safe-harbors-under-the.

National Partnership for Women and Families Survey, Engaging patients and families: How consumers value and use health IT, December 2014. https://www.nationalpartnership.org/our-work/resources/health-care/digital-health/archive/engaging-patients-and-families.pdf.

Otsuka, Digital-signaling medications were first approved for an Otsuka pharmaceuticals/proteus product, 2017. https://www.otsuka-us.com/discover/articles-1075.

Privacy Rule (45 CFR 164) at 164.524, as amended by Congress in the Health Information Technology for Clinical Health Act (HITECH) section 13405(e). HITECH was part of the American Recovery and Reinvestment Act, Public Law No: 111–5. February 17, 2009. https://www.congress.gov/111/plaws/publ5/PLAW-111publ5.pdf., https://www.ecfr.gov/cgi-bin/text-idx?tpl=/ecfrbrowse/Title45/45cfr160_main_02.tpl (accessed January 16, 2021).

Robert Horne and Lucia Savage, In the digital era, payment reform is key to shaping a modern medicare program, Health Affairs Blog, February 22, 2021. https://www.healthaffairs.org/do/10.1377/hblog20210218.976675/abs/.

Rock Health. Q3 investment report, 2020. https://rockhealth.com/reports/q3-2020-digital-health-funding-already-sets-a-new-annual-record/.

Ronald Standler, Response of law to new technology, August 12, 1998. http://www.rbs2.com/lt.htm.

Sean Duffy, et al., When in person care is plan B, *The New England Journal of Medicine* 378, 2018:104–106. doi: 10.1056/NEJMp1710735.

Shubham Singhal and Cara Repasky, The great acceleration in healthcare: Six trends to heed, September 2020. Available at: https://www.mckinsey.com/industries/healthcare-systems-and-services/our-insights/the-great-acceleration-in-healthcare-six-trends-to-heed.

Sirina Keesara, Andrea Jonas, and Kevin Schulman, Covid-19 and health care's digital revolution, *The New England Journal of Medicine* 382, 2020: e82. doi: 10.1056/NEJMp200583.

Suresh Mani, Shobha Sharma, Baharudin Omar, Aatit Paungmali and Leonard Joseph, Validity and reliability of Internet-based physiotherapy assessment for musculoskeletal disorders: A systematic review, *Journal of Telemedicine and Telecare*, 2016: 1–13. Available at: https://cens.cl/wp-content/uploads/2020/04/paper-internet-bases-physiotherapy.pdf.

The "21st Century Cures Act: Interoperability, Information Blocking, and the ONC Health IT Certification Program" promulgated by US Department of Health and Human Services Office of the National Coordinator for Health IT is published at 85 Federal Register page 47099 and following on August 4, 2020 and creates or amends regulations found at Title 45, Code of Federal Regulations, part 170.

The Breach Notification Rule is found at Title 45 Code of Federal Regulations Pa4t 160 and Subpart D of part 164.

The HIPAA rule on Encryption is found at title 45 Code of Federal Regulations, subpart D of part 164. Specifically, 45 CFR 164.312(a)(2)(iv), which characterizes the requirement of end-to-end encryption as "addressable.", 2021.

The T.J. Hooper, 53 F.2d 107 (S.D.N.Y. 1931); on appeal The T.J. Hooper, 60 F2d 737 (2d Cir. 1932).

Tom Wheeler, Internet capitalism pits fast technology against slow democracy, Brookings TechTank (blog), May 6, 2019. https://www.brookings.edu/blog/techtank/2019/05/06/internet-capitalism-pits-fast-technology-against-slow-democracy/.

US Department of Health and Human Services, Center for Medicare and Medicaid Services, Medicare Program: Hospital Outpatient Prospective Payment and Ambulatory Surgical Center Payment Systems and Quality Reporting Programs; New Categories for Hospital Outpatient Department Prior Authorization Process; Clinical Laboratory Fee Schedule: Laboratory Date of Service Policy; Overall Hospital Quality Star Rating Methodology; Physician-Owned Hospitals; Notice of Closure of Two Teaching Hospitals and Opportunity To Apply for Available Slots, Radiation Oncology Model; and Reporting Requirements for Hospitals and Critical Access Hospitals (CAHs) To Report COVID-19 Therapeutic Inventory and Usage and To Report Acute Respiratory Illness During the Public Health Emergency (PHE) for Coronavirus Disease 2019 (COVID-19), Amending various provisions of

Title 42, Code of Federal Regulations, starting with part 410. 2021 Physician Fee Schedule and other payment rules, published 85 FR 84543, December 28, 2020. https://www.federalregister.gov/documents/2020/12/29/2020-26819/medicare-program-hospital-outpatient-prospective-payment-and-ambulatory-surgical-center-paymentCMS.

US Department of Health and Human Services, Office of Human Research Protections, Belmont Report, 1977. https://www.hhs.gov/ohrp/regulations-and-policy/belmont-report/index.html.

US Department of Health and Human Services Office of the Inspector General, Medicare and State Health Plan Program: Fraud and Abuse; Revisions to the Safe Harbors Under the Anti-Kickback Statute, and Civil Monetary Penalty Rules Regarding Beneficiary Inducements, published at 85 Federal Register page 77684, December 2, 2020, amending Title 42 Code of Federal Regulations, Parts 1001 and 1003, https://www.federalregister.gov/documents/2020/12/02/2020-26072/medicare-and-state-healthcare-programs-fraud-and-abuse-revisions-to-safe-harbors-under-the; and 85 FR 77492 (Medicare Program; Modernizing and Clarifying the Physician Self-Referral amending Title 42 Code of Federal Regulations part 411, https://www.govinfo.gov/content/pkg/FR-2020-12-02/pdf/2020-26140.pdf.

US Department of Health and Human Services, Office of the National Coordinator for Health IT, Examining oversight of the privacy & security of health data collected by entities not regulated by HIPAA, July 2016. https://www.healthit.gov/sites/default/files/non-covered_entities_report_june_17_2016.pdf.

US Department of Health and Human Services, Office of the National Coordinator for Health IT, Transmittal letter of the Privacy Tiger Team of the Health Information Technology Policy Committee to the National Coordinator for Health IT, September 1, 2010. https://www.healthit.gov/sites/default/files/hitpc_transmittal_p_s_tt_9_1_10.pdf.

US Department of Health and Human Services, Office of the National Coordinator for Health IT, 21st Century Cures Act Final Rule (ONC API RULE). https://www.healthit.gov/curesrule/overview/about-oncs-cures-act-final-rule.

US Department of Health and Human Services, Office of the National Coordinator for Health IT/OCR Fact Sheets on exchange of PHI for Health Care Operations, 2015. https://www.healthit.gov/sites/default/files/factsheets/exchange_health_care_ops.pdf.

US Department of Health and Human Services, Office of the National Coordinator for Health IT/OCR Fact Sheets on exchange of PHI for Treatment. https://www.healthit.gov/sites/default/files/factsheets/exchange_treatment.pdf.

US Department of Health and Human Services, Proposed modifications to the HIPAA privacy rule to support, and remove barriers to, coordinated care and individual engagement, 86 Federal Register 6446, January 21, 2012. https://www.federalregister.gov/documents/2021/01/21/2020-27157/proposed-modifications-to-the-hipaa-privacy-rule-to-support-and-remove-barriers-to-coordinated-care.

MANAGING RISKS
TO SUCCESS

Chapter 9

Managing Implementation Risk for Successful Mobile Medicine

Eric Svetcov
Medigram

Allison J. Taylor
Thought Marketing LLC

Matthew Perez
Cybersecurity Professional

Contents

DOI: 10.4324/9781003220473-13

Introduction

To gain full value from the use of mobile devices and simultaneously protect the networks, systems, and data within a hospital environment is a challenge that requires an extraordinary amount of discipline and imagination to succeed as well as a measured level of "cat herding." It would be nice to presume a greenfield implementation; however, the reality is that most organizations will want to approach the implementation of mobile medicine as a re-implementation, as mobile devices are already present. Reaching an improved future secure mobile communications state will require collaboration, integration of several important perspectives, rigor in approaching the implementation, leveraging leading practices across several security domains, and at least a touch of diplomacy and organizational psychology to keep a diverse set of stakeholders marching in the same direction.

When considering the implementation risk and the methods to mitigate that risk, it is important to reach back to the skills gained from your parents or initial adult role models—teaching you how to perform your first risk assessment prior to crossing a street—while integrating your educational and professional experience performing more formal risk assessments. A successful mobile medicine rollout will reward you and the organization through improved patient care and clinical satisfaction, but it will not be easy. Success in mobile medicine has been elusive for many, though many rewards will be granted to the leaders. You will save thousands of lives and reduce disability by reducing time to treatment, and significantly enhance both safety and well-being of your clinician workforce by enabling them to get their work done wherever they are and in a timely manner. This is critical when a leading cause of preventable death is still a delay in information. At the same time, a mobile medicine rollout may be one of the most challenging endeavors you will ever pursue; however, if you lean hard on your experience, leading practices that can be found in these pages, and the diversity of thought and background within your own workforce, it is possible to succeed where others have failed.

In this chapter, we will discuss the risks, mitigation strategies, and monitoring and measurement techniques that can serve as signposts on your successful journey.

Unique Risks Introduced by Implementing Mobile Medicine

Static solutions, systems that are connected using wires, and the inevitable build-up of dust surrounding computers and systems that remain in place for months, years, or even decades are a thing of the past. Over the years, stationary medical devices have sprouted wheels and have gained an element of mobility. However, until Star Trek like communicators became everyday devices—until battery and processor technology miniaturized and became more powerful—the wired medical device remained at the essence, merely a semi-mobile tethered solution. Until recently, the mobile medical device was nothing more than a stationary device that was just easier to move from room to room by virtue of being on wheels and having network connections pre-wired to tether the device when it arrived at its new, stationary, resting place. Kind of like a laptop was to a desktop computer.

We would like to still be living in the figurative age of castles and moats (without the fleas, disease, inadequate sanitation, and dearth of clean water) with restricted ingress, or entry and egress, or exit of persons (in our case, data) via a drawbridge, we are now living in and facing a borderless, open environment where the CIO cannot control who comes and goes from the buildings. The now tetherless mobile devices are able to come and go freely as patients, visitors, doctors, nurses, staff, and even support animals (pets?) move haphazardly around the modern medical facility. Your doctors, nurses, and staff demand the ability to quickly and easily connect their personal device to your network in order to communicate via voice calls; video conference with family, friends, and colleagues; update social media; and even play games during brief interludes of personal relaxation. At the same time, visitors (patients) freely venture into the hospital with implanted devices that seek to connect to your network and provide medical telemetry that can potentially provide the lifesaving information their doctor requires. This is all while a potential bad actor who happens to have relatively free access to public areas of the facility opens up their laptop and emulates an evil twin of your wireless network. Further, this bad actor then encourages unsuspecting employees and visitors to connect to their devices instead of the secure hospital network. The requirement to be open and welcoming and to provide both communication and critical medical services via your wireless network is fraught with risk.

From a risk perspective, it is important to realize that there is a balance that will need to be achieved. The first step is to realize that by being too risk averse, you potentially run the risk of doing too much and potentially negatively impacting medical outcomes or creating grumbling among your staff (neither are desirable, but you definitely do not want to be the cause for an adverse impact to patients). On the flip side, it is important to do enough to protect your personnel and patients from both malicious insiders and outsiders as well as potential environmental impacts.

Leveraging Frameworks to Understand Risk (e.g. ISO 27005, FAIR, ISO 31000, NIST SP 800-37)

It is absolutely critical to engage in a well-considered risk assessment that is both compliant with the requirements of your locality (e.g., HIPAA in the United States and the NHS Data Security and Protection Toolkit in the United Kingdom) and conforms to leading practices as well as to your internal risk management methodology.

When looking at risk, it is important to perform an assessment that makes sense to you and your management team and lends itself to helpful risk-based decision-making. Because risks associated with mobile medicine are potentially more complex than the risks that you have historically addressed, it is worthwhile to take a moment to re-evaluate the risk management methodology that you have been pursuing at your organization. If improvements can be made to make a better, more informed, risk-based decision regarding appropriate controls, including risk avoidance and risk transfer, then take those steps.

While it might seem counterintuitive to delve into a project to re-evaluate your existing risk management methodology, it is worthwhile to explore the leading frameworks to find nuggets of information that might be particularly helpful in understanding the risks of mobile medicine. Take the time now to assess how ISO 27005, FAIR, ISO 31000, or NIST SP 800-37 might be helpful in better understanding your risks. When you last updated your risk management methodology, the risks of mobile computing and mobile medicine may not have been a focus; now these risks are on the front burner and it is possible that you might need to improve or modify how you qualitatively or quantitatively assess risk. The week or even month you spend updating your risk management methodology may result in materially altering how you identify and manage risks for this project.

One area that should be rigorously evaluated is whether it is time to move from or add to a qualitative risk management approach by including or enhancing quantitative risk management. Many organizations have lacked the risk management function maturity to take on a quantitative approach. By complementing existing frameworks by embracing a methodology like FAIR, your organization might realize an enhanced understanding of risk and might better quantify the spending that is appropriate to mitigate the new risks that are being introduced.

Time spent improving or even re-evaluating and making an affirmative decision to retain your existing methodology is time well spent as it will lead to better risk management outcomes by making you more familiar with how you will perform your assessment. By taking this step, the result of your risk assessment will be improved and the decisions you and your organization will be better for it.

Intersection of Governance, Risk, and Compliance with People, Process, and Technology

There is no escaping that healthcare is heavily regulated, and it is essential that the technology organization consider compliance in every action it takes. At the same time, it is also clear that people play a huge role in every decision made within the healthcare arena. These are the two elephants in the room when it comes to any decision made by the organization and it is easy for governance and risk to play second fiddle in the GRC equation while process and technology take a back seat to people. But, it just cannot be that way when considering the impact that mobility introduces into the equation. Success in mobile medicine demands balancing all aspects of Governance, Risk, and Compliance with the People at the center of the equation supported by re-engineered processes required as part of the implementation of new technology.

So, how to deal with this new paradigm? First, look at the technology that you will be facing. Wireless from mobile networks, local wireless networks, and peer-to-peer wireless connectivity and even wired connections need to be considered (mobile wired connections don't only come in on wheels, sometimes they move around on 2 feet). Each solution will require a different approach. Each will require a different level of support and the technologies and techniques for securing them will be different.

Next, understand the business you are in and the business goals and requirements that your stakeholders have for the solution. Security architecture frameworks are built from the perspective of understanding your business requirements and then balancing those requirements with the security solutions that you need to implement and support to mitigate the risks that were found during your risk assessment.

Finally, considering the technology and business goals, look at the people you serve and how they will interact with the technology and how they will be impacted by the security solutions you are putting in place. At this point, you are balancing usability with risk mitigation/security and compliance requirements. The time spent understanding the competing issues and needs is time well spent. The decisions made will significantly impact the program and meeting the unique combination of needs will be critical to your success.

There are two key items to consider at this point as your project takes shape and in preparation for creating the project team—identify the governance team and select the business owner for the project (Table 9.1).

Building a Cross-Functional, Multi-Disciplinary Team for Implementing the Risk Management Program

The strength of your program will depend upon strategic alignment and planning as well as understanding the risks and technology. But, more importantly, will be the people you have on the team working to roll this solution out. Constructing the right team is extremely important.

Table 9.1 Business Owner and Governance

Agree on program/project sponsorship and appoint a program/project board/committee/team with members who have strategic interest in the program, have responsibility for the investment decision making, will be significantly impacted by the program, and will be required to enable delivery of the change	Program/ project governance
Verify that a business owner has been nominated as the designated owner for target data used in the solution, and is responsible for making risk-based decisions and access approvals for the solution	Business owner

Source: Svetcov, Medigram, Inc. (2021).

Table 9.2 Medical Enterprise Requirement Categories

Create project team	Project team
Nominate project manager	
Nominate architect	
Nominate development lead	
Nominate QA/test lead	
Nominate information security lead	
Nominate privacy	
Nominate operational lead	
Nominate business stakeholders [AT1] (e.g. legal, HR, Healthcare Delivery)	

Source: Svetcov, Medigram, Inc. (2021).

And, then keeping the team aligned despite competing interests is going to lend a bit of complexity to this bit of cat herding. The key to this entire process will be keeping the team you build focused on the outcome while avoiding the potential stresses that will naturally occur because of competing interests by the stakeholders. The core team at a minimum should look something like this (Table 9.2).

Include a Diverse Set of Perspectives within the Team

Team selection is extremely important. One of the problems many projects can have is the lack of perspective and diversity of opinion. This can result in a failure of imagination when building a solution to the many problems that you could face while rolling out your mobility program.

When contemplating your team design, do not attempt to staff the team with people just like yourself. You will end up building in confirmation bias from the start as people just like you will generally support and advocate for the same solutions you already are advocating. It is important to surround yourself with very smart people from a variety of backgrounds, educational experiences, and life experiences. This will lock in a team capability that prioritizes a diversity of opinions to evaluate and select from over a single path without an ability for someone to point out the pitfalls of that path in advance to head off avoidable difficulties.

This can be interpreted as requiring a certain number of women and men and a certain number of various racial/ethnic backgrounds, though that is not the intent. What is important is that you have a suitable amount of diversity to ensure that there are team members who can and will speak up and point out a potential lack of perspective. Should you include both men and women? Yes. Should you include people with a variety of backgrounds that can bring an alternate perspective to the table? Yes. Do you include frontline medical personnel, staff, and administrators? Absolutely. The solution needs to meet a diversity of needs and a variety of use cases. It is important to integrate this diversity into your solution and decision-making process as well.

Lastly, is it important to have the technical capability built into the team? Absolutely, this is essential. And, where possible, make sure that you include as much diversity as you can into your technical team too. If your technical team is made up of seven Java engineers with Computer

Science degrees from the same school, a certain amount of flexibility of perspective would be lost. Mix up the team even if you lose some veteran talent, make sure that differing opinions can find their way to the technical team as well.

Compliance, Privacy, Security, Legal, Front Line, Back Office—They All Have a Place at the Table

Role-based diversity is also important for Mobility projects, which will affect all levels of the organization and create new and interesting challenges from a legal, compliance, regulatory, risk, and business perspective. Making sure that some of your more specialized business teams have a seat at the table is essential.

If you think about it, a mobility project will introduce complex legal and privacy issues as people connect to your systems and personal and medical data traverses your wired and wireless network. It is absolutely essential that legal, privacy, and security not only have a seat at the table but actually have a voice during all phases of the project. You cannot wait to include legal, privacy, and security until after a decision is made regarding the solution for this type of Mobility project. Their voice needs to be there from the very beginning before a step down the path becomes a fait accompli and legal, privacy, and security face a Sisyphean task to remake the decision and processes.

Deciding who is part of your project team and who has input into the program is important to consider; however, whether they are a core project team member or a stakeholder, receiving input from individuals across the organization is critical (Table 9.3).

Run It Like a Project—In Accordance with the Organization Project Management Methodology

In order to avoid introducing unnecessary project risk, run your mobility program like every other project in your organization. If your organization follows a formal Project Management methodology built upon PMBOK (Project Management Body of Knowledge), PRINCE2 (Projects IN Controlled Environments), or any other Project Management methodology, it is critical to run this project using your organizational methodology along with integrating the expertise of your Project Management Office (if you have one) into the oversight of the project. If your organization does not have a formally documented Project Management methodology, it is appropriate to take the time to develop one for this project if not for your organization.

As part of running like a project, it is extremely important to make sure that after you have validated the business owner and built the project team and identified stakeholders that requirements

Table 9.3 Stakeholder Input Plan

Identify key stakeholders beyond those individuals involved in program/project sponsorship, the board/committee/team, and business owner	Stakeholder input
Confirm the program/project mandate with sponsors and stakeholders. Articulate the strategic objectives for the program, potential strategies for delivery, improvement, and benefits that are expected to result, and how the program fits with other initiatives	

Source: Svetcov, Medigram, Inc. (2021).

are gathered. Again, it is critical that requirement gathering is comprehensive—please do not just gather technical requirements (Table 9.4).

Once the requirements are gathered, it is important for the project team and stakeholders to validate that the requirements are what is needed to deliver the project, whether the requirements can realistically be delivered, receive stakeholder feedback and then business owner approval of the requirements, and include the security, privacy, and legal stakeholders and project team members to validate the non-functional requirements required to deliver the mobility project (Table 9.5).

Next, it is absolutely necessary to draft your design. Your project team needs to take the time to integrate all of the inputs from previous steps, work with your architecture team and specialized technical personnel, and possibly even have early discussions with possible vendors to determine a likely path forward while drafting the design. This step should not be rushed as some of this work may take a bit of research. When creating the design, it is important to let your diverse team consider a myriad of options for achieving the requirements noted previously and come to a team consensus (or as close to consensus as possible) when creating the design (Table 9.6).

Once the design is confirmed with the Project Team, Stakeholders, and the Business Owner, it is time to evaluate solutions that will satisfy the design requirements. This is where you will

Table 9.4 Requirements Gathering

	Requirements gathered
Gather requirements	
Business requirements	
Security requirements	
Operational requirements	
Compliance requirements	
Technical requirements	
Privacy requirements	
Organizational policy requirements	

Source: Svetcov, Medigram, Inc. (2021).

Table 9.5 Requirements Acceptance Process

	Requirements accepted
Identify, prioritize, specify, agree, and document business functional, technical, and non-functional requirements	
Evaluate how these requirements could be delivered and determine whether organization will build and/or buy a solution	
Have the business owner sign-off on the business functional and technical requirements and the build vs. buy decisions	
Perform information security and compliance review and have information security and compliance participate in creating, reviewing, or approving non-functional requirements	

Source: Svetcov, Medigram, Inc. (2021).

Table 9.6   Project Design

Translate business requirements into a high-level design specification taking into account the organization's technological direction and information architecture	Design drafted
Have the high-level design specifications approved by management to ensure that the high-level design responds to the requirements. Reassess when significant technical or logical discrepancies occur during development or maintenance	
Prepare detailed design incorporating technical and business functional requirements	
Incorporate non-functional requirements (including security requirements) into the detailed design documentation—non-functional requirements will include at the minimum—training requirements, backup requirements, disaster recovery requirements, user access requirements, and requirements for specific security controls	
Have the detailed design approved by the project team and business owner to ensure that they correspond to the reviewed and approved requirements	
Perform reassessment when significant technical or logical discrepancies occur during development or maintenance	
Perform a risk assessment and include the risk treatment plan agreed to and approved by business management and reviewed by the information security team and compliance function	

Source: Svetcov, Medigram, Inc. (2021).

make your build vs. buy decision and will evaluate the variety of potential solutions that you could implement as well as determine how you will be mitigating the risks identified during your risk assessment. It is also important to keep in mind whether you will be putting together multiple solutions (and thus need to integrate solutions together) or whether the solution could be a single solution from a single vendor. Given the complexity surrounding mobile medicine, it is likely that you will be integrating solutions—which is why this is discussed later in the chapter (Table 9.7).

Next, create a project plan along with resourcing for the project. Risks to the project schedule can be significantly mitigated by creating a project plan with resource assignments. It is extremely important to create this level of detail in order to have the appropriate resources assigned when they need to be assigned. It also provides a level of cover by being able to clearly articulate reasons for the project being delayed should resources end up being reassigned because of changing priorities. As with most steps, it is important to communicate the plan to the project team, stakeholders, and the Business Owner for their review, input, and ultimate concurrence with the plan (Table 9.8).

Technical Risk Mitigation Considerations

Thus far, we have been discussing methods to mitigate risk within the project. The next section concerns mitigation of technical risks associated with a mobile medicine program. While reading

Table 9.7   Solution Review

Evaluation of solutions-based upon requirements (this includes build vs. buy decision)	Solution review
Select evaluation process and team	
Create an objective process to evaluate technology solutions— both internally developed and externally procured	
Normalize the findings to determine overall best solution by taking several factors (i.e., features, implementation and ongoing support, cost, etc.) into consideration	
Use a ranking methodology by assigning relative weights to each category before any evaluation takes place	
Evaluation team should have representatives (as appropriate) from IT, Product Management, R&D/Engineering, Operations Engineering, Release Management, Information Security, a Business Representative, Legal, Finance, and others as required	
The evaluation can include presentations, a pilot, a proposal, or a combination of mechanisms to properly score each solution	

Source: Svetcov, Medigram, Inc. (2021).

Table 9.8   Resource Planning

Create a high-level program/project plan with proposed resourcing and timelines to meet the requirements along the timeline requested by the business owner	Baseline plan and resource plan
Confirm funding and resources for the program/project of work	
Convert requirements into actionable user stories	
Update program/project plan to include the identified requirements, user stories, and any resource constraints	
Validate the updated program/project plan meets the timeline required by the business owner	
Identify issues/concerns (risks) that impact completing the program/project plan within the budget, resource, and timeline constraints	
Review updated program/project plan with the business owner (including identified risks)	
Modify program/project plan given business owner feedback	
Receive approval of the updated program/project plan, budget, and resource allocation	
Negotiate with the business owner an appropriate project risk notification and remediation plan for when the project is impacted by unplanned events	

Source: Svetcov, Medigram, Inc. (2021).

through this section, keep in mind the need to balance usability with security, privacy, and compliance. Building a program with onerous security controls will never be successful. Likewise, a program that is quite usable, but completely insecure will result in the organization running into difficulties complying with regulations and preserving patient confidentiality. Achieving balance is a key element of success—usable and secure (or secure enough).

Below we will discuss some of the elements you can adopt or implement (or request that your vendor implements) that will help you mitigate some of your technical risks.

Architecture

Architecture is another area that organizations have frequently developed a formal methodology. If your organization already has a formal methodology for either creating an Enterprise Architecture or Solution Architecture, you should absolutely use that for this project so that you have a common language and common understanding across the organization when discussing the architecture for mobile medicine. If the organization does not have an architecture discipline in place, then it would be useful to adopt an architecture framework or at least adopt some of the principles that underpin good architecture.

TOGAF, Zachman, & SABSA, oh my...

Although there are other enterprise architecture frameworks out there, TOGAF (The Open Group Architecture Framework) and Zachman (Zachman Framework for Enterprise Architecture) are the leading global enterprise architecture frameworks internationally and, along with FEAF (Federal Enterprise Architecture Framework), comprise the leading enterprise architecture frameworks in the United States. Each framework has its own particular orientation. It is worth looking at each of them to see which enterprise architecture framework might work best within your organization. It is very hard to provide a one-size-fits-all recommendation here beyond—the recommendation that you should have one. It should be fairly obvious when you review each of the frameworks what would work best for your organization.

When it comes to security architecture frameworks, only one has gained any sort of global traction, SABSA (Sherwood Applied Business Security Architecture). Although one-size-fits all seldom makes sense (especially in healthcare with the diversity of healthcare environments), this is one case where choice is severely limited. Fortunately, SABSA is quite flexible in its approach. SABSA is about understanding and aligning business requirements and outcomes to Information Security solutions for appropriately managing risk. By understanding business requirements, it is possible to choose and map the right control for the organization to the business requirement. Fundamental to SABSA is the elimination of security controls that do not meet a business requirement.

Build-In vs. Bolt-On—Aligning Business/Operational/Security Requirements

One of the major difficulties associated with information security is including it early in the development of the solution so that security tools, activities, and processes are integrated into the solution from the start. When security is not included early in a project, there is often a last-minute scramble to "bolt-on" security to the implemented solution. The last-minute scramble often results in timeline risk and ruffled feathers as the solution is delayed in order to add security controls after the fact. This typically doesn't just introduce timeline risk, but it frequently results in compromises where information security risks remain in order to reduce the delay that would otherwise be introduced should the security meet the typical risk acceptance threshold for the organization.

The activities outlined in this chapter are designed to avoid this issue by appropriately including a diverse team that includes compliance, legal, security, and privacy functions into the project from the beginning. By also selecting appropriate controls to mitigate risk, it is possible to avoid both the timeline risk and risks associated with making last-minute compromises.

Baking security, privacy, and compliance into the project plan builds in risk mitigation—staff, the solution, training, and budget are appropriately designed in and communicated to all stakeholders. Everyone is on the same page. Functional and non-functional requirements are considered. Personnel (all personnel) are included in the project plan. An appropriate timeline has been created that includes both the functional and non-functional obligations. And, even testing (functional and security testing) is included. Doing this right allows the project team and the business owner of the project to properly communicate the timeline and budget without the risk of having a last-minute security crisis just as the project is about to rollout.

Network Security Controls

Meaningful network security controls are the table stakes of security solutions for mobile medicine. If your organization has not implemented the standard set of network security controls, it is hard to imagine that doing well everywhere else would pay off as effectively as the organization might want it to. If you have had required projects for network security in prior years just not make it above the line to actually get funded, it is probably a good idea to take the time to complete your network security projects and then move forward on rolling out your mobile medicine solution. Trying to complete several network security projects as well as rolling out mobile medicine and additional projects required to make mobile medicine work might not work. This is more about completing the work in the right order to be successful, folding your remaining network security projects into the mobile medicine project—this might extend the project timeline, but building your mobile medicine solution upon a strong foundation is critical to success.

Control across the Network

What do you need to do in order to bring networking under control and have your organization ready to move forward on a mobile medicine project? The first thing is to gain control of your network. These are the types of solutions that you will want to investigate in order to gain control of your network:

1. **Device discovery**: If you have no idea what is on your network, then you will have a tough time applying controls and determining what to do with the device. You absolutely need to know what is on your network today and what is appearing on your network—a tool that provides this level of intelligence will help you gain control of your network.
2. **Network Access Control (NAC)**: Device discovery plays a part in Network Access Control as you need to be able to see what is appearing on your network in order to make decisions regarding what to do with the device. NAC is the ability to control what happens to the device while it is on your network or when it appears on your network.
3. **Posture checking**: The device has appeared and is permitted to be on your network, now it is time to figure out if it is properly patched, has the right security tools enabled, and thus

whether it really belongs. This really is the only way for an untrusted endpoint to gain trust and be allowed to connect with the most sensitive systems and data on your network. Failing a posture check can result in a device being rejected and disconnected or moved to a remediation network so that appropriate remediation steps can be completed and the device can be re-checked and potentially approved.

4. **Network firewall and internet gateway**: This solution can be dynamic based upon the type of endpoint (as determined using NAC) or could be static (anything on this network, these are the firewall rules). Whichever way it is implemented, the Network Firewall is designed to appropriately segregate networks and devices and to allow or disallow traffic based upon pre-configured rules. If there is no business reason for your endpoint to connect to the network containing the database servers, the network firewall will reject all connection attempts from your device to those database servers. If your device is attempting to initiate an outbound connection to an Internet location that is not allowed by the organization, the Internet Gateway will reject that connection.

5. **Network traffic analysis and insider threat protection solutions**: Once your device is on the network, it needs to be continually monitored to determine whether it is behaving the way it should. If it is not behaving in an appropriate way, that inappropriate behavior needs to be flagged for human review or generate an automated response to mitigate the risk.

There are standalone solutions that operate in just one of these five areas and other solutions that encompass all or nearly all of these areas. Integration can be quite useful. If you have not already purchased point solutions for one or more of these control areas, it might be useful to investigate integrated tools (platforms) that integrate several of these items together.

Managing Trusted and Untrusted Endpoints

Trusted endpoints, especially those that you control directly where you control the operating system, user management, applications, and even users/user management, are much easier to manage when it comes to mobile medicine. After all, you know what the endpoint should look like and if it doesn't completely conform to your requirements, you will know immediately and are able to take prompt corrective action steps. For the trusted endpoint, it is absolutely critical to know what the device should look like and validate that it is still in a trusted state. Controls noted earlier in this chapter such as posture checking are critical in helping you determine whether the trusted endpoint is still trustworthy. When rolling out your mobile medicine program it is critically important for you to be able to rely upon your ability to determine whether a trusted endpoint is still trustworthy. Your program will definitely need to address how to provide assurance that trusted endpoints should still be considered trusted.

The problem is the untrusted endpoints. How do you gain visibility of the untrusted device? How do you know what the device is supposed to run and whether it is behaving properly or not? And, can you even believe what the device is telling you or is it attempting to gain access to your environment for malicious or potentially malicious reasons?

Your organization must presume that every single person entering your buildings with at least one mobile device is likely to want to connect to your network. The vast majority of these devices will be untrusted devices (many of them will be mobile phones) that just want to have access to your network in order to in-turn connect to the public Internet. It is likely that your organization will have (or will have soon) a guest wireless network specifically for this type of untrusted device. The more problematic situation is when someone with an implanted or wearable medical device, for instance a glucose monitor, wants to connect and provide information about the patient's health status. Clearly, your organization would like to trust the device and interact with it in order to gather information that would be useful in assisting a physician in making a diagnosis.

Determining how to interact with an untrusted device safely, securely, and how to prioritize the network traffic to/from the device is an extremely important part of this project. Spending time understanding what untrusted devices you will need to interact with and determining a mechanism to do so is extremely important as your organization runs your project. It will undoubtedly be one of the key requirements for your organization's mobile medicine project. Please be aware that it may not be possible to turn an untrusted device into a trusted device. Your solution may need to take into account that the device may never be fully trusted; however, at the same time, your organization will still need to figure out how to deal with the information being provided by the device and determine how to interact without creating unnecessary risk. Integrated platforms that help manage Internet of Things devices may be an answer that can help you bridge the gap between a completely untrusted device and one that can be relied upon at least in part.

Network Vulnerability Assessments/Penetration Testing

Earlier in this section, we discussed posture checking. Part of posture checking will be a network vulnerability assessment of the endpoint. It is important to understand what is and isn't on your network and whether any of your devices present a potential avenue for attack by a malicious threat actor. Regular network vulnerability assessments across your entire network can be helpful in determining whether your endpoints are appropriately secured. This can be performed using automated tools and can be scheduled to run on a regular schedule and alert upon detection of a weakness. This should be considered just good basic mobile security hygiene for your network.

The second part, penetration testing, takes this a step further and should be accomplished also on a regular basis—at least annually. A penetration test is an important process where the controls that are in place are aggressively and systematically tested using both automated tools as well as highly experienced professionals manually attempting to find and exploit weaknesses. The purpose of the penetration test is to identify weaknesses before a similarly highly skilled individual or team attempts to exploit the weakness for malicious reasons. Penetration testing can be performed by an internal team or by a third party. Whichever you choose, the important thing is for the team to be highly skilled at performing penetration testing and especially penetration testing of medical/hospital environments leveraging techniques that both a non-state and nation-state actor might use. Unless you are a very large organization with the need to have a highly skilled internal penetration testing team, it is far more likely that this will be an outsourced endeavor.

When you roll out your mobile medicine program, it is extremely important to implement a regime of regular automated vulnerability assessments (with frequency based upon an internal risk assessment) as well as aggressive penetration testing by a highly skilled team. The combination of automated and manual testing will help your organization validate the success of the security solutions that have been implemented to protect the mobile medicine implementation.

Application Security Controls

It is extremely important to understand how the applications running on mobile devices are to be built and protected. Many people look at a physical healthcare device and just see the device. But it isn't the physical device that will likely be compromised; it is the application running on the

Table 9.9 Develop and Validate User Stories

Organize identified resources into teams to work on the user stories	User stories
Software development occurs in accordance with the formal organization-defined software development process validated against the OWASP ASVS or similar application security framework	
User stories requiring purchase/acquisition of technical solutions follow organizational policies and procedures for technology acquisition	
Non-functional user stories are developed in parallel with the functional user stories with non-functional and functional requirements considered in completing all user stories	

Source: Svetcov, Medigram, Inc. (2021).

device that is most susceptible, and this is an area that can be quite invisible to the organization unless there is an affirmative decision to reduce the risk of insecure applications.

When considering application security, it is important to make sure that the user stories include both functional and non-functional requirements (Table 9.9).

Once the user stories have been created, it is time to perform development. It is important to make sure your development (or the developers of the solution you are acquiring) is performing in accordance with a standard and rigorous process (Table 9.10).

With the methodology in place and the organization committed to operating in accordance with the methodology, it is important to include the following specifics.

Integrating Security into Every Application

There is a step in every project where your organization will need to make a build vs. buy decision. This is the case when it comes to the mobile devices themselves; however, it is very likely that in-house developed solutions will be more the exception than the norm—building the next wearable or implantable device is more likely from a medical device manufacturer than a hospital or hospital network. However, that doesn't mean you cannot hold device manufacturers to a high standard. The device manufacturers want you to implant or provide their device to your patients, this is your opportunity to encourage or even require the device manufacturers to do the right thing.

We all know that software developers are not getting in-depth secure coding technique courses in universities; however, that doesn't mean you cannot require your device vendors to send their developers through a course in secure coding. Additionally, even though your organization isn't doing the majority of development, that doesn't mean you cannot encourage or even require the manufacturers to adhere to secure coding standards such as the OWASP Application Security Verification Standard (ASVS) or Building Security In Maturity Model (BSIMM). Requesting the results of a third-party assessment (audit) of the manufacturer's secure coding program aligned to these frameworks can provide a reasonable amount of information regarding the maturity of the application security program and if the organization hasn't been using one of these frameworks, the implementation of the framework's leading practices will result in positive future risk mitigation.

What is good for your vendors is also good for your development teams as well. Review both BSIMM and ASVS to determine which framework could add value and risk mitigation to your

Table 9.10 Development and Testing Plan

Development is organized in accordance with the identified development methodology	Development
User stories are reviewed and selected for the current development phase	
User stories are assigned to development personnel in a way that is likely to result in completion of the intended work within the timeline of the current development phase	
Developers are assigned appropriate development and quality assurance resources (including infrastructure) to perform development work and developer quality assurance tasks	
Developers perform development tasks in order to complete their assigned work	
Developers check-in code into the appropriate code repository in accordance with organizational development methodology	
Developers perform quality assurance activities and re-work around their assigned work	
Developers perform additional reviews (such as peer code review and peer code testing) in accordance with organizational development methodology	
Independent Quality Assurance (QA) personnel perform QA testing in accordance with the organizational development and testing methodologies (to include unit and integration testing where appropriate) with resources assigned (including infrastructure and automation tools where required) necessary to perform an appropriate level of quality assurance	
Test plans shall include full evaluation of all approved user stories and documented confirmation that all user stories are functionally complete	
Product defects found during independent QA activities are inserted into a "Bug" tracking system and prioritized for re-work	

Source: Svetcov, Medigram, Inc. (2021).

internal development efforts as well. It is useful internally to develop in accordance with a defined methodology as well.

Application Vulnerability Assessments

As with network vulnerability assessments, it is important to also identify weaknesses with the application using specialized tools designed to identify weaknesses that are present in the code (static code assessments) as well as in the running application (dynamic application assessments). Good-quality assurance often does not assess the non-functional requirements as well as your organization might hope. Tools can often fill the gap between functional testing and inexperienced non-functional testing by automating application assessments to identify weaknesses. It is even possible to leverage this type of automated vulnerability testing to find issues prior to QA testing as it is possible to integrate static code assessment into the developer's Integrated Development Environment (IDE). This can save both time and QA resources while reducing defects that need to be remediated later in the development process.

Regular application vulnerability assessments can be performed by a Security QA team or specialized Application Security team within Information Security. There are no one-size-fits-all in creating the function that manages this task, and it really is specific to the organization. The most important thing is that this is included in your process and is performed by a person/team who understands how to operate the tooling and provide input and recommendations to the development team to aid in remediation.

Third-Party Application Penetration Testing

Automated vulnerability assessments definitely have their place, but even now it takes an experienced human to find the more difficult issues within the application. Investing in excellent third-party application penetration testing will pay dividends in avoiding exploits that would otherwise be present and remain undetected by standard vulnerability assessment tools. If acquiring solutions from vendors, this type of testing can be relied upon to demonstrate that the organization has spent the time and effort to secure their application. A review of the methodology and the findings is important to validate that the testing was comprehensive. An important consideration for mitigating risk over time is to rotate through vendors that provide this type of testing as each vendor uses tooling and methodologies that may expose weaknesses that another vendor might miss. As noted elsewhere, diversity of perspectives can be quite useful in mitigating risk.

System-Level Controls

All software runs on systems of some sort. Servers, desktops, mainframes, mobile devices, wearables, implantables, etc. These are all systems running some sort of operating system (iOS, Android, Linux, Windows, etc.). What's important is that we understand the systems and properly configure, manage, and maintain them to prevent (as much as possible) misuse of the system.

Appropriate configuration of the system is important for minimizing the opportunity for potential misuse or exploitation by internal or external bad actors.

Operating System Hardening

Each system that you deploy should have a documented checklist of activities and configuration that need to be set up prior to approval of the change management ticket or another approval process that places the device into production. Start with recommendations from the manufacturer or developer and then add in additional hardening that is appropriate for your environment. No system that you place into production on your network will be ready using just a default install. Even steps like changing the administrative password will be in your system hardening guide—and this and many other hardening steps need to occur prior to any system placed into use. CIS benchmarks can be a good place to start for hardening recommendations of commonly used solutions if you are unhappy with the recommendations from the manufacturer or developer (https://www.cisecurity.org/cis-benchmarks/).

System Security Controls

Removal of administrative rights, implementation of anti-malware solutions, Data Loss Protection, DLP, patch management, asset management software, remote management solutions, host-based firewall, host intrusion detection,…, and the list goes on. These are examples of system security controls that can and should be implemented on each system. Protecting the devices that a mobile medicine product might interact with is going to reduce the likelihood of adverse outcomes.

Spending time to make sure your systems are as secure as they can be using standard system controls is an efficient, low-cost way to improve positive results in your program. The work done here will result in both money and time being saved in your program and will even pay off outside of your mobile medicine project. A recurring theme in this chapter is to look at the use of controls holistically and to consider your overall security approach. Spending time improving system-level controls will reduce overall risk.

Vulnerability Management

Earlier in this chapter, we discussed network vulnerability assessments. These assessments directly feed into your vulnerability management program and are used to validate that appropriate patching is occurring across your environment and that vulnerabilities are being handled. Robust vulnerability management and remediation eliminates many known vulnerabilities that could potentially be exploited by various threats facing your environment. You may not be able to manage an unknown vulnerability effectively, but by eliminating the known vulnerabilities, you are able to improve your security posture and reduce the likelihood of being exploited. This might be a bit of the case of no longer being the low-hanging fruit and bad actors then looking for easier targets—if that's the case, that should be considered a win for you and your team.

Managing Insider Threats

Insiders are difficult to protect against as they are considered trusted personnel and already have access (potentially a lot of access) to your environment; however, they do need to be considered as potential threat actors either because they directly have an interest in exploiting your environment or because they are an easier vector for malicious ingress into your environment and become an unwitting participant in someone else's attempt to exploit your environment and the information, systems, and services you are responsible for.

Having a well-thought-out program to manage the insider threat typically starts with training. Your training program will help your insiders avoid being the unwitting stooge in someone's malicious attempt to compromise you. The Return on Investment is usually quite good for training as it measurably reduces incidents caused by your employees. It doesn't solve the problem of the actual malicious insider, but it certainly should reduce insider exploitation. Including a strong program to segregate duties and provision users with the least privilege to perform their job will additionally reduce the impact of an insider being exploited as the quantity of information will be limited to only what they need to know in order to accomplish their daily tasks.

Manage the Environment: Monitor for Normal Activity/Alert on Abnormal Activity

As noted above, insiders have access and are entitled as part of their job to frequently access, manage, and work with sensitive data. This will also be the case when rolling out a mobile medicine program. There will be individuals with significant access. And, this access can lead to potential improper use. As part of the mobile medicine program, it is important for organizations to evaluate their insider monitoring program and enhance it if the program is already in place or build a program if it is not.

Monitoring for insider inappropriate activity rests primarily upon implementing technology solutions to monitor the entire environment, profile typical baseline behavior, and alert when behavior deviates from historical normal behavior. What might this look like? It could be an alert because the user is touching new systems or new data. It could be alerting because the user is working with larger data sets than normal. It could also be that the user is taking the data and manipulating it in a new way—potentially packaging the solution for egress from the environment.

If your organization's insider threat management program is immature, it can be important to enhance it before you begin stressing the existing monitoring solutions with additional mobile medicine data and devices. During the project planning phase, it can be appropriate to integrate this related project for completion prior to rolling out mobile medicine.

Visitors and Their Devices Can Become Insiders from a Threat Management Perspective

By virtue of how patient wearable and implantable devices as well as typical mobile phones might join your network, these invited and authorized devices can become insiders as well—especially if they are accepted onto an internal network and not just the guest wireless network. When evaluating the insider threat management program, it is important to consider these types of Insiders as well.

Assessment/Audit: Including Continuous Audit

As part of the initial phases of your mobile medicine project, it is essential to think about how you will be monitoring the solution once it is implemented. Technology and processes that will be used to provide oversight into the performance of the program need to be designed into the program from the start. If your organization needs to purchase specialized solutions for monitoring the environment or needs to begin socializing new procedures, these activities take time, effort, and available budget.

The question that needs to be asked regarding each tool you implement and each process you create when building your mobile medicine solution is this: How is our organization going to know that the solution is operating properly? The answer will lead you to the monitoring and measurement solution(s) that you will need to implement.

Continuous Feedback for Security Operations Center (SOC)

Your Security Operations Center needs to be able to react when an adverse event occurs. The monitoring solution that is chosen needs to provide this feedback to the SOC so that they can quickly and efficiently determine if there is an issue and then tools for quickly investigating and arriving at an appropriate remediation solution must be in place so that the issues can be quickly resolved.

It is important to find a solution for monitoring your particular environment, a SIEM or specialized IoT management platform, that can also send alerts and integrate with your ticketing system to automatically create tickets and attach the appropriate information. This will drive improvements to the productivity of your staff and will allow them to spend more of their time adding value as they will be able to quickly resolve an issues they face. Whatever solution is chosen, it needs to be appropriate for your particular environment. When it comes to monitoring, there is no one-size-fits-all solution. Take your time to find the solution that is most appropriate for your organization.

Internal and Third-Party Assessment for Continuous Improvement

As previously mentioned regarding assessments, it is a critical component of a mobile medicine program. Rigorous testing will expose issues in your program and will allow for a feedback loop for future improvements. The reality that most information security professionals understand is that the playing field is continuously changing. Threat actors are becoming more sophisticated and new ways to compromise systems are found every day. If your organization is not assessing your solution on a regular basis, it will be compromised eventually. Yes, even with testing, there is no sure thing; however, there is a reason why most frameworks advocate regular testing—and that is because it works to expose weaknesses and reduce risk.

There is little point in spending hundreds of thousands or millions of dollars on a program for mitigating risk and then not spending a fraction of that to validate that your solution is properly configured and is meeting the goals you originally set.

The question about relying upon internal assessment teams or external (third-party) teams is one of expertise. The internal assessors will know your environment better than an external team; however, the external team will be more experienced compromising environments like yours since that is all they do. Combining the two, internal and third-party assessment, should result in the most comprehensive coverage and drive down the risk to the greatest extent possible. Many organizations will perform internal assessments driven by automated tools on a monthly basis or when significant changes occur and then follow-up with semi-annual or annual third-party assessments that are deeper and more comprehensive. Your assessment regime should be based upon what you are finding during your assessments—run more frequently if you are continuing to find significant defects during each test and run less frequently if you have few or no major defects during each test—frequency and depth of testing should be a risk-based decision.

Integration of Solutions

As mentioned earlier in the chapter, it is extremely unlikely that your organization will find a single product that is able to do everything that is needed to mitigate the new risks that your mobile medicine program will introduce. Sure, there are IoT security platforms that might be useful for your organization and might provide significant coverage; however, there will be pieces—possibly quite significant pieces that are not included. Integration of solutioning needs to be considered from the very start of the project. How will the pieces work together? How will the pieces talk to each other or feed into a centralized repository of information if that is required? How will new solutions interoperate with existing solutions already in place? All of these questions are important and need to be considered from the very start and then as decisions are made, integration needs to be validated. This needs to be well considered from the beginning and integration testing needs to occur as each solution is tested to determine if it will be added to this program of work.

The Whole Is Greater than the Sum of Its Parts Approach: Integration Where Each Piece Adds Value without Creating Controls Operating at Cross Purposes

Integration adds value to a tool. A standalone tool can be useful; however, that same standalone tool properly integrated into your existing toolset will be even more useful. As an example, think of a SIEM (Security Incident and Event Management Tool) that ingests logs, correlates, and alerts. That is quite useful, but it can be even more useful merely by integrating it with a ticketing system. So, instead of just sending an email and hoping someone works on the issues, the SIEM opens a ticket that can now be assigned, tracked/managed, escalated, and confirmed as completed. This will improve the results of the single alert by making sure that it doesn't fall through the cracks. This is where one plus one truly does equal three.

Validate the Solution Post Implementation

Integration testing is hugely important both prior to implementation as well as after the solution has been implemented and operating in your organization's environment. Frequently, the integration testing at implementation is missing important operational context. Taking the time to perform testing after implementation will provide value to either confirm that everything is operating as it should or to point out areas for improvement. You will either gain peace of mind that all is working as it should or have an opportunity to fix issues that truly need to be fixed that you would otherwise potentially not know about.

Finding previously unknown incompatibilities, insufficient shielding of radio signals (interference or bleed to inappropriate locations), inadequate monitoring, or any other previously unforeseen impact prior to putting the solution in production will save you from a potential disaster late in a project. At the end of the project is when it is most critical to identify previously unidentified issues. The organization has invested a tremendous amount of time and effort into a project that is almost at the finish line. You are likely to be getting pressure to go live, make sure your testing is not rushed in the go/no go decision.

Continuous Improvement Approach Drives Iteration Where Necessary to Build Additional Functionality Necessary to Close Gaps

As with much security, there is no opportunity to rest on your laurels. All security frameworks approach security with a lifecycle approach. You plan your security solution, you implement your solution, you validate/assess the solution, and then you take what you learned and improve the solution. Technology changes rapidly, and it is extremely important to continuously evaluate your solutions to ultimately improve patient care. Once you have implemented the updated solution, you start the cycle again. By monitoring and assessing your solution and keeping an eye out for how bad actors are discovering new ways to compromise your environment, you will continuously improve your solution over time with the goal to stay a step ahead of the bad actors.

Metrics

Measuring the activities associated with a mobile medicine program and ongoing operation of the solution once implemented will be important. The question is, what to measure? During the project, it will be essential to track progress against the project plan. After implementation, it will depend at least in part on the implementation; however, there does seem to be a few metrics that you will want to track such as the number of devices on the network (track this over time) by type/category (e.g., guest wireless devices, wearables and implantables, hospital owned/individually owned), incidents, situations requiring human intervention, identified vulnerabilities, operating system, OS version, application version, guest wireless utilization, requests for access to internal networks, and first-time devices. This list isn't exhaustive. There are other metrics that could be tracked based upon technologies that you implement and those that appear in your environment. As your organization makes decisions, metrics should be evaluated for tracking.

What Does Success Look Like?

This is clearly a situation where one size absolutely will not fit all. Each environment is different—solutions are different, mix of devices is different. Clearly, a downward track on vulnerabilities is important. Likewise, manual intervention should be tracked and solutions to reduce that should be identified. Success ultimately will be a downward trend (to some consistent baseline) on metrics that create pain for the organization and an upward trend in areas that are positive for the organization.

What Does the Organization and Board Need to Know—Create Metrics to Track

Most boards want to be aware of problems and how issues are being managed downward. Communicating this to a board shows progress against risk reduction. The board will want to know about the project and project success. Track budget to actuals for the project, track timeline progress, and articulate timeline risk. If your board has not had a chance to review the NACD Cyber-Risk Oversight documentation (the latest version, which is revised every few years), it might be a good place to start a conversation with them to identify areas that they might be interested in understanding—and then build metrics that would help the board make their risk-based decisions.

Conclusion—Managing Risk Never Ends—Consider This Chapter to Be a Continuously Looping Iterative Function—Always Improving, Never Complacent

If it wasn't clear before, it should be clear now that a mobile medicine program will create a significant impact on your organization. But, there is a path that requires planning and perseverance, a multidisciplinary team, diversity of thought and opinion, technical capability, and organizational commitment that will result in success. The reward at the far end is a world-class mobile medicine program that saves lives, improves clinician work experience, reduces adverse medical outcomes that impact quality of life, and drives down cost by efficiently managing the solutions and people under your care.

In short, this program will require intense planning, excellent team building, cat-herding of stakeholders, targeted ongoing assessments, and perseverance. It will be a challenge to be successful; however, by doing it right, you and your organization will have something positive to point to for all of the hard work.

Now is the time to sit down with your team, outline the steps you need to take in order to create the future vision for mobile medicine in your organization, and then leverage this chapter and the book you are holding to move forward into the future. The sooner you begin, the sooner you will be able to take advantage of the promise of mobile medicine in saving lives and returning to health the patients that have placed their well-being in your hands.

Chapter 10

Recognizing Cybersecurity Threats in Healthcare Settings for Effective Risk Management

Allison J. Taylor
Thought Marketing LLC

Contents

The fields of medicine and cybersecurity share a need for voracious learning, continual data-driven vigilance, and passionate creativity across diverse talents in order to protect lives, whether from disease or digital threats. For mobile communications in healthcare, cybersecurity risks remain a critical consideration. By surveying and recognizing categories of threats, healthcare leaders can better organize and steward risk management to responsibly limit the severity and impact of cybersecurity incidents.

Two fundamental truths are helpful for healthcare leaders to recognize:

1. The volume and likelihood of threats have increased.

    The World Economic Forum ranks a cybersecurity failure as a "clear and present danger" in the next 2 years as of 2020 and has previously ranked cybersecurity in its top five global risks (World Economic Forum, 2020). Those of us active in the field point to several conditions of great concern that are leading to this reality:

    - Advanced hacking tools used by elite actors (known as Shadow Brokers) were released into the public domain in recent years (Schneier, 2017), increasing the abilities of a far broader and larger set of threat actors to infiltrate networks and penetrate devices for data theft, disruption of services, or financial blackmailing.

DOI: 10.4324/9781003220473-14

- Polarizing political environments have further catalyzed existing government-sponsored hacking campaigns, allowing hackers to trial techniques without legal repercussions. While threats in the past may have been solo actors trialing their technical skills, today's threats can include highly motivated and well-funded nation-state and organized crime activities designed to debilitate operations and critical infrastructure.
- Digital transformation and accompanying digital technologies have reached nearly every industry, including those formerly closed off from Internet access. Incented to increase speed and efficiency, many consumer-style technologies have failed to prioritize security, creating many vulnerabilities that increase the attack surface, from hackable devices to unpatched systems all too simple to penetrate to siphon content away.

2. Threats specific to healthcare have increased.

Advisories from threat-tracking organizations point distinctly to the healthcare sector as a target (FireEye, 2021). This has already translated into active threat actor campaigns, as evidenced by recent attacks disrupting healthcare services and accessing confidential data (these are noted in their respective threat category further below, as well as the Bibliography). As COVID-19 reached the US and healthcare institutions became an epicenter, industry publications documented a significant increase in the number of breached records in the healthcare sector, estimating a 273% increase over the same period in 2019 (Jercich, 2020).

Risks vs. Rewards

The many benefits that new technologies can yield must always be weighed against the risks, further pointing to the criticality of establishing a defined, governed security program and risk management specific to your mobile communications initiatives.

Beyond these two basic truths, further understanding some categories of threats and their anatomy can offer healthcare leaders essential grounding, just as fundamental knowledge specific to a medical field is a prerequisite for more specialized care. It will be necessary to then engage with cybersecurity and technology experts who are deeply involved in monitoring and acting quickly on any new security incidents or threat trends.

Threat Categories

Threats to mobile communications can emerge from digital, physical, or socially engineered vectors. While the individual approaches and any combination of approaches will constantly change, there are some common categories of attacks:

Ransomware: Hackers use injected malware, Trojans, or other means to access company systems and lock down data, encrypting it and rendering it unusable. Hackers then extort money from the organization to unlock the data, threatening to destroy it if the ransom is not paid. More advanced ransomware attacks exfiltrate the data before encrypting it, threatening to release it in public if no ransom is paid.

Most concerning in healthcare settings is the disruption of services from these cybersecurity incidents, including delayed treatment. In a case in Germany, a critically ill patient was relocated to another facility 20 miles away when ransomware shut down the primary clinic's systems, costing the patient's life (Miliard, 2020).

As healthcare leaders work with any technology provider, it is important to ask how they back-up and store systems data and applications. Those with advanced security knowledge will build in safeguards and redundancies (physical and digital) to limit the extent of damage that ransomware can inflict. Proper implementation by qualified professionals can also provide disaster recovery and back-up system processes that help you resume services more quickly. Keeping systems up and running means keeping your mobile communications intact.

For research-centric healthcare organizations, targeted either for ransomware, data theft, or other malicious acts, recent security advisories suggest fully isolating systems used for working on or with that research or data. This eliminates Internet access through which attackers either send phishing emails with links to malware, risky websites that stealthily download malicious scripts in the background, and other activities that increase ransomware likelihood.

Social engineering: Your employees can be a weak link in your mobile security since they know the ins and outs of your organization, especially the finer details about how processes work. Hackers may send phishing emails to extract pre-attack data such as mobile phone OS types, geolocation data, email naming structures, and Wi-Fi network types. In social engineering attacks, hackers may pretend to be patients or customers asking questions through email, in order to gain further organizational information or complete a task on an internal system (Healthcare Business & Technology, 2020). Advanced attackers may leverage natural language processing (NLP) technologies to trick your personnel into turning Wi-Fi systems off or otherwise configuring them to be useless. NLP is used by the good guys and the bad guys. It understands patterns a person uses in digital media, and for hackers, enables malicious actors to impersonate others – a boss, a colleague, for example – provoking the trusting employee to take an action.

Training your employees with baseline cybersecurity knowledge, together with ongoing updates, can make them aware of how their behavior introduces risk to the overall organization. As you consider mobile rollouts, ensure your provider supports risk assessments and other checks and balances that can uncover weak links before they are exploited. Expert mobile communications teams can also build in layers of defenses with processes and human verification to further protect critical information and workflows. Hiring practices can also be updated to screen for tech-savvy, cyber-aware personnel.

Denial of service: Hackers may flood computer networks with traffic to overwhelm systems and cause all dependent services to crash. Hackers may also exploit vulnerabilities such as default passwords on Wi-Fi networks to access administrative rights and deny services. In the case of a children's hospital, a well-known hacker group intentionally disrupted Internet service, causing a week-long outage and $300,000 in remediation costs (Center for Internet Security, 2021)

As healthcare leaders work with technology providers for mobile communications, it is essential providers are fluent in mobile networks specifically and have designed security considerations with those networks in mind. Ideally, they are also familiar with current mobile device trends that could contribute to inter-related outages. Particularly as the number of device types changes and the apps and services on them are updated daily, having teams with expert mobile knowledge can significantly impact and help reduce your level of risk.

Compromised medical devices: As human-machine integration continues, the reliance on devices such as glucose monitors and pacemakers becomes a matter of life and death. Attackers continually battle-test medical devices to find vulnerabilities they can exploit, and communities of hackers focus exclusively on these device types. This is different than just hacking a network and its services, and requires physical-digital skills as well as healthcare institution knowledge. In addition, as the product development trend of merging mechanical and digital continues, the threat likelihood increases that digital interfaces will be exploited to impact physical functionality (or vice versa). Chips with Bluetooth Low Energy may be susceptible to exploitation, according to recent FDA updates, and papers from the annual hacker conference Black Hat readily explain insulin pump exploitation (Radcliffe, 2011).

Wi-Fi-connected devices deliver convenience and mobility, and thus require associated security to reduce risk. Consider what device types are on your network and how seriously that device maker takes security. Some leaders choose to standardize on trusted medical suppliers with diligent security practices, while others prefer using heterogeneous devices to diversify the risk of compromise.

A reputable healthcare technology partner will also cross-check systems and networks that can impact devices to ensure vulnerabilities such as default device passwords are more difficult to reach and exploit. Experts in cybersecurity monitor alerts and updates on newly discovered vulnerabilities and can patch or update your devices to limit threat impact.

Mobile application exploitation: Similar to device exploitation, these attacks leverage vulnerabilities in software or connected software components to access other device resources. A majority of FDA-approved medical apps tested by a third party only 4 years ago did not even adequately meet OWASP top risks (Siwicki, 2016).

Trusted suppliers with a mission to deliver secure software will ensure you have correct patches, updates, and hotfixes as part of your service and may offer further hardening recommendations. Keeping software updated and passwords frequently changed is common hygiene to limit vulnerability exploits and further related malicious behavior.

Malicious users: Guests bringing their mobile phones inside your healthcare organization's physical borders can digitally, then laterally move from that guest network to your vital networks. Malicious user attacks can be driven by motivated nation-state actors, competitors, disgruntled patients or their family members, or unstable employees. Just as medical practitioners are trained to spot domestic abuse as a patient presents for other purposes, understanding common activities of malicious mobile users can improve how well your organization manages this risk (e.g., alerting staff, changing processes, integrating data/systems for detection). Example malicious user activities:

■ Beyond a guest walking into your facility, hackers parked near your wireless network perimeter can find WiFi coverage areas that are "bleeding" beyond your facility's physical walls and use them to attempt penetration. Physical security measures such as gating access to parking lots and tracking vehicles can aid in reducing this risk, together with layering in digital defenses.

■ Data theft is a much more well-known activity performed by malicious users. Data can also be sent to third-party systems or diverted for further exploitation. Medical insurance fraud and obtaining medical services through false identity are two drivers creating a "market" for stolen patient health information. Credential harvesting is not necessarily data theft by the same definition, but it is another lucrative approach for criminals who can sell or leverage these digital "keys" to perform more advanced attacks. Ensuring multiple layers of defense and encouraging cross-team communications and integrated processes, together with incentives to call out suspicious activity, may lower risk.

■ While mobile phones do not typically have a USB slot, they do use USB battery chargers. A growing area of concern is either malicious charging cables intentionally shipped with vulnerabilities (e.g., from nation-state actors) or mobile phone charging cables plugged into enterprise networks to initiate a variety of malicious activities. These can include exfiltrating data, shutting down a system, or quietly changing application or administrator settings just by installing a specific type of loaded USB charging cable that appears benign. Segmenting your network, standardizing on device platforms and other techniques can be introduced to manage these risks.

Technology partners who monitor threat trends will perform mobile implementations to the most current best practices and may offer support services for further security monitoring. It is essential to remember that attack types change constantly. Staying connected to specialists can provide the advantage of early warning and mitigation.

Crypto mining: Like any computing resource, healthcare institutions represent a metaphorical gold mine to hackers seeking ways to mine cryptocurrency by using someone else's computing power. Drains on servers can impact mobile operations. Resource exploitation hacks like crypto mining can be stealth and can require specific monitoring to uncover, most notably looking for performance changes on either the devices or the services delivering to that mobile device (Shaw, 2019). While not typically intended to steal data (mining focuses on electricity and compute power), such inappropriate mining can trigger regulatory security notifications \. In one case, crypto mining software was discovered on an EHR server at a health institution, requiring notification to 20,000 individuals that their PHI had been exposed.

Mobile initiatives may not be directly impacted by these various types of threats but may experience indirect operational consequences. Reputable mobile healthcare specialists are aware of such integrated security risks and can provide recommendations and ongoing guidance. As you design and deploy important mobile communications, you can equally support the most important healthcare goal of doing no harm.

Staying Current through Access to Talent and Ecosystems

While this chapter highlights current threats, it will be obsolete the moment a new creative hacker is motivated to do harm, whether for personal gain or on behalf of a well-funded sponsor. Healthcare leaders will want cybersecurity subject matter experts who are deeply familiar with the sector, and who regularly monitor advisories and alerts from government institutions. In the US, these are entities include the Cybersecurity and Infrastructure Security Agency (CISA), the Federal Bureau of Investigation (FBI), and the US Department of Health & Human Services, as well as security sector information sharing groups and threat feeds.

To stay current and lead with data and knowledge, healthcare leaders can stay tapped into healthcare cybersecurity circles as well as establish security leads throughout their mobile initiatives. Security leads can pay attention to not only technology risks, but issues introduced by people or processes.

At the board level, experts in cybersecurity and operational cybersecurity leaders can offer perspectives as well as links to field specialists and knowledge circles. Consider Qualified Technology Expert (QTE) certified leaders (Zukis, 2020), who have been trained in digital and cybersecurity risk oversight (Digital Directors Network).

More broadly in your talent base, security expertise can come from trusted suppliers who are passionate about privacy and security together with the Hippocratic Oath. Look to cutting-edge innovators who can translate domain depth across multidisciplinary teams and can simplify your requirements to deliver across process, people and technology. Just as you adjust hiring to screen out high-risk employees, establish security criteria for your supply chain providers. As one innovator described it, how can you lower the number of security "fouls" on your team and across your organization (Douville 2019)?

This extends to security leadership among your partners and suppliers in terms of mindsets and values. Does your partner's CEO prioritize security, to the point of holding back a product if it does not meet healthcare setting requirements? Does she/he fund secure development lifecycle work among their engineering teams? Other chapters in this book highlight the importance of company culture, leadership communication, and other factors that will, in the end, impact your organization's level of risk. Other chapters can also provide specific information about device risk and other related cybersecurity topics.

Overall, open communication and constant information sharing among your stakeholder groups can help ensure proactive steps are taken, such as including security training in your mobile roll-out or knowing who to call when something suspicious is noticed. All of these steps should be aligned to your mobile risk management program that details objectives, governance, metrics, and other guiding frameworks. With the right layers of defenses in place, the significant benefits of mobile communications – especially saving patient lives – can be experienced while the risks are carefully navigated.

References

Center for Internet Security. "DDoS attacks: In the healthcare sector." Accessed February 27, 2021. https:// www.cisecurity.org/blog/ddos-attacks-in-the-healthcare-sector/.

Digital Directors Network. "Systemic risk, failure and change: DDN, NIST and security scorecard." Last accessed February 27, 2021. https://www.digitaldirectors.network/cpages/home.

Douville, Sherri. "Privacy and security violations in healthcare are like the personal fouls of football." November 12, 2019. Last accessed February 27, 2021. https://sherridouville.medium.com/privacy-and-security-violations-in-healthcare-are-like-the-personal-fouls-of-football-74675e37ce3d.

FireEye. "A global reset: Cybersecurity predications 2021." Last accessed February 27, 2021. https://www.fireeye.com/current-threats/annual-threat-report/cyber-security-predictions.html.

Healthcare Business & Technology. "Social engineering attacks in healthcare." Last accessed September 2020. https://www.healthcarebusinesstech.com/social-engineering-attacks-healthcare-cybersecurity/.

Jercich, Kay. "UHS hospital chain hit with apparent Ransomware attack." *Healthcare IT News*, September 29, 2020. https://www.healthcareitnews.com/news/uhs-hospital-chain-hit-massive-ransomware-attack.

Miliard, Mike. "Hospital Ransomware attack leads to fatality after causing delay in care." *Healthcare IT News,* September 17, 2020. https://www.healthcareitnews.com/news/hospital-ransomware-attack-leads-fatality-after-causing-delay-care.

Radcliffe, Jerome. "Hacking medical devices for fun and insulin: Breaking the human SCADA system." *Black Hat Conference*, Research paper, 2011. https://media.blackhat.com/bh-us-11/Radcliffe/BH_US_11_Radcliffe_Hacking_Medical_Devices_WP.pdf.

Schneier, Bruce. "Who are the shadow brokers?" *The Atlantic.* May 23, 2017. https://www.theatlantic.com/technology/archive/2017/05/shadow-brokers/527778/.

Shaw, Gienn. "Cryptomining threats grow stronger for healthcare organizations." *Health Tech Magazine*, June 7, 2019. https://healthtechmagazine.net/article/2019/06/cryptomining-threats-grow-stronger-healthcare-organizations.

Siwicki, Bill. "8 out of 10 mobile health apps open to HIPAA violations, hacking, data theft." *Healthcare IT News,* January 13, 2016. https://www.healthcareitnews.com/news/8-out-10-mobile-health-apps-open-hipaa-violations-hacking-data-theft.

World Economic Forum. "Global risks perception survey 2020." January 15, 2020. Last accessed February 27, 2021. https://www.weforum.org/reports/the-global-risks-report-2020.

Zukis, Bob. "Succeeding in a world of risk." *Interview by Allison J. Taylor. LIFT Podcast,* August 25, 2020. Audio, 2:34. https://www.thoughtmarketing.com/business/succeeding-in-a-world-of-risk/.

Chapter 11

Risk Considerations for Mobile Device Implementations

Mitchell Parker

IU Health

Contents

While tablets had been in use for years in healthcare, health systems only started taking notice when physicians went to the Apple Store and bought iPads. After years of mobile devices being tested out and failing, this was the one that worked and was not a nightmare to use. The term BYOD, for Bring Your Own Device, was coined. In the case of healthcare, it was Brought Your Own Device, as CIOs soon found out that the medical staff already had them. Often, they were connected to the network, running Citrix or Remote Desktop, and being used in clinical practice to run software without the support of the IS department. This was a complete change from the days of the PalmPilot or Windows Mobile, which physicians and residents alike loved to hate.

When mobile devices originally entered the healthcare landscape in the 1990s, they came as devices that were tethered to PCs for their major functions. The Palm Pilot, Compaq iPAQ, and Dell Axim handhelds used in healthcare environments were glorified note and order takers that required a PC and docking station to fully function. Mobile devices such as the first glucometers required those too. Blackberries were incredibly secure and met HIPAA requirements for secure message transmission; however, they didn't work in buildings. If you worked in a hospital, you'd see residents clustered around windows looking to get a signal to use their devices. Pagers, which did, worked where interference made mobile phone usage impossible. The devices in use were put in place to supplement the work clinicians did. However, there was no consideration for risk or security. They were there to supplement clinical workflow as a companion to the PC. Security wasn't a concern as these devices did not even have network access. Healthcare was vaguely aware of HIPAA. Electronic Medical Records (EMRs) were not pervasive. These devices were there mainly to augment paper. In many ways, they are the precursors to the EMRs today.

DOI: 10.4324/9781003220473-15

In 2007, that all changed. The introduction of the iPhone and its desktop-class Safari web browser opened up numerous possibilities. The applications that doctors had been developing for the kiosk desktops on inpatient units and mobile workstations now fit in the palm and, most importantly, did not require a tethered PC and its numerous support issues to work. These devices worked on hospital wireless networks, could send and receive corporate email and, unlike the Blackberry handhelds, had full browser functionality. This was both the death knell for older devices and the expansion of possibilities for new ones. It was finally possible to bring together the two technologies attempting to knock out paper-based medical records, mobile devices, and EMRs. Applications for the major EMR systems soon followed. The promise of the PalmPilot or laptop on the unit helping reduce paper was going to be fulfilled.

Due to applications like REDCap and the desktop browser functionality, it was very easy to adapt existing workflows and technologies to mobile. However, Blackberry had been operating at a very high level of security since 2003, when the Department of the Navy approved them for use in a DOD environment (Hernon, 2007). Apple, however, had to address multiple security concerns with iOS. It can be argued that Apple didn't reach feature parity with Blackberry until September 17, 2014, when iOS 8.0 was released (Preece, 2014). According to Elcomsoft, who writes security and forensics software for iOS devices, the major change was that Apple no longer had the encryption keys to decrypt devices (Katalov, 2015). Encryption was now based on the user's screen lock passcode. Apple had taken 11 years to reach the same level of security functionality that Blackberry had in 2003. During that time period, however, Apple became pervasively deployed in healthcare and had presented lowered security.

Google had developed the Android operating system, which is based on Linux, for its devices. According to Statcounter, for the December 2019–2020 time period, it was the most popular mobile operating system, with 72.48% market share to Apple's 26.91%, and 0.61% for everyone else (Statcounter.com, 2021a). There are billions of devices out there with the Android operating system. However, according to the paper The Android Platform Security Model, there was a major release of Android that greatly improved its security (Mayrhofer, 2020). Android 7.0, released on October 7, 2016, according to Verizon, introduced File-Based Encryption to allow for usable encryption on devices (Verizon, 2016). Android has had significant security improvements with every release, and this paper goes through how the model has evolved toward process isolation and least privilege since its inception.

The issue is that Android users simply don't get the latest versions. According to Statcounter, for the time period from December 2019 to 2020, Android 10, the latest release, had 42.77% of the overall market share (Statcounter, 2021b). For that same time period, Apple iOS had 57.69% for iOS 14.2, its latest version (Statcounter, 2021c). The previous version, iOS 13, comparable to Android 10, had 14.6% combined (Statcounter, 2021c). Android devices, despite the larger market share, do not get updates at the same rate. According to Dieter Bohn, in his article, *Google Can't Fix the Android Update Problem*, the individual Android vendors are responsible for packaging and supplying device updates, not Google (Bohn, 2019). Carriers also want to verify these updates. There are diminishing returns for keeping older devices updated. They have made significant efforts, but this is an area where they lag. Apple, because they control the entire ecosystem, can push out updates for older models without waiting for manufacturing partners.

This brings to light a very important concern. Mobile devices did not effectively reach security parity with their desktop versions until 2014 if they ran iOS, or 2016 if they ran Android on the latest devices. PalmPilots and mobile devices ran without effective security that met HIPAA standards for over 20 years. We have tried to implement mobile solutions without considering the risks. In many cases, we've implemented extensions of secured EMR environments on mobile devices without the security of the desktop versions. Mobile devices together with EMRs helped solve the problem of paper. Now we can add Risk Management to that pair to create a triad of patient protection.

This chapter will start by asking the important question about what is a mobile device implementation in healthcare, and what are we looking forward to post-COVID? We will discuss what we are trying to solve with risk management, especially new threat scenarios that emerged during the COVID-19 crisis. We explain what makes it so different, and what components present risk. Methods to address them through technical and non-technical means will be explained, including techniques to address security through the application and authentication stacks internally and externally. Continually evaluating solutions for risks comes next. After the SolarWinds debacle, we will explain methods to integrate into daily operational processes that enable the ability to more easily detect and address risks.

Too often the emphasis is on eliminating risks. Like many other items in life, it is not possible to remove all risks with 100% certainty. What is possible is to take actions that reduce risks and develop responses and actions to effectively mitigate the remaining percentages. Cyber attacks have rippling effects across the clinical enterprise. It's important to know how to plan to manage their risks. When these devices emerged in the clinics, they were there to augment workflow. Now they are a critical component of it. Knowing these use cases is a great place to start.

The two most prevalent use cases for mobile devices in the healthcare process today are with mobile EMR access and secure messaging. One of the major advantages of mobile devices is that they have enabled doctors and caregivers to access medical records to make quick assessments from their phone or tablet from anywhere they have a network connection. In the words of a former clinical chair of Radiology at an academic medical center, it frees doctors from having to spend time around a computer when they are on call. It means they can attend their children's games. It gives caregivers a higher quality of life. It also allows for experienced personnel to assist in making decisions remotely.

Messaging allows clinicians to coordinate and communicate together, facilitating N:N communication between groups to improve workflow and care. Secure messaging helps address issues where distributed teams can all interact at once. It also allows ad-hoc teams split between facilities to work together. This includes care teams that are at different hospitals, offices, or even in different states to work together on complex cases.

More recently, due to the COVID-19 pandemic, there have been multiple resource constraint issues. Chief among them has been the need to reduce infection risk while preserving scarce Personal Protective Equipment (PPE). One of the ways to accomplish this task has been to leverage the use of mobile and wireless devices in the inpatient setting to reduce the barrier between caregivers and COVID patients. The need to monitor high blood glucose levels caused IU Health, the largest health system in the state of Indiana, to utilize the Dexcom G6 monitors with Samsung Galaxy smartphones to monitor this (Jones, 2020). This allowed endocrinologists to monitor patients while preserving scarce PPE.

In addition to that, patients have been sent home to free up hospital beds for people suffering from COVID. Atrium Health successfully implemented a remote monitoring program called Hospital At Home to do just that (Terry, 2020). This necessitates the use of mobile devices to monitor patients in their homes.

Now that we have examples of how mobile devices are being used in the environment of care, no matter where it is, we need to understand what we're trying to solve for. Mobile devices did not follow a standard path for intake into the environment like an EMR or new MRI. They were brought in to augment and automate tedious manual processes that took time away from patient care. We need to frame our solution set for mobile device risk management around what the expectations are now for them, as opposed to what they were when Palm Pilots on the unit were a new item. These are full-fledged computers with a different user interface and Internet connectivity.

Mobile devices, before the advent of EDGE and 3G connectivity, used to be behind a firewall or isolated. While there were cellular data networks available when these devices started appearing, many of them were connected via Wi-Fi as that was the fastest connectivity method. Also, it was the only one that worked in many hospitals. There were some devices that were being used from homes, such as Resmed CPAP machines (Resmed, 2020). Patient logging and clinical feedback on chronic conditions such as COPD also became a use case given solutions like HGE Healthcare's monitoring platform (HGE Health, 2021).

COVID-19 has accelerated the move of devices out of the hospital into the home and to remote sites. Many of these devices were not designed to function outside of a hospital or closed network. Mobile device usage means that more transactions happen on the Internet, instead of an Intranet or hospital network. The 21st-century Cures Act Final Rule requires the use of Fast Health Interoperability Resources (FHIR) version 4.0.1 to interchange data (US President, 2020). This means that implementations of mobile devices need to be secured down to the transaction level. We need to solve for security of the entire stack, not just put it all behind a firewall or network segment like we did when implementing these devices in an inpatient setting.

What makes it different is that due to the open nature of API interchange, we need to provide countermeasures at all levels, not just at the proverbial Network, Data Link, and Physical layers of the OSI model (Figure 11.1).

The hostile environment is now everywhere, not just outside the gates. This is a live implementation of Zero Trust principles, which is a concept that organizations should not automatically trust anything inside or outside its perimeter and verify anything and everything trying to connect before granting access (Pratt, 2018). It translates to don't trust anyone or anything implicitly.

This means that every component can present risk. If it can be broken, it will be. The recent Software Supply Chain attack on Solarwinds indicates the level of core network damage one of these can incur (CISA, 2021a). Solarwinds Orion, according to the United States Cybersecurity and Infrastructure Support Agency (CISA) advisories, monitors networks (CISA, 2020a). CISA indicates that the levels of infiltration and risk from running an infected version are so great that the core passwords of the enterprise authentication system most enterprises use, Microsoft Active

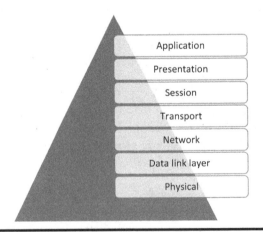

Figure 11.1   The OSI model (Adapted from Parker [2021].)

Directory, must be changed. As we discussed earlier, mobile devices themselves present a risk vector through their own software supply chain issues, specifically with Android devices. Security configurations of these devices also need to be considered.

For securing connectivity between devices and corporate networks, Virtual Private Networks are often used. One of the most dominant vendors for this is Cisco. This year presented significant vulnerabilities in their products, the most severe which could allow hijacking of connections (Osborne, 2020). This demonstrates risks here that have to be considered.

The transmission mode and methods, which encompass the use of Transport Layer Security and secured network protocols, also need to be considered. Secure network transmission protocols have an expiration date due to underlying vulnerabilities being found in the base network libraries. For example, due to the use of cryptographically broken hashing algorithms, the Transport Layer Security protocols, versions 1.0 and 1.1, have been considered insecure and removed from Google Chrome, version 84 (Google, 2020a). OpenSSH, which is the main secure remote access tool used by Linux, UNIX, and BSD, also has significant vulnerabilities in older versions and needs constant maintenance and patching to keep current. According to cvedetails.com, 14.3% of them allow for security bypasses (Cvedetails.com, 2021). Constantly evaluating these for risks is a must, as remote access tools such as Citrix, VMware Horizon, and Microsoft Remote Desktop Protocol (RDP) utilize TLS or SSH as an encapsulation method to protect the underlying data from device to its ultimate destination endpoints.

The destination endpoints, better known as remote access servers, also present a risk factor all of their own. These servers run specialized versions of Windows, Linux, or FreeBSD. They not only need all the updates for the underlying operating system, but they also need to have current secure protocols and secure code for the remote access components. The vulnerabilities that Citrix reported in September 2020, which include those remote access components, are indicative of the types of vulnerabilities remote access devices can have (Citrix, 2020).

Virtual Desktop Interfaces, better known as VDI, are a technology where a desktop operating system, usually running Windows, runs as a virtual machine in a data center. According to TechTarget, this virtual image is delivered over the network to an endpoint device (Rouse, 2020). This happens over a secure protocol, which includes Independent Computing Architecture (ICA) for Citrix-based solutions, PC over IP (PCoIP) for VMWare, and Remote Desktop Protocol (RDP) for Microsoft-based ones. These present the view of an internal desktop or application to an outside viewer. They are dangerous because they expose the corporate desktop over a lower-level secured network protocol to mobile devices.

Abstracting to a higher level, we have Fast Health Interoperability Resources (FHIR), an Application Programming Interface (API) standard maintained by Health Level 7 (HL7) International (HL7, 2019). This API uses eXtensible Markup Language (XML) and JavaScript Object Notation (JSON) to provide methods by which applications can interchange patient data. It is utilized by Apple Health, Samsung, and numerous other vendors (Apple Corporation, 2021) (Rhew, 2018). Version 4.0.1 of the standard has been adopted by the Center for Medicare and Medicaid Services (CMS) as the standard for the 21st-century Cures Act Final Rule (Landi, 2020). This rule also means that patients will have access to their medical records as part of the MyHealthEData initiative using FHIR 4.0.1 (CMS, 2020).

APIs have three risk areas of concern. The first is with the security of the APIs themselves. Many of these can fall victim to the same types of attacks that plague other web-based systems, including SQL Injection, automated bots scanning for vulnerabilities, credential theft/phishing, cross-site scripting, man-in-the-middle attacks, or insecure network protocols. Andrew Marcus, in his presentation from DevDays 2018, Security on FHIR, goes over these and potential mitigations in detail (Marcus, 2018). The other issue he discusses is the importance of keeping the Operating System and Libraries that host the APIs up to date and secure. He also discusses not running code that you do not know the provenance of, as code injection can also exfiltrate data.

While the APIs often run on Windows or Linux, mobile devices can run on a number of operating systems. The two that get encountered most are Apple's iOS/iPad OS, which are based on Mac OS, and run on the iPhone, iPad, and iPod Touch, and Android from Google, which runs on phones, tablets, Zebra handheld devices, and Internet of Things devices. However, other common operating systems in the space include Blackberry's QNX, Wind River VxWorks, Green Hills INTREGRITY, Windows Internet of Things edition, and embedded Linux. Legacy installations can include Windows Mobile, which Microsoft has stopped development on and is no longer supported. Updating a mobile operating system outside of iOS/iPadOS or Android can be difficult, as many of them require connectivity to a host computer to update. Performing live updates on many of these devices is not as easy as it is with iOS or Android. The same goes for the underlying libraries, many of which are the same as the ones on the servers. The risk here is that outdated devices can have many of the same vulnerabilities and that the ability or methods to properly update them may not be there. Also, many of these libraries used are Open Source ones such as Network Time Protocol (ntp), GNU C Library (glibc), or Busybox that are ported to individual platforms and take significant work and testing to keep updated on them. While the use of Open Source has great benefits, the amount of work taken to keep them secure and up to date on platforms may not be an advantage as much as standardization is.

Another great concern is with the use of third-party system components for critical functions such as the TCP/IP networking stack. Many companies that licensed Wind River's Interpeak stack and never updated it found themselves in an unenviable position due to a 16-year-old vulnerability (Wind River, 2021; CISA, 2020b). This meant that devices that never had a risk analysis done for updating software, or never meant to have their software updated, were now vulnerable to a critical issue that affected the basic communication foundation they use. Updating these devices took significant work on the parts of numerous vendors. The medical device security vendor Armis identified several, including BD and Spacelabs (Seri, 2019).

Insider Threats are still a major threat to these devices. As many of them do not have the same level of logging and auditing on the devices as a conventional desktop system, it is possible to log into these systems and exfiltrate data from the device memory or storage cards. The same types of insider threats that CISA has identified for regular applications also apply to mobile installations (CISA, 2021b). Just because the form factor is different does not mean different rules apply. The disconnection by default from standard networks means that it's easier to do and more of a risk factor than ever.

Now that we've discussed these risks, what can we do to help address these risks? There are many people who think that we've gone years without doing anything and nothing's wrong. With the impending moves to very high-speed wireless in 5G and other multi-gigabit cellular technologies, and multi-gigabit Wi-Fi, this is a good time. The differences between corporate networks and remote will further blur, and technologies like Software-Defined Wide-Area Networking (SD-WAN) will allow corporate or enterprise connectivity anywhere at these speeds.

Understanding risk starts with understanding the environment that mobile devices will be used in, and the overall solution that they will be part of. When evaluating risk mitigation procedures, it's important to know this and use this as part of the evaluation criteria as certain solutions will just not work in the given environment or with the given technologies. One size does not fit all, and the solution chosen for office automation may not work in the clinical environment.

As part of the environment, it is important to understand how the mobile solution will be leveraged. There will be numerous usage scenarios. Catalog these and understand them. Know what the mobile solution will be used for in detail. Understand how team members use mobile devices as part of these use cases. Model them and leverage Use Case Diagrams to better comprehend the entire picture. Jeff Hawkins did this when he developed what became the PalmPilot, as Leander Kahney discussed in his article "The Philosophy of the Handheld" (Kahney, 2017). If the person who developed one of the first mobile technologies used in healthcare to help automate workflows can do this, then we can too.

Understanding the environment, use cases, and usage patterns puts organizations in a better place to conduct a Failure Mode and Effects Analysis (FMEA) for each of the defined use cases. The management chapter goes into greater detail about how to conduct one. The output from the FMEA analyses will be knowledge of where failures are most likely to occur in mobile device system implementations.

Include these outputs as materials for the risk assessment and overall risk management plan for the organization. However, first, develop risk management plans for the most likely failure scenarios. Also develop alternate mode operations and procedures for addressing what happens when the system or devices are not there. The tragic domestic terrorism attack on the AT&T data center in Nashville in 2020, which disrupted public safety communications across the Southern US, along with ransomware attacks, demonstrates how vulnerable our infrastructure is, especially for mobile devices (Mangrum, 2021).

We need to start building our own infrastructure. One that is built on identity. Identity Management (IDM), according to CSOOnline, is about defining and managing the roles and access privileges of individual network users and the circumstances in which they are granted or denied those privileges (Martin, 2018). It is based on the concept of one digital identity per individual. This identity must be maintained, modified, and monitored throughout the lifecycle. The goal is to grant access to the right people to meet the right business need (Martin, 2018). The HIPAA Security Rule, 45CFR 164.308 (a)(3)(i) requires the use of policies and procedures to ensure that all workforce members have appropriate access to Protected Health Information (Legal Information Institute, 2021a).

These policies and procedures need to outline procedures for the authorization and supervision of workforce members that work with Protected Health Information (PHI). They also need to provide methods by which access to PHI is deemed to be appropriate. They also need to provide for de-provisioning access when no longer required. 45CFR 164.308 (a)(5)(i) requires security awareness and training for the workforce. This includes acceptable and unacceptable use. 45CFR 164.308 (a)(1)(ii)(D) requires procedures to regularly review system activity. 45CFR 164.308 (a)(1)(ii)(C) requires a Sanctions Policy to apply appropriate sanctions against workforce members that violate policies and procedures. These are required before putting in software to automate the Identity Management process. If you do not have these in place, you're not following the tenets of HIPAA, and you're letting the software run your business.

While IDM is normally associated with a software package that manages centrally located identities within directory stores, it is an automation process augmented by them. IDM and Identity Access Management (IAM) systems provide the technologies and software needed to automate provisioning and de-provisioning users, creating and deleting roles, assigning and removing identities from roles, auditing of actions taken, and reporting on actions, role assignments, and system status. The Directory Service, normally a system like Microsoft Active Directory or Okta, is designed to be a storage system for identities, roles, and assignments. It also provides a directory interface to look up users via a protocol like Lightweight Directory Access Protocol (LDAP) and methods by which authentication and authorization take place.

Sitting on top of the Directory Service and LDAP can be additional services to allow other services, such as third-party providers like Google or Microsoft 365, to authenticate and authorize identities. These include SAML, the Security Assertion Markup Language, which allows for transferring identity data between the Identity Provider, usually based on the Directory Service, and the Service Provider, normally a service like Microsoft 365 or Google (Lloyd, 2020). This does not transfer passwords or credentials, which reduces risk. The most prevalent use of SAML is by the EZproxy software supplied by the Online Computer Library Center (OCLC) (OCLC, 2020). EZProxy provides a SAML interface from library systems to access numerous paid academic journal sites. It allows people to sign into their university or company and allows access to what the organization is entitled to without having to sign in again.

Another method for allowing third-party application access is OAuth2. It's an authorization framework that allows applications to obtain limited access to user accounts on an HTTP-based service such as Facebook, GitHub, or Digital (Anicas, 2014). Fast Health Interoperability Resources (FHIR) also uses OAuth 2 as the authentication method for Application Programming Interfaces (APIs) (HL7, 2018). This is the authentication scheme that patient-facing applications will use. Future standards, such as IEEE/UL P2933, Trust, Identity, Privacy, Protection, Safety, and Security (TIPPSS), will also leverage OAuth2 for Internet of Things (IoT) connectivity (Hudson, 2020).

What this means is that Identity Management, in addition to being a requirement for team member access, is now also going to be very important for patients as part of compliance with the 21st-century Cures Act Final Rule using OAuth2. There needs to be good processes and procedures for associating patients with digital identities. These digital identities will be used to authenticate through third-party applications such as Apple Health to allow them to download their own data. An Identity Management System is no longer a nice-to-have. It is a requirement for being able to manage patient identities so that they can download the medical records they are entitled to under that identity. Guardians, parents, and other interested third parties who are entitled to these make this sufficiently complex enough to make this a base requirement for even the smallest organization. If your organization is not capable of doing this on their own, please find a third party capable of helping you address these needs.

Identity Management also provides the base needed for assigning security profiles and configurations to devices. Ultimately, the entitlements provided to the user need to extend to the devices. The dependency on identity is where we start. There have to be good policies and procedures based on the HIPAA Security Rule before IDM and authentication work is completed to be able to effectively use it.

Dependencies on external applications and services over the Internet and keeping those services updated are the major concerns. Oftentimes applications have external dependencies on third-party libraries. Managing the applications and libraries together is often a very difficult and complex task. The example of the numerous runtimes that Windows desktop or Linux applications require is not an example to follow. Encapsulating all possible dependencies in deployed mobile device applications and services by incorporating libraries in an Apple XCode project or Android Studio project will help reduce that complexity and allow for more simple updates and upgrades of apps if there are security concerns (Google, 2020b; Bucholtz, 2020). Utilizing a good set of frameworks and APIs that come as part of a package, such as Google Play Services or specific Apple iOS versions also reduces complexity (Google, 2020b). The goals are to make it easier to manage deployment and upgrades and keep complexity to a minimum.

Another way to reduce this complexity is to manage it for the users using Mobile Device Management (MDM). According to Gartner, it includes software that provides software distribution, policy management, inventory management, security management, and service management for smartphones and media tablets (Gartner, 2021). Some solutions, such as Jamf and Microsoft Endpoint Manager, extend this to laptops or tablets running MacOS or Windows (Jamf, 2021; Microsoft, 2021). MDM requires good identity management to be in place to provision entitlements and services to users' devices based on their roles.

Organizations use MDM to provide applications and services to devices they own, and also users' personal devices, better known as Bring Your Own Device (BYOD). This also provides a better way for organizations to protect their assets. Only the applications and services managed by an organization fall into the scope of MDM. This means that it can be configured to only manage those applications, and not the users' personal information, email, or photos. The use of alternate mail programs, such as IBM FIberlink's MaaS360 SecureMail or Microsoft Outlook, instead of Apple Mail, Gmail, or device-provided programs, makes it easier to compartmentalize email access (IBM Security Learning Services, 2021).

MDM is also used to provide custom applications not delivered through the Apple App Store or Google Play stores. It checks security configurations of devices to ensure that insecure devices are not allowed access to company resources. It also can push out security updates of applications to devices. Jamf and Microsoft Endpoint Manager can also push out security updates for MacOS and Windows, respectively. It can also be used to provide licensing information for apps that are licensed per user or device.

When a user separates from an organization, the only ways to make sure that they do not take information with them on mobile devices are through wiping entire devices or selectively wiping through MDM. The solution that does not involve wiping someone's personal data that is not connected with their employment is the latter.

There is a lot of fear, uncertainty, and doubt over device management with BYOD. People are concerned that companies will have access to their information. Meanwhile, there are applications such as TikTok that have permission to entire devices and networks (DeGrippo, 2020). The only way to combat this is to have a plan that explains the following:

- Mobile Device Management applications have less permissions than commonly used applications such as TikTok, Facebook, or Instagram. They do not have permission to access personal data.
- All access to devices by administrators is audited, and unauthorized device accesses will be treated as violations of the Acceptable Use Policy and subject to Corrective Action. If you are part of a healthcare organization, these policies are required by the HIPAA Security Rule (Legal Information Institute, 2021b) and should already exist.
- These applications only manage the applications provided to connect to the organization's data. They will not touch personal email, photos, text messages, or services.
- Your organization has to have separate encapsulated applications for business use, including secured messaging. Do not use the standard applications. Use these instead to provide users additional assurance you are not touching their personal data stored in Mail, Gmail, Photos, or Messages.
- The separate encapsulated applications need to be encrypted and not interact with other applications on the device, and not allow other applications access to their data. This is to prevent data exfiltration.

■ Leveraging Virtual Private Networking for corporate applications through MDM helps detect malicious software and malware that otherwise would not have been detected. As mobile devices normally do not run anti-malware software, this is an additional benefit these solutions can provide to protect users.

Your organization also needs to have a policy in place that incorporates the above into one single policy. It also needs a communication plan to provide effective messaging to the workforce. Team members also need to make themselves available to answer users' questions over MDM and BYOD. Good clear communication and providing substitutes for commonly used applications provide that additional assurance that personal data is not put at risk by using MDM.

As part of securing devices, device encryption must be turned on for devices and for applications. While it is possible to protect against basic attacks, we must assume that devices will be jailbroken and that there will be hostile apps that use security holes to get access. Aleksander Popko, in his article iOS App Security – How to Protect Users' Sensitive Data in Mobile Applications, discusses how to use third-party tools such as Encrypted Core Data SQLite Store and the Realm Database to encrypt data so that other apps cannot get access to it (Popko, 2018). If your application is storing PHI, then you need to have a solution like this in place. If you have a program that allows BYOD, you need to have this for the applications you provision over MDM. All it takes is one hostile app with excessive permissions and your entire MDM security scheme can be bypassed unless you use encryption to protect app data from other applications.

Cryptographic hashing is also critically important. Hashing is a one-way function that cannot be reversed which provides assurance that data has not changed. When you edit data on a mobile device, there always is a concern that the data changed between the device and its ultimate data store. Using hashing for data that was created or changed on a mobile device can be used to prove that data stored on the device is the same as on the data store and that it has not been altered in transit.

Keeping the integrity of public and private keys used in cryptographic transactions is very important. Having someone or something's private encryption key means that you can conduct transactions as them. Not protecting a passphrase means that the secret that was supposed to be shared between Alice and Bob can be viewed by Joe if he has it too. Cryptographic Key Management builds upon Identity Management by generating, associating, and managing cryptographic material and keys associated with identities, systems, and applications. Like Identity Management, it requires excellent security and auditable processes.

The National Institute of Standards and Technology (NIST) has three Special Publications (SPs) that organizations can use to implement cryptographic key security to US Government standards. NIST SP 800-57 Part 1, Revision 1, Recommendation for Key Management: Part 1 – General, provides general guidance and best practices for the management of cryptographic key management systems (Barker, 2020). NIST SP 800-57 Part 2 Revision 1, Recommendation for Key Management: Part 2 – Best Practices for Key Management Organizations, identifies the concepts, functions, and elements common to effective systems for the management of symmetric and asymmetric keys; identifies the security planning requirements and documentation necessary for effective institutional key management; describes Key Management Specification requirements; describes cryptographic Key Management Policy documentation that is needed by organizations that use cryptography; and describes Key Management Practice Statement requirements (Barker, 2019). NIST SP 800-57 Part 3 Revision 1, Recommendation for Key Management, Part 3: Application-Specific Management Guidance, provides cryptographic key management guidance. It consists of three parts. Part 1 provides general guidance and best practices for the management of cryptographic keying material. Part 2 provides guidance on policy and security planning requirements for US government agencies. Finally, Part 3 provides guidance when using the cryptographic features of current systems (Barker, 2015).

These documents provide the steps and procedures your organization needs to properly manage cryptographic keys throughout their entire usage and distribution lifecycles. We anticipate that organizations will purchase key management software and professional services to assist them in this endeavor. The best recommendations we can provide are that they select an organization that is able to help them automate the delivery of cryptographic keys in line with their use cases and needs that do not overly burden end users. They also need a system that is compliant with the requirements in the NIST SP 800-57 document series and is fully auditable.

To make changes to APIs or applications, there needs to be a secured connection between the application and its endpoint. Whether it's a Virtual Private Network (VPN) connection, Transport Layer Security (TLS) version 1.2 or greater connection, or the latest version of OpenSSH with AES-256 encryption, there needs to be that secure tunnel that protects data in transit and from being altered. Vulnerabilities such as Heartbleed, which uses old and vulnerable versions of the OpenSSL library, can allow data to be altered in transit and affect its integrity. To provide effective analysis of network traffic from applications, the use of a VPN that sends data to other network security tools to provide further analysis is recommended.

When using encryption and hashing, secured algorithms and encryption methods are critically important. The use of old and obsolete algorithms such as MD5, TLS 1.0, or SSL 3.0 are just as bad as not encrypting or hashing the data. Algorithms for encryption and hashing have to be known good ones. The National Institute of Standards and Technology maintains a Cryptographic Standards and Guidelines page that provides updated links to the currently supported algorithms (Chen, 2021).

Application Security is also critically important. According to David Strom from CSO Online, Application Security is the process of making apps more secure by finding, fixing, and enhancing the security of apps (Strom, 2020). Making sure the applications you deploy have met minimum security standards is critical. The Open Web Application Security Project (OWASP), who are famous for their Top 10 list of application vulnerabilities, offers two tools that organizations can use to provide better security for their applications (OWASP, 2021). The first, the Mobile Security Testing Guide, provides a comprehensive manual for mobile app security testing and reverse engineering, including how to test mobile apps throughout the lifecycle. The OWASP Mobile Application Security Verification Standard (MASVS) is a standard for mobile app security. Based on their extensive application security experience, it provides a good framework for developers to use. The National Institute of Standards and Technology (NIST) also offers Special Publication 800-163 Revision 1, Vetting the Security of Mobile Applications (Ogata, 2019). This paper outlines and details a mobile application vetting process that organizations can use. The NIST standards are required by federal agencies as part of the Federal Information Security Modernization Act Implementation Project (Ross, 2021). Compliance with these is required for doing business with the US Federal Government or any agency that receives funding from them. Ensuring that mobile applications are developed to NIST SP 800-163 Revision 1 and OWASP MASVS standards is a good first step toward ensuring good security. Adding in encryption of sensitive application data, hashing of created or modified content, Mobile Device Management, and keeping to NIST standards for encryption and hashing will provide a much more secure experience.

Keeping it secure is the hard part. Security isn't just one and done. It's a continual process to evaluate the entire solution and all dependencies for vulnerabilities, address them, and deploy fixes. Having a good operational management plan to check for, develop, address, and deploy solutions for discovered issues is a requirement. Solarwinds has taught us that ensuring the entire software supply chain is as free as possible from critical vulnerabilities, especially in third-party components, is very important. It's difficult to shift between Development, Security, and Operational Management cycles continually. Vulnerability Management and keeping watch on dependent components continually, especially applications, operating systems, supporting libraries, and encryption standards, is now a requirement. As we tell people, all it takes is one presentation at Black Hat or DEFCON to demonstrate that what you thought is secure is not, and that you need to be prepared to deal with that eventuality.

IBM's Red Hat division, in their piece, What is DevSecOps, discusses this process, and how it helps address managing the software development lifecycle in a better way (IBM Red Hat, 2021). DevSecOps integrates security and automated testing throughout the entire software lifecycle, along with least privilege, short and frequent development cycles, centralized identity management, component isolation through containerization or microservices, encryption of data between apps and services, and secured Application Programming Interface (API) gateways. The use of true DevSecOps, as opposed to companies that say they do it, provides significant security advantages. It also provides for more rapid and automated resolution of security issues, along with automated testing as part of the process. The use of the NIST and MASVS standards to help validate a DevSecOps lifecycle along with encryption provides a method by which more isolated mobile applications and services can be developed.

DevSecOps won't catch everything. Utilizing the Failure Mode and Effects (FMEA) Analysis, we need to look at the data generated by the application and put in place monitoring to address monitoring for potential fraud scenarios. This includes users' ability to make changes that they do not have permissions to, excess views, excess data manipulation, and/or unauthorized viewing of friends and family. The recommendation is to use that analysis in a joint session with customers to identify potential sources of fraud and to develop automated methods to detect this fraud across systems. This will be a continual process. Logging and auditing all changes made by users is a basic requirement to be able to conduct this testing. It will change continually throughout the lifecycle as changes are made.

Automated monitoring also extends to network security. The SolarWinds incident brings up several methods by which we can detect potential security issues. Monitoring the application for ingress/egress traffic from unknown sources, which can be done with a good Virtual Private Networking (VPN) solution that outputs logging data to a Security Incident and Event Management (SIEM) system capable of analyzing network traffic and a Mobile Device Management (MDM) solution that forces VPN traffic, is capable of enforcing this control for applications. Having that SIEM capability and a good supporting VPN infrastructure for mobile applications is a requirement. Also, logging and checking DNS queries for potential DNS tunneling and exfiltration are also critical. Using a VPN here will also help address this. Finally, checking certificates for validity and logging their usage is also important. A lot of applications just pass certificates through without checking for their validity or erroring out when they find a different or invalid one. Don't let the mobile applications you depend on be like them. Good defensive application programming along with routing traffic via a VPN to guard against Border Gateway Protocol (BGP) hijacking and Domain Name System (DNS) hijacking attempts will provide a significant deterrent against this attack type.

If your organization chooses a development or management methodology, continual vulnerability management is a requirement. While DevSecOps automates this and provides an excellent framework, it does not do all of the work for you. You will also need resources that are allocated to DevSecOps that are not overloaded with other work that are able to devote time and attention to security. Too often security resources are loaded onto team members that are already allocated to other work, and both their primary work and security work suffer because of it.

Continual Vulnerability Management requires the use of the DevSecOps concept of continual code analysis and remediation for security issues. It also requires someone to continually watch for vulnerabilities up and down the Software Supply Chain, including Operating System, Application, and Third-Party Library and Component vulnerabilities. It requires continual vulnerability scanning of the development, test, and production environments, and of the deployed applications themselves. Plans need to be developed, tracked, and executed for addressing discovered issues. The HIPAA Security Rule, 45CFR 164.306(a)(1) and (2), requires organizations to protect against any reasonably anticipated threats or hazards to the security or integrity of protected health information and ensure its confidentiality, integrity, and availability (Legal Information Institute, 2021b).

Periodic risk assessments that undertake a technical and nontechnical evaluation of an organization's conformance to the standards of the HIPAA Security Rule are required under 45CFR 164.308(a)(8) (Legal Information Institute, 2021a). These risk assessments are also required in response to environmental or operational changes that affect the organization's security policies and/or procedures. In other words, you don't need to do a risk assessment for security patches, code fixes, or operating system updates. However, if you change your workflows, policies, or procedures, you do. If you make a major application or operating system change, you will need to.

Another way to determine the risk exposure of mobile solutions and aggressively address them is by using Purple Teams. According to Daniel Miessler, an author and security professional, in his article, *The Definition of a Purple Team*, there are three teams involved in protecting and defending information assets against adversarial attacks (Miessler, 2019). The Red Team emulates the Tactics, Techniques, and Procedures (TTPs) used by adversaries in a continual and evolving manner to test the security of the organization. The Blue Team is assigned the responsibility of defending the network and assets by understanding adversaries' TTPs and evolving the organization's capabilities to effectively defend against them. The Purple Team is designed to enhance the effectiveness of both by sharing information between them to maximize their combined effectiveness (Miessler, 2019). This means that Red Teams share their TTPs with the Blue Team, and that the Blue Team shares how they can detect and mitigate against TTPs. Even though the two teams are diametric opposites, their combined strength is significantly higher with collaboration.

This approach in terms of mobile applications aligns with DevSecOps and continual monitoring by providing additional inputs by which the Red Teams can find new avenues of exploiting existing assets, and the Blue Team can build defenses across the entire development pipeline. These can be quantified and measured through management metrics demonstrating the TTPs utilized to test the organization's security, the number successfully defended against, and the number that required additional work to address. The work can be quantified in risk management plans developed to address discovered issues.

One other item that can be incorporated into Purple team tests for wireless security is scanning the wireless spectrum for pager and unsecured wireless technologies. There have been numerous cases where unprotected PHI has been found being transmitted over the air (Donovan, 2018). This means that there are still applications and legacy data that have not been transferred over to more secure means of communication. Discovering these so they can be remediated is very important to ensuring continual security of patient information.

There are no good risk management plans without operational management plans. Understanding use cases well enough to have FMEA plans means that you need corresponding operational plans to document daily operation. This includes daily operation, identity management, maintenance, security management, vulnerability management, and the DevSecOps lifecycle. It does not need to be complex. It just needs to be written, documented, approved, and followed. Using a wiki, Sharepoint, or collaboration site to develop these plans allows organizations to focus on documenting what is important, not getting lost in minutiae. Make sure that your team has operational plans and procedures for their mobile applications documented. If your team is going to do an FMEA analysis, it's not difficult to complete it and document the rest.

We must build to analyze. If we need to figure out what is been occurring with a mobile application and associated services, we have to have all that information available to perform analysis. Utilize a Security Incident and Event Management (SIEM) system as a base to store logging and auditing data. Store critical log data in the app whenever possible and store it centrally in the SIEM. Log data and data points every time Protected Health Information is read, changed, or deleted. Also, make sure to store cryptographic hashes of the additions and changes to be able to successfully compare. Utilize the VPN and network logging, we discussed earlier to be able to discover and analyze network issues and anomalies. Use the results of the anti-fraud analysis and reports as a base to be able to further analyze logging data for potential fraud. Use discoveries from the Purple Team to analyze past traffic and logging data for anomalies. Incorporate Identity Management to determine if someone is acting outside their entitlements.

Analysis is a continually evolving process. It will need at least one dedicated resource to examine stored log data from across mobile solutions and associated infrastructure to be able to appropriately operate and discover potential issues. Being able to review logs and actions taken to determine issues is critical to maintaining the confidentiality, integrity, and availability of the solution.

When Jeff Hawkins put that block of wood in his pocket and acted through potential use cases, the world was a much simpler place. Mobile devices did not have complex high-speed network connectivity or significant processing power. EMRs were still mostly on paper. Wi-Fi did not exist. Mobile devices didn't have significant processing power or the ability to run desktop applications. Virtualization did not exist in a meaningful form outside of the data center. Giving medical records to patients meant making photocopies, not setting up an OAuth2-compliant Identity Management solution to deliver them over an XML-based Application Programming Interface.

Technology has evolved to be much more complex than when these solutions were originally conceived. The risk management processes used to address these solutions did not have a corresponding evolution. This chapter was designed to guide organizations through what the use cases are for mobile solutions, what we are trying to solve for using them, why they are different, what components present the most risk, and how to address them using technical and non-technical means. The overall goal is to present in one place the risks that organizations face with mobile and API-based solutions, and how to address them to the ultimate benefit of the patients and themselves.

References

Anicas, Mitchell. "An Introduction to OAuth 2." DigitalOcean, July 21, 2014. https://www.digitalocean.com/community/tutorials/an-introduction-to-oauth-2.

Apple Corporation. "Healthcare - Health Records." Apple, Accessed January 13, 2021. https://www.apple.com/healthcare/health-records/.

Barker, Elaine. "Recommendation for Key Management: Part 1," NIST Special Publication 800-57, Institute of Standards and Technology, Gaithersburg, MD, 2020. doi.org/10.6028/nist.sp.800-57pt1r5.

Barker, Elaine B., and Quynh H. Dang. "Recommendation for Key Management Part 3: Application-Specific Key Management Guidance," Special Publication (NIST SP), National Institute of Standards and Technology, Gaithersburg, MD, 2015. doi: 10.6028/nist.sp.800-57pt3r1.

Barker, Elaine B., and William C. Barker. "Recommendation for Key Management Part 2: Best Practices for Key Management Organizations," Special Publication (NIST SP), National Institute of Standards and Technology, Gaithersburg, MD, 2019. doi: 10.6028/nist.sp.800-57pt2r1.

Bohn, Dieter. "Google Can't Fix the Android Update Problem." The Verge, September 4, 2019. https://www.theverge.com/2019/9/4/20847758/google-android-update-problem-pie-q-treble-mainline.

Bucholtz, Stephen. "Using a Static Library in an IOS App." Accusoft, February 21, 2020. https://www.accusoft.com/resources/blog/using-static-library-ios-app/.

Center for Medicare and Medicaid Services (CMS). "Fact Sheet Interoperability and Patient Access Fact Sheet." CMS, March 9, 2020. https://www.cms.gov/newsroom/fact-sheets/interoperability-and-patient-access-fact-sheet.

Chen, Lily. "Cryptographic Standards and Guidelines: CSRC." CSRC, January 7, 2021. https://csrc.nist.gov/projects/cryptographic-standards-and-guidelines.

Citrix. "Citrix Application Delivery Controller, Citrix Gateway, and Citrix SD-WAN WANOP Appliance Security Update." Support Knowledge Center, September 18, 2020. https://support.citrix.com/article/CTX281474.

Cvedetails.com. "Openbsd Openssh : Vulnerability Statistics." Openbsd Openssh: CVE security vulnerabilities, versions and detailed reports. Accessed January 13, 2021. https://www.cvedetails.com/product/585/Openbsd-Openssh.html?vendor_id=97.

Cybersecurity and Infrastructure Security Agency (CISA). "Emergency Directive 21-01." cyber.dhs.gov, December 13, 2020a. https://cyber.dhs.gov/ed/21-01/.

Cybersecurity and Infrastructure Security Agency (CISA). "ICS Medical Advisory (ICSMA-19–274-01)." Cybersecurity and Infrastructure Security Agency CISA, January 7, 2020b. https://us-cert.cisa.gov/ics/advisories/icsma-19-274-01.

Cybersecurity and Infrastructure Security Agency (CISA). "Insider Threat - Cyber." Cybersecurity and Infrastructure Security Agency CISA. Accessed January 13, 2021a. https://www.cisa.gov/insider-threat-cyber#:~:text=The%20Department%20of%20Homeland%20Security,mishandling%20physical%20devices.%E2%80%9D%20Threats%20can.

Cybersecurity and Infrastructure Security Agency (CISA). "Supply Chain Compromise." Cybersecurity and Infrastructure Security Agency CISA. Accessed January 13, 2021b. https://www.cisa.gov/supply-chain-compromise.

DeGrippo, Sherrod. "Understanding the Information TikTok Gathers and Stores: Proofpoint US." Proofpoint, January 8, 2020. https://www.proofpoint.com/us/blog/threat-protection/understanding-information-tiktok-gathers-and-stores.

Donovan, Fred. "IT Worker Uncovers Hospital Pagers with Poor PHI Data Security." HealthITSecurity, June 26, 2018. https://healthitsecurity.com/news/it-worker-uncovers-hospital-pagers-with-poor-phi-data-security.

Gartner, Inc. (Gartner). "Definition of Mobile Device Management (MDM) - Gartner Information Technology Glossary." Gartner. Accessed January 13, 2021. https://www.gartner.com/en/information-technology/glossary/mobile-device-management-mdm.

Google, Inc. (Google). "Chrome Platform Status." TLS 1.0 and TLS 1.1- Chrome Platform Status, November 14, 2020a. https://www.chromestatus.com/feature/5759116003770368.

Google, Inc. (Google). "Overview of Google Play Services | Google APIs for Android." Google, December 16, 2020b. https://developers.google.com/android/guides/overview.

Health Level 7 International (HL7). "SMART App Launch: Scopes and Launch Context." visit the hl7 website, November 13, 2018. http://www.hl7.org/fhir/smart-app-launch/scopes-and-launch-context/.

Health Level 7 International (HL7). Overview - FHIR v4.0.1, November 1, 2019. https://www.hl7.org/fhir/overview.html.

Hernon, Mike. "Black Berries and CACs Get Connected." CHIPS Articles: BlackBerries and CACs Get Connected. October-December 2007. https://www.doncio.navy.mil/chips/ArticleDetails.aspx?ID=2881.

HGE Health. "Solutions." HGE Health. Accessed January 13, 2021. https://www.hgehealth.com/our-impact.

Hudson, Florence. "P2933 – Clinical IoT Data and Device Interoperability with TIPPSS Working Group." June 15, 2020. https://sagroups.ieee.org/2933/.

IBM Red Hat. "What Is DevSecOps?" Red Hat - We make open source technologies for the enterprise. Accessed January 13, 2021. https://www.redhat.com/en/topics/devops/what-is-devsecops.

IBM Security Learning Services. "Tips, Tricks, and Helpful Features: MaaS360 Secure Mail Guide." IBM Security Learning Services. Accessed January 13, 2021. https://www.securitylearningacademy.com/mod/book/view.php?id=13829&chapterid=666#:~:text=MaaS360%20Secure%20Mail%20is%20an,protection%20(DLP)%20security%20controls.

Jamf, Inc. (Jamf). "Jamf Pro: Mobile Security: Casper Suite." Jamf. Accessed January 13, 2021. https://www.jamf.com/products/jamf-pro/.

Jones, Sarah. "New IU Health Pilot Program Protects Most Vulnerable Health Care Workers and Patients." wthr.com, November 17, 2020. https://www.wthr.com/article/news/health/new-iu-health-pilot-program-protects-most-vulnerable-healthcare-workers-and-patients/531-4c2d7edc-1cbc-41e2-9953-f2dd056e1129.

Kahney, Leander. "The Philosophy of the Handheld." Wired. Conde Nast, June 4, 2017. https://www.wired.com/1999/10/the-philosophy-of-the-handheld/.

Katalov, Vladimir. "Extracting Data from Locked iPhones". Elcomsoft Blog, November 13, 2015. https://blog.elcomsoft.com/2015/11/extracting-data-from-locked-iphones/.

Landi, Heather. "CMS' New Interoperability Rule Requires Major Changes for Payers, Hospitals: Here Are 6 Key Elements." FierceHealthcare, March 9, 2020. https://www.fiercehealthcare.com/payer/cms-interoperability-rule-requires-major-changes-for-payers-hospitals-here-are-key-timelines.

Legal Information Institute. "45 CFR § 164.306- Security Standards: General Rules." Legal Information Institute. Accessed January 13, 2021a. https://www.law.cornell.edu/cfr/text/45/164.306#a.

Legal Information Institute. "45 CFR § 164.308- Administrative Safeguards." Legal Information Institute. Accessed January 13, 2021b. https://www.law.cornell.edu/cfr/text/45/164.308.

Lloyd, Holly. "How SAML Authentication Works." Auth0, June 30, 2020. https://auth0.com/blog/how-saml-authentication-works/.

Mangrum, Meghan, and Donovan Slack. "Nashville Bombing Reveals US Communication Networks' Vulnerability; Officials Demand Answers on How to Secure Them" USA Today, Gannett Satellite Information Network, January 2, 2021. https://www.usatoday.com/story/news/nation/2021/01/02/nashville-bombing-debate-how-secure-communication-networks/4111859001/.

Marcus, Andrew. "Security on FHIR." Asymmetrik, Inc., November 14, 2018. https://www.devdays.com/wp-content/uploads/2019/03/DD18-EU-Andrew-Marcus-Security-on-FHIR-v1.1-2018-11-16.pdf.

Martin, James A., and John K. Waters. "What Is IAM? Identity and Access Management Explained." CSO Online, October 9, 2018. https://www.csoonline.com/article/2120384/what-is-iam-identity-and-access-management-explained.html.

Mayrhofer, Rene, Jeffrey Vander Stoep, Chad Brubaker, and Nick Kralevich. "The Android Platform Security Model." Google, December 14, 2020. https://arxiv.org/pdf/1904.05572.pdf.

Microsoft Corporation (Microsoft). "Microsoft Endpoint Manager Overview." Microsoft Docs. Accessed August 11, 2021. https://docs.microsoft.com/en-us/mem/endpoint-manager-overview.

Miessler, Daniel. "The Definition of a Purple Team." Daniel Miessler, June 29, 2019. https://danielmiessler.com/study/purple-team/.

Ogata, Michael, Josh Franklin, Jeffrey Voas, Vincent Sritapan, and Stephen Quirolgico. "Vetting the Security of Mobile Applications," Special Publication (NIST SP) 800-163 Rev. 1, National Institute of Standards and Technology, Gaithersburg, MD, 2019. doi: 10.6028/nist.sp.800-163r1.

Online Computer Library Center (OCLC). "EZproxy: Access and Authentication Software." OCLC, December 3, 2020. https://www.oclc.org/en/ezproxy.html.

Open Web Application Security Project (OWASP). OWASP Mobile Security Testing Guide. Accessed January 13, 2021. https://owasp.org/www-project-mobile-security-testing-guide/.

Osborne, Charlie. "Cisco Releases Security Fixes for Critical VPN, Router Vulnerabilities." ZDNet, July 17, 2020. https://www.zdnet.com/article/cisco-releases-fixes-for-critical-vpn-router-vulnerabilities/.

Popko, Aleksander. "IOS App Security: How to Protect Users' Sensitive Data in Mobile Applications." Netguru Blog on Mobile, May 11, 2018. https://www.netguru.com/blog/ios-app-data-security.

Pratt, Mary K. "What Is Zero Trust? A Model for More Effective Security." CSO Online, January 16, 2018. https://www.csoonline.com/article/3247848/what-is-zero-trust-a-model-for-more-effective-security.html.

Preece, Caroline. "iOS8 Download Release Data Arrives." ITPro, September 17, 2014. https://www.itpro.co.uk/general-data-protection-regulation-gdpr/ios-8-download-release-date-arrives.

Resmed, Inc. "AirSense™ 10 Elite CPAP Device: ResMed Healthcare Professional." Healthcare Professional, November 9, 2020. https://www.resmed.com/en-us/healthcare-professional/products-and-support/devices/airsense-10-elite/.

Rhew, David. "Samsung Backs Open API Pledge for Healthcare Data Interoperability." Samsung Business Insights, December 13, 2018. https://insights.samsung.com/2018/12/13/samsung-backs-open-api-pledge-for-healthcare-data-interoperability/.

Ross, Ron. "FISMA Implementation Project - Protecting the Nation's Critical Information Infrastructure." Accessed August 10, 2021. https://csrc.nist.gov/CSRC/media/Presentations/FISMA-Implementation-Project-Protecting-the-Nation/images-media/Workshop-1.pdf.

Rouse, Margaret. "What Is Virtual Desktop Infrastructure? VDI Explained." SearchVirtualDesktop, TechTarget, October 20, 2020. https://searchvirtualdesktop.techtarget.com/definition/virtual-desktop-infrastructure-VDI.

Seri, Ben. "Vulnerabilities in Medical Devices Prompt FDA & DHS to Issue Advisories." Armis, October 29, 2019. https://www.armis.com/resources/iot-security-blog/urgent-11-update/.

Statcounter.com. "Mobile Operating System Market Share Worldwide." StatCounter Global Stats. Accessed January 13, 2021a. https://gs.statcounter.com/os-market-share/mobile/worldwide#monthly-201911-202011.

Statcounter.com. "Mobile & Tablet Android Version Market Share Worldwide." StatCounter Global Stats. Accessed January 13, 2021b. https://gs.statcounter.com/os-version-market-share/android/mobile-tablet/worldwide#monthly-201911-202011.

Statcounter.com. "Mobile & Tablet IOS Version Market Share Worldwide." StatCounter Global Stats. Accessed January 13, 2021c. https://gs.statcounter.com/os-version-market-share/ios/mobile-tablet/worldwide#monthly-201911-202011.

Strom, David. "What Is Application Security? A Process and Tools for Securing Software." CSO Online, September 2, 2020. https://www.csoonline.com/article/3315700/what-is-application-security-a-process-and-tools-for-securing-software.html#:~:text=Application%20security%20is%20the%20process,apps%20once%20they%20are%20deployed.

Terry, Ken. "'Hospital at Home' Increases COVID Capacity in Large Study." Medscape, November 18, 2020. https://www.medscape.com/viewarticle/941173.

US President Proclamation. "21st Century Cures Act: Interoperability, Information Blocking, and the ONC Health IT Certification Program." Federal Register, May 1, 2020. https://www.federalregister.gov/documents/2020/05/01/2020-07419/21st-century-cures-act-interoperability-information-blocking-and-the-onc-health-it-certification.

Verizon Wireless. "Nougat (7.0) for Android™." Verizon Wireless, October 7, 2016. https://www.verizon.com/support/android-nougat-os/?adobe_mc=MCMID%3D2427072118606232097322783009039195914 9%7CMCORGID%3D843F02BE53271A1A0A490D4C%2540AdobeOrg%7CTS%3D1608 497620&mboxSession=bd850318159d436f9e5c477db6088209.

Wind River, Inc. "Security Vulnerability Response Information." TCP/IP Network Stack (IPnet, Urgent/11). Accessed January 13, 2021. https://www.windriver.com/security/announcements/tcp-ip-network-stack-ipnet-urgent11/.

Chapter 12

Security in Motion: Protecting Devices and Data on the Move

Jeff Klaben

Santa Clara University Schools of Law School, Engineering, and Business

Contents

DOI: 10.4324/9781003220473-16

Introduction

In this moment, envision that you are experiencing a personal health crisis. Something feels wrong. Perhaps it is tightness in your chest with constricted breathing. Whatever the symptoms, your body is sending warning signs. It is providing enough information to convince you that you require the immediate attention of a healthcare professional. Could it be a heart attack, pulmonary embolism, unstable angina, COVID-19 infection, panic attack, or just heartburn?

Imagine that you end up in a hospital emergency room as a patient with doctors, nurses, and support staff intent on helping you. To systematically rule out the most life-threatening conditions and make an accurate diagnosis, your doctor uses data points from a variety of sources, including intake forms, imagery from ultrasound and CT scans, medical computing and diagnostic equipment, lab tests, vital sign monitoring, electronic medical records, and patient interviews. When pieced together effectively, this disparate collection of data forms a more cohesive story about your health. To quickly and efficiently create, ingest, analyze, share, protect, and manage this data, a variety of systems and methods are required.

You and your healthcare team may also utilize a variety of tools to continue gathering and contextualizing your health information, to keep communicating and collaborating, and to define and manage a long-term treatment plan. Mobile devices offer many immediately useful capabilities that can enable both you and your healthcare team to move forward with greater context and confidence. Patients with a pacemaker could use technology like the Medtronic MyCareLink Smart Monitor to avoid an ER visit entirely. This combination of an inexpensive medical device for reading cardiac data and an accompanying mobile device app can support rapid sharing of heart device data with a doctor – even when the patient is remote or on the move (Medtronic 2021). However, precious information (and the lives it represents) can be subject to significant risk when mobile devices and data are on the move.

This chapter explores ideas on maximizing the benefits of mobile computing in medicine while minimizing unintended side effects. Our goal is to equip stakeholders of mobile medical computing environments with tools to communicate system goals and collaborate more effectively to manage risk. This involves establishing some consistent language, methods, and models to organize our thinking about risk, strategy, and system architecture. Above all, our primary focus is bridging from conceptual technical and management frameworks to practical ideas that have immediate applicability. With this in mind, we explore several key elements and perspectives on a healthy information system, including:

- Learning from System Failures
- Creating a Trustworthy Mobile Computing Environment
- Leading Organizational Culture
- System Objectives, Control Objectives, and Managing Risk
- Identifying and Characterizing Devices
- Managing Identity and Access Control
- Assessing and Governing
- Fostering Interdisciplinary Collaboration

Together, these elements offer a starting point for developing a game plan to protect a mobile computing environment. When we pull it all together, we can envision the sense of reassurance, confidence, and ultimately trust in the systems that we hope to rely upon.

Learning from System Failures

Mobile technology can enable both a patient and their healthcare team to respond and mitigate risk more quickly. During a health crisis, patients with a Medtronic MyCareLink Smart Monitor might be able to share critical cardiac data with their doctor and avoid an ER visit entirely. Any remote medical device and this general category of technology can introduce new forms of risk. Successful exploitation of device vulnerabilities could result in an attacker modifying or fabricating data from an implanted cardiac device. An attack could involve uploading corrupt data to the network used by physicians for patient care. Further, an attacker could remotely execute code on the patient's Smart Reader device, which could then allow control of a paired cardiac device (Cybersecurity & Infrastructure Security Agency 2020). When a malicious cyber-attack has the potential to be fatal, an inevitable question arises. Are these mobile technologies worth the risk?

Patients who choose (or attempt) to avoid the use of mobile devices in their care may also encounter other security and privacy risks during a visit to the ER. Imaging system vulnerabilities are now cause for immediate concern. A critical vulnerability recently discovered in a prominent brand of medical imaging devices is emblematic of this risk. These vulnerabilities allowed remote code execution and access/alteration of sensitive patient data, including Protected Health Information (PHI) on Healthcare imaging devices including MRI, Ultrasound, Advanced Visualization, Interventional, X-Ray, Mammography, Computed Tomography, Nuclear Medicine, and PET/CT devices (Alder 2020). These vulnerabilities are rated as critical because they are remotely exploitable and only require a low level of skill level to exploit (Cybersecurity & Infrastructure Security Agency 2020). The US DHS Cybersecurity and Infrastructure Security Agency (CISA) also stated that

> If exploited, these vulnerabilities could allow an attacker to gain access to affected devices in a way that is comparable with the company's (remote) service user privileges. A successful exploitation could expose sensitive data ... or could allow the attacker to run arbitrary code, which might impact the availability of the system and allow manipulation of PHI.

When combined, these device-level vulnerabilities and broader risks impacting medical technology ecosystems are compounded.

Even seasoned risk management experts could not predict the perfect storm of 2020 that drove medical and IT practitioners to sheer exasperation. The confluence of global pandemic, unplanned remote work, political and economic instability, and public protests about social justice contributed to feelings of frustration, isolation, detachment, and desperation by healthcare and IT professionals, patients, and other stakeholders. By year end, these challenges were paralleled by a scourge of incidents in the digital world. Stealthy computer viruses enabled attackers to quietly ravage government and private networks for months before massive, wide-reaching cyber-attacks and data breaches were detected. Experts struggled to form a comprehensive understanding and mitigation strategy for the cascade of data breaches that seemingly started with SolarWinds, a provider of computer network management tools. This supply chain style attack then escalated by spreading SUNBURST malware to roughly 18,000 SolarWinds customers (Krebs 2020). The SolarWinds/ SUNBURST debacle offers an immediate realization for many: the game of nation-state level cyberattack and defense is evolving beyond the skill or capability of many enterprise information technology teams.

Researchers, including those at the University of Michigan and University of California, continue to uncover weaknesses in medical devices and the environments in which they operate. They explain the crux of the ongoing challenge: "preventing hackers from disabling or taking control of electronic devices is an ongoing challenge because malicious actors tend to be steps ahead of researchers and manufacturers" (McGee, 2020a). Securing these systems can feel like a moving target. How can stakeholders adopt a more effective and resilient approach to securing mobile devices and data on the move?

Creating a Trustworthy Mobile Computing Environment

As discussed throughout this book, mobile computing can enable and empower healthcare providers and recipients to more fully participate in the delivery of care. Mobility can enable a multitude of new capabilities, including:

- Accessing, transmitting, updating, and validating medical and system data
- Agent-based augmentation of clinical practitioners
- Collecting and transmitting biomedical signal data
- Coordinating care and service delivery
- Diagnosing
- Facilitating emergency response
- Monitoring for adherence to medication or treatment
- Patient education, self-monitoring, intervention, and behavior design
- Provide real-time services
- Remote patient activity monitoring and telehealth
- Remote/robotic surgery
- Tracking patient location and activity
- Video-based consultation

Mobility can clearly add valuable capability, but at a price. Additional layers of system complexity and risk demand some thoughtful consideration. A meaningful examination of mobile device security starts by recognizing that these devices do not exist in isolation. To avoid catastrophe and create trustworthy systems, a broader perspective can lead to a more complete solution and ultimately to greater trust.

Strategy

Some describe the digitally connected mesh of devices that store, use, and transmit medical data in and across healthcare environments as the Internet of Medical Things (IoMT), while others mention mHealth (Mobile Healthcare) Systems. Regardless of monikers, it is helpful to recognize the technology ecosystems and variety of systems and services with which mobile devices connect and interact. A broader view enables a more integrated and holistic approach to security.

A broader view also allows us to see the ugly warts and control gaps that can spoil systems that seemed otherwise ideal and secure in theory. Ultimately, establishing and maintaining protection of the systems and information in our healthcare delivery environments is about choosing to see these flaws, irrespective of who is responsible for shortcomings or suboptimal management practices. An effective strategy addresses traditional IT, mobile, cloud, clinical engineering, building automation, and supply chain systems that handle sensitive data or operations. This applies whether sensitive data touches these systems by design or inadvertently. Data management and data analytics practices are also in scope, as these are often at the heart of advanced clinical capabilities. Finally, it is vital that we find the right words to articulate our strategy effectively. The precise and intentional use of language will enable us to share these ideas and move forward together – from a conceptual strategy to true action.

Language and Communication

Finding a common language is a key ingredient to effectively engage stakeholders, to develop a systemic view of embedded technologies and information systems, and to ultimately deliver the intended outcomes of a healthcare system. Unfortunately, language is still perceived as an obstacle:

> The current confusion in the nomenclature and classification hinder telemedicine research… it frustrates our efforts to reach a reasonable understanding of what we already know and what we need to know. Equally important, it impedes progress toward development and implementation of a research agenda geared toward reaching answers to questions regarding the true benefits and costs of telemedicine.
>
> *Cameron et al. (2017)*

Fortunately, individuals don't have to be formally trained technologists to participate in strategic conversations and decision-making about the application of technology to solve clinical, business, and organizational problems. If we agree that the goal of creating a trustworthy mobile computing environment is best served by a holistic approach, then it reasonably follows that some level of common understanding amongst stakeholders is worth pursuing. Together, they can articulate vision, problem statements, requirements, use cases, control objectives, system architecture, and verification methods. This involves language, mindset, and frameworks.

Leading Organizational Culture

As described above, system failures can bring a sense of instability, pessimism, and reluctance to embrace new technologies. Our mobile device security strategy and those tasked with protecting valuable or sensitive data will inevitably be tested. Fortunately, mindset is something that a talented leader can shape. By doing so, they also shape the behavior that follows.

Leaders can encourage conscious, concerted, systematic thinking and enable folks to avoid or break out of counterproductive mindsets and behavior. They can establish common goals and incentives to avoid catastrophe. Leaders can teach folks that it is a choice to act responsibly and avoid crisis. They can proactively look for the warts on seemingly perfect systems by seeking and addressing "bad" news through activities like threat modeling and network penetration testing. They can choose to recognize that all information technology tools are, in a way, also security tools.

Organizational leaders can chart a course to a more constructive state of mind and an effective mobile device security strategy. Through thoughtful, structured, and committed action, even (and especially) in the most difficult circumstances they can transform a mobile device security strategy into a success story about confidence, resiliency, trust, and clinical efficacy. When they enact these practices in ways that consistently guide people (and the organizations they form), they lay the groundwork for effective, sustainable organizational governance.

Frameworks

There is no singular strategy or approach to achieve an organization's goals for a trustworthy mobile computing environment. Rather, a framework of considerations, possible solutions, and tradeoffs is offered. NCR corporation's first Chief Information Security Officer (and this author's mentor), Ralph Stahl Jr. offered the basis for this framework decades ago (Stahl Jr. 1997). Stahl's focus was on the mobile computing user, and his framework addressed many core elements that are still equally relevant today. He organized his framework into four primary sections: availability and continuity, integrity, confidentiality, and new technology considerations.

Stahl's model of security services for system availability is still an excellent starting point, as it includes awareness of operational schedules, physical protections, device identification, reliability of power and connectivity, communication tools, service continuity, data backup, and system loss and recovery. His advice was also pragmatic and prescient:

> Security procedures, guidelines, and practices accepted by end users must enable them to do their jobs. If end users interpret security to be a roadblock, they will often find ways to circumvent security requirements. To ensure that this does not happen, the security practitioner should spend time learning the problems and security concerns of users. ... This practice enhances understanding of the remote access conditions, and assists the security practitioner in developing more effective security practices.

After over two decades, a framework can continue to offer valuable guidance, but practitioners must also avoid following them singularly or blindly. CIO and biomedical engineer, Giuliano Pozza explains that to effectively evaluate, implement, and operate new technologies, practices in clinical environments must be routinely updated and based on a collection of relevant frameworks:

> Presently, the IT department has a set of core methodologies for governance and security (e.g., IT Infrastructure Library [ITIL], COBIT 5, ... [ISO]/ [IEC] ISO/IEC 27001), while clinical engineering is working on a different set of methodologies (e.g., a health technology assessment [HTA]). This was fine a few years ago, when diagnostic equipment was purely machines. Now, the data-capture devices (such as medical devices with their MDDS) and automation technologies are mostly software-defined and software-controlled.

Pozza (2018)

Written and unwritten organizational charts are also important frameworks in this context. An organization's culture is shaped by efforts to create a common understanding about the roles and responsibilities within and across the organization. This can be dynamic and often involves a healthy (or at least unavoidable) tension. On the one hand, it can be uncomfortable for organizations to deviate from known, predictable organizational structures. On the other hand, it can be equally uncomfortable for cybersecurity leaders to jostle for the right home between departments and functions, especially in the midst of operational disharmony or preexisting organizational misalignment.

To reliably deliver on the promise of mobile computing in medicine, effective organizational alignment and governance remain vital throughout the lifecycle of these systems. Organizations that intend to create an effective governance structure for mobile medical computing should look broadly at the scope of systems and data that mobile computing devices interact with and the respective organizations and stakeholders tied to these systems. If calling upon a new mix of experts and stakeholders is necessary, so be it. Focus on the end results and do what works to get it right.

System Objectives, Control Objectives, and Risk Management

Whatever we call it, our mobile-enabled healthcare information system was created for a reason. These systems essentially exist to assist in managing and extracting value from data – to help patients. Access to more data, more quickly can enhance this value – especially when it is well curated and protected. The volume of this data continues expanding and with more access to more data, and these advances often come with the hidden price of greater risk.

The challenge is how to paint more accurate predictions about risk. How do we gain greater knowledge and perspective about current state and potential risks, requirements, and possible solutions? Ongoing efforts to interact with stakeholders and to research and understand some of the macro trends in healthcare are a helpful building block. At a minimum, this may provide greater capacity to describe a system's desired target state in terms of both control objectives and healthcare outcomes. Where control objectives may span across Trust, Identity, Privacy, Protection, Safety, and Security (TIPPSS).

Data growth is an example of a technology trend that continues to increase in relevance. Understanding the nature of the data growth (along with accelerating threats) is important because it is a significant factor in compounding risk. This growth of data "encompasses all types of data, from structured data in the electronic medical record (EMR) to unstructured and imaging data. However, imaging and unstructured data, the worst condition from a security standpoint, are the real fuel of this data explosion" (DeGaspari, 2014a,b).

Where, how, and what data is being used and stored, and where it is on the move? A simple exercise can also help us think about the threats that mobile computing in medicine may face. Start by envisioning the exciting breakthroughs in healthcare that advances in technologies like cloud computing, big data and analytics, Internet of Things (IoT), AI, imaging, sensors, and wearables might bring. Next, envision leaving the intended path of this technology adoption, to encounter the downsides. Think about:

- What could go wrong?
- Are trade-offs evident?
- Where can data go?
- How are restrictions monitored and enforced?
- What types of attacks are worth understanding more deeply because they are likely to recur?
- Who can provide access to store, modify, or move data?
- Who can change the way systems behave?
- Can you anticipate virtual replacements for any common clinical activities?
- How is access to protected patient data restricted?

Risk management requires both quantitative and qualitative elements. It also requires the right mindset. For example, an assessment of risks relating to interactions between mobiles devices and personal computers might consider that an investigation "into the software updaters of five of the most popular PC manufacturers – found that all had … security problems that would allow attackers to hijack the update process and install malicious code on victim machines" (Zetter 2016).

Similarly, an often unpopular but rigorous mindset is that generally, the fewer people who have access to confidential data, the less risk there is that said confidential information may be improperly disclosed. If this is a control objective that the organization supports, it's probably a good idea to formally record it as a policy or standard. Standards can provide clarity and reduce avoidable questions and conflict. Regardless, the best way to start a discussion with stakeholders.

Another lesson that is already emerging from the SolarWinds/SUNBURST event described above is that returning systems to a trustworthy state can be incredibly difficult, time consuming, expensive, and strategically distracting. There may be no time like the present to recognize that this may be as good as it gets. This may be the very best time to start appreciating and fighting to maintain the order that exists when systems are freshly deployed and trustworthy. Beyond this, in the future, it could become financially infeasible to return to the level of system trust that currently exists.

Identifying and Characterizing Devices

Adopting commonly recognized language and frameworks enables more consistent characterization and management of mobile devices (and connected systems). With consistency and sufficient detail, we may uniquely identify devices and organize them into groups. Group-based management techniques allow for more efficiency throughout the lifecycle of system management. Let's start with a few definitions from recognized, authoritative sources.

Mobile Devices

A portable computing device that: (1) has a small form factor such that it can easily be carried by a single individual; (2) is designed to operate without a physical connection (e.g., wirelessly transmit or receive information); (3) possesses local, non-removable or removable data storage; and (4) includes a self-contained power source. Mobile devices may also include voice communication capabilities, onboard sensors that allow the devices to capture information, and/or built-in features for synchronizing local data with remote locations. Examples include smartphones, tablets, and E-readers (National Institute of Standards and Technology 2020).

Medical Devices

As described by the US Food and Drug Administration (FDA), medical devices range from simple tongue depressors and bedpans to complex programmable pacemakers with microchip technology and laser surgical devices. In addition, medical devices include in vitro diagnostic products, such as general-purpose lab equipment, reagents, and test kits, which may include monoclonal antibody technology (US Food and Drug Administration 2019).

If our goal is to create a trustworthy environment to use mobile devices for clinical purposes, we must expand our perspective. These definitions can get blurry when we consider that these systems may depend upon, be managed by, or connected to separate control or storage devices, laboratory management systems, supervisory control and data acquisition (SCADA) systems, or robotics in a variety of different settings. "For example, the Therapy Imaging and Model Management System

(TIMMS) is a complex system to integrate and manage heterogeneous medical devices, clinical information systems and components of computer-assisted surgery in the operating theater" (Lemke and Vannier 2006).

Connected storage devices highlight the importance of considering data in motion. Industry researchers identified over 45 million unique medical images that were openly accessible via the Internet on "about 2,000 unprotected connected storage devices with ties to medical centers, hospitals, clinics and doctors' offices – large and small – in 67 countries." In many instances, the leaking devices were network-attached storage (NAS) and exposed data included patient X-rays and CT scans containing electronic Protected Health Information (ePHI) (McGee 2020b).

Internet of Things (IoT) and the Convergence of Interconnected Systems

The Internet of Things encompasses a variety of devices and functions. Generally, this can include "things having identities and virtual personalities operating in smart spaces using intelligent interfaces to connect and communicate within social, environmental, and user contexts" and may be defined as "a world-wide network of interconnected objects uniquely addressable, based on standard communication protocols" (Ray 2018). These systems can pose a significant risk to goals of Trust, Identity, Privacy, Protection, Safety, and Security but are more likely to be overlooked by more rigorous IT governance practices within an organization. Examples include interconnected sensors and other components of smart building control systems such as lighting, heating, ventilation and air conditioning (HVAC), physical access control, video surveillance, and refrigeration control systems.

Device Capabilities

These devices can include advanced capabilities such as context awareness based on current or prior information collected by directly or indirectly connected sensors. Other capabilities include embedded mobile communication and intelligent or coordinated decision-making. Certain devices can be identified by other smart devices or by connected networks.

These devices may also share stored data and other attributes and identifiers, such as IP address, Uniform Resource Identifier, or descriptions of the device's capabilities. These IoT systems may also have adaptive interfaces that are based on context, such as environmental variables or user behavior. Device interfaces may also allow users to query other devices, monitor status, or enable remote control (Ray 2018). Effective risk management will consider various device interfaces and communication capabilities as well as operating states and behavior patterns. Additional considerations are the context or trusted zones within which the device is operating, along with the categories of data it is collecting, storing, processing, or analyzing.

Behavior Patterns and Recommendations

Everything that offers a promise of greater value can introduce the risk of that value being misdirected or subverted for the benefit of malicious actors. Risks such as unauthorized data access, destruction, modification, interruptions in availability, manipulation of decision-making systems, and loss of patient trust. Before something goes wrong, it can be helpful to know:

■ Do these systems interact by design?
■ Could they interact inadvertently?
■ What is the worst-case scenario and business impact if systems malfunction?

Having a baseline for expected behavior of systems and devices can be particularly useful, but how can we determine what is normal behavior after things are already operating?

Analytic tools can be used to establish a baseline to understand the expected patterns of behavior, connections, and data transfer activities that mobile devices may routinely perform. Using techniques to detect and compare these baselines with real-time analysis of network and system activities will make it possible to effectively and more consistently detect unusual or anomalous activity that can be an indicator of a compromise. Indicators of compromise (IoCs) may also be shared to more quickly detect potentially nefarious activity. Machine learning techniques are becoming increasingly important to effectively and quickly identify the behavior of adversaries.

On *us-cert.cisa.gov*, the Cybersecurity & Infrastructure Security Agency (CISA) provides a number of recommended practices, including Improving Industrial Control Systems Cybersecurity with Defense-in-Depth Strategies. Additional mitigation guidance and recommended practices are publicly available on the ICS webpage on us-cert.cisa.gov in the Technical Information Paper, ICS-TIP-12-146-01B – Targeted Cyber Intrusion Detection and Mitigation Strategies. Examples of suggested leading clinical practices include:

- Ensure proper segmentation of the local hospital/clinical network and create explicit access rules based on source/destination IP/port for all connections, including those used for remote support. Specific ports to consider may include those used for TELNET, FTP, REXEC, and SSH
- Utilize IPSec VPN and explicit access rules at the Internet edge before forwarding incoming connections to the local hospital/clinical network
- Impact analysis and risk assessment prior to deploying defensive measures

CISA further recommends that organizations observing any suspected malicious activity should follow their established internal procedures and report their findings to CISA for tracking and correlation against other incidents.

Managing Identity and Access Control

Ongoing attention is required to maintain control over mobile devices and data on the move. Identity and Access Management (IAM) is the lynchpin to systematize and automate these controls. An effective IAM system combines technical capability, lifecycle management, and enforceable policy.

As highlighted in Figure 12.1, a centralized repository for identities can enable more streamlined management of user and system accounts and login credentials, reduce redundant sign-on requirements, and support self-service functionality, such as password reset. Multi-factor authentication capabilities can be aligned to enable consistent policies and management across applications and services on mobile devices, on-premise systems, and cloud-based services. These systems can be designed and implemented with resilience measures to mitigate risks of service disruptions from disaster or malicious attack. Lifecycle management capabilities can enable greater diligence and efficiency by automating repetitive activities, offering role-based access management controls, and enhancing monitoring, reporting, and visibility of system activity and policy compliance for IAM system administrators.

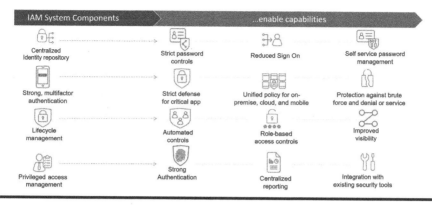

Figure 12.1   Core architectural components of an IAM system (Klaben 2018).

As hypothetical cyberattacks have become the new normal, the process of rolling-out new computing and security capabilities requires greater diligence. Evolving attack techniques require corresponding risk management strategies. Proactively adopting methods to reduce attack surface during deployment, build critical skills, validate cloud service implementation, and leverage identity intelligence for threat detection and response can prevent chaos. As I discussed during an Oktane industry conference presentation (Klaben and Tugnawat 2018), the core architectural components of an IAM system shown in Figure 12.1 may also be viewed as a key system element to protect from malicious attack.

Assessing and Governing

The Information Systems Audit and Control Association (ISACA) explains that governance "ensures that stakeholder needs, conditions and options are evaluated to determine balanced, agreed-on enterprise objectives to be achieved; setting direction through prioritization and decision making; and monitoring performance and compliance against agreed-on direction and objectives." Governance involves setting and enforcing policy, assessment, and verification.

Distinct policies and standards may be required for various elements of mobile medicine computing and delivery environments, for example:

- Medical staff and human resource practices
- System development and lifecycle requirements
- System security planning and management
- Control objectives and requirements
- Data storage and database management practices
- Data models for collection, storage, and analysis
- Service and quality management
- System validation and compliance
- Change control
- Mobile device and software security
- Medical devices configuration and maintenance standards
- IoT and sensor standards

- Web services and microservices standards
- Cloud and analytics services and software usage
- Decision-making and AI ethics practices
- Data transmission methods
- Data privacy
- Record keeping and data retention
- Supply chain and service provider management
- Remote access and monitoring
- Protocols for remotely controlled medical activities
- Risk assessment, system assessment, and remediation
- Incident response

Mobile devices refer to any mobile phone, smartphone, or tablet as defined by NIST. The following are examples of identity and access management related standards that can be applied to the use of mobile devices

- Mobile devices must be configured with a minimum password/passcode/PIN length to access the device
- Mobile devices must be configured to disable the device for a certain or indefinite period of time after a predefined number of failed login attempts.
- Mobile devices must be secured with a password-protected screen lock when left unattended and must be configured to automatically lock after a certain period of inactivity.
- The use of devices that are jailbroken or have been altered to disabling built-in protections is not permitted. Modification of device functionality must be reviewed or approved by the organization.
- Mobile devices must use approved forms of user authentication (e.g. user IDs, passwords, and authentication tokens/devices) to access the organization's non-public information.

For example, a policy stating: "when using mobile devices, organizational data may only be created, processed, stored, and communicated on personal devices running organizationally approved mobile device security software" requires key elements to be in place to make it an enforceable policy. Capabilities in identity and access management such as mobile device provisioning and deprovisioning and sanitization of physical devices are crucial to turn policy intentions into effective controls. Further, increased risk may be the result of when mobile devices are improperly identified or improperly associated with an organization or specific policy.

Criteria and methods for verifying the correct design and operation of controls are another key aspect of governance. Security assessment and risk management for new technologies can be increasingly challenging because of the increasingly interconnected nature of these technologies. Coordination between a variety of stakeholders may be required to ensure that sufficient expertise in various systems and approaches is included during assessment, architectural design, implementation, and operation. Similarly, to create a comprehensive and holistic governance model, the interrelationships and dependencies between system elements require consideration.

Empowering Interdisciplinary Collaboration

The Emergency Care Research Institute highlighted cyberattack as the top hazard for medical devices. Therefore, ECRI recommends that IT professionals be aware of the specifics of medical devices, and clinical engineers be trained in the essentials of IT security (ECRI Institute 2021). But why stop there?

As discussed, systems are becoming increasingly interconnected and interdependent. The teams that manage the clinical systems and medical devices, customer support, physical security, plant and facilities, technology networks and infrastructure, robotics, applications, information security, supply chain, and governance can no longer afford to operate independently. These groups must find ways to collaborate and manage risk effectively. How do we teach cross-disciplinary collaboration in proactive ways?

After having served as a CISO multiple times, this question has continued to trouble me. I concluded that teaching could be a force multiplier, by educating the next generation of engineers and technologists on the foundations of cybersecurity. After teaching graduate courses in cybersecurity management and computer forensic investigation as a part-time, adjunct instructor, I seized an opportunity to design a course that could break new ground. So, I designed a course to answer the question through simulated real-world scenarios and fact patterns that couple collaboration techniques with real-world challenges in cybersecurity and data privacy. This is what I am teaching now (Santa Clara University 2019).

This was also an opportunity to do something that has not been done before, to build upon what I have learned from mentors, and to bring together students from four separate academic departments. Empowering individuals with self-awareness and the tools to overcome communication breakdowns between different professional functions (and personalities), and to learn to rely upon each other. They will be ready to enhance trust and build organizational resiliency. I hope that you find similar tools to overcome vulnerability and moments of uncertainty and move on to moments of confidence in mobile device security for your organization.

References

Alder, Steve. 2020. HIPAA Journal, December 9. Accessed December 21, 2020. https://www.hipaajournal.com/critical-vulnerabilities-identified-in-more-than-100-ge-healthcare-imaging-and-ultrasound-products/.

Cameron, Joshua D., Arkalgud Ramaprasad, and Thant Syn. 2017. "An ontology of and roadmap for mHealth research." *International Journal of Medical Informatics* 100: 16–25.

Cybersecurity & Infrastructure Security Agency. 2020. ICS Medical Advisory (ICSMA-20-345-01), December 10. Accessed January 10, 2021. https://us-cert.cisa.gov/ics/advisories/icsma-20-345-01.

DeGaspari, John. 2014a. Healthcare Informatics, September 22. Accessed December 18, 2020. www.healthcare-informatics.com/article/managing-data-explosion.

DeGaspari, John. 2014b. Healthcare Innovation: Managing the Data Explosion, September 22. Accessed February 15, 2021. www.healthcare-informatics.com/article/managing-dat-exlposion.

ECRI Institute. 2021. 2021 Top 10 Health Technology Hazards. Accessed February 24, 2021. www.ecri.org /2021hazards.

Klaben, Jeff, and Surbhi Tugnawat. 2018. Conference Proceedings: Oktane 18, May 24. Accessed February 11, 2021. https://youtu.be/zVbIVqomVuI.

Krebs, Brian. 2020. Krebson Security, December 20. Accessed December 21, 2020. https://krebsonsecurity.com/2020/12/solarwinds-hack-could-affect-18k-customers/.

Lemke, Heinz U., and Michael Vannier. 2006. "The operating room and the need for an IT Infrastructure and Standards." *Journal of Computer Assisted Radiology and Surgery* 1(3): 117–121.

McGee, Marianne Kolbasuk. 2020a. 2 Tales of Device-Related Risks to Patients, December 16. Accessed December 18, 2020. https://www.healthcareinfosecurity.com/2-tales-device-related-risks-to-patients-a-15613.

McGee, Marianne Kolbasuk. 2020b. Healthcareinfosecurity.com, December 16. Accessed December 21, 2020. https://www.healthcareinfosecurity.com/2-tales-device-related-risks-to-patients-a-15613.

Medtronic. 2021. MyCareLink Smart US, February 17. Accessed February 17, 2021. https://www.medtronic.com/us-en/mobileapps/patient-caregiver/mycarelink-smart-us.html.

National Institute of Standards and Technology. 2020. Computer Security Resource Center. Accessed December 30, 2020. https://csrc.nist.gov/glossary/term/mobile_device.

Pozza, Giuliano. 2018. ISACA Journal, May 1. Accessed January 4, 2021. https://www.isaca.org/resources/isaca-journal/issues/2018/volume-3/healthcare-securitythree-paradoxes-and-the-need-for-a-paradigm-shift.

Ray, Partha Pratim. 2018. "A survey on Internet of Things architectures." *Journal of King Saud University - Computer and Information Sciences* 30(3): 291–319.

Santa Clara University. 2019. New Multi-Disciplinary Course Improves Communications Among Silicon Valley Professionals, May 16. Accessed December 18, 2020. https://www.scu.edu/news-and-events/press-releases/2019/may-2019/new-multi-disciplinary-course-improves-communications-among-silicon-valley-professionals.html.

Stahl Jr., Ralph. 1997. Virtual Office (Mobile User) Security. Auerbach Information Management Service 83-02-16.

US Food and Drug Administration. 2019. Is the Product a Medical Device? December 16. Accessed December 21, 2020. www.fda.gov/MedicalDevices/DeviceRegulationandGuidance/Overview/ClassifyYourDevice/ucm051512.htm.

Zetter, Kim. 2016. Wired.com, May 31. Accessed December 21, 2020. https://www.wired.com/2016/05/2036876/.

ASPIRATIONAL TO OPERATIONAL: RAPIDLY UPGRADE PEOPLE SKILLS

5

Chapter 13

Personality Intelligence and Communication: Communicating Trust through Relatability and Personality Intelligence—Conversations with Key Stakeholders

Anthony Lee and Mamie Lamley

Heroic Voice Academy

Contents

DOI: 10.4324/9781003220473-18

Welcome to the training room! All the previous chapters have prepared you with content to take into presentations and conversations with key stakeholders. The purpose of this chapter is to prepare you for these speaking opportunities (Figure 13.1).

Here is an overview of your journey to the stage:
1. **The value of trust:** A story of building a new trust infrastructure
2 **Emotional intelligence:** Connect with hearts and minds in your audience
3. **The connection triangle:** Message delivery skills that create a connection
4. **The message blueprint:** A solid foundation for your presentations
5. **Shared values:** The critical element for creating trust
6. **Personality intelligence:** Communication strategies for elevating trust and relatability
7. **The message portfolio:** Frameworks to storyboard your presentation
8. **Practice like a professional:** Get in the Gym

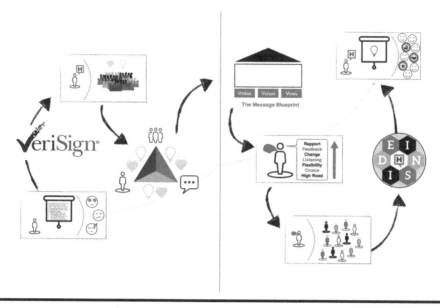

Figure 13.1   The Heroic Voice Journey. (Adapted with permission from Anthony Lee, Heroic Voice Academy [2018].)

Figure 13.2   From VeriSign, Inc., Public domain, via Wikimedia Commons.

The Value of Trust

A Story of Building a New Trust Infrastructure

On the Internet, nobody knows you're a dog.

– Paul Steiner

Paul Steiner, a cartoonist for "The New Yorker," drew one of the most well-known cartoons in the Internet's early days. The comic was published in July 1993 when there were 130 websites (cite Matthew Gray, MIT, *http://www.mit.edu/people/mkgray/growth/*).

The Internet was expanding from the worlds of academics and government into the public domain. By the beginning of 1996, the number of websites had grown to 100,000 (also – Matthew Gray).

Recognized as a source of unlimited commercial potential, the Internet and many companies were launched to capitalize on Internet-related technologies. One of those companies was VeriSign, a company I joined in 1996 (Figure 13.2).

VeriSign's founders recognized that e-commerce would remain a "good idea," but it lacked critical elements for widespread adoption by businesses and consumers. There were existing examples of digital transactions such as wire transfers and credit card machines. These transactions were considered secure and took place on private networks that large well-known financial institutions managed.

When digital transactions take place between any two individuals, the customers could realize the potential of e-commerce. Amazon sold its first book in 1995 and ended the year with $511,000 in sales. Many companies had visions of becoming the "next Amazon," but they would have to overcome two significant challenges to achieve substantial sales numbers through their websites.

The first challenge was to gain the public's attention and required a significant amount of money dedicated to marketing departments. The objective was to maximize the number of visitors to their website. The increase in website traffic measured the success of a marketing campaign. Sales departments could use the number of visitors and begin to make revenue forecasts.

The second challenge was getting the visitor to purchase and consumers who were wary of sharing their credit card information online. Handing a credit card to an employee of a restaurant, supermarket, or department store was a typical transaction. Giving a credit card number to a stranger on the other end of a computer screen was an entirely different matter.

There were fears about the authenticity of the website. Did it truly belong to the company it claimed to represent, or could it be an impostor using a fraudulent website? There were fears about the security of the transaction. Could the credit card information be digitally intercepted and then used for fraudulent transactions?

VeriSign's mission was to address and solve these problems regarding consumer confidence. They worked with all the major web browser companies to introduce the concept of a digital certificate. VeriSign would be responsible for the authentication and issuance of these certificates to the websites' legitimate owners.

When consumers visit websites with a digital certificate, a padlock icon is displayed, confirming its authenticity and an encrypted connection. The padlock icon also gave consumers the confidence to make an online purchase.

With digital certificates the key to unlocking the potential of e-commerce, the marketing department at VeriSign still faced challenges in gaining widespread adoption. During my presentations to potential customers, I used our marketing material to teach the importance of web server certificates. I used comprehensive slides to explain the value of encryption and how it protected each transaction. The topics of security, authentication, and privacy resonated with a small minority of each audience in every presentation. Because the messages did not connect with the entire audience, the adoption of technology was extremely slow.

Looking deeper, the marketing department realized that their message was too technical. They decided to change the technical message by including emotional messaging. The outcome was a 2.5-minute video, "The Value of Trust," which became the company tagline. Shifting the focus from encryption to trust allowed the messages to become more relatable and empathetic. Specific sections of the video spoke to a broader range of values, including community, family, opportunity, excitement, technology, and the big picture.

The new messaging succeeded because it focused the audience's attention on business transactions and customers beginning to shift to online transactions. The e-commerce examples included online shopping, travel, banking, and insurance. Other models also highlighted examples where information privacy was important: emails, contracts, purchases, and health.

Having relatable examples helped audiences understand situations where we wanted to continue experiencing trust, security, and privacy. Prospective partners and customers quickly grasped the problem we were solving and envisioned themselves as leaders in the new digital business world. In 3 years, we had signed 23 partners accelerating the pace of e-commerce.

VeriSign's story is a beautiful example of how they built a brand new trust infrastructure to support the emergence of e-commerce. You now have the opportunity to create the next trust infrastructure for the world of mobile computing. In the following sections, we will share with you communication tools and practices that will fully prepare you for conversations with your stakeholders.

Emotional Intelligence

Connecting with the Hearts and Minds in Your Audience

The function of leadership is to produce more leaders, not more followers!

– Ralph Nader

Powerful conversations happen when you connect your audience's hearts and minds. Precision in your presentation creates a learning experience for all audiences. Whether you are speaking to 1 or 10,000, you must make a connection. Connection to your message demonstrates your passion and desire to communicate trust by incorporating high emotional intelligence and relatability (Figure 13.3).

Emotional Intelligence (EI) is the heart of communication mastery. It is essential when you build trust and are required to deliver results to patients and their families, clinicians, or other stakeholders. It is also crucial when high-stakes conversations involve managing risks, enabling organizational effectiveness, or adhering to regulatory protocol and compliance.

As medical professionals, having high EI coupled with empathy gives you the ability to recognize your emotions, understand what they are telling you, and help you see how your emotions impact others. EI considers others' perceptions and feelings and allows you to engage through excitement, predictability, expertise, logic, and authentic connection.

Relatability integrated with EI brings the mind and heart element into every presentation and conversation. It strengthens your audience's connection and helps identify shared values which communicate that you care about the same things. With diverse audiences, varying circumstances, and the desire to mitigate risks and avoid escalation, it will be vital for you to exercise preparedness to provide a quality response and meaningful content, which integrates "what is important" to the

Figure 13.3   Connecting to your audience's hearts and minds. (Adapted with permission from Anthony Lee, Heroic Voice Academy [2018].)

listener. We will talk more about relatability in our section called the *Connection Triangle*, a tool that delivers your message with precision, emotion, and connection.

The Connection Triangle

Message Delivery Skills to Connect with Your Audience

> Nobody cares about how much you know until they know how much you care.
>
> *– Heroic Voice Academy*

As a sales engineer with Verisign, one of my earliest mistakes was delivering great technical presentations that failed to connect with the audience's hearts. I did a great job teaching the importance of encryption, digital certificates, and server authentication. However, I forgot to address the executives' emotional experience in the room, who were in charge of protecting their company's data and reputation.

Most experts take the stage prepared with a wealth of information and ready to share their vast knowledge with an audience. However, the quantity of information that a presenter brings to the stage has little to do with delivering a successful presentation. Great communicators know that expertise plays a small part in a successful presentation. What other skills do world-class presenters bring to the stage?

The Heroic Voice Academy's Connection Triangle is a framework for success in any high-stakes conversation or presentation. When executives master these six skills – relatability, empathy, comprehension, engagement, passion, and expertise – they consistently connect with their audience's hearts and minds.

The three points of the triangle represent the presenter, the audience, and the message. When delivering presentations, we can call on specific skills from the connection triangle to strengthen the presenter-audience connection, the presenter-message connection, and the audience-message connection (Figure 13.4).

The first leg of the triangle connects the presenter to the audience. This leg consists of a pair of conversation skills, **relatability**, and **empathy**. With the gift of relatability, presenters can demonstrate how much they know about their audience. Before speaking, a presenter can use online research, phone interviews, or in-person visits to gather information to integrate into a presentation.

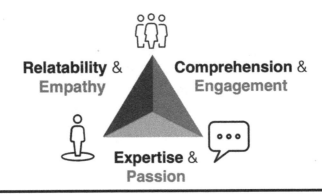

Figure 13.4 The connection triangle creates a connection with individuals and groups. (Adapted with permission from Anthony Lee, Heroic Voice Academy [2018].)

With the skill of empathy, presenters can demonstrate how much they care about the audience. The process begins by learning about the audience's story of struggle and then listening for the negative emotions that surface during the conversation. By identifying these emotions, a presenter shows a level of emotional intelligence that results in credibility and trust.

The second leg of the triangle connects the presenter to the message. This leg includes a pair of presentation skills: **expertise** and **passion**. As previously mentioned, expertise is partially defined by how much a presenter knows. The challenge for the expert presenter is curating a precise and concise amount of content for the audience.

A common mistake that expert presenters make is bringing too much information to the stage. They squeeze a large amount of data into a fixed amount of time. They illustrate the depth of their knowledge, believing that this elevates their credibility. What happens is that the audience experiences information overload, absorbing only a small portion of what the presenter shared.

Presenters express passion for demonstrating how much they care about their topic. One of the ways to do this is by speaking with energy and excitement. They bring the information alive by sharing with a vocal variety that intrigues and entertains.

The third leg of the triangle connects the audience to the message. We call this the magic leg because it educates individual members of the audience and empowers them to share your message with others, creating an exponential ripple effect for your message. On this third leg, we find the skills of **comprehension** and **engagement**.

> I hear, and I forget. I see, and I remember. I do, and I understand.
>
> *– Confucius*

Presenters often make the mistake of making comprehension the responsibility of the audience. Unfortunately, it is a shared task. The presenter brings their best teaching skills to the stage, and the student gets their active listening skills and full attention. Consider using accelerated tools to help your audience quickly absorb new knowledge.

Invest the time to develop all six of the Connection Triangle skills. Watch videos of your favorite presentations, and identify when specific skills are incorporated. When a message delivery skill inspires you, try it out during your rehearsal sessions. Better yet, find an executive communications coach to elevate the skills you wish to acquire.

The Message Blueprint

A Solid Foundation for All Your Presentations

> You can't build a great building on a weak foundation. You must have a solid foundation if you are going to have a strong superstructure.
>
> *– Gordon B. Hinkley*

A lesson from the VeriSign story is that technical expertise and competency only work when a solid messaging foundation is in place. When messaging from the "Value of Trust" campaign was added to the technical presentation, it elevated audience interest and attention.

The elements of Vision, Values, and Vows form the foundation of our Message Blueprint. Use this foundation to design presentations and facilitate great conversations. When you start with this solid foundation, you take your audience through a journey to know your vision, understand your values, and trust your vows (Figure 13.5).

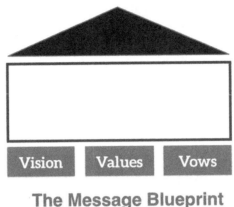

The Message Blueprint

Figure 13.5 The message blueprint, a solid foundation for all your presentations. (Adapted with permission from Anthony Lee, Heroic Voice Academy [2018].)

Vision is your "Big Picture" of the future that you are committed to creating. When you share your vision with clarity and passion, you can enroll others who wish to travel to the same destination. When you look to the future, possibilities are unlocked with your new trust infrastructure.

Values are your "Brave Stand" for what is most important to you and how you make decisions. Everything that you do with intention elevates your values. When you share your values, you connect with audience members who care about the same values. With a new trust infrastructure, what values will be elevated in the world?

Vows are your "Bold Promise" to the world. It is your commitment to bring the best of your abilities and skills to each situation. When you share your vows with your team, family, company, partners, and investors, they know exactly how they can count on you to lead them into the future. How much time and energy are you willing to commit to the creation of a new trust infrastructure?

How can you incorporate these elements into a first conversation? Begin by using a storyboard to illustrate your vision, values, and vows. Have these images in your head as your talking points. Use your improvisational skills to use them during a first conversation, and your reward will be a second conversation (Figure 13.6).

Slide 1: Your Big Picture

Create a simple sketch that represents your "Big Picture." Help your audience see what you see. Use this sketch to empower your audience to learn your vision and teach it to others. Point out specific details in your illustration that sparks the mind and warms the heart. Imagine a time in the future when your trust infrastructure is fully operational, what pictures of the future would you bring back to share to create interest and excitement.

Slide 2: Your Brave Stand

Look back at your sketch and identify the values that have been restored or elevated. Ask your audience to identify the personal values they see in your picture. Lead a conversation around the shared values that you have identified.

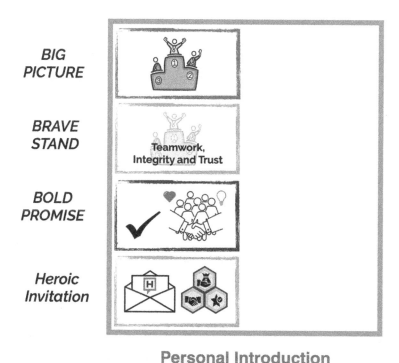

BIG
PICTURE

BRAVE
STAND

BOLD
PROMISE

Heroic
Invitation

Personal Introduction

Figure 13.6 Personal introduction storyboard. (Adapted with permission from Anthony Lee, Heroic Voice Academy [2018].)

Slide 3: Your Bold Promise

Your Bold Promise is how you define "All-In." Think of the last time you fully committed to a mission or a goal. You will likely find a story that illustrates your willingness to do "Whatever it takes." These stories show your character and integrity and give your audience social proof that they can place their trust in you.

Slide 4: The Heroic Invitation

By sharing all three of these foundation pieces, you will have answered the most critical questions in the minds of your audience. Vision tells your audience where you are going. Values define what is most important to you. Vows are how your audience can count on you. The audience will be open to giving you their attention for the rest of your presentation or their time for a second conversation.

Shared Values

The Key Element for Creating Trust

The most valuable business commodity is trust.

– Richard Branson

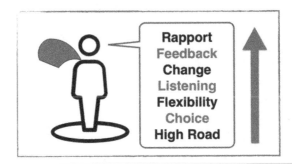

Figure 13.7 **The heroic mindset – 7 principles of trust in communication mastery. (Adapted with permission from Anthony Lee, Heroic Voice Academy [2018].)**

Heroic Voice Academy bases trust on mutual respect, responsibility, integrity, high emotional intelligence, and intentional action. We believe the capacity of your voice defines the power of your mission. As experts in your field, the self-mastery of communicating trust is vital in a framework to connect with patients, colleagues, and executives.

Shared values are essential to the overall success for yourself and your organization. It is the balance and alignment of company culture, vision, and mission with the individuals and community they work with and serve. Although shared values mean different things in various institutions, the bottom-line result influences people's behavior and attitudes. Let's start by introducing you to the seven principles we follow here at Heroic Voice Academy. These principles add value, responsibility, logic, and authenticity to how leaders like yourself communicate trust through shared values (Figure 13.7).

The Heroic Mindset: 7 Principles of Trust in Communication Mastery

Communicating trust is intentional and creates insight into various perspectives. The following principles, when implemented, can guide you in building connection and rapport.

Principle 1: There Are No Resistant Audiences - Only Inflexible Communicators

The meaning of communication is the response you get. Choosing the right words, tone, and actions is only the first step. Delivering them well is the second step, and the final step is ensuring your audience receives them positively. When someone is resistant, it is a sign of a lack of rapport and connection, and it is your responsibility to correct and continue. Be the first to demonstrate trust by building rapport. Know what is essential to your audience and integrate. Whether you are the executive or administrator or a frontline team member, when people know their best interest is the priority, trust gets established. To ensure there is no resistance, learn to communicate consistently with clarity, confidence, and composure.

Principle 2: There Is No Failure, only Feedback

Incorporating feedback is the key to generating consistent support, reputation, and monetization (Heroic Voice Presentation ROI). Leaders who practice open communication with their team, incorporate best practices, eliminate inefficiencies, and access creative expressions provide ideal opportunities for feedback to be shared positively and organically in an environment that fosters growth, success, and collaboration.

Principle 3: Great Leaders Ignite Change

Great Leaders ignite change that produces an ecological transition suitable for all parties - creating a world that works for everyone. Staying open-minded and listening allows people's voices and opinions to count. To ignite change, leaders and influencers "show-up" by continuing to edify and inspire their team. They practice transparency with integrity and follow-through on all promises.

Principle 4: Listen to Understand!

Practice intentional listening to understand and not to respond. Be fully present and respect the other person's model of the world and meet them where they are. World-class leaders invest significant time to understand their clients and team members. As you read the next section on various communication personalities, pay attention to the diversity in which each person wants you to hear them.

Principle 5: The Person with the Most Flexibility Wins

The person with the most behavioral flexibility will control the conversation in the room. A great conversationalist or presenter can deliver flawlessly during rehearsals; however, no number of practice sessions can thoroughly prepare for interaction with a live audience. Behavioral flexibility includes humor, improve, confidence, and composure. To assist you in framing more efficiently, find out what your team, organization, or culture wants and be open to suggestions.

Principle 6: We Have a Choice!

Leaders design and spark change and leave room for choice. When designing a talk, be sure to leave the audience with an option to change. Resistance comes when someone feels they have no choice. Agreement happens when the leader resonates with the values and vision presented – and they choose to change.

Principle 7: Take the High Road

- Surround yourself with other world-class leaders
- Give picture scenarios
- Details in a step-by-step sequence
- Show them you care
- Incorporate excitement and opportunity
- Integrate Don Miguel Ruiz's *The 5 Agreements*

The opportunity to trust takes time and effort. The collaboration of trust and shared values is a process designed to expand, grow, and develop yourself and others. It is the bond that develops communicating consistently with clarity, confidence, and composure. It models shared leadership at all levels, with teamwork at the forefront. It also exemplifies your level of intention and commitment to yourself and others.

Personality Intelligence

Communication Strategies for Elevating Trust and Relatability

One of the most simplistic and successful personality coding systems we integrate into our training to communicate trust, create relatability, and connect in <90 seconds is the revolutionary B.A.N.K.® methodology developed by Cheri Tree. We met Cheri, Founder, and CEO of Codebreaker Technologies Inc., over 9 years ago and adopted her concepts, artificial intelligence application, and practices into our Heroic Voice framework and training.

In an earlier chapter, you learned about *Social Character Differences* and how various groups (Farming-Craft, Industrial Bureaucratic, Knowledge-Interactive) interact based on a socioeconomic base, social character, and ideals. What we are about to introduce is not based on social character or psychology. Instead, Cheri created it on BUYology, the science of buying or "buy-in," a scientifically validated assessment and methodology. Instead of assessing who you are, she built it on the perspective of who the customer or client is, based on the four personality types: Blueprint, Action, Nurturing, and Knowledge.

B.A.N.K.® got its beginnings in sales, and Cheri created this opportunity to help her close more deals in less time, improve communication skills, and build relationships. As the creator and genius behind Codebreaker's Personality Coding Technology, Cheri is known worldwide. Both Forbes.com and Entrepreneur.com published an article on her. She has also been a keynote speaker at the United Nations Artificial Intelligence for Good Conference, Harvard University. She has the backing of research from San Francisco State University in three white papers.

Today, we use this revolutionary methodology to prepare global impact leaders and executives like yourself to develop a Heroic Mindset to communicate consistently with clarity, confidence, and composure. To compose Heroic Messages that teach your audiences about your values, vision, and vows. To Speak your Heroic Voice to guide your audience to learn about, care about, and connect to your message, and to practice with Heroic Devotion to create trust by demonstrating your level of intention, commitment, and excellence.

Using this detailed, yet straightforward step-by-step system for getting more Yeses, you can implement a return on investment, which gains support, reputation, and monetization in your position and business. B.A.N.K. helps to also fast-track connections and rapport with your diverse audiences.

Let your audience determine your presentation.

– Tony Robbins

Although personality typing has been around for thousands of years, none that we have worked with (DISC, MBTI, etc.) has ever told us why people make buying decisions or say "yes" during the sales process or why people attract and sometimes attack (Figure 13.8).

When presenting to groups, it is important to know that individuals in that audience will respond differently to your content. You may find that each part of your presentation resonates differently among the audience members. To understand the difference in responses, let's take a look at the different set of values in your audience (Figure 13.9).

B.A.N.K.® Personality Intelligence

The next section shares how powerful this toolset can be in preparing you for high-stakes conversations, speaking opportunities, and closing more sales or results in less time. Learning these

Figure 13.8 Shared values – create relatability with the sets of values in your audience. (Adapted with permission from Anthony Lee, Heroic Voice Academy [2018].)

Figure 13.9 Communication profiles – speaking to the four major value sets in your audience. (Adapted with permission from Anthony Lee, Heroic Voice Academy [2018].)

four profiles will fine-tune your delivery and create relatability with high emotional intelligence when engaging in conversation, emails, or text. You can also incorporate these value sets in scripts, checklists, websites, and marketing copy.

As you read through each of the value sets, have a pen and paper ready to write up a list of people you see as a match for each personality. Knowing the nature of the people who surround you can change how you speak, treat, and act with others.

B.A.N.K.® Blueprint Personality

People with a Blueprint Personality expect everyone to follow the rules and be on time. Blueprints place high value on organization, time management, explicit details, and predictable systems with no risk. You gain their trust through proven authority. Blueprints tend to see through the lens of right and wrong and run an agenda-driven meeting with efficiency, structure, and responsibility.

Blueprint personalities hold people accountable and are disciplined in their careers. Change is not a strong suit, and planning requires scheduling and a budget. Excellent written details are a must.

Blueprints resonate with our Message Blueprint because it is a system with detailed instructions on how to compose presentations for leadership conversations. When preparing to engage in a conversation, incorporate some of the values mentioned to capture their attention.

A critical acronym to remember when engaging Blueprints is S.Y.S.T.E.M., and it stands for **S**ave **Y**ourself **S**ome **T**ime **E**nergy and **M**oney. Use this in your language and writing.

Who on your staff or in your life is a Blueprint? What actions can you take to ensure that your communication is concise, efficient, structured, and systemized?

B.A.N.K.® Action Personality

Action personality types are optimistic and act on instinct. They live for "the sizzle," and unlike the Blueprint, they do not like details. They want the bottom line, and in bullet point fashion! It is all about the energy, hands-on learning, and they have a "What's in it for Me!" attitude.

Additional Action values are:

- Profit driven
- Freedom
- Open to opportunity and enjoy the competition.
- Flexible, fun, and spontaneous
- Risk takers

This personality loves celebrity endorsements, the center of attention, and immediately acts when they recognize an opportunity. When they engage, they do it with "gusto." They make decisions quickly and with their gut. They are great negotiators, and many are attracted to their energy and lifestyle.

Actions resonate with our Presentation ROI because it is a way to measure and celebrate their success by generating money, support, and reputation contributing to the bottom line. When you write, text, or email an action personality, be short and to the point. When engaging in conversation, give them the "bottom-line" and leave out boring details.

Do you have any action types in your circle of associates, family, and friends? How can you show up for them to uplevel their goals?

B.A.N.K.® Nurturing Personality

Nurturing personalities are primarily kind, generous, and diplomatic people. They have a tremendous love for community and relationships, often putting others' needs first. The values important to a nurturing person are:

- Authenticity and significance
- Contribution and teamwork
- Personal growth and high emotional intelligence
- Ethics, morality, and harmony

Nurturing personalities live for connection and believe in supporting and empowering others to be their best. Because their currency is people, you want to emphasize what you stand for and how joining you will make a difference in the world. Nurturing people resonate with our Heroic Voice Connection Triangle because they value tools that help them create community and build long-term relationships.

When talking with a nurturing personality, you want to show them you care more about them and NOT the money. Emotions may run high for this personality, and you must offer high Emotional Intelligence when conversing with Nurturing personnel.

Who in your office, family, or friends is a builder of relationships and consistently contributes to others? Recognize them and show them with kindness, and they will assist you in building a fantastic team!

B.A.N.K.® Knowledge Personality

The knowledge personality type trusts logic and reason above all. Being the smartest people in the room, they love to debate and question your competence and expertise. Science, data, and proof are what they live for, and if you do not make sense, they will challenge you. They map out a strategy at a macro level and are precise in speech, and notice contradictions. The knowledge person thrives on seeing the big picture, long-term results, and universal truths. They pride themselves on self-mastery, intelligence, and accuracy.

Staying within their budget and giving them time to complete their due diligence help them make the smartest decision possible. When a knowledge personality says, "I have to think about it," they tell the truth. Give them time to process the data and extra time to talk it through. When they can see the logic and intelligence, they will be "on-board" with you.

The knowledge personality resonates with the Heroic Voice Message Portfolio because it gives them the Big Picture of the seven core leadership questions outlined below. It is also a framework to achieve self-mastery in conversational leadership.

Who in your life is logical and intelligent and strives to be the smartest person in the room?

Elevate Your Conversational Leadership Skills

As a leader, make your primary objective to connect with your audience. Invest the time to learn and master these four personalities. Level-up your presentation ROI and always be authentic with your audience. The vision we hold for you is to ignite, inspire, and influence. Lead with integrity and strengthen your communications to generate intentional support, money, and reputation. Empower people to define their vision, values, and vows to align their mission with clarity, purpose, precision, mastery, and connection.

In the upcoming section, you will discover the framework to storyboard your presentation and be prepared to have those high-stakes conversations with ease and grace!

The Message Portfolio
Frameworks to Storyboard Your Presentation

It's not about answering the question right. It's about answering the right question.

– *Heroic Voice Academy*

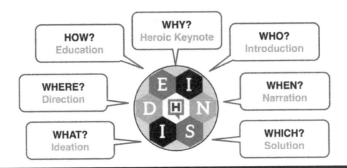

Figure 13.10 The message portfolio and the seven leadership questions. (Adapted with permission from Anthony Lee, Heroic Voice Academy [2018].)

Seven Leadership Questions

As leaders, we are responsible for answering questions from our team, stakeholders, and supporters. In the Heroic Voice MasterClass, we prepare executives to answer the seven leadership questions that communicate trust, create connection, and build relationships (Figure 13.10).

- Who are you?
- When have you succeeded?
- Which do you recommend?
- What is possible?
- Where are we going?
- How will we get there?
- Why is this important?

A Portfolio of Leadership Conversations

The Message Portfolio is a collection of presentations that answers each of the leadership questions. As you prepare to deliver presentations about a new trust infrastructure, the question you will be answering is "Where are we going?"

To answer this question, the leadership conversation we will be using is "Direction." The storyboard for a "Direction" conversation consists of seven slides. These slides guide your audience through a sequence of topics. The goal for this presentation is to generate approval and support for your proposed direction (Figure 13.11).

Slide 1: Where Are We Today?

Use this opening slide to connect immediately with your audience. Show that you can relate to what they are going through and how they feel. Share your personal experiences as well. What are the problems and costs for not having an adequate trust infrastructure?

Slide 2: Where Are We Going?

Focus your audience's attention on the positive future you are creating together. Your audience looks to you to have a clearer vision of the future. Be clear and specific with your details to connect

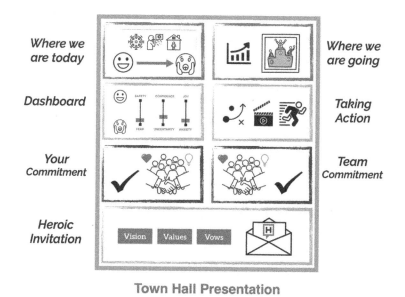

Town Hall Presentation

Figure 13.11 Storyboard example for a "direction" conversation. (Adapted with permission from Anthony Lee, Heroic Voice Academy [2018].)

with their hearts and minds. What does a future look like when this new trust infrastructure becomes a reality.

Slide 3: The Dashboard

The Dashboard slide shows the emotional and financial state of an organization, team, or family. A dashboard indicates that you are interested in both the mental health and the financial health of your audience. Sharing your dashboard readings will demonstrate technical and emotional intelligence with your audience, elevating their confidence in you.

Slide 4: Taking Action

Skillful articulation of the dashboard prepares your audience to be more receptive to your plans and strategies. Teach them the specific actions to take and the best practices to follow.

Tip:
1. Be transparent.
2. Give answers you do have.
3. Commit to finding the solutions you don't.
4. Use your values to guide your critical decisions and actions.

Slides 5 and 6: Commitments from You and Your Team

Commitment is the bold promise to bring the best of your energies and skills to the mission. Think of how President Kennedy inspired the best efforts of American scientists, engineers, and astronauts to win the space race.

Start by sharing your commitment with your audience. When your team witnesses your high level of commitment and dedication, they will be inspired to follow the lead, and be open to your invitations.

Slide 7: The Heroic Invitation

Conclude your presentation by asking your audience to participate in your mission. Make a heroic invitation to your audience. Ask them to contribute money, support, or reputation to fuel your mission.

Practice Like a Professional

Get in the Gym

Amateurs look for inspiration; the rest of us just get up and go to work.

— Chuck Close

Speaking is a competitive sport. World-class athletes and performers dedicate time to the gym to bring their very best to the game and the stage. As global impact leaders, we invite you to adopt a lifestyle of practice and develop your voice into an instrument of change.

The following are some best practices of world-class professionals.

Frequency

Practice Often. The audience is investing time to learn from you. Honor every minute that the audience has given you, and bring your very best. Our very best clients have rehearsed hundreds of times before they step on stage at TEDx, South by Southwest, and Industry Conferences. This frequency of practice results in the consistent generation of Presentation ROI: money, support, and positive reputation.

Feedback

We use the following feedback framework in all of our workshops, training programs, and coaching sessions. Our executive communication coaches provide high-quality feedback that fosters the rapid integration of new skills and significant improvement levels.

- **Part 1**: What worked?
  - Capture all the best practices that happened during the rehearsal
- **Part 2**: What didn't work?
  - Remove anything ineffective or inefficient.
- **Part 3**: Creative options?
  - Brainstorm creative (not corrective) options to play with

Professional Training

If you are new to the journey of leadership and communications, we highly recommend entry-level programs like ToastMasters. Their programs do a great job teaching the basics of public speaking, and their students can start to develop a lifestyle of practicing for the stage.

As you grow in your leadership career and take on regular high-stakes speaking opportunities, we invite you to join us in our presentation gym. Our executive programs are designed to develop, nurture, and unleash your Heroic Voice. By mastering the message delivery skills from our Connection Triangle, your voice will have the power to communicate trust, create connection, and build relationships.

Heroic Voice Resources

- **Learn about your favorite subject**: YOU. Get a customized personality report that gives you your code, likes and dislikes, what makes you say YES to someone or NO, triggers and tripwires that drive you to buy or not buy into someone or a product. Learn more at: *https://crackmycode.com/HeroicVoice*
- Join us in our **Presentation Gym** for:
- **Group workouts**: The Heroic Voice MasterClass
- **Individual workouts**: Private Coaching
- **Individual sprint**: Keynote Preparation
    Learn more at *https://www.heroicvoice.com/services.*

Chapter 14

Cultivating Belonging and Creating Access: A Chapter on Diversity, Equity, and Inclusion

Asha S. Collins, PhD
Idexx

Kate Liebelt
AbbVie Inc.

Contents

Introduction

Race-related tragedies in America in 2020 and 2021, coupled with the COVID-19 global pandemic, have amplified awareness of deep racial inequity in our society and ignited intense national dialogue about systemic racism. Now more than ever, Americans have become deeply aware of the complex challenges faced by black and indigenous people of color ("BIPOC") (Garcia, 2020) in our communities, and particularly our health care system. Healthcare leaders in hospitals, health systems, enterprise healthcare technology companies, and mobile medicine start-ups have a unique opportunity and responsibility to address diversity, equity, and inclusion in their organizations and drive a sense of belonging and access among patients and employees. "Belonging" and "access" are key ingredients to achieving diversity, equity, and inclusion: "belonging" is creating the sense that employees and patients feel safe to present their authentic selves at work and in the patient care setting, and "access" refers to giving equitable opportunity and permissions to patients and employees regardless of ability or experience, and striving toward equal representation. Healthcare leaders are positioned to model critically important behaviors and deeply embrace and invest in the social, workforce, and economic imperative for DEI. Hospital executive teams and leaders of mobile medicine product and service companies should understand the return on DEI investment across key social, reputational, and financial dimensions. This chapter aims to support healthcare leaders in exploring DEI, "belonging," and "access" relevant to the healthcare industry and particularly mobile medicine by:

1. Framing the dynamic forces shaping a renewed approach to the design, implementation, and measurement of DEI programs in healthcare with an emphasis on mobile medicine.
2. Defining the social and business imperative of DEI, and the competitive advantage driven by a proactive, thoughtful approach to DEI in healthcare organizations.
3. Examining the unique role healthcare leaders play as individuals, and as the leaders of executive teams in supporting their organizations in making progress on DEI goals.

This chapter was written to educate and inspire healthcare leaders with the hope they will feel further compelled to act in defining and executing DEI strategies for their organizations, for it is up to them to lead DEI in our industry to enable a sustainable workforce and the greatest impact for patients.

Dynamic Forces Driving DEI in Healthcare

Occasionally, there is a news story about a storm along the coastline of an ocean or lake that is so powerful it disrupts water levels and reveals the remnants of shipwrecks and sunken vessels emerging from the depths of the water. In the year 2020, COVID-19 can be compared to such a storm, revealing fractures in our nation's healthcare delivery system and a lack of unity around American societal views on DEI:

■ The COVID-19 global pandemic has exposed fragmented health care access and health inequities for Black, Indigenous, and people of color, BIPOC resulting in more COVID-19 cases and deaths across non-white populations. For example, the pandemic killed 1 in 1,000 Black Americans (over 50,000 lives) as of fall 2020 (Stanley-Becker & Sun, 2020; The Atlantic, 2020).

■ The pandemic has placed tremendous pressure on the US economy resulting in negative effects on the social determinants of health for non-white populations (Norris & Gonzales, 2020).

■ Additionally, systemic racism in our law enforcement has been amplified via a series of well-documented tragic acts of physical violence against BIPOC, particularly Black

Americans. Non-white Americans are increasingly reporting negative, discriminatory experiences as revealed in a recent Pew Research Center Survey (Ruiz, Horowitz, & Tamir, 2020).

Looking ahead, organizations must demonstrate awareness of the broader, longer-term trends of our country's demographic shift and respond with agility. US Census Bureau predicts we will become a majority-minority country by 2045. Specifically, the multi-racial population is projected to be the fastest growing over the next several decades, followed by Asians and Hispanics (Frey, 2018). Furthermore globally, the fastest growing countries and economies by the middle of this century will also be populated by Black and Asian populations (McCrindle, 2020). Organizations that understand these trends and build agile, thoughtful strategies based on the philosophy of "belonging" and "access" to meet the needs of their stakeholders (patients, employees, vendors, and other stakeholders) will survive and thrive in these fast-changing times.

Healthcare DEI Imperative and ROI

These dynamic shifts lead us to the conclusion that effective DEI practices are required for the future sustainability and success of companies. The critical need for efficacy in DEI is even more pronounced for companies that produce digital and technology products, including mobile medicine products and services. Effective DEI practices will be required to attract the best talent and to secure the biggest and most influential customer segments. Younger and future employees, who are the source of company innovations and the next generation of leaders for our companies, are more diverse than their predecessors and they are requiring different incentives to be recruited and retained at companies (Quillen, 2018; He, 2019). In the same vein, customers for digital and technology products around the globe will be more diverse than ever before and will require more nuanced marketing strategies to ensure their voices are heard and their needs are met (Quillen, 2018; McCrindle 2020). This shift in demographics and values means that the companies that will have and maintain market leadership will be ones that can cater to these segments and cater to them in a manner that embraces diversity and broad inclusion in ways that have not been done before. Companies that fail to employ such strategies will also falter in the market. It is a 21st-century imperative.

DEI Practices as Tools to Win the War for Talent

Future workforce leaders, workers born from 1980 and onward (i.e., Millennials/Generation Y and Generation Z) are requiring different cultural norms and workforce benefits than previous generations (He, 2019; Barkley, 2017; Cone 2016 study). Culture is more important to these generations than our current or previous generation of leaders. Moreover, top talent prioritize being able to bring their "authentic, whole self" to work over salary and stock options. Being able to bring their "authentic, whole self to work" translates to requiring a workforce culture that is inclusive. Specifically, a workforce that embraces multiple identities, intersectionality; a workforce culture that allows individuals of diverse experiences, intelligences, working styles to thrive and succeed with advancement opportunities. This can only be done if a company has intentionally implemented practices and intentionally reinforces practices of inclusion. Further to inclusion, very specifically, a recent survey found that 72% of Generation Z individuals in the workplace saw racial equality as one of the top two important workforce issues (Barkley, 2017). The companies that can establish practices that embody these principles (authenticity, inclusion, racial equity) will be the companies that will be able to **secure and retain** top talent. This is especially critical in an era where talent, especially engineering and product development talent, for digital and technology products and services is fierce and the pipeline for this talent is not projected to be able to meet the needs of the market (Kosenko, 2020). Companies will continue to be in fierce competition to bring and keep the best talent. Data indicate that having a robust, intentional DEI strategy set of practices will help companies win this war (Interview with Jami McKeon led by Natalie Bertram, 2020).

DEI Practices as Tools to Win the War for Customers

Just as there is a shift happening with future workforce leaders, there is a similar shift happening with key, influential customer segments for technology products. While there are many customers still focused on function and purpose as the primary driver for purchasing decisions, the most influential demographic segments driving technology consumption are consumers that prioritize company values as a key driver for selecting products (Frey, 2018). An increasing number of customers indicate that their purchasing decisions are informed as much by-product function, as by company values (Haller, Lee, & Cheung, 2020). These are the same population segments that value environmental sustainability, community consciousness, and racial equity; at the same time, this most influential customer segment represents a breadth of racial and ethnic diversity not previously seen (Quillen, 2018). To capture these customers, especially at an age that will drive brand loyalty, companies need to demonstrate their commitment to environmentally friendly practices and sustained efforts of inclusion; they need to drive nuanced marketing efforts that speak to the broad diversity of these customers and exhibit community citizenship that shows caring beyond profits. This means that DEI efforts cannot stop at internal efforts. Robust DEI efforts that will be rewarded by the market are required for external users, customers, and stakeholders. Efforts to demonstrate inclusion must have strategies for internal talent acquisition and retention, as well as customer acquisition and retention. One without the other will not suffice. The landscape is shifting and to succeed companies need internal and external robust, visible, and effective DEI strategies and practices.

The shifts that are increasing pressure for internal talent and for external customers collectively mean that it is a company's fiduciary responsibility to create and implement robust inclusion strategies and actions. It has been shown repeatedly that companies with more diverse leadership outperform those with less diversity (Hunt, 2015). Additionally, as customer demographics shift, being able to connect with diverse customers will dictate the extent of commercial success, especially for technology products. Ignoring these clear market indicators is not social irresponsibility, it is fiduciary irresponsibility and negligence. Robust DEI strategies and plans are required to maximize sustained returns for shareholders and stakeholders.

DEI Practices as Tools for Best Practice Corporate Governance

The spotlight is being put on DEI efforts due to recent socio-political events, changing demographics of customers and the talent pool, but also due to recent reporting requirements for Corporate Boards (Ashton & Westerhaus, 2020). Specifically, key entities that influence corporate governance from Nasdaq to Institutional Shareholder Services (ISS), State Street Global Advisors (State Street), and Glass Lewis have announced reporting requirements regarding the diversity of company corporate Boards and subsequent actions that may be taken for boards that are not diverse. In December 2020, Nasdaq announced their proposal to the US Securities and Exchange Commission (SEC) that Nasdaq-listed companies: (1) annually publish self-identified gender, race, and LGBTQ+ status of Board members; and (2) have at least two diverse directors on the Board – one female self-identified and the other that is from an underrepresented minority group (Nasdaq, 2020). The proposal further includes that if companies do not meet these guidelines, an explanation would need to be provided. Likewise beginning in 2021, ISS will begin highlighting corporate boards across the Russell 3000 and S&P 1500 that do not have any racial and/or ethnic diversity and ones that do not openly disclose such information (ISS, 2020). In subsequent years, ISS may recommend voting against the chair of the Nominating & Governance Committee for such Boards if there continues to be a lack of racial and/or ethnic diversity in Board membership. They are not alone in moving from establishing reporting requirements to establishing voting actions based on the lack of corporate board diversity. Glass Lewis and State Street Global Advisors have stated that they will begin voting against Chairs of Nominating and Governance Committees that do not have certain diversity representation on their Boards (Ashton & Westerhaus, 2020). State Street focused on companies in the S&P 500 and FTSE100 will begin voting against Chairs of the Nominating and Governance Committee based on diversity disclosures and Board representation. In 2021, State Street will vote against Chairs of the Nominating & Governance Committee that do not disclose the racial and ethnic makeup of the Board. Beginning in 2022, State Street will vote against the Chair of the Nominating & Governance Committee for these companies that do not have at least one director from an underrepresented minority group on the Board. Similarly, from January 2022 onward, Glass Lewis will recommend voting against the Chair of the Nominating & Governance Committee of any Board that has less than two women directors (for any board with more than six members). This rise in corporate governance entities taking a stance on inclusion reflects the growing understanding that diversity is not just about social justice, but is a matter of best practice that drives the highest performance that is in the best interest of shareholders and stakeholders alike. Executives would be wise to take these bellwether efforts to heart and move with urgency to define DEI efforts across their own enterprises to drive business performance and ensure they are driving these efforts vs. reacting to further mandates.

Role of Healthcare Leaders in Cultivating Belonging and Access

Healthcare leaders can drive DEI, belonging, and access today by modeling behaviors to drive the creation and execution of impactful DEI strategies. Self-awareness and empathy are increasingly critical leadership traits needed to create an environment of belonging and access.

Modeling DEI Behaviors

Formally, healthcare leaders are responsible for both setting the strategy for diversity, equity, and inclusion efforts, as well as executing on the organizational vision and delivering results supported by data (Mills, Middleton, & Sachar, 2019). They serve as a bridge connecting the broadest set of stakeholders: the board, employees, the community, and vendors/suppliers. Healthcare leaders at future-ready, marquee organizations drive diversity, equity, and inclusion with both a governance and talent lens. They lead the charge in routine evaluation of the organization's processes and practices from a top-down perspective, asking such questions as:

1. Do our board, leadership, and staff recruiting practices reflect an inclusive approach?
2. Do we have programs in place to sponsor and mentor diverse talent?
3. Do we have the right channels of communication in place to connect and engage with staff?
4. Do we track and monitor the right data (e.g., Supplier Diversity) to support our organizational objectives?

To fulfill this role, healthcare leaders must demonstrate self-awareness, empathy, and core values aligned to the organizational mission and the broader societal imperatives around DEI. These types of leaders are more likely to understand and model behaviors that reduce implicit and explicit bias (Richardson, 2019). Leaders who have overcome adversity – embraced their failures and committed to challenging themselves by pursuing opportunities outside of their professional and personal comfort zones – will emerge as industry leaders and build admirable, high-performing teams and organizations. Research conducted by Juliet Bourke and Andrea Titus revealed that inclusivity-minded, self-aware leaders demonstrate a combination of six signature traits (Bourke & Titus, 2020):

■ **Visible commitment**: They articulate an authentic commitment to diversity, challenge the status quo, hold others accountable, and make diversity and inclusion a personal priority.
■ **Humility**: They are modest about capabilities, admit mistakes, and create the space for others to contribute.
■ **Awareness of bias**: They show awareness of personal blind spots, as well as flaws in the system, and work hard to ensure a meritocracy.
■ **Curiosity about others**: They demonstrate an open mindset and deep curiosity about others, listen without judgment, and seek empathy to understand those around them.
■ **Cultural intelligence**: They are attentive to others' cultures and adapt as required.
■ **Effective collaboration**: They empower others, pay attention to diversity of thinking and psychological safety, and focus on team cohesion.

Hiring committees and search firms will increasingly pursue candidates for leadership roles that demonstrate these attributes. The late Bernard Tyson, Former Chairman and CEO Kaiser Foundation Health Plan, Inc. and Hospitals, was a model for healthcare leaders working to champion diversity. In a 2017 interview, he celebrated his organization's achievements around DEI in a *Harvard Business Review* article on championing diversity (Johnson, 2017), reporting:

■ In 2016, more than 60% of the total workforce (of 186,497 employees) were members of racial, ethnic, and cultural minorities, and more than 73% were women.
■ More than 50% of the management and professional positions were held by racial and cultural minorities and 75% were held by women.
■ 50% of the Executive Medical Directors group were women and 29% of the Health Plan Organization's C-Suite were women.

Tyson explained they achieved these results "through deliberate planning, development of current talent, and outreach within the communities that they serve." The intentionality of healthcare leaders, coupled with thoughtful talent development and stakeholder engagement, will help organizations be positioned to exceed stakeholder and industry expectations.

Designing and Executing DEI Strategies

Healthcare organizations are seeking support for DEI strategy development in these unprecedented times, and demand for diversity consulting to organizations across the country is growing at an accelerated rate (The Economist, 2020). Healthcare organizations, key players in the mobile medicine ecosystem, have an important role to play in advancing diversity, equity, and inclusion in our industry. Healthcare organizations are uniquely positioned at the intersection of healthcare delivery/technology. Healthcare leaders are adopting and innovating around mobile solutions to drive patient centricity, employee engagement, clinical quality, and operational efficiency (Shah, 2017). In parallel, healthcare organizations are acting on their obligation to address social determinants of health (Sullivan, 2019). Given this complex remit of arguably the greatest importance, many healthcare leaders are understandably receiving increased pressure from the communities they serve and their employees to create sustainable programs to support diversity, equity, and inclusion with a holistic and agile approach:

- Hospitals are increasingly investing in social determinants of health, and methods of capturing and reporting on these investments as well as measuring the impact on health outcomes are maturing (Horwitz, Chang, Arcilla, & Knickman, 2020).
- To support BIPOC employees, some healthcare organizations are assessing current diversity programs and starting to strategically invest to expand program scope and impact. The American Hospital Association's Institute for Diversity and Health Equity has published Health Equity, Diversity, and Inclusion measures for Hospitals and Health Systems to understand key metrics for the organization and the community (Institute for Diversity and Health Equity, 2020).

These examples demonstrate positive movement in the right direction. However, social pressure may prematurely expedite the speed at which healthcare organizations are trying to fix the problem of systemic racism, leading to unintended consequences. plan at a US health system leading to a gap in vaccinations for younger front-line healthcare workers: the institution's resident physicians raised grave concern with the vaccine deployment plan. Further, trust between administrators and employees was eroded and will need to be rebuilt to continue to fight the pandemic as a cohesive team (Bernstein, Beachum, & Knowles, 2020). This unfortunate situation demonstrates the risks associated with rolling out a plan too quickly in an effort to move fast. To solve for the inequities that plague our healthcare system, we implore healthcare leaders to:

1. Invest both resources and time to understand underlying problems in depth
2. Leverage the abundance of data available to design solutions and interventions, as we well as measure and monitor impact and inform future decision-making
3. Strive to develop solutions that are fit-for-purpose and sustainable at the community, organization, employee, and patient levels
4. Nurture a "continuous improvement" mindset to diversity, equity, and inclusion within their organizations, their communities, and our industry

Healthcare leaders must seek to understand the intricately intertwined social and economic impacts of a healthy population.

Healthcare Industry Associations Support for DEI

> At America's hospitals and health systems, we want to make sure everyone feels seen and included – from the frontlines to the boardroom. And we're working hard to ensure that our patients feel valued and recognized as the unique individuals they are.
>
> *– Rick Pollack, CEO, American Hospital Association*

Healthcare industry associations such as the American Hospital Association have increased investment in awareness, education, and advocacy efforts to empower healthcare leaders to drive diversity, equity, and inclusion efforts in their organizations:

■ The Institute for Diversity and Health Equity focuses on providing equitable care for all persons and advance healthcare diversity, equity, and inclusion.
■ The Institute for Diversity in Health Management is a not for profit that works to expand career opportunities for ethnic minorities.

Both organizations partner with members of the American Hospital Association as well as collaborators such as health insurance companies to advance their commitment to delivering care for all and creating more inclusive work environments. Similarly, the American Medical Association has invested in education and advocacy programs to advance inclusion at the individual, organization, and community levels:

■ The AMA Center for Health Equity is committed to embedding equity across AMA's practices, process, action, innovation, organizational performance, and outcomes, and hired a Chief Health Equity Officer to lead this charge.
■ AMA challenges health leaders to consider the root cause of health inequity in their "Prioritizing Equity" YouTube series.

The Healthcare Information Management Systems Society ("HIMSS") launched the Global Health Equity Network to advance health and wellness for all individuals globally. This diverse community of leaders within HIMSS connects to share insights, best practices, and tools with an emphasis on supporting underserved groups in the healthcare information and technology sector, with an emphasis on Black and LatinX communities.

We predict industry associations will continue to play a key role in working with their members and stakeholders to develop solutions and resources for their membership and the communities they serve.

Conclusion

In this chapter, we have introduced ideas in hopes of challenging healthcare leaders to look beyond the traditional perceptions of the definition of DEI in the healthcare organizations and the communities they serve. We explored the concepts of "belonging" and "access" in organizations and demonstrated the impact on value creation for all stakeholders including the board of directors, employees, customers, and communities. Finally, we provided perspectives on the design and execution of sustainable programs to foster belonging and access, and the hospital executive's role in driving the success of these programs through self-awareness and modeling these behaviors for their executive teams and stakeholders.

References

Ashton, K., & Westerhaus, V. (2020, December 14). Turning up the heat on board diversity and E&S risk oversight: Quick guide to ISS and glass lewis 2021 proxy season updates. JD Supra. Retrieved from https://www.jdsupra.com/legalnews/turning-up-the-heat-on-board-diversity-89113/.

Barkley. (2017, February 1). Getting to know gen Z: How the Pivotal generation is different from millennials." https://www.barkleyus.com/wp-content/uploads/2019/05/FC_GenzResearchReport.pdf.

Bernstein, L., Beachum, L., & Knowles, H. (2020, December 18). Stanford apologizes for coronavirus vaccine plan that left out many front-line doctors. *The Washington Post*. Retrieved from https://www.washingtonpost.com/health/2020/12/18/stanford-hospital-protest-covid-vaccine/.

Bertram, N. (2019). The big interview: Jami McKeon, Morgan Lewis Firm Chair. Chambers Associate. Retrieved from https://www.chambers-associate.com/the-big-interview/the-big-interview-jami-mckeon-morgan-lewis-firm-chair.

Bourke, J. & Titus, A. (2020). The key to inclusive leadership. The US Census Bureau. Retrieved from https://hbr.org/2020/03/the-key-to-inclusive-leadership.

Cone. (2016). Cone communications millennial employee engagement survey. https://www.conecomm.com/research-blog/2016-millennial-employee-engagement-study.

Frey, W. H. (2018). The US will become 'minority white' in 2045, census projects. The US Census Bureau. Retrieved from https://www.brookings.edu/blog/the-avenue/2018/03/14/the-us-will-become-minority-white-in-2045-census-projects/.

Garcia, E. S. (2020). Where did BIPOC come from? *The New York Times*. https://www.nytimes.com/article/what-is-bipoc.html.

Haller, K., Lee, J., & Cheung, J. (2020). Meet the 2020 consumers driving change. IBM Research Insights. https://www.ibm.com/downloads/cas/EXK4XKX8.

He, E. (2019). For younger workers, old-school pay and perks are not enough. *Forbes*. https://www.forbes.com/sites/emilyhe/2019/08/07/for-younger-workers-old-school-pay-and-perks-are-not-enough/?sh=61f2beed5dce.

Horwitz, L. I., Chang, C., Arcilla, H. N., & Knickman, J. R. (2020, February). Quantifying health systems' investment in social determinants of health, by sector, 2017–2019. Health Affairs. Retrieved from https://www.healthaffairs.org/doi/full/10.1377/hlthaff.2019.01246.

Hunt, V., Layton, D., & Prince, S. (2015, January 1). Why diversity matters. https://www.mckinsey.com/business-functions/organization/our-insights/why-diversity-matters.

Institute for Diversity and Health Equity. (2020). *Health Equity, Diversity & Inclusion Measures for Hospitals and Health Systems*. Chicago, IL: American Hospital Association. Retrieved from https://www.aha.org/system/files/media/file/2020/12/ifdhe-inclusion-dashboard-FINAL.pdf.

Institutional Shareholder Services (ISS). (2020). www.issgovernance.com (Accessed February 1, 2021).

Johnson, S. (2017). What 11 CEOs have learned about championing diversity. *Harvard Business Review*. Retrieved from https://hbr.org/2017/08/what-11-ceos-have-learned-about-championing-diversity.

Kosenko, N. (2020). The software developer shortage in the US and the global tech talent shortage in 2021. Daxx.com.

Mills, D., Middleton, R., & Sachar, H. (2019, April 3). Driving diversity and inclusion: The role for chairs and CEOs. Harvard Law School Forum on Corporate Governance. Retrieved from https://corpgov.law.harvard.edu/2019/04/03/driving-diversity-and-inclusion-the-role-for-chairs-and-ceos/.

Nasdaq. (2020, December 1). Nasdaq to advance diversity through new proposed listing requirements. https://www.nasdaq.com/press-release/nasdaq-to-advance-diversity-through-new-proposed-listing-requirements-2020-12-01.

Norris, K., & Gonzales, C. (2020, November 1). COVID-19, health disparities and the US election. *EClinical Medicine*, 28, 100617.

Quillen, A. (2018, June 4). The workforce's newest members: Generation Z. ZeroCater. Retrieved from zerocater.com/blog/2018/06/04workforce-newest-members-generation-z/.

Richardson, K. (2019, January 10). Implicit bias: The importance of self-awareness for patient care and in the workplace. Medical Group Management Association. Retrieved from https://www.mgma.com/data/data-stories/implicit-bias-the-importance-of-self-awareness-fo.

Ruiz, N. G., Horowitz, J. M., & Tamir, C. (2020, July 1). Many black and Asian Americans say they have experienced discrimination amid the COVID-19 outbreak. Washington, DC: Pew Social Trends. Retrieved from https://www.pewsocialtrends.org/2020/07/01/many-black-and-asian-americans-say-they-have-experienced-discrimination-amid-the-covid-19-outbreak/.

Shah, S. (2017, October 23). Understanding smart hospitals and why most aren't there yet. *Healthcare IT News*. Retrieved from https://www.healthcareitnews.com/blog/understanding-smart-hospitals-and-why-most-arent-there-yet#:~:text=%E2%80%9CSmart%20hospitals%20are%20those%20that,or%20available%20earlier%2C%20to%20achieve.

Stanley-Becker, I., & Sun, L. H. (2020, December 18). COVID-19 is devastating communities of color: Can vaccines counter racial inequity? *Washington Post*. Retrieved from https://www.washingtonpost.com/health/2020/12/18/covid-vaccine-racial-equity/.

Sullivan, H. R. (2019, March). Hospitals' obligations to address social determinants of health. *American Medical Association Journal of Ethics*. Retrieved from https://journalofethics.ama-assn.org/article/hospitals-obligations-address-social-determinants-health/2019-03.

The Atlantic. (2020, December 22). The pandemic is showing black people what they knew all along. Patrice Peck.

The Economist. (2020, November 28). Social unrest has fuelled a boom for the diversity industry. Retrieved from https://www.economist.com/business/2020/11/28/social-unrest-has-fuelled-a-boom-for-the-diversity-industry.

United Nations. (2020). Organization for economic co-operation and development, McCrindle. Generation Alpha, February 1, 2021. https://mccrindle.com.au/wp-content/uploads/Gen-Alpha-2020-digital-1.pdf.

ENVISION YOUR ORGANIZATION'S MOBILE TECH-ENABLED FUTURE

6

Chapter 15

Evidence-Based Leadership Practices That Accelerate Transformation

Shreya Sarkar-Barney, PhD
Human Capital Growth, California

Alec Levenson, PhD
Center for Effective Organizations, University of Southern California

Kristine Dery, PhD
Massachusetts Institute of Technology, Center for Information Systems Research

Jennifer J. Deal, PhD
Center for Effective Organizations, University of Southern California

Contents

DOI: 10.4324/9781003220473-21

Leticia's blood sugar has dropped to a level that is dangerously low. She is running the risk of falling into a coma. Her aging husband Raul makes an anxious call to their advice nurse. The incoming call system routes the call to a Spanish speaking nurse making it easy for him to communicate. Because Leticia has linked her Continuous Glucose Monitor (CGM) to an app on her mobile phone, the advice nurse quickly reviews her readings while speaking with Raul. She recommended a few remedial steps brining rapid relief to Leticia and averting the need for a hospital visit. With the hospital managing COVID-19 patients, it is better for patients and staff if the condition can be managed remotely. Within 30 minutes, Leticia's condition was stabilized. The whole time, the nurse was able to keep an eye on her blood sugar readings through the CGM app and see Leticia through the camera. Thus, Leticia's emergency was managed very quickly using technological aids, keeping her out of the hospital, and the ambulance staff available for other emergencies.

What could have been another mortality statistic, instead became a success story.

Leticia's great outcome requires more than just the application of new technologies. Healthcare providers have to work in new ways. Business rules around delivering advice and actions have to be radically revised, and leaders need to frame their decisions very differently as they access more data and insights about the patient and employee/provider experiences. These shifts have implications for leaders across the organization. In particular, they have significant implications for the role of the CIO.

Today the CIO's role cannot be just a functional head who implements new technology. Instead, CIOs must be visionary leaders. Together with the rest of the business, they need to provide leadership in how digital technologies can transform the business model of healthcare in ways never before possible, shifting day-to-day medical practices to improve patients' health, the workflow for staff, and the financial position of the organization. Intimate knowledge of what it takes to deliver efficient, effective, and high-quality healthcare together with digital skills means that contemporary CIOs in healthcare are focused on delivering a great experience for both the patients and the medical doctors and staff.

Historically the CIO's role was to be the leader of all matters related to technology, essentially a functional head leading a siloed group of technology experts that serviced the business. Because of the increasing span of technology within medicine, over the last decade, the role of the healthcare CIO has morphed into one of a strategic business leader, where the goal is not just to ensure adoption and management of technology infrastructure but to help lead the organization in healthcare innovation. Today's C-suite leaders are expected to be skilled at both envisioning the future and delivering operational excellence, and the CIO is no exception. They must not only have domain expertise in their core area but be adept at orchestrating the strategy, business operations, and people as a cohesive system.

Although the exact numbers are debated, a leading cause of death in a US hospital is due to hospital-borne illness or misdiagnosis and mistreatment, all of which can be prevented (Gorski, 2019). About 66.5% of personal bankruptcies in the US are due to medical issues and healthcare bills (Himmelstein et al., 2019). While patient safety, quality of care, and costs are clearly the primary concerns of all healthcare leaders, the solutions are complex and simply getting better at existing processes, and financial prudence is not the answer. Ultimately new ways of working, improved options for delivery of patient care, and more effective partnering will be needed to transform healthcare to achieve more consistent and better-quality outcomes. Data, ubiquitous computing, and processing power will enable humans and machines to work together to solve problems in ways previously unimaginable. Leaders will therefore not only have to be domain experts but, more importantly, they will need to apply technical, organizational, and leadership skills to support and enable high-performing teams empowered to solve complex problems in an ever-changing world.

This chapter provides evidence-based guidance on what healthcare CIOs can do through their leadership to help their organizations deliver better healthcare outcomes. We address how leaders need to conceptualize and optimize digital transformation efforts by orchestrating the triad of technology, people, and operations.

This chapter has three focus areas:
1. The challenges of healthcare and implications for leadership
2. The new healthcare CIO role
3. Evidence-based guidance for healthcare leaders

The Challenges of Healthcare and Implications for Leadership

While it's reasonable to assume that keeping up with the latest technology is perhaps the highest priority for healthcare CIOs, the reality is more complex. The ultimate goal for any technology is that it helps reduce costs and/or increase patient care quality. Yet, if CIOs focus only on those objectives within their own organizations, they face a huge risk of having their internally focused decisions overridden by the marketplace or government regulators. The challenge facing CIOs and healthcare leaders more broadly is that they have to solve the immediate challenges facing their organizations while simultaneously watching out for industry-level pressures and trends.

The challenge of balancing the organizational-level view of strategy with the industry-level view is particularly acute for healthcare because of the constant threat that regulators will impose solutions that could undo the leadership's decisions within the organization. This is a significant concern for healthcare and technology because of the public health benefits of having technology systems that work seamlessly not just within each organization, but also across organizations; without that, patient care can suffer dramatically any time treatment crosses organizational lines, which is the case for the overwhelming majority of patients in the US So rather than wait for the government to tell healthcare leaders how to use technology to solve those pressing challenges, truly strategic leaders need to embrace the challenges of reducing cost and increasing patient care quality across the entire industry to ensure the choices they make today will be most closely aligned with what society needs.

Here are some of the major issues facing today's healthcare systems in the US, and the potential challenges facing the CIO:

Poor Population Health, Overly Expensive Healthcare, and Racial and Socioeconomic Inequality Create Healthcare System Challenges for the Strategic Management of Data and Digital Partnering

The US lags behind 16 peer countries in life expectancy, infant mortality, obesity, sexually transmitted diseases, and drug-related deaths (2013 Institute of Medicine report: US Health in International Perspective: Shorter Lives, Poorer Health). Simultaneously, America's health-status gap across racial and socioeconomic lines is not closing. Moreover, the COVID-19 pandemic has highlighted in stark terms what we have known for years: low-income communities and people of color continue to have worse healthcare and outcomes, and the structural inequities were exacerbated by COVID-19 (Johnson, 2016). Blacks and Hispanics have been hospitalized and are dying from COVID-19 at much higher rates than other racial groups.

Growing health disparities across race and socioeconomic status have reached alarming levels (Holden et al., 2016). According to a 2016 study published in the *Journal of the American Medical Association* (JAMA), for the poorest American men aged 40, life expectancy was the same as similarly aged men in Pakistan and Sudan (Chetty et al., 2016). There are two notable findings from the study. First, being poor in a wealthier region (e.g., New York City, San Francisco) was associated with a longer life expectancy than those in less wealthy areas. Second, the richest 1% live an average of 10 years longer than those in the bottom 1% of the income distribution. This suggests there is a lack of uniform access to healthcare, and for those who have access, healthcare often is unaffordable. Driving healthcare equity is of national importance. Healthcare leaders can no longer just be concerned with the metrics of success within their institution but instead need to look at the health indicators of their communities to judge their success.

The typical metrics of healthcare outcomes include patient experience, timeliness of care, the effectiveness of care, readmissions, safety, mortality, and efficient use of medical imaging. These standardized metrics are used to compute the CMS star rating, which consumers can use to compare hospital performance. Missing from these metrics is a focus on community health. Indicators of community health and well-being can be of added value as they show healthcare systems' involvement in prevention and investment in health of the community. CIOs can play an important role by designing systems that not only capture metrics specific to their organization but also include activities deployed in partnership with community organizations.

Emerging healthcare organizations such as Oak Street Healthcare are particularly focused on improving health outcomes, especially in the most underserved communities. Their operating model revolves around leveraging data to optimize operations for a specific community rather than a one-size-fits-all approach. While this approach requires a high initial cost of set-up to invest in a robust operational IT backbone, it is paying off with a 26% decrease in hospital readmissions as patients gain better access to affordable primary care (Siwicki, 2019). Investments in technology have supported improved payment systems, opportunities to digitally partner for better care, and opportunities to reduce costs. By shifting from a pay-for-service model to a monthly service fee, they can seamlessly combine telehealth, face-to-face visits, remote patient monitoring, and in-home care to deliver more preventative and targeted care. Integrated systems, ubiquitous data, and digital offerings are critical to both the patient and employee experiences.

In order for healthcare systems to start to close the gap, the capabilities of new technologies offer opportunities to gain greater transparency into which populations and individuals in the organization's client pool are at greater risk of experiencing poor health outcomes. For example, greater transparency into medication adherence, one of the contributors to unequal health outcomes along racial and socioeconomic lines (AHRQ, 2009), provides opportunities for human interventions to improve patient outcomes. Longitudinal community data can be used to increase practitioners' understanding of adherence patterns and inform organization-wide goals focused on closing the gaps.

Telehealth and Healthcare Digitization Are Likely to Result in More Hybrid Models of Patient Care, Which Will Create Challenges for CIOs to Deliver Omni-Channel Systems

Medical systems that are part of a fee-for-service model are oriented to provide only the care and treatments for which they are paid. Medical systems that work on a whole-health model (where they get paid the healthier, they keep patients) see the benefit of more time-efficient approaches such as email and virtual visits.

Prior to the COVID-19 pandemic, many health insurance systems wouldn't reimburse for telehealth visits. The sudden shutdown of in-person treatment for almost everything except for emergency room visits forced a sudden reckoning by both payers and providers that rapid approval and testing of telehealth delivery options were needed. The speed of change was almost breathtaking: according to a survey conducted in July 2020 (Landi, 2020), 80% of US physicians had conducted a virtual patient consultation in the previous 3 months—up from 39% in April and 9% in early March, when the use of virtual consults was unchanged over 2019 levels.

Yet despite the rapid deployment and acceptance of telehealth options, 20% of physicians still had not used telehealth during the past 3 months, with the top reason cited being the possibility of diminished quality of care (49%).

Those physicians also cited liability risks (44%) and concerns about privacy/data security (29%) as reasons why they did not offer virtual consultations. Some practices do not offer virtual consultations, according to 29% of those physicians. Doctors' concerns also extended to reimbursement (21%) and establishing the relevance of telehealth to their specialty (21%).

Among those physicians surveyed in June and July who said they had conducted virtual consultations in the past 3 months, about half (52%) said they would likely continue to do so after COVID-19 mitigation measures have ended.

Telemedicine—delivered through handheld devices that have been ubiquitous for more than a decade—is finally being reimbursed at parity to in-person visits by Medicare, and Medicaid and private health plans have followed suit. State medical boards, *previously bound by professional license regulations*, are now more readily recognizing medical licenses across state lines to enable the healthcare workforce to travel to problem areas where they are needed.

With most healthcare organizations now embracing telemedicine—and more liberal payment policies enabling it—we anticipate that traditional hospitals and medical groups will serve as strong competitors to the disrupters that are using all-virtual models. That's because patients who still value seeing a doctor in person when necessary will likely gravitate toward local organizations that offer an omni-channel approach to care delivery where the patients can choose the channels that work best for them. This is likely to be a combination of in-person, in-home, and virtual settings. These omni-channel approaches offer many new ways of serving patients where and when they need care. However, the challenges for the IT leaders are significant as they evolve and replace existing legacy systems to build sustainable, reusable components that can record and share key patient data regardless of channels. In order for this business model to be seamless for patients, it must also be easy for medical practitioners to gain easy access to records, data, and insights. In this way, patients are afforded better choices, while the practitioners have real-time access to the information, they need to deliver better and more consistent outcomes.

Innovations in Healthcare Delivery Models Are Challenging Traditional Business Models

The fee-for-service healthcare delivery model remains the dominant approach in the US, though it is continuing to face pressure to evolve. Value-based healthcare delivery models such as accountable care organizations (ACOs), patient-centered medical "homes," and hospital value-based purchasing (NEJM Catalyst, 2017) are growing in importance as options that all healthcare systems may need to adopt. Many healthcare systems have already transitioned a significant portion of their healthcare delivery model to a value-based approach, and hybrid models are common. These hybrid models often blur the distinction between where fee for service ends and value-based approaches begin. Since fee-for-service will likely gradually decrease in importance, but not suddenly disappear, the technology systems implemented to support the new value-based models will need to continue to be built in parallel to the ones that support fee for service, allowing interoperability among the systems. This is challenging for CIOs to deliver value at scale while keeping costs under control.

At the same time, the focus on patient outcomes in value-based models will also require building and integrating technology solutions that capture more detailed patient information while simultaneously complying with ever-evolving HIPAA and data protection regulations. Since mobile apps are becoming a primary interface for patients to interact with healthcare delivery and monitoring of their outcomes, mobile systems will have to be included in the value-based technology systems architecture. Ultimately, the trends toward more value-based delivery models along with the increased societal pressure to improve population health and decrease racial and socioeconomic healthcare outcome disparities should converge, creating greater pressure on healthcare providers and their CIOs to build and maintain systems that can grow and evolve to meet the new needs.

However, in order to meet those converging needs, CIOs need to recognize and address the digital divide—disparities in technology access among lower-income communities which also are disproportionately nonwhite. Broadband internet access and usage of the most up-to-date smartphones are substantially lower in these communities, creating large barriers to accessing the internet- and mobile-based options for interacting with their physicians and the health systems. This increases the demands on CIOs to build and maintain systems that work just as easily for older generation phones and computers—and allow for community-based options for the many people who don't have reliable access even to older technologies which can be located in community centers, libraries, houses of worship, etc.

The challenges of the digital divide are only partly about access to technology and are also related to socioeconomic disparities in the ability to access and respond to digital systems easily. For example, during the COVID-19 pandemic, states, cities, and counties set up online systems for finding and registering for vaccine appointments, only to discover that the people who could access and use the systems with ease were disproportionately white and wealthy. A large part of the problem was the technical barriers to accessing the online systems. But there was also a large non-technical element: lower-income nonwhite people are disproportionately employed in jobs where they have to be at work in person (cannot work virtually from their homes) and could not be constantly looking at their cell phones to grab the vaccine appointments when they became suddenly available online. CIOs must therefore be aware and proactively look for socioeconomic and racial disparities in both technical access, and the ability to use the systems' full functionality.

The pandemic has created an opportunity with shifting of regulations to meet the current need, rapid digitization, and increased respect for healthcare in the public's eyes, while longer-term trends toward value-based healthcare models continue and are likely to accelerate in the coming years. CIOs must not waste this moment. This is the time to leverage the momentum and help bring sweeping changes to the practice of medicine and patient care, one that is powered by data and mobility, and not restricted to the confines of seeing patients face-to-face inside a medical care facility, and which makes greater use of models other than fee for service.

The New Healthcare CIO Role

How the CIO Role Has Changed

It is not a surprise that even compared with 10 years ago, there has been a significant evolution in the CIO's role. In the 1980s and 1990s, this role was primarily responsible for project management and technology implementation. Most healthcare organizations during this time focused on implementing electronic health records. Technology experts call this the first phase of digitalization. In tracking 25 years of evolution of the role, Chun and Mooney (2009) state these were the times when the CIO's role was primarily a functional head position.

Parallel to the evolution of the CIO's role, the early stages of electronic medical records focused almost exclusively on standardizing and sharing of existing data within healthcare systems, conversion of handwritten notes and other non-coded data into coded fields for ease of access and classification (and ultimately, analysis), and improvement of billing. Though substantial progress has been made in evolving those systems, today there is still great room for improvement, especially in the delivery of patient care. This means that for most CIOs, a substantial amount of work lies ahead in partnering closely with the senior executive team to move their organizations to effectively leverage new digital technologies and platforms to start to improve care delivery in a meaningful way across the healthcare system.

Over the years, the CIO's role has expanded to involve strategic partnering. This shift parallels an increased sophistication of technology use across healthcare organizations. The second phase of healthcare technology adoption has been marked by an increased emphasis on system integration and optimization. Although this shift began a couple decades ago, it continues to be the focus of most healthcare organizations. In this phase, the CIO's role has been to ensure system adoption and meeting the technology and data needs of the various stakeholders. Aligning across hospitals and units to drive a common way of operating is key for technology implementation. This alignment requires CIOs to act as influencers, working with their cross-functional peers to deliver valued organizational outcomes. It is important to note that it is not just technology that must be optimized. Healthcare entities must continually adapt to changes in regulatory requirements and shifts in population healthcare needs.

The expectations of the CIO's role will continue to morph with the emergence of advanced technology and changes in societal expectations. CIOs today are expected to operate in a business co-leader capacity. Some of the more advanced healthcare systems are in the third phase of technology adoption where the focus is on big data analytics, mobile-enabled devices, cloud computing, and social engagement. The ability to harness vast amounts of patient and system data presents a myriad of opportunities, including enabling healthcare leaders to make evidence-based decisions particularly in new and emerging disease conditions. Today it is already possible to harness healthcare data using artificial intelligence to deliver faster and more accurate insights. The current and future challenges for healthcare organizations lie in identifying the right places to introduce these AI-driven insights into organizational processes, and the subsequent adoption by physicians and the clinical staff.

Taking advantage of the new insights provided by digital technology requires much more than focusing on the technical issues of deployment and integration of software and hardware. Fundamentally it's about the work design itself—the way care is structured and delivered within the healthcare organization and beyond to the larger ecosystem. Designing a system that leverages technology to improve patient outcomes and organizational processes requires a close strategic partnership between the CIO and the other organizational leaders who own the healthcare delivery processes to understand both the needs of patients but also the needs of the healthcare providers and support functions across the organization.

Despite the emerging trends, not all organizations are ready to embrace the new CIO role. Old ways of operating are keeping some organizations from moving toward a more strategic orientation. According to Joe Peppard, in some organizations, information technology is seen as a necessary resource but not one that increases value. He notes "we're often involved far too late or in the latter stages and we're not hearing some of the early dialogue" (Peppard, 2010), which puts the CIO in a reactive position from which it's hard to lead strategically and proactively. Today's CIOs must establish themselves as strategic partners in the business, a trusted advisor to the CEO, and an integrator across business silos. This is best done by leading with a business-first perspective as opposed to a functional head perspective.

A People Centric Approach to Leading

In today's healthcare environment, CIO roles demand both a patient-centric approach and a healthcare worker approach. Research from MIT CISR shows that organizations that focus on making it easier for their employees to do their work also deliver vastly superior customer satisfaction (Dery and Sebastian, 2017). Not only does the CIO need to be constantly in touch with the changing needs of patients, but also the requirements of physicians, and the clinical staff, as well as the people who staff and run the rest of the non-clinical support systems that are essential to healthcare delivery (such as sanitation, food service, and maintenance). Strategic CIOs focus on a range of capabilities (digital and physical) designed to raise both the voices of their patients and healthcare workers to identify the speedbumps. In more traditional work environments, the CIO has a more reactive role in resolving problems as they emerge; however, in a digital world, the CIO is looking for ways to get information that can predict when problems are likely to emerge and get ahead of them.

Strategic healthcare leaders succeed by taking a more holistic approach to the patient experience. Rather than focusing on healthcare delivery on a procedure-by-procedure basis, they recognize that success comes from a more nuanced approach to the whole patient experience. Creating technology-based products and solutions that meet patient needs for the highest quality outcomes while meeting affordability goals requires that patient care be reimagined as end-to-end experiences or journeys. Patient journey mapping, just as with customer journey mapping in other businesses, must also include the experience of the physicians and medical staff to deliver better experiences in ways that are sustainable, consistent, and affordable. Journey mapping or other ways of shifting from products to experiences requires all business leaders, but particularly the CIO, to create cross-functional teams that can unlock a better understanding of the needs of patients in new ways to identify the organizational capabilities necessary to meet them. These teams iterate in rapid cycles to ensure that they can pivot solutions to meet changing and often unexpected challenges.

Most recently, the healthcare system has been focused on the COVID-19 pandemic. Before that, there were pressing societal healthcare needs including the opioid crisis, diabetes, cancer, and heart disease, to name a few. To fully comprehend the systemic implications of the rapidly changing healthcare needs associated with these complex issues, CIOs need access to data and systems to build a rapid understanding of the needs of patients, their families, their home context, and their culture. Our interviews with healthcare leaders demonstrated that while next-generation technologies are necessary, they are not sufficient to deliver better outcomes, particularly in crisis situations. Instead, success comes from the design and effective implementation of those technologies and tools to equip the physicians, the patient care teams, and even the patients themselves with the data and insights to make better decisions.

These decisions are not made in a vacuum, and so the CIOs in healthcare are constantly balancing multiple competing stakeholders and perspectives, and finding a way to optimize all of the divergent priorities. For example, the CEO and the CFO may be most concerned with revenue and the CMO with medical outcomes. It is easy to prioritize the interests of the loudest or the most influential stakeholder, usually the CEO, yet easy does not guarantee the right approach for the organization's mission and long-term success. What is required of the CIO in this environment is a dedicated focus on IT governance. What decisions about IT need to be made, who gets to make these decisions, and what management structures, processes, structures, information, and tools are needed to ensure that they are effectively implemented (Marchand and Peppard, 2013). This is where the strategic CIO's political savvy and ability to influence are essential. The CIO must take on the diplomatic role that synthesizes across all the organizational priorities and aligns interests around the most important ones, which in healthcare is typically safe, high quality, affordable patient care that is also profitable.

In contrast with other industries, another particular challenge for healthcare CIOs is the special role that physicians play in both delivery and organizational-level decision-making about business processes. In many other industries, the frontline personnel who are central to the critical work are less involved in many decision-making processes, though their input is often sought before a decision is made. In those industries, when the organization makes the decision to implement protocols and deploy technology to improve business processes, the frontline personnel typically have no choice but to go along with the execution of the new protocols and technology or face punitive consequences. In healthcare, by contrast, frontline physicians retain the power to either actively or passively resist decisions made from the top down without their full consent and buy in because they are ultimately responsible for patient care. This power is bolstered by the decentralized structure of many US healthcare organizations, and because of the history of fee-for-service billing.

One reason for the continued power of physicians within the system is because they are ultimately responsible for patient care. Even when part of a larger system, the individual physicians are both legally and perceived to be morally responsible for the care of their patients. Therefore, physicians feel both legally and morally bound to make sure that systems are created in a way that is most conducive to enabling them to be successful in delivering the best possible patient care.

The duty of care physicians have to their patients is further complicated by the fact that many physicians aren't employed by the organizations where they work. As recently as the 1980s, only one quarter of physicians in the US were direct employees of a hospital or healthcare system, or members of a physician practice owned by such entities. By 2018, that figure had almost doubled, but remained less than a majority at 46% (Kane, 2019). Thus, today around half of all physicians maintain legal autonomy from the healthcare systems in which they work, and thus do not have to commit and comply with decisions by the leaders of those systems as readily as regular employees have to.

Even where physicians are directly employed, decentralized decision-making is a hallmark of the US healthcare system because of the fee-for-service model. Physicians are expected to make positive patient care decisions and routinely do so without having to consult with anyone else. That decentralized approach filters up to the specialty level, with specialist groups consulting with each other, but less likely to consult with unlike specialties because of the substantial differences in the work itself. There is little direct collaboration among specialties, except for the complex cases where treatment requires real-time consultation and joint decision-making.

In the small number of systems where value-based care is the foundation for all patient care, such as Kaiser Permanente, collaboration and information sharing are a core part of the delivery system. In these systems, information technology is a foundation first and foremost for sharing information that is central to patient care; in contrast, in systems that traditionally were predominantly fee for service, information technology was first used to create efficiencies in billing, and patient care considerations have been addressed later on in the evolution of the systems.

Decentralized decision-making is becoming more common in healthcare systems as larger systems acquire smaller systems, standalone hospitals, and physician practices. This shift introduces the classic challenge of integration of both management and information systems, which is an issue for all mergers and acquisitions. However, because healthcare is delivered locally and there are few to no economies of scale when coordinating care across geographies, there is less pressure to create tight integration of all business processes and information systems in healthcare mergers than in many other industries.

Ultimately, healthcare administrators, including CIOs, have primary responsibility for making many key decisions about processes, systems, and technology that span the enterprise, but they have to be keenly aware of how those decisions are received by the physicians and their perception about how the decisions affect the physician's ability to deliver quality care. If the physicians see a conflict among the systems, technology, and patient care, they can act both directly and indirectly to undermine those decisions, including rejecting the system outright. Thus it is essential for CIOs to engage key stakeholders throughout the physician community from the start of any key project to ensure their influence has maximum impact on their projects' success.

The ability of physicians to potentially override patient care decisions imposed by centrally administered systems is particularly important in a fee-for-service model when the technology negatively impacts the flow of patients to a doctor and/or restricts the doctor's ability to order expensive procedures. Such restrictions may be optimal from the perspective of others in the system—the patients, the non-medical administrators, and society/the government—but they can directly negatively impact both patient care and physician compensation in a fee-for-service model. The negative impact on physician compensation creates deep conflict between what the physicians view as in their personal best interest (in terms of both autonomy and compensation) vs. what non-medical administrators believe is most lucrative or best from a healthcare delivery system perspective. Any digital technology that a CIO seeks to install without the buy-in of physicians, even with the blessing of administrators and other medical staff, runs the risk of being dead on arrival. To avoid turf wars, the CIO must look to align with the physician leaders on the important priorities for the organization. Having shared priorities can increase the chance for collaboration in the design and implementation of systems. One challenge with this approach is that it may slow down progress or restrict the number of priorities a CIO can realistically pursue. Ultimately, it's about narrowing down to only those priorities that are essential and making the right trade-offs.

The role of the CIO is even more complex in healthcare compared to other industries. Not only are patient needs rapidly changing, but the dynamics of doctors and other healthcare workers are complex and challenging. While it may be possible to conceptualize a best-in-class system, a CIO may be forced to settle for what is feasible. Designing and leading cross-functional teams that can iterate constantly around the needs of all stakeholders and find solutions within the guardrails of the IT governance framework is critical in these complex environments.

Evidence-Based Guidance on Leadership

Healthcare leaders have the responsibility to take a systems approach to addressing organizational needs. The challenges are too big and the crisis too urgent for them to take an incremental or siloed view. Healthcare at its foundation is a "complex adaptive system" in which the interplay of a large number of different factors affects both patient and organizational outcomes (NASEM, 2019; Plsek and Greenhalgh, 2001). This is why the World Health Organization has advanced systems thinking as the standard in health system interventions and evaluation design by providing tools and guidance (De Savigny and Adam, 2009).

Improving any one thing by itself is less likely to deliver results: it is the orchestration across different organizational elements that ultimately drives better outcomes. The starting point is the strategy and future direction of the organization. Laying out how the organization should transform to the desired future state is the starting point for successful organizational change. For example, studies show that highly effective leaders skillfully orchestrate four key elements of their work to deliver excellence: strategy, transformation, operations, and people (Yukl et al., 2002; Antonakis and House, 2014). Here we take that overall category of "people" and differentiate between internal stakeholders (the workforce, consisting of the physicians, medical staff, and all support staff and functions) and external stakeholders (patients, payers/health insurers, and government/regulators).

Related evidence comes from Smaltz et al. (2006) who conducted a multiphased study designed to uncover the specific behaviors associated with CIO role effectiveness. Study participants were contacted using the Healthcare Information and Management Systems Society (HIMSS) member directory with 136 responses from top management team members representing 106 organizations. The findings provide prescriptive guidance on the types of behaviors CIOs can benefit from engaging in to drive better outcomes. The study measured CIO effectiveness by obtaining ratings on 24 role expectations associated with the CIO role, with the ratings provided by members of the top management team (CEO, COO, CFO, etc.). Some of the role expectations included actions such as "develop and implement an IT strategy plan that aligns with the organization's strategic business plan," "be intimately involved in business strategic planning and decisions," "build and maintain an IT staff with skill sets that match your current and planned technology base," and "establish electronic linkage to external entities (insurance payers, private physician offices, suppliers, etc.)." The behavioral role descriptors matched many of the examples we got from the healthcare interviews we conducted.

There are many models of organization design and effectiveness that can help guide leaders as they navigate the challenges of managing the complex organizational system and their role in it. Ones that are commonly used include Galbraith's Star model, McKinsey's 7S, and similar systems views such as the NIST Baldridge categories of strategy, leadership, operations, customers, and workforce capability. In this section, we review evidence that comes from the literature and our interviews and organize the ensuing guidance using categories similar to those of NIST Baldridge.

Strategy

Leaders have a number of roles with regard to strategy. For CIOs, two of the most important roles they play within their organization in the strategy space are that of strategist and business model advocate. Strategist refers to the CIO's role as a strategic business partner with the specific goals of helping the organization succeed both today and in the future by innovating using IT-based solutions, clinical workflow, business process redesign. To that end, they help shape the organization's mission and vision, and influence and inform the strategic plan.

Closely related to strategy formulation is identifying the right data and insights. In the past, CIOs could pour over spreadsheets of data and dashboards produced by their various internal systems and use that to formulate plans. Yet today, strategy no longer is confined to the walls of single healthcare delivery systems. Accessing information such as new treatment methods, technology solutions, or operating models is essential for strategic success. For this, CIOs must have a network of experts with whom they maintain regular connections. They also should have proficiency in drawing insights from information sources such as population health data, community data, etc.

Compared to the past, the risks associated with misjudging the future state can have grave consequences. For instance, in 2020 alone, 47 hospitals shuttered their operations in the US (Ellison, 2020). This was accompanied by sizable losses to both those who relied on the services and the healthcare workers employed by those hospitals. Could these closures have been prevented? Some may attribute such closures as a healthy sign of market forces operating. Another perspective is that the leadership could have found ways to repurpose the facilities to address the demands had they been attending to the signs that were starting to emerge by late 2019.

Leaders have an important role in laying the building blocks for the future; however, no one can see the future perfectly. The best prepared are more likely to survive and thrive. During the COVID-19 pandemic, systems that had made bets on and invested in telemedicine adapted quickly with barely any loss in service delivery. This ability to make good bets on the future is an important leadership skill. It requires expertise in assessing risks and returns of various choices. Experts recommend the practice of metacognition to hone this skill (Marshall-Mies et al., 2000). Constantly evaluating choices and decisions either by themselves or with their teams is essential for fine-tuning the art of making bets (Marshall-Mies et al., 2000). A leader must also remember the role of luck and serendipity. Some decisions may have worked in their favor due to chance. At other times, the most judicious decision-making may result in a poor outcome. Creating psychological safety in the work environment and operating with humility and resilience are essential for better decision-making.

A key part of strategy is innovation. The pressure to innovate in providing safe and cost-effective healthcare is coming from multiple sides. Government regulators and watchdogs are increasing pressure and requirements for organizations to adopt new value-based models, while similar pressure is coming from organic innovation by disruptors such as virtual providers and business models such as the ones developed by Narayan Health.

India-based Narayan Health's mission is to bring compassionate healthcare at an affordable cost to the masses. The system performs more heart surgeries than the Cleveland Clinic and Mayo Clinic combined, at a fraction of the cost, and with comparable health outcomes. The secret to Narayan Health's success is a highly efficient operation that is inspired by organizations such as Walmart and McDonalds. According to Narayan Health's COO, Viren Shetty, their system amortizes costs of equipment and other infrastructure by maximizing its usage. For instance, open-heart surgeries are performed by two teams of doctors. Junior residency doctors perform the lower-risk procedures such as the opening and closing of the heart, and expert surgeons perform the main tasks. Using this method, the most expensive resource is utilized where it matters the most, which increases throughput in the system, and can dramatically reduce unit costs and the prices charged to patients and payers.

Healthcare CIOs have a unique role in rapidly enabling the organization through technology. One good example comes from healthcare startup Oak Street Health that operates primarily in disadvantaged communities. At the beginning of the COVID-19 pandemic, their biggest challenge was finding ways to bring healthcare to those who do not use a smartphone. Through a rapid transformation of their operating model, the vast majority of patients' visits are now over the phone or through video visits.

Leadership

Healthcare leaders work both with their own teams and with many other stakeholder groups both within and outside their organization. Many organizational outcomes are driven by how the leader engages with their peers and team members, and the relationships they develop both within and outside the organization. From navigating barriers such as legacy systems and uneven digital maturity to aligning across divergent priorities, the CIO's path to leadership effectiveness is not easy and goes well beyond the knowledge of technology. An effective, strategic healthcare leader must have the tools and the capacity to orchestrate people, structures, and systems to deliver affordable and high-quality patient care in an increasingly dynamic world.

CIOs work in partnership with other C-Suite leaders as agents of culture change. They set the standards for the digital talent the organization attracts, engages, grows, and retains. Organizations that employ most of their digital talent as full-time staff and executives outperform their competitors on most measures of value (Dery et al., 2018). These firms are more innovative, faster to market with new customer-facing products and services, and more profitable on average than their competitors. Given that IT teams are notorious at plugging talent gaps and boosting teams with contractors, the move to more dedicated, internally staffed full-time teams can seem counterintuitive. This is further exaggerated by the fact that many IT workers favor freelancing careers, and large traditional medical facilities are often challenged in their ability to attract good people in a highly competitive talent market. Research at MIT Center for Information Systems Research identified that the most effective way to shift the balance of digital talent to more full-time employment models is to invest in the experience of people to do their work more easily and effectively (Dery et al., 2018).

The CIO's ability to deliver the best possible healthcare workers' experience of work will facilitate the engagement and growth of their staff to be more innovative, create opportunities for growth and development, and facilitate the stability of cross-functional teams to deliver on patient-centric products and services. The strategic CIO creates a culture that embraces a digital mindset and is closely aligned with the strategic priorities of the organization. They are particularly cognizant of the divergent preferences of a multigenerational workforce and implications on the adoption of new technologies.

To be effective, CIOs also need to build partnerships with their peers in other healthcare organizations, as well as with community leaders, vendors, and service providers. For example, the CEO of Narayan Health, Dr. Devi Shetty, had a relationship with Indian Space Research Organization (ISRO) which resulted in Narayan health being able to build out telehealth centers for rural locations in India that leverage ISRO's satellites for communication. This partnership was supportive of both organizations' goals in that it both subsidized the cost of the satellites and facilitated substantial improvement in health in rural India. It has also provided a critical health option for patients during the COVID-19 pandemic. This would not have happened without the partnership orientation of leaders at Narayan Health.

Ed Marx, former CIO at the Cleveland Clinic, offers a helpful leadership perspective for developing human-centered business strategy. In an interview reported in HIMMS, he shared this important advice to CIOs:

> You need to be spending the bulk of your time with the business – whether it's shadowing clinicians, understanding the detailed nature of supply chain or HR processes, understanding all aspects of the business, whether it's the operational, clinical or business components. You need to be able to blend in and speak as if you were one of them.
>
> *Sullivan and Miliard (2018)*

In our organizational consulting, we hear a similar sentiment echoed across industries. Today's CEOs are expecting their C-suite partner leaders to think holistically about the business and staff, rather than focusing on the needs of their specific function alone.

In healthcare, leading transformation often entails dismantling institutional barriers or deeply held beliefs about medical care. The unique challenge for CIOs is not identifying the right technology solution, of which many exist, it is in arriving at a solution that is accepted, adopted, and workable. This may require settling for a less than ideal solution from a technical perspective, but one that is more likely to be used. A moderately good solution that is widely adopted is likely to be a better outcome for clinical care and business success than a perfect solution that no one will use. No technology implementation can be successful without adoption and resulting behavior change. This challenge is similar to the classic case of the format wars between two competing technologies in the days of the videocassette recorder (VCR): Sony's Betamax format was the superior technology from a technical standpoint, yet it lost out to the VHS format which was embraced by a broad coalition of manufacturers, retailers, and content producers.

Balancing multiple stakeholder priorities is essential to effective strategic leadership for CIOs. Most healthcare systems have multiple hospitals, units, and specialties. Each hospital may have its own governing board. Healthcare leaders often say that aligning priorities at a system level is an involved task. In the absence of such alignment, even the best plan can fall apart. The alignment process invariably involves giving priority to some part of the organization before others. To make that work, the leadership needs to be aligned with the prioritization and be able to articulate why that prioritization is best for both clinical care and the business.

In our conversation with Narayan Health, making judicious decisions about where and what to digitize played a critical part in transforming the organization. Because their most prominent efforts in digitization began with the Intensive Care Units (ICU), they prioritized clinical care. Knowing the organization's focus on providing compassionate and affordable care helps one see why such as choice is not out of the ordinary. Physicians were aligned with the changes, seeing that investing in aggregating ICU system data in a single dashboard enabled the physicians to make faster decisions about their patients. It also enabled remote monitoring which meant that doctors could address adverse conditions from a distance, cutting down the time between identifying the problem and treating it. This technology shift resulted in better outcomes for the patient, as well as increasing throughput and lowering costs per patient because of an increase in the number of patients who could be effectively monitored simultaneously. Being able to closely monitor patients at a distance has also been of unexpected assistance to the physicians and other clinical staff during the COVID-19 pandemic, reducing exposure of clinical staff while maintaining a high standard of care.

Operations

The CIO's role is ultimately responsible for keeping the systems running as a well-oiled machine, anticipating breakdowns, and preparing for contingencies. In addition, they must keep ahead of the ubiquitous cycle of planned obsolescence and new technology adoption.

CIOs help ensure the safety, reliability, and consistency of services. Healthcare systems are often an amalgamation of doctors' offices, ambulatory care facilities, and hospitals. The doctors themselves often are independent agents who operate with significant autonomy. Ultimately the physicians, staff, and administration must integrate for effective patient care. CIOs can provide leadership and direction for integrating across all of these groups of people and the systems that support them, influencing change while ensuring the needs of each stakeholder group are addressed.

CIOs also are stewards of the information systems, data, and resources needed to deliver high-quality patient care. They are required to ensure data integrity and quality while complying with HIPAA, GDPR, and other jurisdictions' privacy protection laws. For example, considerations related to data security and privacy are becoming increasingly important. In a recent incident in Germany (discussed further below), hackers succeeded in rerouting an ambulance to a longer route which resulted in the patient's death.

Because of how critical the role of technology is in patient care today, CIOs are responsible for influencing the technology security consciousness across the organization, encouraging safe technology behaviors, and ensuring technology systems are protected at all times. Any violation of HIPAA policies can result in significant fines and loss of trust and reputation. In this way, CIOs also contribute significantly to the organization's brand.

While delivering team-based patient care is common healthcare operations, there is an increasing demand for expanding the team involved in team-based care beyond the boundaries of a single healthcare organization. This expansion may involve developing partnerships with ancillary service delivery organizations for non-critical care such as physiotherapy or behavioral health. According to healthcare analyst, David Johnson, medical institutions that operate with the mission of delivering service through collaborative teams or in partnership with other institutions deliver better outcomes (Johnson, 2016). Examples of such partnerships include medical foundations such as the Mayo Clinic. The team-oriented approach to delivering care through doctors who are employed by the system results in increased information sharing and follow-through on protocols. Such organizations usually deliver better patient outcomes due to their additional focus on preventative care.

CIOs play an important role in enabling such partnerships by making the process more seamless using technology. When clinical staff have the resource to look up outside services and schedule appointments, they ensure that patients are more likely to follow through on the treatment procedures. Creating a frictionless system should be the goal of all technology solutions.

Cybersecurity is a real and present concern for healthcare organizations and their CIOs. A recent incident in Germany highlights the vulnerabilities of healthcare systems to cyberattacks. On September 11, 2020, paramedics were transporting a 78-year-old patient to the local university hospital for an aortic aneurysm. Mid-way the paramedic was informed that the emergency department was closed, and the patient was redirected to a hospital 32 miles away, which delayed medical care by an hour. Sadly, the patient died. Investigations revealed that a ransomware attack had brought down the hospital infrastructure and resulted in the cancellation of several hundred medical procedures. Examples such as this highlight that even essential institutions such as healthcare are not immune to cyberattacks. Protecting an organization is not just a matter of adopting better security technology. Hackers are known for exploiting behavioral vulnerabilities in the system. This requires training employees on adopting safe behaviors to maintain the security of systems.

Customers: Patients, Payers/Health Insurers, and Regulators/Government

An important role of the CIO is in helping determine when and where technology can make a difference in serving the overall mission of the organization and the needs of stakeholders: patients, payers/health insurers, and regulators/government. Implementing the best available technology may not be the best choice if it does not lead to adoption and the right outcomes for the external stakeholders. Strategic CIOs are good at reading organizational strengths and weaknesses and projecting where technology is likely to produce the best return for the external stakeholders.

Although a CIO's role is several steps removed from treating patients, staying in close touch with the needs and circumstances of patients is essential for optimizing patient experience through digitization and data. Patient's stories can inspire new thinking on how previously disconnected systems can be brought together to unleash untapped potential in data and insights.

In his talk at Stanford Big Data 2015, Christopher Longhurst describes the case of a 13-year-old girl who was life flighted to the Lucile Packard Children's hospital. Doctors were at a loss for how best to address her condition. The treatment plan in adults for her condition was well understood, but the risk and benefit ratio in children was unknown. The fallback in such cases is to use the best judgment by the team of doctors. The physician in-charge in this case took a slightly different approach. Instead of relying on clinical judgment, the medical team isolated data from similar pediatric patients to determine the relative risk of the procedure. The data-based insights informed the treatment plan, which ultimately allowed the medical team to minimize any adverse effects. The Institute of Medicine has since begun recommending smarter clinical decision support systems to deliver safer and most cost-effective patient care.

The point of emphasis in this story is not just about a better approach that is driven by data-based insights, but that all innovation starts with a deep understanding of the people healthcare serves and wanting to make their situation better. Following that initial experiment with data, Stanford commenced working with Apple to gather patient data and build dashboards for remote monitoring of patients.

Just as important as the orientation toward patients is the orientation toward payers/health insurers. Every point of contact between the healthcare system and the health insurer is an opportunity for digital innovation and transformation. Two current examples are real-time authorization and price quotes, and improved billing efficiency and accuracy. Consider real-time authorization. A big problem with healthcare delivery within the fee-for-service model is the uncertainty both the patients and physicians have regarding which services will be covered and how much they will cost patients. A robust real-time authorization system would provide virtually instantaneous responses regarding coverage and net cost after discounts and deductibles are taken into account.

Strategies for implementing real-time authorization start with the payers, not the healthcare systems, because it's the payer's work processes and systems that have to undergo the most fundamental transformation. Yet, the close interdependency between the IT systems of both sides means that success cannot be achieved without substantial transformation of systems and processes on the health care provider side as well. While the healthcare CIOs may take the lead in driving evaluation and adoption of such changes, they must work in close partnership with clinical and office staff because every IT system and protocol change requires staff to learn new processes and behaviors. Building that workforce capability (see below) is essential to any successful change or transformation.

Similarly, a strong relationship with government/regulators is also essential for the CIOs to enable strategic success for the organization. Continuing the example of real-time authorization, CIOs must confront the reality that each health care organization works with many different health insurers, each with their own strategies, systems, and desires to beat the competition and improve their market share. If the CIO takes into consideration only the immediate relationship between their organization and the health insurer without looking at the system as one that includes regulatory organizations, they could be taken by surprise by new regulatory expectations.

Just like the Betamax vs. VHS format war in VCR technology from a generation ago, one health insurer may come up with an outstanding, efficient, and technologically superior solution to real-time authorization. Yet if a large enough group of other insurers and provider organizations band together to promote a technically inferior approach, they might still win over the regulators through sheer power in numbers and compelling arguments about economies of scale combined with patient protection. Thus successful CIOs must maintain strong orientations simultaneously toward patient needs, the economics and dynamics of the payer relationships, and the priorities and trends among regulatory bodies.

Workforce Capability

Hospitals are buildings, walls and floors. Hospitals don't treat people. Doctors do.

Dr. Clive Fields, CEO of Village Family Practice (VFP)

CIOs have a key educator role to play with the top management team and leadership throughout the organization with regard to how information technology can address the needs of the enterprise and enable the strategic vision to be enacted. Creating a future-ready workforce to effectively deliver the digital strategy requires CIOs to focus on both the digitalization of work and digital fitness. In more traditional firms training is mapped to roles or future career progressions. In the digital era, we need to empower employees to make better decisions by leveraging technology, data, and shared knowledge (Dery et al., 2020). This means staying up to date on the technology options, making these options accessible and easy to apply to multiple problems, educating the leadership team on the implications of the options, and helping teams make informed technology choices for the enterprise. It also means ensuring the end users—the physicians, clinical staff, and all other operations and facilities management staff—are up to date and fully capable of using the various functionality of the digital technology systems and have the skills to enable them to work in ways that are more aligned with more iterative, cross-functional approaches to decision-making.

CIOs face a critical choice of where and when to invest in new technology. The organization's mission and values can provide important guidance. At Narayan Health, the focus on delivering high-quality patient care at an affordable cost translates into improving the experience of the physicians so they can spend time treating patients rather than trying to make the systems work for them. As discussed earlier, one of Narayan Health's areas of technological investment has been in pulling together data from disparate systems in the ICU into a dashboard. By improving the usability of the data, Narayan Health has improved the decision quality of the ICU staff. It has also allowed for remote monitoring of patients based at their hospital in the Cayman Islands by the staff in India.

COVID-19 has accelerated the digitization of healthcare. To fully embrace digitization, CIOs must invest in growing staff capabilities to leverage new technologies, including methods for overcoming the fears and concerns of some physicians and medical staff.

At UC Davis, all staff in the hospital setting are equipped with tablets, and as each action in the workflow is recorded in the system which triggers the next steps for the clinical staff. For example, if the bed for a new patient is not ready, the transporter who is bringing in the patient is alerted. All subsequent processes are electronically adjusted to prevent backlogs in the system. Running an efficient technology-enabled system such as UC Davis both requires extensive staff training on the systems and procedures, and for staff to feel motivated and inspired to deliver. While some leaders believe their job begins and ends with deploying efficient systems, running an efficient system is more than the technology, the workflow, and the training guide. An efficient system engages the hearts and minds of the people involved, and the staff feels ownership in delivering the organization's mission. This requires an intentional effort on the part of the leader to inspire and motivate their teams, particularly in times of intense work pressure. Research on transformational leadership has recommendations for specific leader behaviors in this domain (see Antonakis et al., 2011; Avolio and Bass, 2001).

One of the biggest current challenges in healthcare is employee burnout. According to a 2021 report by NSI Nursing Solutions, 10% of nurses are looking to leave the profession and 22% to retire sooner (NSI Nursing Solution, 2021). Because of the direct link between clinician burnout and healthcare safety and quality, preventing burnout has become an important national healthcare priority. In 2019, 32 institutions and foundations sponsored a study on "Taking action against clinical burnout" (National Academies of Sciences, Engineering, and Medicine (NASEM), 2019). According to the study, a key reason for high levels of stress and burnout among clinicians is poor design of technology (e.g. electronic health record systems that require additional time for record entry). This has direct implications for the work of the CIO. There is an urgent need for better healthcare technologies geared toward work simplification. One of the healthcare leaders we interviewed was specifically recruited from the automobile industry where it is common to implement technologies to minimize errors and prevent delays. Forward looking healthcare organizations such as Virginia Mason are looking to the famed Toyota production system to borrow ideas for optimizing healthcare operations (Branch, 2020). Such efforts are not only beneficial to the overall functioning of an organization, but they also reduce workload and emotional exhaustion for staff members, enabling them to deliver better patient care.

Of course, focusing on fixing only one part of the healthcare delivery system will not solve the burnout problem by itself. Many different aspects of the healthcare environment have to work together in an integrated way to prevent, reduce, or mitigate burnout and improve professional well-being (Shanafelt and Noseworthy, 2017). CIOs need to understand that bigger picture and how their work on the technology infrastructure has to seamlessly integrate with the work of their peer leaders to reduce stress and burnout.

Research to date indicates that successful systems-oriented strategies (National Academies of Sciences, Engineering, and Medicine (NASEM), 2019) will include making improvements in clinician workload and clinical workflow, providing more usable technologies that are focused on clinicians' needs, and developing organizational structures and processes that better support clinicians and the interdisciplinary care teams in which they work (Bodenheimer and Willard-Grace, 2016). Individually focused interventions such as group discussions and mindfulness education can be complementary to system interventions, which include the technology components that are the domains of the CIOs.

Conclusion

The healthcare CIO role has evolved from a functional leader to a critical member of the executive team leading the business. With that shift, the role of CIO has changed in fundamental ways.

First, the technological needs of the organization must be integrated with the strategic priorities of the business, staff, regulators, and external stakeholders. CIOs need to take an outside-in view when determining the focus of their work, assessing population and community health needs to design systems that are adaptive and responsive to the times. Second, success as a CIO is measured based on the success of the business. Metrics and KPIs are based less around the implementation of technologies and more around innovation and widespread adoption of human-centric systems that ease the work of physicians and clinical staff to deliver superior patient care. Third, CIOs must engage cross-functional teams in continuous learning to ensure that they are effectively evaluating and refining digital capabilities to enable their organizations to fulfill clinical and regulatory requirements while setting up the business for success. Fourth, healthcare CIOs need to work closely with the business to actively design and support high-functioning teams that embody new ways of working to deliver the highest possible levels of patient care. In a modern healthcare system, CIOs are at the fulcrum of leading their organizations into the next generation of healthcare. Being intentional and strategic about their leadership will accelerate that journey.

References

AHRQ. (2009). https://digital.ahrq.gov/sites/default/files/docs/page/10-0010-EF.pdf.

Antonakis, J., Fenley, M., & Liechti, S. (2011). Can charisma be taught? Tests of two interventions. *Academy of Management Learning & Education, 10*(3), 374–396.

Antonakis, J., & House, R. J. (2014). Instrumental leadership: Measurement and extension of transformational–transactional leadership theory. *The Leadership Quarterly, 25*(4), 746–771.

Avolio, B. J., & Bass, B. M. (Eds.). (2001). *Developing Potential Across a Full Range of Leadership Tm: Cases on Transactional and Transformational Leadership*. Psychology Press: Hove, UK.

Bodenheimer, T., & Willard-Grace, R. (2016). Teamlets in primary care: Enhancing the patient and clinician experience. *The Journal of the American Board of Family Medicine, 29*(1), 135–138.

Branch, Z. (2020). Q&A with Dr. Gary Kaplan. 425 Magazine. Retrieved from https://425magazine.com/qa-with-dr-gary-kaplan/.

Chetty, R., Stepner, M., Abraham, S., et al. (2016). The association between income and life expectancy in the United States, 2001–2014. *JAMA, 315*(16), 1750–1766.

Chun, M., & Mooney, J. (2009). CIO roles and responsibilities: Twenty-five years of evolution and change. *Information & Management, 46*(6), 323–334.

De Savigny, D., & Adam, T. (Eds.). (2009). "Systems thinking for health systems strengthening". World Health Organization.

Dery, K., Beath, C., & Woerner, S. E. (2020). "Equipping and empowering the future-ready workforce", MIT CISR Research Briefing XX-12, December 17. https://cisr.mit.edu/publication/ 2020_1201_FutureReadyWorkforce_DeryWoernerBeath.

Dery, K., & Sebastian, I. (2017). "Building business value with employee experience" MIT CISR Research Briefing No XVII-6, June 15. https://cisr.mit.edu/publication/2017_0601_Employee Experience_DerySebastian.

Dery, K., Van der Meulen, N., & Sebastian, I. (2018). "Employee experience: Enabling your future workforce strategy" MIT CISR Research Briefing No XVIII-9, September 20. https://cisr.mit.edu/publication/2018_0901_DigitalTalent_DeryVanderMeulenSebastian.

Ellison, A. (October 16th, 2020). 47 Hospital closed, filed for bankruptcy this year. Hospital CFO Report. Retrieved from https://www.beckershospitalreview.com/finance/47-hospitals-closed-filed-for-bankruptcy-this-year.html.

Gorski, D. (2019). Are medical errors really the third most common cause of death in the US? (2019 Edition). Science-Based Medicine. Retrieved from Are medical errors really the third most common cause of death in the US? (2019 edition) | Science-Based Medicine.

Himmelstein, D. U., Lawless, R. M., Thorne, D., Foohey, P., and Woolhandler, S. (2019). Medical bankruptcy: Still common despite the affordable care act. *American Journal of Public Health, 109*, 431–433.

Holden, K., Akintobi, T., Hopkins, J., Belton, A., McGregor, B., Blanks, S., & Wrenn, G. (2016). Community engaged leadership to advance health equity and build healthier communities. *Social Sciences (Basel, Switzerland), 5*(1), 2.

Johnson, D. W. (2016). Market vs. medicine: America's epic fight for better, affordable healthcare, 4sight Health.

Kaiser Permanente. (June 6, 2019). Partnership houses Oakland homeless. Kaiser permanente Northern California media relations. https://lookinside.kaiserpermanente.org/partnership-houses-oakland-homeless/

Kane, C. K. (2019). Updated data on physician practice arrangements: For the first time, fewer physicians are owners than employees, American Medical Association, AMA Economic and Health Policy Research. https://www.ama-assn.org/system/files/2019-07/prp-fewer-owners-benchmark-survey-2018.pdf.

Landi, H. (2020). In rush to embrace telehealth, many physicians still have concerns about quality of care, survey finds, September 10, FierceHeathcare.com. https://www.fiercehealthcare.com/practices/rush-to-embrace-telehealth-many-physicians-still-have-concerns-about-quality-care-survey.

Marchand, D. A., & Peppard, J. (2013). "It cannot be only the CIO's responsibility" HBR July 19. https://hbr.org/2013/07/it-cannot-be-only-the-cios-res.

Marshall-Mies, J. C., Fleishman, E. A., Martin, J. A., Zaccaro, S. J., Baughman, W. A., & McGee, M. L. (2000). Development and evaluation of cognitive and metacognitive measures for predicting leadership potential. *The Leadership Quarterly, 11*(1), 135–153.

National Academies of Sciences, Engineering, and Medicine (NASEM). (2019). *Taking Action against Clinician Burnout: A Systems Approach to Professional Well-Being.* National Academies Press: Washington, DC.

NEJM Catalyst. (2017). What is value-based healthcare? January 1, Catalyst.nejm.org https://catalyst.nejm.org/doi/full/10.1056/CAT.17.0558.

NSI Nursing Solution. (2021). 2021 RN labor market update, February. Retrieved from https://www.nsinursingsolutions.com/Documents/Library/RN_Labor_Market_Update.pdf.

Oak Street Health. https://www.fiercehealthcare.com/practices/how-oak-street-health-has-changed-post-covid-19.

Peppard, J. (2010). Unlocking the performance of the chief information officer (CIO). *California Management Review, 52*(4), 73–99.

Plsek, P. E., & Greenhalgh, T. (2001). Complexity science: The challenge of complexity in health care. *BMJ, 323*(7313), 625–628. https://doi.org/10.1136/bmj.323.7313.625

Shanafelt, T. D., & Noseworthy, J. H. (2017, January). Executive leadership and physician well-being: nine organizational strategies to promote engagement and reduce burnout. *Mayo Clinic Proceedings* 92(1), 129–146).

Siwicki, B. (2019). Oak Street Health decision support system reduces readmission by 26%. *Healthcare IT News.* https://www.healthcareitnews.com/news/oak-street-health-decision-support-system-reduces-readmissions-26.

Smaltz, D. H., Sambamurthy, V., & Agarwal, R. (2006). The antecedents of CIO role effectiveness in organizations: An empirical study in the healthcare sector. *IEEE Transactions on Engineering Management, 53*(2), 207–222.

Sullivan, T., & Miliard, M. (2018). Meet the modern healthcare CIO: A business leader that is casting off their traditional IT role. https://www.healthcareitnews.com/news/meet-modern-healthcare-cio-business-leader-casting-their-traditional-it-role.

Yukl, G., Gordon, A., & Taber, T. (2002). A hierarchical taxonomy of leadership behavior: Integrating a half century of behavior research. *Journal of Leadership and Organizational Studies, 9*(1), 15–32.

Chapter 16

TIPPSS for Facilitating Connected Healthcare Interoperability

Ken Fuchs
Draeger Medical Systems, Inc.

William C. B. Harding
Medtronic

Florence Hudson
FD Hint, LLC, New York, New York

Mitchell Parker
IU Health

Contents

The four walls are gone with medical devices and the Internet of Medical Things (IoMT). We have reached the point where these devices that are so important for patient care no longer depend upon the physical buildings where care is traditionally rendered. Instead, with the rush to outpatient care hastened by COVID-19, medical devices have moved to people's homes and to other facilities. We also have the challenge of people's own smartphones being used in the care process.

Advances in mobile technology have enabled the evolution of medical devices from being primarily in healthcare facilities to escaping to the world at large. The processing power of mobile

DOI: 10.4324/9781003220473-22

devices including medical devices has increased substantially, so much so that devices that needed to connect to computers within the hospital for processing power now have significant amounts of processing power and memory on their own. Medical devices used to be self-constrained infra-structures running their own proprietary protocols and depending upon interface servers to trans-late proprietary communications protocols into Health Level 7 (HL7) or DICOM interchange formats. Now medical devices are capable of outputting data in interpretable interoperability for-mats such as the HL7 superset of Fast Health Interoperability Resources (FHIR), directly. They do so over wireless and cellular networks, which opens the risk of these devices operating in hostile territories and increasing the attack vectors for data and device security. This is as opposed to their traditional hard-wired environments, which started as directly connected interfaces, moving to serial, then Ethernet and Wi-Fi, and now over cellular data networks such as LTE or 5G. Medical care has gone mobile, and it's not going back.

Healthcare interoperability standards such as HL7, DICOM, and now FHIR have significantly improved how organizations and devices can interchange data. The HL7 Clinical Document Architecture (CDA) does an excellent job of capturing context and data (Fonseca et al., 2007). The new generation of medical devices utilizes FHIR and other APIs to populate Electronic Medical Records (EMR) systems, sometimes directly. There has been significant improvement in transport-layer security, specifically with the inclusion of Transport Layer Security (TLS) in the DICOM specification and FHIR reference implementations.

There is now a need to ensure that the devices themselves and the data they transmit meet minimum standards for security and extend that implied trust from the four walls to wherever the devices are being utilized. Deloitte estimates that IoMT will be a $158 billion USD market in 2022 (Taylor et al., 2018). This translates into millions, if not billions, of devices being used in the care process, including smartphones that belong to patients.

This will necessitate the use of intelligent systems utilizing Artificial Intelligence (AI) and Machine Learning (ML) to be able to manage and ensure the security and provenance of data interchanged with the IoMT. These solutions depend on the integrity of processes that generate the data used by them to be accurate. This is important for the systems that will consume the data for patient care, analysis, and analytics. It is also important for systems that will use that data for intelligent systems for anomaly detection and security. It is critical that the data be as accurate as possible for the intelligent systems that aggregate data from multiple devices about multiple subjects for clinical decision support and analytics. There has been research on intelligent systems attacks that caused perturbations which were significant enough to cause a misdiagnosis, such as the one described in the paper CT-GAN: Malicious Tampering of 3D Medical Imagery using Deep Learning (Mirsky et al., 2019). Researchers at Ben-Gurion University in Israel were able to add and remove evidence of medical conditions using a 3D Generative Adversarial Network. This paper also notes that the security of modalities themselves, along with the Picture Archiving and Communication Systems (PACS) used to store the images, is also a concern. Use of advanced technologies such as Augmented Reality (AR), Virtual Reality (VR), and Mixed Reality (MR) in the healthcare world can add risk as well. Medical devices and health technology systems require accurate data and excellent processes to ensure data integrity. Data from the IoMT will feed these systems and be an integral part of their usage.

The leverage of mobile and new technologies requires security that adapts to new scenarios. We are not going to extend the four walls of a facility out to numerous new devices. We need to focus on security controls that can provide a good operating picture of the devices and data gener-ated on behalf of patients to improve their quality of life. Utilizing the Trust, Identity, Privacy, Protection, Safety, and Security methodology, better known as TIPPSS, to manage the security of these devices and the data they interchange will provide a means to do so.

This chapter will first go over the need for a clinical IoT framework driven by real needs, and how the TIPPSS framework can improve outcomes. Next, the realities of complex healthcare data interchange and interoperability with the Internet of Things will be discussed. Finally, we will discuss how material in other chapters can help with implementing TIPPSS in your organization, and how to leverage a learning organization to best educate all stakeholders.

A Clinical IoT Framework: Driven by Real Needs

The TIPPSS Framework has six key principles (Hudson, 2019):

- **Trust**: Allow only designated people/services to have device or data access
- **Identity**: Validate the identity of people, services, and "things"
- **Privacy**: Ensure device, personal, sensitive data kept private
- **Protection**: Protect devices and users from harm – physical, financial, reputational
- **Safety**: Provide safety for devices, infrastructure, and people
- **Security**: Maintain security of data, devices, systems, and people

TIPPSS requires us to take a holistic view of the use cases and scenarios where and how devices will be used in the care process.

In all cases, TIPPSS factors such as security, privacy, and safety must be considered in the design and implementation of these solutions. We must ensure that we are only allowing people or things with an entitlement to utilize this data access to it. This is demonstrating trust. People, services, and things need to affirmatively assert who they are (Identity) against a known credible data source and be able to be cross-checked. This is also critically important given both the proliferation of multiple devices, and the numerous amounts of people, institutions and systems involved with the care process that can possibly be granted access. This data must be kept private from anyone other than the intended use case actors or systems. The devices and things must protect and keep their users safe from harm, be it from a malfunctioning device or from other conditions that cause failure. The Management and Leadership Distinctions Required chapter covers the use of Failure Mode and Effects Analysis (FMEA) as a risk mitigation technique to augment Protection and Safety. Security is pervasive and has to be considered throughout the entire lifecycle. The protection of data, devices, people, and things from a multitude of threats is a significant undertaking. The Management and Leadership and Mobile Device Risk Management chapters cover techniques which organizations can use to assess and address risk while effectively managing these solutions.

While the term Mobile Medicine has tended in the past to be associated with mobile access to static patient records, we see an increasing need and desire to get "real-time" access to patient data. It is also safe to say that the COVID-19 Pandemic has acted as a catalyst in accelerating and catalyzing an evolution that was already in progress. Access to real-time patient data is enabled by what we have termed the Clinical Internet of Things (IoT). Our goal, in this section, is to provide some examples of environments and use cases where the Clinical IoT complements the practice of medicine.

The invention of the Continuous Glucose Meter (CGM) represents a breakthrough for diabetics, allowing them to manage their diet and insulin more precisely. The meter consists of a body-worn sensor and a "receiver" which can be a special manufacturer-provided device or a smartphone running a specific app. One of the challenges that we encounter today is the exchangeability of sensors. Each sensor manufacturer uses proprietary communications approaches so that the patient cannot just use a sensor from another manufacturer if needed. What happens if a user needs to replace the device sensor because it stopped working, or it was lost, or it expired and the user can no longer get a replacement for their normal device?

Extending the example, the receiver and/or smartphone can communicate with Internet-based applications which allow another caregiver or healthcare practitioner to view the CGM data as often as necessary. This is especially important if the patient is challenged due to age or some other disability. The Clinical IoT is intimately involved in these solutions. Enabling communication from the sensor to the receiver and enabling communication from the receiver to consuming applications using the Internet. It is also possible to envision that the sensor, someday, could communicate directly to the internet. How is data shared with the healthcare practitioner or primary care physician (PCP) if their system is not compatible or interoperable with the chosen device? Of course, issues such as TIPPSS need to be considered in these medical applications.

A Clinical IoT trend, which has been accelerated by the COVID-19 Pandemic, has been the transition of acute care from the hospital to Long-Term Acute Care (LTAC) facilities and/or the home. This has given rise to the advent of remote monitoring services. One simple example which we are probably all familiar with is the "I've fallen and can't get up" scenario. There are many ways this is being deployed, including the use of special fobs that the user can use to send out an alarm. These have become more sophisticated to the point that they may automatically detect falls with the capability of using specialized fobs or accelerometers in smartwatches such as the Apple Watch (insert ref here). In all cases, the Clinical IoT is involved in these solutions using various wireless technologies to ultimately use the internet to communicate with the monitoring service provider. Note that the reliability of these systems is a function of the fall detection algorithms (a form of AI) as well as the coverage of the wireless technology.

Extending this example would be a seriously ill patient that is being taken care of at home. This patient may need ECG, blood pressure, temperature, SpO_2, and other parameter sensors. In addition, that patient may be on some therapy delivered by an infusion device, respiration device, etc. Ideally all these sensors, in addition to video and audio feeds, participate in the Clinical IoT and can be monitored and controlled remotely by the monitoring service provider or hospital-based command center. Of course, the challenge is responding in a timely way to adverse events. Increasing the use of AI to track a patient's status may provide early warning systems to predict and anticipate potential adverse events, or sense events in real time, which may allow intervention before things get too bad.

We should also note that this type of Clinical IoT integration is done in the hospital environment as well. The electronic Intensive Care Unit (eICU) is an ICU that has local staffing but is also remotely monitored by ICU specialists to support the local staff. The remote ICU specialists can track the patient vitals and other parameters, as well as interact with the local caregivers and patients (if they are conscious).

In dealing with severely infectious patients, healthcare workers (HCWs) are at a significantly greater risk of infection than the overall population due to their frequency and time in contact with the infected patients. The HCWs will enter the patient room to administer care to the patient and manage the therapeutic equipment. This management of the patient's therapy may require frequent device adjustments which may be delayed due to the need for the HCWs to protect themselves by donning PPE prior to entering the patient room and doffing the PPE upon leaving. This donning and doffing process can exceed 15 minutes depending on the specific PPEs used. A recent study (Suen et al., 2018) reported times of 7 minutes for donning and 10 minutes for doffing, with the doffing process providing the opportunity for "considerable" self-contamination.

Infectious diseases confer a synergistic burden on and risk to the patient due to the requirements for isolating the patient (Abad et al., 2010) including poorer care and impaired coordination of care (Mehrotra et al., 2013), significantly fewer HCW and family visits relative to patients not on precautions (Morgan et al., 2013), increased rate of adverse events (Stelfox et al., 2003) and increased depression (compared to other inpatients) (Day et al., 2011). The use of remote control and monitoring can be used to eliminate some treatment delays, reduce the infection risk to the HCW, and help preserve the limited supplies of PPE and improve patient care.

Critically ill patients with an infectious disease will often require monitoring with physiologic monitors and therapeutic support with ventilators and infusion pumps. As previously explained, entering the room to view parameters or adjust any settings can require 15 minutes for something that may take <1 minute. Clinical IoT technology can provide remote access to view parameters and adjust settings thereby increasing efficiency, saving the costs of the PPE, and most importantly increasing the safety of the HCW.

In implementing such a solution both the manufacturer and the hospital deployment team must consider numerous requirements in order to keep the patient safe including the key elements of TIPPSS (Trust, Identity, Protection, Privacy, Safety, and Security). Another scenario that is highlighted by the pandemic was the need to create ICUs overnight where there were none the day before. In addition to the logistics of finding space, obtaining equipment, running electrical and plumbing, etc., much of the critical patient care equipment would come from sources such as the strategic stockpile or just donations from veterinarians, cosmetic or other surgical practices, etc.

Normally, integrating these medical devices with the hospital IT infrastructure would be a months' long process which usually involves a device integration team from a third-party vendor or the Electronic Medical Record (EMR) vendor. In the absence of time, these devices were still deployed but patient charting was done manually thereby impacting the productivity of the clinical staff and not taking advantage of any Artificial Intelligence (AI) or Clinical Decision Support (CDS) tools that would improve the care of these patients. In addition, if these devices are "data islands" remote access to the data is not possible which disables the ability to remotely view the patient's status and requires going to the bedside with the accompanying issues of PPE, PPE donning and doffing and HCW safety. Having Clinical IoT devices which follow specific interoperability protocols which enable "Plug and Play" information exchange would address this challenge. The important aspects of TIPPSS must also be considered.

Healthcare is not just about clinical devices; a holistic healthcare solution may encompass commercial and industrial IoT as well as Clinical IoT devices. For example, knowledge of environmental factors such as air quality, UV index, humidity, etc. at the very local level can be very useful to patients with asthma, chronic obstructive pulmonary disease (COPD) and other diseases. Tapping into local environmental sensors in addition to traditional clinical sensors such as heart rate, respiration rate, temperature, etc. using the IoT can create a more complete picture for the patient and provider.

Implanted devices continue to get more intelligence and are more connected. They can capture and report events to remotely located clinicians. Clinicians may have the ability to remotely change the settings on the implanted devices based on these reports as well as other biological measurements reported from sensors on the patient. It is essential that these "things" communicate in a secure, trusted, and safe manner.

Healthcare is currently very crisis oriented. Typically, patients obtain care only after they suffer an adverse event. Clinical and Biological IoT will support connectivity of person connected sensors and devices which will support the continuous monitoring of people before they become patients. This data will be processed in real-time by AI-based algorithms which will be able to detect changes in health status before a health crisis occurs. Of course, early detection of issues will also lead to better outcomes. This, we believe, is the objective of smartphone and smartwatch manufacturers.

The objective of TIPPSS, in these scenarios, is to ensure that the data from smartphones, smartwatches, and other devices are effectively protected from its generation to its ultimate disposition. Numerous devices which we may or may not completely control will generate data used in the care process. Its usage has to be governed by principles that respect privacy, protection, safety, and security, and lead to better outcomes overall.

Realities in Connected Healthcare and Clinical IoT

If you were to walk into a modern ICU, you may expect that the devices are integrated with the chosen EHR (Electronic Health Record), feeding the EHR with vital signs, infusion pump data, ventilator data, etc. What you may not realize is that this is not always the case due to the amount of work and resulting cost that goes into making this happen – too much work. Device integration is challenging primarily since while most device vendors provide a digital interface, these interfaces are for the most part proprietary. This means that while they are "interoperable" they are examples of "dysfunctional interoperability". The recently signed 21st-century Cures Act Final Rule is a step forward in aligning organizations on a common data interchange Application Programming Interface (API), Fast Health Interoperability Resources (FHIR) version 4.0.1, with Oauth2 as the authentication standard, and Transport Layer Security (TLS) as the secure transport (CMS HIIG, 2021).

Interoperability is a complex topic that is multilayered as shown by the following table (Tolk et al., 2007):

As you can see from Table 16.1, achieving full "functional interoperability" is a multilayered effort. For the most part, today's devices are interoperable at Level 1 and potentially at Levels 2 and 3. They support a Common Communication Transport such as Ethernet, Wi-Fi, Bluetooth, and TCP/IP or equivalent as the communication protocol. While they typically support some sort of syntactic and semantic interoperability, they are not "Common" in that it is typically every device for itself. The better devices may support some form of common protocol such as HL7 or IEEE 11073 (Level L2) or, better yet, an IHE DEV profile (Level L3) (more about those follows). We are far away from taking a medical device off the shelf, plugging it into the IT network, and having it feed data to the EMR or interact with other devices on the network without considerable effort and expertise by device integration specialists.

Image data needs to be grouped into the same scope as general text data, where just as the saying goes, a picture is worth a thousand words. Or more specifically, an image of something that might uniquely be used to identify a person or a trade secret (e.g., a process, formula, or method). Furthermore, as we consider extended reality (XR) technology, then things like digital twins, visual recordings, and visual streaming represent data that needs the same level of protection as that of typical text data. Lastly, with advancements in AI/ML, high-speed image processing has enabled the recognition of individuals (e.g., faces and identifying marks/tattoos), where the ability to manage the results of such systems is needed. Otherwise, we can imagine that those individuals who need the protection of their identity the most might be at risk.

In current healthcare environments, facilities, and organizations, technology and humans are expected to work together to establish standards, securely exchange data, and transform a massive amount of healthcare data into digestible facts and insights that will benefit patients, healthcare

Table 16.1 Levels of Interoperability

Level	Interoperability Layer Name	Premise	Information Defined	Contents Clearly Defined	Focus
L6	Conceptual interoperability	Common conceptual model	Assumptions, constraints, etc.	Documented conceptual model	Composability
L5	Dynamic interoperability	Common execution model	Effect of data	Effect of information exchanged	
L4	Pragmatic interoperability	Common workflow model	Use of data	Context of information exchanged	Interoperability
L3	Semantic interoperability	Common reference model	Meaning of data	Content of information exchanged	
L2	Syntactic interoperability	Common data structure	Structured data	Format of information exchanged	Integratability
L1	Technical interoperability	Common communication protocol	Bits and bytes	Symbols of information exchanged	
L0	No interoperability	No comm.	N/A	–	–

Source: Adapted from Tolk et al. (2007).

research, and healthcare organizations. The ability to transform data is presently accomplished using methods such as non-standardized electronic health records/medical records (EHR/EMR) and data protocols that connect the vast array of dissimilar healthcare components. Transforming the data from the point of collection to the point where it is used to make health-related decisions requires that human or machine-generated errors not be present, and that the information be available in a timely manner as solution response time could literally impact a patient's life or death. Correspondingly, current manual methods of data collection require the use of the EHR to connect dissimilar healthcare technology, exposing the problems associated with increased human error and a reduced ability to maintain data and patient security.

To resolve the issues of interconnectedness between healthcare components, businesses and government organizations worked to create standard methods for reducing paper-based healthcare records. Those methods are characterized by EHR/EMR systems where in addition to representing a foundation for standardizing data, they also stimulated improvements in data security. Respectively, the collection and movement of data between dissimilar healthcare technology using EHR are analogous to trying to empty the oceans with a teacup or are symbolically considered a band-aid, such that the variability between third-party EHR systems renders the concept of standardized healthcare technology as unachievable.

Respectively, variability between solutions is an issue where the absence of a standard communications method for transforming data will result in data instability across the multitude of dissimilar technology. For example, the issue of variability is significant when examining how data is taken from handwritten patient records, an X-ray analysis, or from a capture of patient vitals, and when combined with records that were collected from other healthcare organizations, result in lost or inaccurate data. The variations in data collection and the issues associated with aggregating data into a single patient record occur due to the integration of healthcare solutions and processes that lack common standards for communication and digital compatibility with existing technology. We have excellent messaging integration with DICOM, PACS, HL7, and FHIR. However, context and workflow have been the Achilles' heel of integration, despite the HL7 CDA standard.

One of the oldest implementations of a standard solution is the Picture Archive and Communication System (PACS), used in radiology (Khaleel et al., 2018). This solution consists of four components. These are the image acquisition devices (better known as modalities), the communication networks, the PACS archive and server, and the integrated display workstations. The communication network is high-speed to communicate between the modalities, PACS archive and server, and the workstations. PACS is focused on decreasing the time it takes for physicians to make qualified diagnostic imaging decisions. It is designed to interface with a Radiology Information System and hospital Electronic Medical Records systems.

Imaging, messaging, and communication are done utilizing the Digital Imaging and Communications in Messaging (DICOM) protocol, codified as ISO 12052 (MITA, 2021). DICOM was established as a protocol in 1993. Its main focuses were to establish a common protocol for exchanging imaging data format and correspondence information (MITA, 2021). The American College of Radiology and National Electrical Manufacturers Association (ACR-NEMA) started work on what became this protocol in 1982 (Khaleel et al., 2018).

DICOM conformance can be validated using the DVTK Open Source toolkit (DVTk, 2021). This project has two main contributors – ICT Group and Philips. This toolkit allows companies to test their products for the appropriate level. The conformance statement itself follows a template format specified by NEMA that covers networking, media interchange, character set support, and security (DICOM Standards Committee, 2021).

DICOM itself is an imaging-specific data interchange protocol. Health Level 7 (HL7) is a comprehensive framework and set of standards for the exchange, integration, sharing, and retrieval of Electronic Health Information (Health Level Seven International, 2021a). This group was founded in 1987. Its name is a reference to Level 7 of the OSI networking model, which is the application level. They have a comprehensive set of standards that cover all aspects of interchange. These include Clinical Document Architecture (CDA), which specifies the structure and semantics of clinical documents for the purpose of exchange between healthcare providers (Health Level Seven International, 2021b). These also include Fast Health Interoperability Resources (FHIR), which builds an Application Programming Interface (API) on top of HL7 to allow interoperability between all stakeholders. FHIR is the standard that the 21st-century Cures Act is based upon.

HL7 also cross-approves standards with the American National Standards Institute (ANSI) and International Standards Organization (ISO) (Health Level Seven International, 2021c). This ensures that there are US and international standards for conformance. This is important when utilizing these devices in non-US markets. It also allows device manufacturers to use one set of standards when addressing regulatory bodies worldwide. Due to their cross-approval of standards with ISO, they are considered the standards bearer along with DICOM.

Along with HL7 and DICOM, standards work has been ongoing in the field of medical and personal health device interoperability for multiple decades in IEEE (Institute of Electrical and

Electronic Engineers) as well as IHE (Integrating the Healthcare Enterprise). In IEEE, this work has been primarily addressed in the IEEE 11073 Standards Committee (SC) which focuses on clinical device interoperability. The goal is to achieve plug-and-play connectivity which includes message formats, device discovery, data nomenclatures, and information modelling reaching into Level 4 and beyond in our interoperability model. This committee has two Working Groups (WGs): Point-of-care Device (PoCD) WG and Personal Health Device (PHD) WG.

The PoCD WG focuses on medical devices typically used in hospitals such as ventilators, infusion devices, patient monitors, etc. These devices are typically installed and maintained by clinical engineering professionals. This committee also maintains the overall nomenclature (11073-10101) and the base information model (11073-10201).

The PHD WG focuses on simpler connected devices that could be used by people outside of the hospital environment including weight scales, pulse oximeters, blood pressure cuffs, medication monitors, etc. These devices would typically be purchased and maintained by the patients themselves, though we are starting to see concepts such as "hospital at home" where a commercial enterprise is providing this service for more acutely ill patients.

Despite the considerable body of work accomplished by the IEEE, commercial adoption of these standards has been minimal. It has become obvious that the "if you build it they will come" approach has not been working. Recently the not-for-profit Center for Medical Interoperability (CMI) has been created to aggregate the purchasing power of healthcare organizations to favor open solutions that are compliant with published standards and specifications. Even with the involvement of CMI, this does not address the need for organizations to address this using an overall architecture that aligns with the stated missions of care providers.

The usage of the TIPPSS framework aligns the excellent work done with existing standards with the need to align them to patient protection. TIPPSS is the bridge between technical standards that explains why they matter.

In addition to the HL7 work previously cited, there is also an HL7 Healthcare Devices (DEV) working group. This committee has focused on making sure that the general HL7v2 or HL7 FHIR standards support any special device needs. It does not create any separate standards.

IHE creates specialized "profiles" of existing standards (such as HL7 or IEEE 11073) to address specific healthcare integration challenges. IHE work on devices is handled by the DEV Domain which is structured as three different programs: DPI – device point of care integration, PCH – Personal Connected Health, and PCD – Patient Connected Devices. IHE DEV published profiles have been relatively well accepted and adopted. They include the DEC profile which is used for communication between device gateways and healthcare IT systems, the ACM profile for communication of clinical device alerts, and PIV which supports medication administration via infusion devices.

Health and safety risks are areas that we might consider as already being addressed as general functionality of a medical device or system. However, there are aspects of medical solutions where accidents or unexpected events can put a patient's health at risk, and thus there is a need to protect the patient's safety. Even if the best care is exercised by a patient in the use of their medical solution, there are conditions that might require the solution provider to build in capabilities that provide a patient with protection for scenarios that are less than nominal. For example, a patient with an implanted pain therapy device can override the safeties of their device, which if not properly managed could result in negative consequences. That said, building in the capability to measure therapeutic response might enable the device to determine the thresholds that are safe or unsafe for a person's unique physiology, and thus limit the ability to cause serious harm.

When it comes to device and human safety, there are numerous scenarios to consider. Specifically, safety might mean reducing the potential threat to a patient, if the power source of a solution becomes unstable, or where accidental damage might cause an uncontrolled chain reaction or systemic failure. On the other hand, safety may be compromised when a medical device is unable to protect its transmission and receipt of protected data that might be intended to control the solution. Accordingly, though it is impossible to anticipate all potential risks, it is important to ensure that there are no backdoors or unsecured methods that would enable either intentional or accidental disruption of data transmissions.

There are many potential threat vectors and incidents which we need to consider in maintaining safety and security for the device and patient. These include but are not limited to: signal hacking/hijacking/disruption; device interoperability with other technology such as patient programmers, mobile devices, and other wearable technology; accidental device disruption such as an electromagnetic (EM) field generator or other device that could interfere with a device's normal functionality (e.g., MRI, keyed radio, radiation, and magnets); device/sensor failure or performance degradation as a result of poorly managed power, charging, and control. That said, it is important to keep in mind that not all disruptions to a medical device's functionality are intentional. For example, it is easy to propose that a pain therapy device (near the patient's skin) or insulin pump (attached to a piece of clothing) could be damaged due to an accident or as a result of poor judgment. Accordingly, it might be necessary to build into those devices fail-safe functionality, such that the device cannot harm the patient, in the event that the device suffers a catastrophic failure.

Implementing TIPPSS Governance

Creating TIPPSS governance requires having excellent organizational governance across the organization. This is not something that can just be segmented to product development. There are organizational skills your team needs to effectively utilize it. This starts with developing a learning organization to be able to develop a culture of continual improvement. From there, building a governance structure to manage intake, projects, and prioritize work is important. The "Management and Leadership" and "Mobile Device Risk Management" chapters cover in detail the steps you and your organization can take to implement the overall management and risk management techniques needed to implement TIPPSS. These management techniques apply whether you are a device manufacturer, payor, or provider, with the goal to provide a transparent, safer, and more secure experience for patients and their advocates. The next step after reading this is to apply what you have learned and be an advocate for it by implementing it in your organization and framing your processes around its core principles.

Boundaries for the Internet of Things and Medical Devices have gone past the traditional four walls. TIPPSS provides the framework, when combined with effective management techniques and risk management, to effectively use mobile devices in this new environment. Keeping TIPPSS top of mind throughout the entire lifecycle can lead to better outcomes. Our challenge is to ensure that we follow through to do just that.

References

Abad C, Fearday A, Safdar N. Adverse effects of isolation in hospitalized patients: A systematic review. *Journal of Hospital Infection* 2010;76(2):97–102.

CMS HIIG. Reducing provider and patient burden by improving prior authorization processes, and promoting patients' electronic access to health information. CMS, January 20, 2021. https://www.cms.gov/Regulations-and-Guidance/Guidance/Interoperability/index#SMART/OAUTH%202.

Day HR, Perencevich EN, Harris AD, Himelhoch SS, Brown CH, Gruber-Baldini AL, Dotter E, Morgan DJ. Do contact precautions cause depression? A two-year study at a tertiary care medical centre. *Journal of Hospital Infection* 2011;79(2):103–107.

DICOM Standards Committee. DICOM PS3.2 2020e - conformance. Accessed January 24, 2021. http://dicom.nema.org/medical/dicom/current/output/chtml/part02/PS3.2.html.

DVTk organisation ("DVTk"). DVTk, a must have for anybody working with DICOM! Accessed January 24, 2021. https://www.dvtk.org/.

Fonseca JM, Mora AD, Barroso P. The web and the new generation of medical information systems. Outcome Prediction in Cancer. Elsevier, September 28, 2007. http://www.sciencedirect.com/science/article/pii/B9780444528551500167.

Health Level Seven International. About Health Level Seven International | HL7 International. Accessed January 24, 2021a. http://www.hl7.org/about/index.cfm?ref=nav.

Health Level Seven International. HL7 products: Master grid. Accessed January 24, 2021b. http://www.hl7.org/implement/standards/product_matrix.cfm?ref=nav.

Health Level Seven International. Introduction to HL7 Standards. Accessed January 24, 2021c. https://www.hl7.org/implement/standards/.

Hudson FD. Harnessing advanced technology innovations today and into the future. *The 15th International Conference on Emerging Technologies for a Smarter World*, November 6, 2019. https://www.cewit.org/conference2019/speakers/_Powerpoints/CEWIT%202019%20FDH%20v2-%20Hudson.pdf.

Khaleel HH, Rahmat RK, Zamrin DM. Components and implementation of a picture archiving and communication system in a prototype application." *Reports in Medical Imaging* 2018;12:1–8. doi:10.2147/rmi.s179268.

Medical Imaging Technology Association (MITA). "About DICOM: Overview." DICOM. Accessed January 24, 2021. https://www.dicomstandard.org/about.

Mehrotra P, Croft L, Day HR, Perencevich EN, Pineles L, Harris AD, Weingart SN, Morgan DJ. Effects of contact precautions on patient perception of care and satisfaction: A prospective cohort study. *Infection Control & Hospital Epidemiology* 2013;34(10):1087–1093.

Mirsky Y, Mahler T, Shelef I, Elovici Y. CT-GAN: Malicious tampering of 3D medical imagery using deep learning. *28th USENIX Security Symposium*, June 6, 2019. https://arxiv.org/pdf/1901.03597.pdf.

Morgan DJ, Pineles L, Shardell M, Graham MM, Mohammadi S, Forrest GN, Reisinger HS, Schweizer ML, Perencevich EN. The effect of contact precautions on healthcare worker activity in acute care hospitals. *Infection Control & Hospital Epidemiology* 2013;34(1):69–73.

Stelfox HT, Bates DW, Redelmeier DA. Safety of patients isolated for infection control. *JAMA* 2003;290(14):1899–1905.

Suen LKP, Guo YP, Tong DWK, et al. Self-contamination during doffing of personal protective equipment by healthcare workers to prevent Ebola transmission. *Antimicrobial Resistance & Infection Control* 2018;7:157.

Taylor K, Steedman M, Sanghera A, Thaxter M. Medtech and the internet of medical things." Deloitte United States. Deloitte UK Center for Health Solutions, September 12, 2018. https://www2.deloitte.com/global/en/pages/life-sciences-and-healthcare/articles/medtech-internet-of-medical-things.html.

Tolk A, Diallo S, Turnitsa CD. Applying the levels of conceptual interoperability model in support of integratability, interoperability, and composability for system-of-systems engineering. *Journal of Systemics, Cybernetics, and Informatics* 2007;5(5):65–74.

Closing Thoughts

Why Is Mobile Medicine So Hard?

Perhaps it's human nature to believe that one size fits all, or one size fits most. Where this is not true is where the opportunities are which are also the gaps in medical technology. It would be much simpler and more convenient if the same software that worked on desktops in stationary use cases also worked for mobile medicine. But it doesn't. What do we do then? While this is a daunting technical challenge, the bigger challenges turn out to be ones of workflow change management and the people, culture, and governance adaptations required to unleash the potential of mobile medicine.

There are many reasons why thus far, there has been little success for mobile applications in medicine. Much of it stems from a lack of understanding by most of the tech workforce of a totally different world which means new requirements. Much of the tech world lives in a world of their own – their own buildings, their own infrastructure, their own connectivity, with people at times with their own homogenous technology-related skills. In the rest of the world and the real world, technology that the tech sector develops doesn't automatically plug and play into new use cases. Beyond medicine, we've seen this in multiple industries including aerospace and autonomous vehicles. These gaps, by the way stifle progress of data and AI in a similar way to mobile in medicine specifically.

In the background, there is no technology industry that has been focused on succeeding in this mobile medicine context. Industries involved include but are not limited to wireless, networking, software, and consumer smartphones. While providing valuable products, none of these industries seem to put a serious investment into medicine even by one metric, workforce training dollars. This is required for driving value out of last mile technologies and systems of engagement. If you look at BioPharma and Medical device companies, you'd potentially be shocked to learn about the time, priority, and resources they invest in upskilling their workforce in the relevant areas of medicine and regulatory compliance. No technology industries are doing that now in any appreciable way. Second, no technology companies whose core technologies address mobility have built significant capabilities for delivering enterprise-grade software as a service, let alone medical-grade software. This is why you can't look to the technology sector to lead mobile medicine! Many SaaS companies want to say that their originally desktop product addresses mobile medicine but the proof is in the performance of the apps when the physician is in a no or low connectivity area, which are ubiquitous in healthcare.

Many healthcare systems have dabbled in mobile projects and for them the questions become many. Why doesn't the same software that always worked in the office work everywhere on mobile phones? How do I manage the phones? What are the privacy constraints? What are the security issues? To get value out of it, we need to change workflow. What is the right governance for this? Who are the right people to lead this? What leadership do I have to bring to this? Can this be done like every other Healthcare IT project? The answer to the latter question is, a simple No. Traditional healthcare IT systems of record designed for billing and reporting, or file storage don't have enough in common with systems of engagement like useful mobile applications. The latter would have even less in common with cloud storage, analytics or AI, search, and other similarly stationary use cases of computing. So why is mobile medicine hard?

The first reason: Mobile changes jobs. It changes how people behave and work. For this reason, the people and the teams need to evolve and change along with the workflows, all parties including vendors, customers, and partners. Otherwise, there is no value created for either the organization or the users without this transformation.

The second reason: There is little success in mobility for medicine, and really much of the generalized deskless workforce to help health system leaders leverage lessons learned to capitalize on the promise of mobile. As a result, leaders committed to their digital and mobile future need to pave the way. You need to expect hurdles, be ready for them and pride yourself on facing them and overcoming them. Hence the word "Overcoming" in the title.

What does this mean for the leader? It means you are on a journey of self management, personal life performance improvement, discovery, learning, and eventual mastery to build our skills and knowledge base and team of teams to meet the potential and challenges of mobile medicine.

Having a fresh lens is key. Anytime you're thinking about a mobile workflow, one should take a critical look at any existing or desktop technology's real ability to meet all of the requirements and, at the same time, take a sharp look at the needs of those physician users. While the usability is examined, the privacy and security that medicine and patients deserve need to also be part of the plan and execution. Real respect for privacy and security is based on nuanced, medically relevant risk management and comprehension, not flashy ads.

Anticipate the future technological landscape that can improve patient outcomes and clinician satisfaction at the same time. This will push you away from a tendency to force existing solutions into new workflows where they don't fit. Think about the capabilities you need to have and to build both within yourself and your team of teams to serve humanity with leading-edge, life-saving, and life-enhancing technologies. Adapting is never easy but it's necessary. Make it "uncool" to be comfortable with the status quo in your organization. We must change ourselves and our teams of teams to design the future technological landscape that will make a real difference to clinicians, patients, and their families. It's hard, but don't settle and don't let "it's too hard" win. Tackling what's required for mobile medicine will position you to be ready to integrate value from additional innovations such as IoT and wearable robotics. Embrace that future, we need all of the clinical workforce augmentation we can create. Think about what our patients actually need. They don't need what amounts to toys. They need actionable, timely, reliable, secure information. The clinicians also need that to deliver the best care. To augment the workforce means taking a hard look at the requirements and understanding the risks and what's at stake, and boldly building for that. It's not sitting on the sidelines because "it's too hard". Many hands make less work and many hands built this resource for you. We hope this book provides the beginning of a foundation for you together with your team of teams to envision, execute, and build on your mobile medicine future with confidence. I look forward to learning from you, both from our failures and then celebrating our successes.

Sherri Douville

Wearable Robotics, Enterprise AI, IT, & IOT, and Cyber Security and Risk Glossary

If it is said that language is a bridge, then in order to build bridges between historically disparate disciplines and industries, we need to start with some common language. That is why we are pleased to present you with a glossary of the least common terms that are found in this book.

Brittany Partridge
Clinical Applications
UC San Diego Health

Anti-malware solutions: Offerings designed to protect a business by monitoring data transferred via networks for a variety of potential threats. It also detects and removes threats to protect your entire organization and your customers.

Asset management software: A software program used to track inventories, hardware devices, software, and other software. The system also helps in asset lifecycle management. The software can track assets at all stages right from purchase to disposal. The system helps to optimize the process of asset management.

Artificial Intelligence (AI): The theory and development of computer systems able to perform tasks that normally require human intelligence, such as visual perception, speech recognition, decision-making, and translation between languages.

Atrial fibrillation (AFib): Irregular and sometimes fast heartbeat that occurs when the two upper chambers of your heart experience chaotic electrical signals.

Augmented Reality (AR): A technology that superimposes a computer-generated image on a user's view of the real world, thus providing a composite view.

Autonomous: Independence in one's thoughts or action, technology that can function without being constantly told what to do by a human.

Biological Internet of Things (BIoT): Network of biological things that is embedded with sensors, software, and other technologies to connect and exchange data with other biological things, devices, and systems over the internet.

Biometric: Measurement and statistical analysis of people's unique physical and behavioral characteristics.

Bluetooth Transmitter (BT): Bluetooth is a short-range wireless technology standard used for exchanging data between fixed and mobile devices over short distances using UHF radio waves in the ISM bands, from 2.402 to 2.480 GHz, and building personal area networks.

Clinical Internet of Things (CIoT): IoT devices used solely for medical research or devices that have been previously approved for medical applications by a governing body. This differentiates such devices from those that are currently used as consumer-end IoT devices for wellbeing.

Data Loss Protection (DLP): Solutions that help a network administrator control the data that users can transfer. DLP products use business rules to classify and protect confidential and critical information so that unauthorized users cannot accidentally or maliciously share data, which would put an organization at risk.

dFMEA: Design failure mode and effect analysis (DFMEA) is a systematic group of activities used to recognize and evaluate potential systems, products, or process failures.

Doffing: To Take Off.

Donning: To Put On.

EKG/ECG: Is a test that measures the electrical activity of the heartbeat.

Extended Reality (XR): Referring to all real-and-virtual combined environments and human-machine interactions generated by computer technology and wearables, where the 'X' represents a variable for any current or future spatial computing technologies.

FAIR: Factor Analysis of Information Risk (FAIR) is a taxonomy of the factors that contribute to risk and how they affect each other.

Goniometer: An instrument for the precise measurement of angles.

Host intrusion detection: An offering that analyzes the activities on or directed at the network interface of a particular host.

Host-based firewall: Software that runs on an individual computer or device connected to a network.

Internet of Bodies (IoB): An extension of the IoT, connecting the human body to a network through devices that are ingested, implanted, or connected to the body in some way. Once connected, data can be exchanged, and the body and device can be remotely monitored and controlled.

Internet of Medical Things (IoMT): The collection of medical devices and applications that connect to healthcare IT systems through online computer networks.

Internet of Things (IoT): A collection and exchange of information between disparate devices. This includes electronics, software, sensors, actuators, and network connectivity that directly integrates the physical world with software, allowing for remote sensing and control. The number of connected devices exceeds the world's population.

Interoperability: Is the ability of different information systems, devices, and applications (systems) to access, exchange, integrate, and cooperatively use data in a coordinated manner, within and across organizational, regional, and national boundaries, to provide timely and seamless portability of information and optimize the health of individuals and populations globally (HIMSS Definition).

ISO 27005: A set of standards from the International Organization for Standardization (ISO) and the International Electrotechnical Commission (IEC) that provides guidelines and techniques for managing information security risks. ISO/IEC 27005 is designed to assist in the implementation of information security based on a risk management approach and is part of a larger set of standards in the information security management system (ISMS), the ISO/IEC 27000-series.

ISO 31000: A family of standards relating to risk management codified by the International Organization for Standardization, ISO 31000: 2018 provides principles and generic guidelines on managing risks faced by organizations and is intended to be customizable to any context.

Machine Learning (ML): The use and development of computer systems that are able to learn and adapt without following explicit instructions, by using algorithms and statistical models to analyze and draw inferences from patterns in data.

mAh: The capacity of batteries is indicated as XXXX mAh (milliampere/hour). The formula for calculation is as follows: Capacity (milliampere/hour) = discharge (milliampere) × discharging time (hour).

Mesh Network (MeshNet): A local network topology in which the infrastructure nodes (i.e. bridges, switches, and other infrastructure devices) connect directly, dynamically, and non-hierarchically to as many other nodes as possible and cooperate with one another to efficiently route data from/to clients.

Mixed Reality (MR): Medium consisting of immersive computer-generated environments in which elements of a physical and virtual environment are combined.

Mockup: A model, drawing, or replica of a machine or structure used for instructional or experimental purposes.

NIOSH: The National Institute for Occupational Safety and Health (NIOSH) is the United States federal agency responsible for conducting research and making recommendations for the prevention of work-related injury and illness. NIOSH is part of the Centers for Disease Control and Prevention (CDC) within the US Department of Health and Human Services.

NIST SP 800-37: NIST Special Publication 800-37 is the "Guide for Applying the Risk Management Framework to Federal Information Systems" and was developed by the Joint Task Force Transformation Initiative Working Group. It aims to transform the traditional Certification and Accreditation (C&A) process into the six-step risk management framework (RMF). Further, the RMF is used to select the appropriate subset of security controls from the control catalog from the NIST Special Publication 800-53.

Patch management: A structured process for updating systems and software with new pieces of code. Patches fix vulnerabilities that may leave your system open to hackers, address problems in the programs you use, or add new functionalities to them.

pFMEA: A methodical approach used for identifying risks on process changes. Process Failure Mode and Effects Analysis (PFMEA) looks at each process step to identify risks and possible errors from many different sources.

Piezo/vibration stimulation: An ultrasonic vibrator that has a compact mechanism to produce vibratory stimulation on human skin using a pin array driven by a single piezoelectric actuator.

PPE: Protective clothing, helmets, goggles, or other garments or equipment designed to protect the wearer's body from injury or infection.

Prototype: A first, typical or preliminary, initial model of something from which other forms or iterations are developed.

Remote management solution: Managing a computer or a network from a remote location. It involves installing software and managing all activities on the systems/network, workstations, servers, or endpoints of a client, from a remote location.

Semantic (interoperability): The ability of computer systems to exchange data with unambiguous, shared meaning.

Sherwood Applied Business Security Architecture (SABSA): Is a framework and methodology for enterprise security architecture and service management. SABSA is a model and a methodology for developing risk-driven enterprise information security architectures and for delivering security infrastructure that supports critical business initiatives. The primary characteristic of the SABSA model is that everything must be derived from an analysis of the business requirements for security.

SpO_2: Oxygen saturation is a measure of the amount of oxygen-carrying hemoglobin in the blood relative to the amount of hemoglobin not carrying oxygen.

Strain gauge: A device used to measure strain on an object. Strain is the deformation or displacement of material that results from an applied stress.

Subrogation: A term describing a right held by most insurance carriers to legally pursue a third party that caused an insurance loss to the insured. This is done in order to recover the amount of the claim paid by the insurance carrier to the insured for the loss.

Syntactic interoperability: Allows two or more systems to communicate and exchange data when the interface and programming languages are different.

TOGAF: The Open Group Architecture Framework (TOGAF) is the most used framework for enterprise architecture. It provides an approach for designing, planning, implementing, and governing an enterprise information technology architecture. TOGAF is a high level approach to design. It is typically modeled at four levels – Business, Application, Data, and Technology – and is oriented toward existing or past technologies.

Transcutaneous Electrical Nerve Stimulation (TENS): Involves the use of low-voltage electric currents to treat pain. A small device delivers the current at or near nerves, via electrode pads placed directly on the skin.

Virtual Reality (VR): The computer-generated simulation of a three-dimensional image or environment that can be interacted with in a seemingly real or physical way by a person using special electronic equipment, such as a helmet with a screen inside or gloves fitted with sensors.

Zachman: An ontology or schema to help organize enterprise architect artifacts such as documents, specifications, and models. The framework considers who is affected by the artifact, such as the business owner, and weighs that against the issue or problem being addressed. The Zachman Framework is aimed at organizing and analyzing data, solving problems, planning for the future, managing enterprise architecture, and creating analytical models.

Z-Wave: A wireless communications protocol used primarily for home automation. It is a mesh network using low-energy radio waves to communicate from appliance to appliance.

Index